blue
rider
press

HUSTLING
HITLER

ALSO BY WALTER SHAPIRO

*One-Car Caravan: On the Road with the 2004 Democrats
Before America Tunes In*

HUSTLING HITLER

The Jewish Vaudevillian Who

Fooled the Führer

WALTER SHAPIRO

BLUE RIDER PRESS

an imprint of Penguin Random House

New York

blue
rider
press

An imprint of Penguin Random House LLC
375 Hudson Street
New York, New York 10014

Copyright © 2016 by Walter Shapiro
Penguin supports copyright. Copyright fuels creativity,
encourages diverse voices, promotes free speech, and creates a vibrant
culture. Thank you for buying an authorized edition of this book and
for complying with copyright laws by not reproducing, scanning, or
distributing any part of it in any form without permission. You
are supporting writers and allowing Penguin to continue to
publish books for every reader.

Blue Rider Press is a registered trademark and its colophon
is a trademark of Penguin Random House LLC

Library of Congress Cataloging-in-Publication Data

Names: Shapiro, Walter.
Title: Hustling Hitler : the Jewish vaudevillian who fooled
the Führer / Walter Shapiro.
Description: New York : Blue Rider Press, an imprint of
Penguin Random House, 2016.
Identifiers: LCCN 2016010868 | ISBN 9780399161476 (hardback)
Subjects: LCSH: Bernstein, Freeman, 1873–1942. | Jews—New York
(State)—New York—Biography. | Swindlers and swindling—United
States—Biography. | Businessmen—China—Shanghai—Biography. |
Nickel—History—20th century. | Germany—Commerce—History—
20th century. | World War, 1939–1945—Germany. | Entertainers—
New Jersey—Bayonne— Biography. | Shapiro, Walter—Family. |
BISAC: BIOGRAPHY & AUTOBIOGRAPHY / Historical.
Classification: LCC F128.9.J5 S47 2016 | DDC 338.092—dc23
LC record available at http://lccn.loc.gov/2016010868

Printed in the United States of America
1 3 5 7 9 10 8 6 4 2

Book design by Amanda Dewey

TO MERYL

You are the words and *the music.*

TO MY FATHER

Salem Shapiro, 1909–2004

If only . . .

Lee Shubert, the theatrical impresario, was ankling down the Canyon the other sundown and ran into Freeman Bernstein, a Main Stem character.

"What are you doing?" queried Mr. Shubert.

"Oh, I'm just trying to pick up a fast dime," said Bernstein.

"What's a fast dime?"

"A fast dime," was the reply, "is better than a slow quarter, any time!"

—*Walter Winchell column, April 29, 1930*

1

In February 1937, Freeman Bernstein was in the coin. After years of kiting checks, pawning his diamond cuff links, and putting the touch on old pals, Freeman was staying in the best hotels in California without worrying about being bounced if he couldn't come up with the cash to square his account by Friday. A year earlier, Freeman didn't even have the money to take the train from New York to Toronto without putting the touch on someone else to pick up his fare. Now he was traveling by limousine with his prized terrier, Benny, keeping him company in the backseat as he smoked his equally prized Corona Corona cigars. As Freeman himself would later write, looking back on this halcyon period, "I was now located in the most ideal spot in California . . . that place, as you know, is Hollywood, the city of glamour and what have you."

He had been in California for seven months—and not a peep had been heard about that grand larceny indictment back east. It wasn't like Freeman was hiding or playing hard to get. In fact, he was so public that he gave an interview to the *Los Angeles Times* while luxuriating in film-colony splendor at the El Mirador Hotel in Palm Springs. As Freeman understood from his days hustling cards in first-class salons on transatlantic liners, appearance trumps reality. So when he crowned himself the Jade King of China, no one questioned him about the details of the investiture ceremony. For Freeman, who was peddling jade, rubies, star sapphires, and a few iffy diamonds, nothing beat the free advertising from the *Los Angeles Times* headline: "'Jade King' Visiting in Desert Tells of Rich Burma Mines."

When he moved on to Hollywood, an Oriental potentate like Freeman knew where to stay—the Garden of Allah on Sunset Boulevard. The stucco main house (originally built for silent movie star Alla Nazimova) and the twenty-three secluded guest villas exuded high-class cachet. Another attraction was the hotel's anything-goes reputation, symbolized by its well-known disdain for hiring a house detective. Everyone in Hollywood had heard about the night an inebriated Tallulah Bankhead wandered around the pool nude and the time when a pixilated Robert Benchley was delivered back to his villa in a wheelbarrow. In fact, while Freeman was a registered guest at the Garden of Allah in mid-February, Salvador Dalí arrived with his waxed mustache and his new wife, Gala, dramatically announcing that he had come to California to paint a portrait of Harpo Marx.

Freeman, whose formal education stopped around the fifth grade, was no intellectual. So it's hard to imagine him devoting much brain power to pondering Dalí's obsession with Harpo Marx as a surrealistic icon. The blond starlets lolling around the pool were undoubtedly more alluring to Freeman, though at sixty-three years old, with a physique more resembling a table than Gable, his interest probably remained theoretical. Anyway, he had his eye on a different blonde, who was living four miles away in the Ravenswood Apartments. Freeman had precious, semiprecious, and, well, bogus stones to sell—and his target was the highest-salaried actress in Hollywood. Mae West had asked him to come up and see her sometime.

Their original connection has been lost in the grease-paint blur of the early days of vaudeville. In her autobiography, *Goodness Had Nothing To Do With It*, published in 1959, Mae West recalled being told by her agent that Freeman Bernstein "says you played in some of his theaters as a child actress." That was pretty much what she scrawled that night at the Ravenswood on an autographed picture for the Jade King: "To Freeman Bernstein, who was my first agent at the age of 10 years old."

When Mae West was ten in 1903, Freeman had just opened his first office as a vaudeville booking agent on Broadway south of Longacre Square (soon to be renamed Times Square) and was simultaneously managing the twelve-hundred-seat Trocadero Music Hall in upper Manhattan, promising in his ads to bring "high class vaudeville" to an area struggling to become the Coney Island of northern Manhattan. He certainly knew from child stars, booking performers like eight-year-old La Petite Mignon and the youthful dancers Eva and Harry Puck to the consternation of the do-gooders from children's aid societies.

Mae West's life did not lack for colorful characters, but even for her Freeman stood out. She lavished four pages of her autobiography on him, though it remains unknown what else she may have lavished on the Jade King when he came to call on the evening of February 18. As she recalled, "He had a sandpaper voice, and a ludicrous habit of repeating words and phrases. 'I'm known as the Jade King—the Jade King,' he told me, 'and I heard you are interested in precious stones—precious stones like star sapphires—star sapphires.'"

Freeman's scam was to mix high-quality gems with the kind of gewgaws that you might find in a Cracker Jack box. Feigning ignorance about star sapphires, the Jade King warbled over the beauty of flawed white stones with off-color stars, while casually ignoring the fine jewels with the proper cornflower hue. After displaying his best rubies, Freeman offered to also sell her a shimmering diamond (okay, it was a $65 zircon he had brought back from Asia) for the rock-bottom, only-for-you-Mae price of $10,000.

The actress, who had written and starred in *Diamond Lil*, knew her way around paste as well as pasties. She had furnished her living room to enhance her beauty (a curved floor-to-ceiling mirror subtly increased height and reduced heft) and her sense of drama (three white polar-bear rugs on the floor). But when it came to gems, Mae West craved reality, not illusion. Whipping out her own jewelry scale, she accepted Freeman's price for the rubies and the best sapphires. "Aren't you going to take the white ones?" Freeman asked dejectedly as she wrote the check. "Everyone likes them the best— the best." Mae West, who gave herself the last word in her autobiography, replied, "Then you should have no trouble selling them."

Still, when Freeman left the Ravenswood around midnight, he must have been basking in the bejeweled luster of his night at Mae's. He had her autograph on both a photograph and a much-needed check. Sure, he was momentarily stuck with the flawed white sapphires and the authentic zircon. But Hollywood was his kind of tawdry town, filled with gullible actresses and the gift-giving men who loved them—and neither group was known for conducting negotiations armed with their own jeweler's loupe. Freeman had his limousine, his chauffeur, his dog, his Corona Corona cigars, and the heavenly bed that would eventually be awaiting him at the Garden of Allah.

If he were back in New York, Freeman would have headed for Lindy's, the Hotel Astor, or some other Times Square joint to see who was around, what the gab was, and who might be impressed by his embellished tales of Mae West. In early-to-someone's-bed Los Angeles, the land of the six a.m. studio call, the Brown Derby at the corner of Hollywood and Vine was virtually the only round-the-clock, see-and-be-seen spot. That was where Freeman was heading when his limousine attracted the attention of two refugees from a Raymond Chandler novel—plainclothes detectives Johnnie Erickson and Jack Koehn of the fugitive squad of the Los Angeles Police Department.

You can just picture them in bruised fedoras, ketchup-dotted ties, and shiny, ill-fitting suits with cigarette ash on the lapels and conspicuous bulges underneath to show they're packing heat. Erickson might have been complaining about his ulcer again—the one that nearly killed him back in '35. Or been bragging about the tip that sent him to that rooming house on South Main where he nabbed George Mortensen, the pickax killer from Utah, without firing a shot. Koehn, even though he was pushing forty and was a detective lieutenant just like Erickson, was the junior partner on the team. Still, it was almost the one-year anniversary of Koehn's biggest collar—using tear gas to smoke out Abraham Redlick (known in the papers as the "Frisco Kid"), who was on the lam from a jewelry store stickup in Pittsburgh.

Career criminals wanted for armed robbery and berserk murderers cowering in crummy rooming houses fed the headline-grabbing prominence of the Los Angeles fugitive squad. But why were Erickson and Koehn tailing Freeman Bernstein, whose only violent act ever was to yell into a telephone? Who had tipped them off where the Jade King of China was holding court?

Maybe, as they claimed, the two detectives got lucky in arresting Freeman by tailing a limousine that was cruising through Hollywood in a suspicious manner. The police may have been quietly monitoring Mae West's apartment building in gratitude for her outspoken 1934 court testimony attacking thieves and racketeers preying on the motion-picture industry. It is conceivable that the Garden of Allah, for all its promises of privacy, had a bellhop or two who dished the dirt to the cops. Or Erickson and Koehn could have been tipped off by one of Freeman's many creditors back in New York, especially Stephen Meade, a bankrupt metals dealer who had hired private detectives to try to get his money back.

But the most likely explanation was that Freeman Bernstein—whom *Variety* once described as "the small-time agent with the big time nerve," who promoted his extravagant hustles on four continents, who believed in the P. T. Barnum power of bunkum and ballyhoo—simply couldn't hide in plain sight. Finding Freeman in Hollywood required about as much detective work as locating Lou Gehrig at first base at Yankee Stadium.

A veteran at being handcuffed, Freeman submitted to arrest peacefully, but not quietly. His time-tested strategy at these moments was to drop every name he could. He bragged to Erickson and Koehn that he was coming from Mae West's apartment and told them, "I put Mae on stage thirty years ago," brandishing the signed photograph as evidence of his VIP status. Looking up at the towering neon sign at Hollywood and Vine heralding Pantages movie palace, Freeman proudly informed his police escorts that he used to be a vaudeville booking agent for Alexander Pantages himself. Of course, what Freeman didn't know was that on the night that this Hollywood theater opened in 1930, Pantages, facing sexual assault charges, was reduced to listening to the red-carpet festivities on the radio from the Los Angeles County Jail. Which was also where Freeman would be spending the night.

From the moment that Erickson and Koehn waved a fugitive warrant in his face, Freeman must have been asking himself, "Which fugitive warrant?"

He thought that he had cleared up that business in Boston about the Irish festival, a fellow named Roger O'Ryan who looked suspiciously like him, and the missing gate receipts. And was it really Freeman's fault that he had cashed someone else's bum check because he ran short of funds running a sports book at the New Yorker Hotel? Anyhow, he was on probation for that one. Or maybe it was that bogus Canadian nickel deal with the Nazis that the New York DA's office had jumped on like they were getting a second helping of pork chops at a boardinghouse. Freeman had an airtight alibi for that one—or, at least, when viewed in a certain light, a pretty good explanation. And, anyway, who's going to get arrested in Hollywood in 1937 for bilking Adolf Hitler?

In Freeman's mind, the origins of the fugitive warrant were a coin flip. But it turned out that it was the Nazi nickel that bounced off his limousine and landed him in Erickson and Koehn's custody for a little ride downtown.

Once delivered to the hall of justice, Freeman, like the two thousand other prisoners housed in the county lockup, began his incarceration by being booked, fingerprinted, and mug-shot on the tenth floor. His jailers took away the wad in his wallet and the Mae West check, but they returned $5, which, given the way that Freeman played cards, was more than enough. A jailhouse trusty then escorted Freeman to the supply room where he was given a mattress, blankets, a miniature pillow, a small chunk of homemade soap, plus the aluminum cup and spoon featured in all prison movies. Okay, it wasn't the Garden of Allah. But to Freeman, it certainly beat that 1921 mix-up in Brussels when he was led through the streets in handcuffs and left to rot for three days in a dungeon known as "the Tunnel."

The next morning, wilted from a night in the cells, Freeman—still in his dark suit and patterned tie, and desperately needing a shave—met with the boys from the papers in a flurry of flashbulbs. The L.A. police put on a show like they had just nabbed Ma Barker and her boys.

Captain Jack Trainor, who headed the fugitive squad, played the Hitler card, claiming that Freeman Bernstein had defrauded agents of the German Reich out of $272,000. The supposed scam was that Bernstein had promised the Nazis high-grade Canadian nickel, but instead delivered to Hamburg scrap metal in the form of old tin cans, rusted railroad tracks, and discarded baling wire. Reveling in the latest triumph of the fugitive squad, Trainor dramatically declared that Freeman Bernstein "had been sought far and wide—throughout the world—for six months at the insistence of the German buyer."

Trainor fantasized about headlines like "Capt. Trainor's Fugitive Squad Nabs Swindler After Worldwide Manhunt." But those front-page dreams vanished as soon as the reporters got a crack at the prisoner. Freeman's performance was a cross between W. C. Fields and Fibber McGee with a little bit of Sydney Greenstreet thrown in for class. After introducing himself as a longtime vaudeville booking agent for the likes of Alexander Pantages and John Considine, after casually mentioning that, yes, he first put Mae West on the stage, Freeman proudly announced that all over the Orient, from Manila to Shanghai, he was known to one and all as "the Jade King."

Then Freeman Bernstein, in a voice like a foghorn, gave the lowdown on that Hitler thing: "When I was in Germany last year," he boomed, while puffing a borrowed cigar from behind a desk at police headquarters, "Adolf Hitler was on bended knee begging me to help him get some nickel which was so terribly hard to get in that country. Goering, one of his chief aides, did some pretty hard begging. And I promised to do the best that I could to do what they wanted and I did."

Freeman may have sensed from the quizzical expressions and eye rolls by the newspaper boys that he was going too far with the Führer-is-my-friend braggadocio. So Freeman adopted a new role as the aggrieved international businessman, claiming, "Adolf Hitler got just exactly what he paid for in that deal—scrap steel and nickel, and I'll prove it." Swearing that he would never sign the extradition papers that would send him back to New York, Freeman ended with a variant of a line that he had frequently resorted to throughout his checkered career: "Hitler ain't got a thing on me."

They certainly hadn't a thing on Freeman when it came to publicity. Thirty-five years in the limelight—all those interviews with Sime Silverman for *Variety*, all those stunts like announcing a match race for Man o' War in London and an exhibition bout for Jack Dempsey in Mexico City—had made him a hit-maker of the headlines. And the first paper to hit the streets with the story, the Friday, February 19 edition of the *Los Angeles Evening Herald and Express*, set the tone for all subsequent California press coverage of Freeman, Adolf Hitler, and the ersatz nickel.

"Bernstein's Deal with Hitler" was the headline. But it was the over-banner in bold type that told the story Freeman's way: "Embarrasses Der Fuehrer." What could be funnier than an American guy named Bernstein with multiple chins pulling a fast one on the

Nazis? That comic-strip story line appealed to the makeup editor of the *Herald and Express*, who laid out the front page with a picture of Freeman on the left ("Adolf Hitler Got Just Exactly What He Paid For!") and a frowning photo of the German chancellor on the right ("Fuehrer Adolf Hitler 'Hooked' in Buying Nickel from Mr. Bernstein, Claim"). In this Hollywood yarn, it wasn't hard to figure out who to root for.

As the Friday afternoon edition of the *Herald and Express* was rolling off the presses, Freeman finally got his day in court. By the luck of the draw (and clearly someone other than Freeman had cut the cards), the case was assigned to the biggest prig on the municipal bench, the Honorable Clement D. Nye. Just four months earlier, in September 1936, Judge Nye wielded the gavel the night they raided Minsky's, or, at least, the Los Angeles edition of the traveling burlesque troupe. Calling the production "revolting," Nye sentenced the manager of Minsky's to 180 days in jail without bail. When Alice Kennedy, one of the ecdysiasts from Minsky's, began sobbing melodramatically in the courtroom, the judge fined her $300 on the spot. In short, Judge Clement D. Nye was not the kind of guy you wanted standing between you and the electric chair.

Despite Freeman's top billing, he barely had a speaking part in court. After the prisoner formally refused to voluntarily return to New York to stand trial, Judge Nye, in a burst of punitive ferocity, set bail at $50,000, the equivalent of more than $800,000 today. Freeman's lawyer, John E. Ford (not the film director who had just released *Mary of Scotland* with Katharine Hepburn), protested and the judge grudgingly agreed to reduce the amount to a still hefty $25,000. "That ought to hold anyone arraigned for anything short of murder," Ford said. "Besides, Bernstein's good friends Joseph Schenck and John W. Considine will guarantee the bond."

Three decades earlier in Manhattan, Schenck had built the Fort George Amusement Park as a rival to Coney Island. Freeman's Trocadero Music Hall adjoined the sprawling attractions at the end of the Amsterdam Avenue trolley line. Now Schenck had been reborn as Hollywood royalty after launching 20th Century-Fox with Darryl Zanuck. In fact, the night of Freeman's arrest, Schenck had given a dinner with Zanuck in honor of Admiral Byrd—the Antarctic explorer temporarily stateside and getting no closer to frostbite than baked Alaska—featuring guests like Douglas Fairbanks, Charles Boyer, Eddie Cantor, and Ernst Lubitsch.

Considine, though in his midseventies and ailing, was more Freeman's kind of guy. As Joe Laurie Jr. wrote in his misty remembrance, *Vaudeville: From the Honky-Tonks to the Palace*, "John Considine was one of the most colorful characters in show business. He could handle a gun like Wild Bill Hickok and could play pool like Hoppe." Not to mention the minor detail that Considine had shot and killed the corrupt former police chief of Seattle in a drugstore brawl in 1901—and got off on grounds of self-defense. Running one of the few independent first-class wheels in vaudeville, the Sullivan-Considine circuit on the West Coast, he first hired Freeman as a booking agent in 1906. And Considine proved to be Freeman's most loyal friend through the coming legal ordeal.

But even $25,000 bail, marked down from $50,000, couldn't be easily raised on a Friday afternoon. Especially with Schenck on the road to Palm Springs to attend a dinner with a shipwreck theme at the Racquet Club along with Ralph Bellamy, Paul Lukas, and Freeman Gosden. And Considine was resting at home with heart problems. So Freeman was still stuck on the wrong side of the jailhouse bars as he met a reporter from the *Los Angeles Times*.

When a man knows he's going to spend the weekend in the Los

Angeles County Jail, it concentrates his mind wonderfully. Freeman had spent the prior twelve hours perfecting his patter. "I should've sent Hitler a carload of papier-mâché," he groused. "Actually, he got what he bought. Scrap iron and nickel. Not much nickel, but some." The Jade King also expressed his fears that he would be shot if he returned to Nazi Germany and hinted that retirement might be a safer course of action. But first there was that small misunderstanding with the New York City district attorney's office. "I'll fight them," Freeman thundered. "They haven't got a case."

His performance over, Freeman begged the gentleman from the *Los Angeles Times* for a cigar. It didn't have to be a Corona Corona; any cigar would do. Disconsolately, he accepted the reporter's cigarette instead. Lighting up, Freeman Bernstein concluded the interview by blowing a perfect smoke ring.

2

Freeman Bernstein, who died before I was born, was my great-uncle.

When I was growing up, my father would occasionally conjure up his uncle Freeman with a mixture of fondness and awe. But the stories never made sense. How could my father, Salem Shapiro—a mild-mannered city planner whose life revolved around zoning hearings and mortgage payments—be intimately connected to a vaudeville promoter, jade dealer, cardsharp, and world-renowned grifter. Freeman was a black sheep who could single-handedly supply a sweater factory. What was he doing on the outskirts of my upright, uptight suburban Connecticut Jewish family?

Compounding the mystery was that when my father told stories, he sounded more like a guy on the rack than a raconteur. He often dropped punch lines and marred narratives with an exasperating fuzziness about key details. As near as I could tell, Freeman parachuted into my father's childhood at erratic intervals, depending on the whim of fortune. When he was broke, Freeman sometimes slept on the sofa of his younger sister, my grandmother Rose

Shapiro (née Bernstein). When he was in the chips, Freeman might return from the Orient with star sapphires for Rose and her six children. As told and retold by my father, the star-sapphire story came with the poignancy of lifelong regret. Freeman ran out of jewels after giving them to his sister, her two daughters, and the three oldest boys. My father, known as "Babe" in the family because of birth order rather than home-run exploits, was left out as the fourth oldest boy.

Looking back, I now realize that Freeman touched an unexpressed part of my father's personality, a world far removed from Rotary Club lunches and PTA meetings. Whenever he talked about Freeman, my father, whose knowledge of show business was on par with his mastery of Gregorian chants, would begin dropping names like an insecure Broadway publicist. But the names referred to obscure vaudeville stars like May Ward (Freeman's wife) and May Yohe (who had once owned the Hope Diamond). Even when I recognized a reference to Sophie Tucker, it came with the outlandish boast that she had lent Freeman money in the last years of his life.

My father's prized tale about his uncle Freeman—a story as plausible as my being a direct descendant of Sitting Bull—featured the scamming of Adolf Hitler. Imagine my teenage skepticism when I heard that Freeman Bernstein, born in Troy, New York, had supposedly pulled a fast one on the Führer. It didn't help my father's case that key plot points kept getting lost in his narrative like a Monopoly set missing the deeds to Marvin Gardens and Baltic Avenue. The facts seemed askew—Hitler wanted a freighter filled with nickel but somehow, because of Freeman, the cargo delivered to the Nazis turned out to be sand. Or maybe, since my father offered several versions, Freeman put high-grade nickel on top of rusted tin cans and the Germans never checked the cargo. The story always petered out at this point, with only shadowy allusions to Freeman's ultimate fate. There was never a thrilling postscript like a grateful FDR summoning Freeman to the Oval Office to ask him to join spymaster Allen Dulles in setting up the OSS.

When I became older and exposed to a dollop of Freud, I recognized the legend of Freeman cheating Hitler for what it obviously was—Jewish wish fulfillment. Even though my parents were neither religious nor caught up in Jewish causes, even though we had no close relatives who died in the Holocaust, the story of Freeman Bernstein, scourge of the Nazis, offered an uplifting alternate narrative to the tear-stained 1930s. In this outlandish fantasy, thanks to the wiles of my father's uncle, our family did our part to defeat Hitler.

A year or so before my father died in 2004, he was rummaging through a box of forgotten family photographs when he unearthed a torn black-and-white snapshot of a rotund man wearing a three-piece white suit and a pith helmet. The Man in the White Suit cradled a lit cigar between the pudgy fingers of his right hand as he leaned back at a comfortable angle in a lawn chair outside a hotel or a guesthouse. But his dark eyes hold the key to the photograph. He was looking warily to the left of the camera, as if some unseen enemy were slithering through the hotel grass. The half smile perched above his triple chins radiated not joy but rather the congenital skepticism of a con artist who wouldn't be conned. The pencil inscription on the back of the snapshot, from the 1930s, read *"Times of Ceylon,"* suggesting that the picture had appeared in a colonial newspaper in Asia.

Freeman Bernstein was, of course, the Man in the White Suit.

This photographic discovery so thrilled my father that I had the tattered picture blown up and framed for him. Part of its appeal was its exoticism—nothing could be farther from leafy Weston, Connecticut, than pith helmets in Ceylon. But the snapshot also spoke to something deeper in my father, a connection, however frayed by time, to a louche life, the adventurous live-by-his-wits path that had always beckoned just over the horizon. So when my father downsized his life to move into an assisted living facility, he insisted on bringing the framed photo with him. And it graced his wall when he died at age ninety-five.

After the funeral, Freeman faded from my memory, the framed photograph from the *Times of Ceylon* consigned to a closet. But a stray 2010 conversation with a visiting Paris-based cousin prompted me to plunge into the closet and move aside a few boxes of books to retrieve Freeman's picture. Staring at the line of his mouth, the angle of his nose, the pitch of his eyes, I saw a resemblance to my father—or maybe I just wanted to.

Impulsively, I typed the distinctive moniker "Freeman Bernstein" into Google, dubious that anything would emerge, aside from, perhaps, a listing for a similarly named podiatrist from Milwaukee. Instead, I was stunned by the collection of recently digitized newspaper articles that popped up on my computer screen. The first clip that I read was the 1937 *Los Angeles Times* account of Freeman blowing a perfect smoke ring as he held court for a reporter at the county jail. The headline said it all: "Broker Denies Bilking Hitler in Metal Deal."

My father was right—and too late I discovered my folly in ever doubting him. Too late. Throughout eternity, those two words have been the saddest lament of sons about their fathers.

Some debts can never be repaid. I will never have the pleasure of seeing my father's face as I tell him that the true story of his uncle Freeman Bernstein—the impresario, the confidence man, the scalawag, the jewel smuggler, and the supremely confident schemer—was far wilder than he could have imagined. All I can offer is this book and the fantasy that my father would have had as much fun reading it as I had in reliving Freeman Bernstein's remarkable career.

In my search for my great-uncle, I also learned some late-in-life truths about myself. As an assimilated Jew, with no interest in ethnicity beyond bagels and smoked fish, I always belittled the genealogical obsession with uncovering family roots. What did I care about the immigrant experience or that my great-grandfather Hyman Bernstein was struggling as an itinerant peddler in Troy at the end of the nineteenth century?

But, as I came to discover, my family's twentieth-century veneer of respectability was as thin as a Freeman Bernstein alibi. There is more to the only-in-America Jewish mythology than brutal hours in a garment factory, Saturdays in a shul studying the Torah, and dreaming that someday your son will become a doctor. Equally important and a hell of a lot more fun were the Hebrew hustlers who learned at an early age that legality can be an elastic concept and honesty works better as a strategy when you are born into membership of the Union League Club. Let the goyim believe the Parson Weems stories about George Washington piously declaring, "Father, I cannot tell a lie. I chopped down the cherry tree." (In the 1920s, Freeman boasted about fleecing the fleeceable by claiming that he possessed the very dollar that Washington threw across the Potomac.)

So I am unduly proud that Freeman Bernstein was my great-uncle. And, in my Walter Mitty moments, I like to think that the music hall programs, the abandoned vaudeville troupes, the betting slips, the pawnshop tickets, the kited checks, the phony business cards, the outlandish schemes, and the zest for living the self-invented life are all entwined with my own DNA. In a sense, I am who I am today because of Freeman Bernstein, the man who hustled Hitler.

3

My American DNA, as is usually the case, began with a ship.

The *James Foster Jr.* was a three-masted packet, built in New York in 1854, regularly plying the Atlantic for the Black Ball Line on the Liverpool route. In 1857, Samuel Walters, considered the finest British maritime painter of his generation, depicted the *Foster* battling a storm as waves crashed over its deck on the outward voyage to New York. In the painting, the sleek packet, riding low in the gray water, cuts through the roiled ocean like a fencing foil. With its ivory sails and its black hull punctuated by a white stripe, the *Foster* exudes debonair black-tie sophistication, even in distress.

That Walters painting sold for $18,750 in New York in January 2014. I like to fancy that if I had known about the auction in advance, I would have been madly waving my paddle to commemorate family history. Instead, the painting now is presumably hanging on the wall of an exclusive men's club or in the den of a retired investment banker who is known around his yacht club as "the Commodore." Had I prevailed in the frenzied bidding—or, to be honest, somehow been allowed to stick $18,750 on a perpetually revolving credit card—I would have treasured this sublime example of maritime art for its subterranean depths.

The subterranean depths of steerage. For sailing the Atlantic in third class on the *Foster* was closer in spirit to the oardom of a Roman galley slave than to the boredom of a modern traveler stuck overnight in a middle seat in coach.

In early 1869, the *Foster* docked in New York after a seventy-eight-day crossing from Liverpool with its crew and passengers ravaged by typhus. Immigrants on what newspaper headlines called "the Fever Ship" told of near starvation and briny water as they received only half their contracted rations, even early in the voyage. According to witnesses, the shipboard hospital was fetid, the doctor was continually drunk, and the only medication he distributed was large doses of castor oil to anyone who complained. The ship's carpenter, who was in charge of distributing food and water, routinely beat passengers with a hammer and a belaying pin. His fury was particularly directed at steerage passengers of all nationalities who had agreed to work off part of their passage as shipboard cooks. An official committee of inquiry found what the *New York Times* summarized as "the culpable negligence of the owners, the indifference of the Captain to the welfare of those placed under his charge, and the atrocious brutality of the carpenter and others to whom he virtually delegated all his authority."

My great-grandfather, Hyman Bernstein, Freeman's father, barely escaped the horrors of the Fever Ship. He arrived in New York in September 1868 on the prior voyage of the *James Foster Jr.* But during the thirty-two-day crossing, the packet was under the command of the same negligent captain and rations were doled out by the same thuggish ship's carpenter. I shudder as I think about the gloom, the stench, and the bedlam of 335 steerage passengers confined for nearly five weeks in a compartment that ran the length of the 191-foot ship with no access to the deck and the only direct light coming from two hatches that were closed in foul weather. Hyman never saw the two late-summer icebergs that were recorded in the ship's log, but, at least, he benefited from gentle westerly winds and calm waters for most of the crossing.

Listed on the ship's manifest as a Polish-born twenty-two-year-old tailor (actually, he was a few years older), Hyman was a demographic oddity. Most of the other immigrants who endured steerage on the *Foster* were British, Irish, or German, with only a handful of Jewish names or Poles. As was often the custom in those days, Hyman left his wife, Yetta, and their one-year-old daughter, Jennie, behind in England to wait until he could raise enough money to pay for their passage.

Trying to envision the moment when my great-grandfather finally cleared immigration at Castle Garden at the foot of Manhattan, I am awash in images from movies like *The Godfather: Part II* and *Hester Street*. These cinematic re-creations are built around frightened immigrants in threadbare coats and workingmen's caps, speaking Italian or Yiddish punctuated by a few words of broken English. Their passion for a new life in a new land is inevitably symbolized by a scene in which they stare longingly at the Statue of Liberty.

As one of 282,189 immigrants to the United States in 1868, Hyman Bernstein arrived too early for many of these Ellis Island clichés to fit. Hyman probably spoke passable English after living in Britain for at least a year. The Statue of Liberty—that beacon to the "huddled masses yearning to breathe free"—would not be dedicated until 1886. After passing the health inspections that accompanied immigration at Castle Garden (Ellis Island did not become the gateway until 1892), Hyman probably had to make his own way down cobblestone streets caked with manure to an address on the Lower East Side. His destination was presumably one of Manhattan's fifteen thousand tenements as the city, bursting its bustle amid the post–Civil War boom, approached one million people.

Okay, here is the moment when I confess that this is not a biography of someone like Averell Harriman or Cornelius Vanderbilt. Hyman Bernstein did not leave behind at the family estate a voluminous collection of memorabilia, nor are his letters from the 1870s on file at the Mudd Manuscript Library at Princeton University. Instead, Hyman's early years in America have been lost to history, as is often the case with the short and simple annals of the poor. Everything that I know about this freshly minted American comes from a handful of documents filled out by bored Irish census takers and harried government clerks unfamiliar with the proper spelling of Jewish names. Piecing together a flesh-and-blood person from these error-filled scraps of paper is akin to reconstructing a prehistoric village based on pottery shards.

The 1870 census shows Hyman Bernstein, now listed as a twenty-two-year-old peddler born in Prussia, living on the Lower East Side somewhere south of Rivington Street and east of Essex Street. He shares the residence with twenty-seven-year-old Meyer Bernstein, also a peddler, and Esther Bernstein, seventeen—and the three of them could have been either siblings or cousins. America had been good to Hyman during those first years in Manhattan: He was listed as having assets of $600 (about $11,000 today), which was more than most of his neighbors.

Hyman's prosperity had its benefits: Yetta and their three-year-old daughter, Jennie, arrived from Liverpool on the steamship *Vir-*

ginia on March 16, 1870. Five years earlier Hyman Bernstein had wed Yetta Shapiro (the two families intermarried so frequently in those days that they could have been honorary residents of West Virginia). Any flimsy claims to Jewish gentility came from Yetta's side of the family: She was the granddaughter of a once-famous eighteenth-century Polish rabbi Josele Shapiro. According to family legend, Yetta was sent as a girl to Berlin to live with an uncle, who was a doctor in the court of the Prussian king Frederick William IV. At some point the family fled to England, and I remember being transfixed as a child by the story that my great-great-grandmother (Yetta's mother) drowned while crossing the English Channel.

At minimum, this unusual itinerary (Poland to Germany to England to New York) helps explain why Hyman and Yetta arrived in America more than a decade before the waves of Jewish immigrants from Eastern Europe and Russia fleeing pogroms. But to indulge in gossamer speculation, I wonder if Yetta's tales about growing up privileged in mid-nineteenth-century Berlin fueled Freeman's sense of entitlement and the unflappable self-assurance that propelled this confidence man through life. I don't want to get too Freudian here (I prefer to be forever Jung), but I have heard vague rumors that the mother-son bond can sometimes be important in Jewish families.

In late 1870, the newly reunited and newly American Bernstein family went up the river. They moved 150 miles to Troy (population: 46,465), a smoke-belching industrial town, just north of Albany on the opposite bank of the Hudson River. As the last spot where the Hudson runs as a tidal river, Troy initially flourished as the terminus of the Erie and Champlain Canals. The Civil War triggered a boom for Troy's steel mills and ironworks. By 1870, the prosperous but never buttoned-down city (the twenty-eighth-largest in America) became renowned for its factories manufacturing shirts and detachable cuffs and collars. A small number of Jews migrated to Troy in the 1850s as peddlers, tailors, and shop owners. In fact, the *Troy Whig*, a local paper, published a "Rosh Hashanah Notice for Citizens" to explain why certain shops were mysteriously closed in the middle of the week.

Why did Hyman and Yetta give Troy a try? Unlike many family questions that I never bothered to ask when I could still get answers, I did quiz my father about their Trojan odyssey—and he was as mystified as I was. If there was a welcoming relative, the grocer listed in the 1870 *Troy Directory* as "P. Bernstein" is the likeliest suspect. But maybe the answer rests with the simple lure of American opportunity—Troy at the height of its prosperity offered jobs and Yetta was pregnant. Samuel Bernstein, the first member of my family to be American born, arrived in early 1871.

Freeman came along two years later—and I know I should offer an emblematic tale or two about his birth, something like the midwife discovering that her best brooch had been pawned during the delivery or Freeman entering the world offering odds on what would be the baby's first words. But because New York State did not record births until 1880, certain minor details about Freeman remain shrouded in uncertainty—minor details like his precise birth date and his given name.

The best source is a June 1875 census conducted by New York State that mangled everyone's name in what was recorded as the "Berenstien" family headed by "Iman," a peddler. The Berenstiens had an older son, "Sanuel," and a second son named "Framen," who was listed as one year and ten months old, suggesting that he was born in August 1873. That census may have been the only time in his life that Freeman resisted the temptation to fiddle with his age.

On his marriage license in 1906, he stripped five years off his age, much like a nervous groom might go to the altar wearing Adler elevator shoes. Freeman gave himself an extra year when registering for the World War I draft. Probably to befuddle United States Customs, Freeman provided five different birth dates (ranging from August 13, 1873, to August 16, 1876) when he returned to New York from international travels during the peripatetic year of 1922. And after his arrest in Los Angeles in 1937, he padded his age by four years to gain sympathy as an elderly gentleman.

As for the name, Freeman was a perfect Dickensian moniker for a freebooter who sailed through life under his own flag. Was it his given name? While the error-prone 1880 U.S. census listed him as "Fredman," he was known as "Freeman Bernstein" when his name first appeared in the *Troy Times* just before his fourteenth birthday. Perhaps Hyman and Yetta wanted to name one child in honor of their arrival in America, although their other four children were given generic nineteenth-century handles (Jennie, Sam, Rose, and Becky). A single offbeat name every generation became something of a family tradition. My father was Salem Shapiro, which was an effort by Rose, Freeman's sister, to Americanize "shalom." The odd coupling of first and last names never worked as intended: Salem Shapiro unavoidably evoked a New England witch trial conducted by men in yarmulkes.

Whatever dreams brought Hyman to Troy were soon dashed. After being listed in the *Troy Directory* as a peddler, Hyman made the big leap in 1877 by opening a variety store on Division Street in the midst of a slum neighborhood that was in transition from Irish to Jewish. Hyman held on to his hard-earned identity as a shopkeeper for a few years before, according to the 1880 census, plunging back to the ranks of itinerant peddlers from which he never

emerged. The family moved virtually every May 1 to another tenement, either to evade the landlord or to save a dollar or two on the
rent. This downward mobility left a lasting imprint on Freeman
and his brother Sam. "After Freeman had been in school about
seven years his father failed in business and he and his brother Sam
were forced to quit school to aid in the family support," wrote old-
time Broadway publicist Maurice B. Haas in a 1937 biographical
sketch that represents the most detailed account of my great-uncle's
early years.

Armed with a fifth-grade education—which is what he admitted to in the 1940 census—Freeman began shining shoes, selling
newspapers, running errands, and learning the art of petty thiev-
ery. The family needed all the help it could get. In 1882, they were
reduced to sharing a back tenement on River Street with a Mrs.
Armstrong whose husband was in the penitentiary. During a
drunken party presided over by Mrs. Armstrong, a reveler set a fire
that destroyed the building and left the Bernsteins homeless. A
year later, the family was burned out of another tenement, but this
time they couldn't blame carousing neighbors. A little after ten
o'clock on a late summer evening, Yetta and her eldest daughter,
Jennie, were sitting on the front stoop when they smelled smoke
and began shouting. Sam was awakened to find his bed on fire—
and leaped out a front window in panic, dressed only in his union
suit. When the fire department arrived, Yetta insisted that some
anonymous stranger had thrown a lighted match through Sam's
window. Officials preferred a more prosaic theory: twelve-year-old
Sam had been smoking in bed.

Religion was the altarpiece of the lives of most of the nearly two
hundred Jewish families in Troy in the 1880s. They lived in tenements and private homes in the lowlands near the fetid Hudson

River, not far from belching ironworks and foundries, but within walking distance of the city's four synagogues.

Freeman later described his father as an Orthodox Jew. But there is no evidence that Hyman was affiliated with a synagogue or a Jewish fraternal organization, although nineteenth-century records are sketchy. Even if Hyman wanted to adjust to America by joining Berith Sholom, a Reform congregation dominated by German Jews, he lacked the money and the pedigree for membership. Yet he may have been too assimilated to fit comfortably in an Orthodox shul filled with Yiddish speakers, even though, I suspect, that was where the family worshipped on the High Holy Days.

Public anti-Semitism was muted in Troy, partly because it was a brawling, self-made, money-mad city with none of the pretensions of Albany, whose social life was dominated by the descendants of seventeenth-century Dutch patroons. Irish mayors of Troy, such as Dennis J. Whelan, sensitive to the immigrant vote, religiously attended synagogue dedications. The *Troy Times* treated Judaism as almost on par with Christianity in such low-key news items as "The completion of the new Jewish synagogue on Division street will make the total number of churches in Troy forty-seven."

Nineteenth-century Troy should not be romanticized as the spiritual home of National Brotherhood Week. A Jewish immigrant's life in Troy could be punctuated by ugly incidents like the one that victimized Hyman in 1883. Lugging his peddler's pack and a satchel on an unseasonably warm late-November day, Hyman was attacked by a group of street urchins hurling stones and presumably anti-Semitic epithets. In desperation, Hyman ran into the nearest open building, a workingman's saloon on Second Street owned by Elezar Bouchard, a French Canadian. Instead of offering the persecuted peddler a whiskey and an Excelsior Pale Ale, Bouchard angrily claimed that Hyman had somehow broken his window. Applying vigilante revenge, Bouchard seized Hyman's pack and satchel worth $125 (about $3,000 today) as compensation.

But the broken-window story ended with a surprise twist. Hyman complained to the Troy police—who believed him, probably because he spoke to them in English rather than Yiddish. That night Bouchard was arrested for theft after the police learned that the barkeep had paid the boys to stone Hyman. The next morning, as Bouchard was arraigned in court, the peddler's pack and satchel were returned to Hyman, who noted that some of its contents were missing. The *Troy Times* in its news story (which was picked up by the *Poughkeepsie Daily Eagle*) stressed the anti–Good Samaritan aspects of the incident with the headline "Paying Dearly for Protection."

A close reading of the Troy police blotter suggests that Hyman wasn't spending his spare hours reading the Talmud or preparing Freeman for his bar mitzvah, an event that, if it occurred, remains unremembered by history. During the Fourth of July celebrations in 1887, Hyman and Sam were at the center of a brawl on River Street that appeared to break down on religious lines—Jews versus Catholics. Arrested along with Hyman and Sam were Napoleon Breton, a French-Canadian carpenter, and the Irish-surnamed Charles Denny. Three months later, the Battling Bernsteins, Hyman and Sam, were back in police court, this time charged with assaulting Louis Monchowski. Sam seems not only to have been fast with his fists but also slow on his feet—especially when pursued by the cops—since in 1890 he was again nabbed for assault.

In contrast, Freeman, perhaps because he was short and stout, always grasped the advantages of fraud over fisticuffs and larceny over lethal weapons.

Fifty years before he was arrested leaving Mae West's apartment in Hollywood, Freeman was picked up by the Troy police in the summer of 1887, putting the first notch on his rap sheet. It all began when the thirteen-year-old Bernstein boy was enjoying the rocky beach by a foundry on Starbucks Island, which was connected to both banks of the Hudson River by a bridge. Like a plucky Horatio Alger hero, Freeman alertly noticed that a man named John Sullivan had generously left $10 in the pocket of his clothes as he took a dip in the filthy river. Understandably, Freeman decided that if the money had to be in a pocket, better the pocket should be his. Equally understandably, the Troy police did not see it Freeman's way.

Appearing as a miscreant before the assistant police magistrate in Troy, Freeman had a stroke of luck—someone in court pointed out that the beach on Starbucks Island was on the Albany side of the river. So Troy didn't have jurisdiction. In his first brush with the law, Freeman got off on a technicality. That early introduction to the complexities of the justice system shaped Freeman's life. Rather than being frightened into becoming a law-abiding youth because of the specter of jail, Freeman realized that there's always an angle, always an escape clause, always a way to beat the rap. And that made all the difference.

Troy also molded Freeman in another lasting way: It taught him envy. Had Freeman grown up on, say, the Lower East Side, the Fifth Avenue mansions of the Astors, the Carnegies, and the Fricks would have occupied an almost imaginary realm as far away from daily immigrant life as the dark side of the moon. Not only did Troy have just one-twentieth of the population of Manhattan, but the upstate city also grew in haphazard ways that obliterated hard lines of social class. Washington Park, a privately owned enclave surrounded by the grand Greek and Gothic Revival homes of industrialists and business leaders, was only two blocks from the Jewish tenements along River Street. As Jack Casey wrote in his meticulously researched novel about Troy in the 1890s, *The Trial of Bat Shea*: "Though it aspires to Victorian elegance . . . Troy can never cleanse the grime and the grit of its furnaces and smokestacks, the sweat and vice of its people. Troy's citizens have built a gracious Music Hall in the center of the city boasting the finest acoustics in the world, yet Troy's daily symphony is one of locomotive and mill whistles, immigrant brawls, and the clang and throb of machinery."

The good life was always visible in Troy—even if it was surrounded by high iron gates. A rare family story that was handed down to me from this period featured my grandmother Rose staring wistfully at the manicured grounds of Emma Willard, the girl's preparatory academy, which was then located in downtown Troy near the Hudson.

Freeman, who had more than a dash of Huck Finn in him, began to roam up and down the Hudson River. As he grew older, Freeman couldn't resist bragging about his early business acumen. When the government in the late 1880s eliminated its stamp tax on imported sulfur matches from Europe, Freeman calculated that he could make a profit from the oversupply. He bought the matches at a discount from jobbers and then resold them to variety stores like the one his father used to run.

Geography guaranteed that Freeman would eventually hoist his peddler's pack filled with cheap matches aboard the Delaware and Hudson Railway for the twenty-five-mile trip to Saratoga Springs. But fate ensured that Freeman arrived during the sixty-day summer racing season. "This move was the finish of a match salesman," Haas explained in his brief 1937 biographical portrait. "Freeman became inoculated with the gambling spirit then and there. His beginner's luck was the turning point in his career. Saratoga in those days was the Mecca for racing fans as well as the sporting fraternity everywhere. Freeman sent his mother more money in one day than he could have sent her in a month selling matches."

When Freeman arrived, the town of Saratoga Springs still reveled in its Gilded Age aura as the favored summer resort for robber barons who considered Newport too staid and boring. The north porch of the United States Hotel, where the rocking chairs were filled with overstuffed men showing off their diamond rings and stickpins, became known as Millionaires' Piazza. The dining room at the Saratoga Club, the premiere late-night gambling mecca, charged prices that made Delmonico's in Manhattan look like a haven for low rollers.

Even though Jews made up about half the summer residents of Saratoga Springs during racing season, leading hotels like the Grand Union adopted a Gentiles-only reservation policy. In 1877, Joseph Seligman, a banker who had just turned down an offer from his close friend Ulysses Grant to become secretary of the Treasury, arrived at the Grand Union expecting his usual suite. Instead, the desk clerk told him that the owner of the Grand Union had decreed "that no Israelites shall be permitted in the future to stop at this hotel." The resulting furor prompted Bret Harte to lampoon the WASP pretensions of the Grand Union Hotel with this bit of doggerel:

You'll allow Miss McFlimsey her diamonds to wear,
You'll permit the Van Dams at the waiters to swear,
You'll allow Miss Decollete to flirt on the stair,
But, as to an Israelite, pray have a care.

No matter how restrictive the social mores of this resort town became, the fortunes of Saratoga Springs still depended far more on wagers than the waters of its spas. Everything revolved around the racing season. But in the early 1890s, it looked like the once-glittering track was headed for the glue factory. Instead of improving the breed, racing at Saratoga had quickly become a matter of improving the greed.

The problem was the track's new owner, Gottfried "Dutch Fred" Walbaum, whom no one would confuse with August Belmont. Dutch Fred raised the $375,000 to purchase Saratoga in 1892 with the help of some of his other business interests in Manhattan—a gambling house on the Bowery, a pool hall in the shadow of the Brooklyn Bridge, and a brothel on the Lower East Side. Prior to taking over Saratoga, Walbaum learned racing by running an outlaw track in northern New Jersey that pioneered doping horses and using electric buzzers for a finishing kick.

Walbaum brought this entrepreneurial spirit to Saratoga, antagonizing titans of the turf like Belmont and Pierre Lorillard. His favored strategy was to run his own horses at Saratoga, bet heavily on them to win, and then cheer them to victory—often under suspicious circumstances. Afterward, Walbaum would chortle, "Yes sir, nobody can beat me. I'm just a sucker for luck." On a memorable afternoon in 1894, Walbaum's sucker-for-luck horses won four straight races, including one in which the favored filly vanished after the weigh-in even though bets on her were allowed to stand. Afterward, the *New York Times* archly noted that Walbaum "had no entries in the last two races, which probably was the only thing that prevented him from sweeping the entire card."

With forty-two saloons, dozens of bookmakers, ten major gambling houses, and, oh yes, sixteen churches, Saratoga Springs was the perfect spot to round out Freeman's education. Reporting for the *New York World* in 1894, Nellie Bly described the scene during that July and August with this fearsome lede: "Saratoga is the wickedest spot in the United States. Crime is holding a convention there and vice is enjoying a festival such as it never dared approach before." (Even though it was written during the heyday of yellow journalism, that purple prose should have made Bly blush red with embarrassment.)

At the track, Freeman could learn the intricacies of gambling from bookmakers as well as from Saratoga's own pari-mutuel system, which had a habit of not always offering full payouts to winning plungers. Telling Freeman's life story in 1937, Maurice Haas wrote, "His personality gained him the friendship of the leading horsemen as well as the gamblers, who would give him inside information that turned out so well that Freeman decided that he was made to be a gambler."

I can see him—part smart aleck, part street urchin, and part math prodigy—ingratiating himself with older bookmakers and maybe even claiming a mythical family connection with violinist Adolf Bernstein, who had led the orchestra at the Congress Hall Hotel for two decades. Freeman's evenings most likely were spent in arduous study at places like Cale Mitchell's gambling house opposite the United States Hotel. As Nellie Bly described the joint, "It is a saloon in the front, and in the rear can be had any sort of gambling from roulette to craps. White and black gamble together, poor and rich."

At Saratoga U, Freeman earned his Ph.D. in bluff, bravado, chips, and chance. For the rest of his life, he played the ponies every day and fantasized about betting coups like the ones that Walbaum pulled off at Saratoga. In 1920, on a return visit to Saratoga, Freeman promised a reporter from *Variety*, "The next good one I hear is going over I'll put down five for you. If I'm flush I'll play ten and make good if you win. I'll even wire you the horse in the morning so you will know I'm not trimming."

Saratoga taught Freeman that no one is so broke that he can't be rescued by a tip straight from the horse's mouth. In 1935, Freeman wrote a story about a fading Broadway promoter who is in hock to his friends, his acquaintances, his loyal secretary, and the hotel in which he's living. (Any of this sound familiar?) But Freeman's alter ego squared it with everyone and even helped some friends down on their luck by secretly training a horse named Blue Money at the beach—and then raked in the coin when the pony galloped home by ten lengths as a fifty-to-one shot in his first race.

In reality, outside of racing season at Saratoga, Freeman was still struggling to put his mark on the world. He helped support the family by selling candy and cigarettes on trains and continuing to make his salesman's rounds peddling matches and sundries. The 1898 *Troy Directory*, which went to press in the fall of 1897, lists Freeman and Sam as salesmen living with their parents on Liberty Street, one long block from the elite enclave of Washington Park.

Any portrait of a con artist as a young man requires a moment when he throws off the shackles of family and convention to seek his fortune. For Freeman, the triggering event was the last great gold rush in North American history. On July 16, 1897, the *Portland*, a ship plying the Alaska fur route, was sighted off the coast of Washington State. Eager for the latest news from Alaska (where telegraph lines were still unknown), the *Seattle Post-Intelligencer* chartered a tugboat to meet the *Portland* on the high seas. The resulting story electrified the world: "GOLD! GOLD! GOLD! GOLD! / Sixty-Eight Rich Men on the Steamer Portland / STACKS OF

YELLOW METAL! / Some have $5,000, Many Have More / A Few Bring Out $100,000 Each."

The miners had struck pay dirt in the Klondike during the summer of 1896, but it took them almost a year to return to civilization because of the frostbite weather and the primitive conditions in Alaska and the Canadian Yukon. Freeman, frustrated that he was still playing for chump change, heard the siren song of the Klondike in news articles in the *Troy Times* that described "poor men made the possessors of fabulous wealth in a single night; stories of thousands of dollars in bright, shining, golden sand taken from the beds of the streams emptying into the Klondike."

But getting there was not half the fun. Return passage on the *Portland* jumped to $1,000 a person. The stampede was on—and every boat on the West Coast from rust buckets to pleasure yachts was headed to Alaska carrying ill-equipped gold-steaders at outlandish prices. Freeman was not only undercapitalized (a lifelong handicap) but also trapped on the wrong side of the continent. He wisely heeded the warnings in the papers that it was already too late in the season to reach the gold fields in the Yukon because there would be no way to beat the first freeze after getting off the boat in Alaska. Instead, Freeman stayed in Troy, probably making a few dollars working the crowds, when President William McKinley visited the city in mid-August. But it is easy to picture the twenty-four-year-old Freeman figuring the angles as he read this advertisement for a jewelry store in the *Troy Times*: "You might dig Klondike gold for less cost if you're lucky, but you won't find it any richer or more brilliant in appearance or purer than the Golden Ware we sell and guarantee."

Hawking jewelry to gold miners seems like the punch line to a joke—the equivalent of selling iceboxes to Eskimos. But Freeman, the future Jade King of China, calculated that a Klondiker, after months panning streams in the frozen wilderness, would want to present a finished bracelet or necklace to his favorite dance hall girl. This oddball business insight left a lasting footprint in the snows of Alaska. Many decades later, a wire editor with a long memory at the *Fairbanks Daily News-Miner* added this sentence to an Associated Press dispatch about Freeman: "In the Alaska gold rush of '98, Bernstein made a small fortune selling jewelry to miners."

During the spring of 1898, Freeman probably made his way to Seattle by train and then took an overpriced steamer up the coast to Skagway, Alaska. Skagway was a brawling, bustling, bet-your-grubstake tent city that was the gateway to the most popular land route to the Yukon, six hundred miles away. This was where Seattle steamers dumped tenderfoot miners, each with nearly a thousand pounds of food and prospecting supplies. But for experienced sourdoughs (miners who survived the brutal winter of 1897), Skagway was where gold dust could be transformed into girls, gambling chips, and gewgaws. In launching his frontier jewelry business, Freeman may have absorbed a few lessons from Soapy Smith, the cheerful hustler who preyed on the gullible in Skagway. Soapy convinced himself that he was performing a public service, since any would-be miner who lost his grubstake within hours of getting off the boat would never survive the rigors of the Klondike. Everything was a con for Soapy, from the $1 maps of the gold fields his henchmen sold at dockside to the $5 charge for farewell telegrams for miners leaving for the Yukon. Since these foolhardy miners hadn't noticed that Skagway, like the rest of Alaska, lacked telegraph wires, Soapy would happily charge them another $5 for a fabricated return message from their loved ones supposedly sent collect.

Fortified by cold cash from Alaska, Freeman was back home

by late 1899. The 1900 *Troy Directory* lists Freeman and Sam as salesmen living with their parents on River Street. But the moment had come for both of them—with Freeman taking the lead even though he was two years younger—to follow the example of so many other Jews eager to put salesman's satchels and peddler's packs behind them.

The Bernstein Brothers were about to enter show business. At the very bottom.

They opened a small amusement park with carnival games in 1900 on the eastern tip of Cuyler Island, the largest of three islands in the Hudson that served as a summer refuge for residents of Albany and Troy. The scheme had only one flaw: The easiest access to reach Freeman and Sam's arcade was to walk along a broad man-made causeway from a much larger park and theater operated by John Weber. Having paid to book a full vaudeville program, a dance band, and special attractions like the balloonist known as Professor Leslie, Weber was eager to puncture the dreams of the Bernstein Brothers to profit from his overflow crowds.

In revenge, Weber erected a barrier in the middle of the causeway, which was owned by the United States Army as part of the Hudson River defenses. That meant that the only way to reach Freeman and Sam's penny-ante arcade was either to swim across the Hudson or to take a long walk from the opposite end of Cuyler Island. Clamoring for justice, Freeman and Sam hired a lawyer to find cause to get an injunction against Weber for blocking the causeway. But the moment that Weber produced a lease for the structure signed by Secretary of War Elihu Root was the moment that Freeman learned that show business was like panning for gold—the glitter matters less than a valid claim.

Freeman and Sam spent the following winter in a small office in

Albany plotting their comeback. The F. & S. Bernstein Company was nominally in the retail liquor trade, but Freeman couldn't bottle up his dreams in an ordinary commercial venture. Channeling his inner Robert Fulton, Freeman set up the grandly named Island Park Amusement and Steamship Company, naming himself manager. The idea was for the Bernstein Brothers to float to the top of the Hudson River summer-fun trade by having their own boats. If Weber wouldn't let their customers walk across the causeway, then a steamship line would allow them to float around it.

They unveiled their plans in a small display ad in the April 20, 1901, edition of the *New York Clipper*, a show-business weekly: "Attractions of All Kinds Wanted . . . The following privileges are for sale: Card Board Doll Games, Fish Pond, Cigar Games of All Kinds . . . We own our own steamboats. Trips made half hourly between Albany and Troy touching on the island. Vaudeville people write for open time." The following week, directly above an ad peddling "PICTURE MACHINES," the Bernstein Brothers made a direct pitch to vaudeville performers: "We want Sister Teams, Single Ladies, also others. All teams must work single or double. Consider silence a polite negative."

That last line sounded like vintage Freeman—pretending that his putative summer theater was so overwhelmed by sister acts and other vaudeville talent that no one had time to send out letters of rejection. In truth, Freeman had to wait until June before even winning permission to dock his two ferries in Troy at a cost of $50 for the season. But he and Sam were rewarded with their first mention in the news columns of the *New York Clipper*: "ISLAND PARK is the name of the new Summer resort on the Hudson River, between Albany and Troy, which will shortly open, under the management of the Bernstein Brothers."

That summer of bottom-of-the-barrel vaudeville, low-rent side-shows, and failing ferries wiped out the Bernstein Brothers. Freeman and Sam soon declared bankruptcy. But as his thirtieth birthday neared, Freeman's ambitions could not be constrained by two-bit towns like Troy and Albany. His ultimate destination was evident from the moment he chose the name for his first amusement park—Camp Manhattan.

4

I t was without a doubt the Fight of the Century—the nineteenth century.

From the moment he unleashed a torrent of blows that sent a battered and bloody John L. Sullivan cascading to the canvas in the twenty-first round, James J. Corbett became America's first beloved sporting hero. The 1892 heavyweight championship, the first fought with padded gloves under the new Marquess of Queensberry rules, had been handicapped as a rout. Few in the crowd of ten thousand in New Orleans expected Corbett, a former bank teller from San Francisco, to endure the ferocity that had made Sullivan America's most feared bare-knuckle brawler. But Corbett, who exemplified "scientific boxing," employed bob-and-weave defensive tactics to wear down the brutish Sullivan, who outweighed him by at least thirty pounds.

Other Gay Nineties sports stars like baseball's player-manager Cap Anson personified coiled rage and underhanded tactics both on and off the diamond. In contrast, the impeccably groomed Gentleman Jim Corbett, who often sported a dress cane, was lionized for both his fast footwork in the ring and his good-natured, boy-next-door charm out of it.

Vaudeville held an obvious allure for Corbett in an era when boxing purses were hard to arrange and harder to collect. Corbett began his stage career by sparring for a round or two, but quickly discovered that, unlike most pugs, he could impersonate an actor. The heavyweight champion toured for three years in a stage vehicle called *Gentleman Jack* in which he played a down-on-his-luck Princeton graduate who is forced to make a living as a boxing instructor. The five-act melodrama climaxed with Jack's prizefight against his villainous archrival at Exhibition Stadium in New Orleans—the venue where, coincidentally, of course, Corbett had knocked out Sullivan.

In 1901, even though he had lost the heavyweight crown to Bob Fitzsimmons and a title bout to Jim Jeffries, Corbett's popularity remained undimmed. The fighter's finances, on the other hand, were being pummeled.

His saloon (Corbett's Bar and Poolroom at Broadway and Thirty-Fourth Street) was briefly menaced by the arrival of hatchet-wielding Carrie Nation in New York, just a few weeks after she was released from jail in Wichita. As Corbett melodramatically wailed to the *Morning Telegraph*, "Ruin my beautiful place! Destroy the mahogany counter and real oak tables! Surely, Mrs. Nation will not be so cruel!" Corbett then lost $12,000 (more than $300,000 today) in the stock market as speculators whipsawed his investment in American Steel. In stand-up-guy fashion, Corbett blamed himself for panicking when he was hit with a margin call. As he ruefully told the papers, "Had I held on I would have retrieved my loss at least in part."

But Corbett proudly stood his ground when the which-side-are-you-on-boys labor wars hit vaudeville. It started when the dominant

Orpheum and Keith circuits attempted to eliminate the independent agents who negotiated salaries and touring schedules for the performers. Instead, the impresarios who ran big-time vaudeville decreed that all bookings must be handled in-house by their own version of a company union, the Association of Vaudeville Managers, which charged performers a 5 percent commission for the privilege of working.

Angry vaudevillians rallied around their fraternal organization, called the White Rats (inspired by a similar English group known as the Water Rats), which tried to become the Wobblies of the footlights. Refusing to sign contracts that included the hated 5 percent fee, the White Rats organized star-studded benefits to support their walkout. The inaugural fund-raiser in New York, at the four-thousand-seat Academy of Music on Fourteenth Street in February 1901, featured thirty of the top names in vaudeville, including Maurice Barrymore (the first of the theatrical Barrymores), DeWolf Hopper (famed for his rendition of "Casey at the Bat"), the comic duo of Weber and Fields (whose specialty was knockabout sketches), and Corbett. The ex-champ, a stalwart of the White Rats, had in recent years turned himself into an adroit monologuist, mixing self-deprecating recollections of his famous fights with endearing Irish family humor.

But the Great Vaudeville Strike of 1901 fizzled as show-business titans like B. F. Keith and Edward Albee held firm. By the fall of 1901, the remaining White Rats, with Gentleman Jim in the forefront, were reduced to hard-cheese rations. Blacklisted on the major vaudeville circuits, Corbett had nowhere to tour. Instead, during the spring and early summer of 1902, he mostly hung around his saloon, often offering free food and drinks to down-at-the-heels White Rats.

Gentleman Jim Corbett—the most popular sporting figure in America—was at liberty.

In 1902, Freeman Bernstein was also at liberty. He had escaped Albany and his dying Hudson River amusement park one step ahead of his many creditors. For a man of Freeman's ambitions, who had been chafing over living with his family in a tenement on River Street in Troy, the inevitable next stop was down the river to the world of big-time vaudeville in Manhattan. But instead of the lights from the necklace of theaters and music halls stretching from Union Square to Forty-Second Street, Freeman had to settle for a solitary candle at Bergen Point, that is, Bergen Point in Bayonne, New Jersey.

As the New York–based *Morning Telegraph* wrote in 1902, "Washington Park, Bergen Point, is about the last place one would pick out as a moneymaker in the vaudeville line." It was on the Hudson all right, directly opposite the remote end of Staten Island. The joke at the time was that Freeman had arranged to build a one-thousand-seat summer theater at Bergen Point because he liked to watch the ferry boats coming in. Other than ferries, the only way to get to the new theater was to take the Bayonne streetcar to the very end of the line.

The hastily constructed Washington Park Amphitheater would never be confused with B. F. Keith's Union Square Theater, Oscar Hammerstein's Olympia Theatre, or the Troy Music Hall. The small stage began puckering immediately after opening night, leaving it as uneven as a corduroy road in frontier America. The two dressing rooms, where the only water came from pails, were each a little larger than a park bench, roughly seven feet long and two and a half feet wide. An act called the Seven Little New Yorkers was canceled midweek because the seven little girls clogged the Lilliputian dressing rooms.

Bergen Point may have been the sticks—the end of the line for streetcars, ferries, and presumably vaudeville careers. But that summer of 1902 made Freeman Bernstein. Virtually everything he later did or became was acted out on a miniature scale in his management of his summer theater on the banks of the Hudson in Bayonne.

As an undercapitalized visionary scornful of traditional green-eyeshade bookkeeping, Freeman was already adept at kiting checks, doubling unpaid loans, stalling vendors, and fleecing the gullible. He possessed an uncanny ability to summon up ready cash, almost always somebody else's.

The angel who bankrolled Bergen Point was Charles Kanter, a thirty-year-old American-born cousin who was attracted to show business after tiring of cutting the pants too long for too long in Manhattan. Instead of leaving the pants business with a traditional insurance fire, Kanter and his partner arranged for a $75,000 bankruptcy in March 1902 after secretly shipping most of their merchandise to North Dakota. Even though North Dakota must have seemed as far away as Siberia to Kanter, he left too many threads behind for the police and was almost immediately charged with grand larceny by a WASP prosecutor who wanted to make an example of him. But somehow the defrocked pants maker, out on bail while awaiting trial, managed to become the prime investor in the construction of the Washington Park Amphitheater.

The fiscal flimflam behind the building of the theater in a former apple orchard on Bergen Point didn't prevent the local newspapers from hailing Freeman as an experienced vaudevillian who would put Bayonne on the entertainment map. The Jersey City *Evening Journal* declared, "Manager F. Bernstein has invested a large sum of money in the erection of the place of amusement and beautifying the grounds and proposes to conduct his place in a strictly first class manner." Opening night, Monday, May 5, was a financial, if not necessarily an aesthetic, triumph. Pricing his tickets at fifteen cents (which would barely get you into the balcony at the Bon Ton Theater in downtown Jersey City), Freeman boasted a sellout by five o'clock, three hours before curtain time.

The Washington Park Amphitheater offered authentic vaudeville performers, most of whom had been playing at the bottom of the bill at major New York houses. The comics (Frank) Martin and (Frank) Quigg were Freeman's first headliners with their sketch called "A Man and a Half," which was built around their respective Mutt-and-Jeff heights. Reviewing a Martin and Quigg performance in New York later that year, the *Morning Telegraph* sniffed, "They are not good . . . using stock jokes and ideas." The comics shared top billing during that first week with the versatile May Yvonne who, according to the *Police Gazette*, "not only sings French character songs but warbles coon ditties and does buck dancing." Freeman couldn't afford true turn-of-the-century stars like Happy Fanny Fields, so he hired Radie Furman, who aped her mannerisms. But, at least, on opening night the crowd at Bergen Point got to hear the Burdock Sisters sing their signature tune, "I Wants a Ping Pong Man."

During the first decade of the twentieth century, as many as three million Americans attended vaudeville each week—squirming seven-year-olds, spooning couples, and snoring grandfathers. For a vaudeville manager, the secret to survival was promoting a new bill each Monday that sounded so alluring that it would bring back last week's crowd.

That's what Freeman tried to do by ballyhooing "TEN ALL-STAR ACTS" for his second week on Bergen Point with an ad in the *Evening Journal* that was three times the size of the promo for the Pan-American Girls at the Bon Ton. Unfortunately, as a fifth-grade dropout, Freeman was more adept at counting gate receipts than spelling. In the first big vaudeville ad of his career, he misspelled the name of his star as "LOUCY MONROE" when, in truth, the singer-comedian was just plain "Lucy." (Freeman made the same error in the *Bayonne Herald*, so it couldn't have been a typo.) Miss Monroe, who had once been an understudy to Flo Ziegfeld's star Anna Held, now imitated her over-the-top Parisian dramatics and her coquettish renditions of specialty tunes like "Won't You Come Play with Me?" The rest of the bill at Bergen Point included a reenactment of the popular *Foxy Grandpa* comic strip; Mabel Delberg billed as a "coon shouter," fresh from touring in *Uncle Tom's Cabin*; and the African American performers John Larkin and Dora Patterson, best known for their 1900 song, "My Drowsy Babe: An Ethiopian Lullaby." Awash in the ready cash from the fifteen-cent admission (ten cents for women and children at the matinees), Freeman soon added five hundred seats to the summer theater by expanding the sides.

But no matter how he played it, Freeman was still in the boondocks in Bayonne (population: 35,295), on the wrong bank of the Hudson River. Sure, his theatrical bills were now listed in show-business newspapers like the *New York Clipper* and the *New York Dramatic Mirror*. But they appeared at the bottom of the listings for Jersey City. The closest to New York City that Freeman could get was an agate-type mention that his theater "attracts a large number of amusement seekers from Staten Island."

Freeman was fast achieving the recognition he craved, but it was in Bayonne, a town where he found it prudent to advertise his shows as "Polite Vaudeville." When he was initiated into the local Elks Club in late May, it warranted a small separate news story. But nothing could erase the stigma of the small time. Even the biggest stars Freeman booked were tiny, like eight-year-old La Petite Mignon (born Sadie Rosenberg), a talented dancer and mimic who had successfully toured as Little Lord Fauntleroy and was promoted as "Direct from the Empire Theatre, London." But mostly Freeman filled his bill with the never-was-and-never-will-bes of vaudeville—talents like J. Royer West (who later hired a man wearing a sandwich board to promote his act to Broadway agents), William Reed ("the Musical Hussar"), Lillian Tyce ("the Real Irish Girl"), and the Gordon Sisters, who, as the *Evening Journal* gushed, "punch the bag like trained fistic champions."

But everything changed for Freeman when in late July he lured a genuine trained fistic champion to Bergen Park—James J. Corbett.

Bored with the saloon business and frustrated that he was stuck on the sidelines as Fitzsimmons and Jeffries were about to meet for the heavyweight championship in San Francisco, Corbett hankered to return to the vaudeville stage. The ex-champ's first stop was a week doing monologues at Patsy Morrison's place at Rockaway Beach, famous for paying the best salaries of any summer theater in vaudeville. Then Gentleman Jim, the pugilist whom the *Evening Journal* described as the "highest priced artist in vaudeville," headed to Bayonne for a week doing two shows a day at the famed Washington Park Amphitheater, where the legendary Freeman Bernstein reigned as manager.

The photograph that I crave, even though it was probably never taken, would show Freeman, the leather-lunged fireplug promoter, greeting the strapping Corbett as he stepped off the Staten Island Ferry at the gates to Washington Park. It would have been midmorning, Monday, July 21, just a few hours before the matinee. A ladies' orchestra was already playing in the Palm Court that Freeman had added to the back of the theater—and the impresario of

Bergen Point might have suggested that his star take a stroll with him around the piazza to build audience anticipation. When Corbett inevitably asked to see the (rippled) stage and the (minuscule) dressing room, it is easy to imagine Freeman heading him off by saying something like "No need, Champ, no need. Work comes later. What you need is to rest. And I've arranged the best hotel room in New Jersey, just about the best anywhere, for your exclusive use. That's a Freeman Bernstein promise—and you can take it to the bank. The hotel is right here on the grounds. And order anything, anything at all. It's all on me, Champ. All on me."

That evening's performance, Gentleman Jim's true debut, fulfilled Freeman's fantasies. Every seat (thirty-five cents for the boxes and a quarter for anything down front, under a new pricing plan) was filled. Some of the well-lubricated gents standing in the back gave off a few raspberries when Corbett came out and started his monologue instead of sparring as they had mistakenly expected. But all it took was one good story about John L. Sullivan to shut them up. When Gentleman Jim stepped off the uneven stage fifteen minutes later, the *Evening Journal* reported, "the audience applauded until the roof beams trembled."

For Freeman, the week only got better. The actress Laura Biggar—who was in the headlines for inheriting more than $1 million from an elderly admirer—came to the theater several times from the nearby sanitarium where she was recovering from nervous exhaustion. Wednesday night, world handball champion Mike Egan made the pilgrimage to Bayonne to see Corbett. Following the performance, the boxer asked Freeman . . . the Freeman Bernstein who had been living with his parents in a Troy tenement . . . to join them for a dinner of champions. The topic that dominated the evening was the Jeffries-Fitzsimmons heavyweight bout slated for Friday. Corbett admitted that he was pulling for Jeffries because the fighter had promised him a rematch if he held on to the crown against Fitzsimmons. The evening ended with drinks, cigars, and pinochle. Even though the card table was the sporting arena where Freeman boasted championship credentials, he shrewdly allowed Egan to win all three hands.

Having Corbett under contract the week of the big fight was a fortuitous break. But Freeman knew that unless you played your cards right, luck wouldn't always be in the cards. In a flamboyant gesture, pushing 1902 technology to its outermost limits, Freeman paid Western Union to run a special telegraph line to his theater on Bergen Point. That way James J. Corbett, the once and hopefully future heavyweight champion, could come onstage after each round in San Francisco to read the wire-service account of which fighter landed battering-ram right hooks and which fighter staggered to his corner bleeding heavily.

As a hustler in a hurry, whose boyhood ambitions had been forged the moment he washed up in Saratoga during racing season, Freeman wanted something more glittering than reigning as a big shot in Bayonne. Gentleman Jim Corbett was Freeman's admission ticket to the other side of the river—his first chance to make his name in Manhattan. On the day of the big fight, the *New York Evening World* proudly announced on the front page that Corbett, "the cleverest man who ever pulled on a boxing glove," would write an exclusive account of the Jeffries-Fitzsimmons battle for tomorrow's edition. As Joseph Pulitzer's flagship paper proclaimed to the world, "Corbett has been making a wonderful hit at Freeman Bernstein's Washington Park Amphitheatre in Bayonne this week, and it is through the kindness of Mr. Bernstein that Corbett is relieved of his contract to him to tell *Evening World* readers about the big fight."

To the outside world, Gentleman Jim Corbett made Freeman.

The *Morning Telegraph* unequivocally declared, "F. Bernstein is making money." A week after Jeffries knocked out Fitzsimmons in the eighth round ("Fitz used bad judgment," was Corbett's verdict in the *Evening World*), Freeman was on to his next scheme. He revealed to the *Evening Journal* that "negotiations are pending" for a year-round theater in downtown Bayonne.

Behind the scenes, though, Gentleman Jim Corbett ruined Freeman.

Even with a week of sellouts, Freeman could not afford to pay the salary for "the highest priced artist in vaudeville" and cover all his other theatrical expenses, including the exclusive Western Union line on fight night. With his creditors circling, Freeman resorted to the credo that he would follow for the rest of his life whenever cornered: Flash equals cash to the credulous.

This has always been the logic behind the confidence man's favorite accessory: a Michigan bankroll, which is a wad of cash fastened by a rubber band with big bills on the outside and counterfeit currency (or even carefully cut paper) underneath. At Bergen Point, Freeman began wearing a flamboyant diamond tie stud, visually implying that if he could afford a $300 piece of jewelry, then any financial problems were a trifle, a misunderstanding certain to be wiped away with an immediate infusion of cash that would arrive tomorrow or, at the latest, the day after. The diamond stud (worth more than $7,800 in today's dollars) came with its own deceptive provenance: It belonged to Freeman's cousin Charles Kanter, the financially pressed pants maker, who had been storing it in the office safe at Bergen Point to hide the sparkling asset from the bankruptcy court.

Even an artful dodger like Freeman eventually had to show

some earnest money to keep the bill collectors from showing up midperformance as (Al) Fields and (Fred) Ward were doing their Hebrew "Izzy and Wazzy" sketch. So Freeman pawned his cousin's diamond stud. The decision to hock the tiepin without permission was classic Freeman—born of both a self-image that he was an honest man temporarily short of capital and an innate optimism that, with a few breaks, he could square everything tomorrow so nobody would be the wiser.

Of course, if the law provided an escape hatch, then Freeman would eagerly clamber down it. In August 1902, Freeman and his brother Sam filed bankruptcy papers in New York (far from the prying eyes of the Jersey papers) for the leftover debts from their failed amusement arcade at Island Park. Appended to that legal filing was Freeman's impressive collection of $4,771 in personal obligations (the modern equivalent of $125,000).

Rather than being chagrined by his bankruptcy petition, Freeman treated his coming financial freedom as if he had been elevated into theatrical royalty. He immediately paid top dollar to show at Bergen Point the Vitagraph motion pictures of King Edward VII's coronation as soon as the film canisters arrived from England. This grand gesture for Labor Day put Freeman's summer theater on par with the Orpheum—Percy Williams's showplace in downtown Brooklyn—which simultaneously began showing the Vitagraph footage of the pageantry at Westminster Abbey. Likening Freeman to vaudeville kingpins like B. F. Keith, the easily impressed local *Evening Journal* gushed, "Manager Bernstein has been compelled to pay an extraordinary amount of money to secure this attraction."

Just three days later, Freeman popped his cork by bringing to Bayonne a live attraction even fiercer than Gentleman Jim Corbett. In fact, rarely had vaudeville produced a greater mismatch between a promoter and his star. For one day only—a matinee and an evening performance—Carrie Nation would be delivering her fiery temperance lectures at Bergen Point. As the *Bayonne Herald* archly noted, "When Manager Bernstein first announced the engagement of Mistress Carrie, many were skeptical as to the appearance of a genuine saloon smasher in a place where the fluid she so strenuously denounces is so much in evidence."

When Carrie Nation arrived early on Thursday afternoon, September 4, at the Washington Park Amphitheater, Freeman proudly escorted her through the waiting crowd to the best hotel room at Bergen Point, the same one where Gentleman Jim drank and smoked just a month earlier. After a lunch that featured steamed clams and ice cream, the termagant of the temperance movement retired for a brief nap. Freeman was clutching his usual lit cigar when he returned with a reporter from the *Evening Journal*. As far as Carrie Nation was concerned, Freeman could have been waving a rum bottle. The agitator, famed for her "Hatchet-ation," sternly ordered Freeman to extinguish it immediately because smoking made men "dopey."

Freeman, who didn't quake freely, spent the day fearful of the wrath of the Nation. The gray-haired anti-saloon crusader came onstage holding a Bible as the crowd of mostly women and children serenaded her with the popular song "Good Morning, Carrie," whose lyrics revolved around plantation life in South Carolina rather than temperance. In her speech, she said with surprising softness, "You have been led to believe that Carrie Nation was a fierce woman who chopped up people with her hatchet. But I am your loving home defender. It breaks my heart to see the signs of the rum-sellers everywhere I go."

It must have broken Freeman's heart that he had to hide his beverage-bearing waiters while Carrie Nation was uplifting the morality of his sellout crowd. And it must have reduced him to tears that he did not share in the concession revenue as his star attraction peddled souvenir hatchets—a dime for ordinary saloon-wreckers and a quarter for deluxe models ornamented with pearls and imitation diamonds.

Carrie Nation's departure for Baltimore the next morning once again left Bergen Point safe for rum sellers. But Freeman was back to where he had been all along—in the minor leagues of vaudeville, still unknown in New York. With intimations of autumn in the air, Freeman was playing out the string on his summer theater, offering standard vaudeville bills just like you might find at the Music Hall in Lewiston, Maine, or at the Frederick, Maryland, City Opera House. In early September, the headliner was Tascott, promoted as "the white man who sings coon songs," who won three encores with his rendition of the just-released "Bill Bailey, Won't You Please Come Home." Another week, Bayonne got its first glimpse of the Great Fialowski, a Russian émigré who imitated animal sounds. Female impersonator Harry Le Clair, known as "the Sarah Bernhardt of Vaudeville," who had been touring as a "wench" since the late 1880s, also arrived with his lush wardrobe of evening gowns to do a pastiche of Ophelia's soliloquies from *Hamlet*.

For Freeman, rescue from oblivion was right around the corner—at Dr. Charles Hendrick's small sanitarium on the grounds of Bergen Point.

Since July, Hendrick had lavished his attention on his most famous patient, the actress-turned-heiress Laura Biggar. In 1897, she had given up her career on the stage (and her marriage to a fellow actor) to spend five years nursing the dying Henry Bennett, a Pittsburgh steel and theater magnate with a horse farm in New Jersey. As the *Chicago Tribune* put it, "Her audience consisted of one bedridden, querulous old man, and she had to spend all day long and every day in seemingly futile efforts to entertain him and keep him from sinking into hopeless melancholia."

Playing the road-company version of Florence Nightingale proved to be Biggar's most compelling performance, with the possible exception of her disrobing scene in *The Clemenceau Case* in 1892, which had initially whetted Bennett's appetite when she appeared at his Bijou Theater in Pittsburgh. Her reward materialized as soon as Bennett's will was filed in April 1902: Biggar was to receive about $1.5 million, depending on the value of a block of downtown Pittsburgh real estate (including the Bijou Theater) and the late Mrs. Bennett's jewelry. The Bennett family responded by contesting the will with headline-making ferocity, employing fifty detectives to make a beggar out of Biggar. The family's fury sent Biggar into the arms of Dr. Hendrick's sanitarium—and soon, as it turned out, into the arms of Dr. Hendrick himself.

Short of cash, Biggar concocted an elaborate ruse to protect herself against a protracted will fight. The devoted Dr. Hendrick helped her bribe a bent New Jersey justice of the peace, Samuel Stanton, to forge a marriage certificate purporting to show that the actress had secretly wed Bennett in early 1898. Then, in a ghoulish twist, Dr. Hendrick claimed that a fifteen-day-old infant who had supposedly died at his sanitarium in late July 1902 was the posthumous son of Bennett. Under New Jersey estate law, this mythical son would have become Bennett's sole heir. And upon the infant's death, the grieving mother, Laura Biggar, would have inherited everything.

The detectives employed by the Bennett family—including two gumshoes who had checked themselves into Dr. Hendrick's sanitarium as patients—discovered that the dead baby had been cynically rented for the occasion and the 1898 marriage certificate was a fake (the crossed-out preprinted date "19—" on the form was a dead giveaway).

Everything unraveled on September 26 in a Long Branch, New Jersey, courtroom scene that would have been judged too implausible for the vaudeville stage. Dr. Hendrick and Stanton were appearing as witnesses for Biggar in a civil suit over Bennett's estate. Suddenly, two deputy sheriffs burst into the courtroom waving criminal warrants to arrest the dumbfounded Dr. Hendrick and Stanton on charges of fraud. The dubious doctor and the unjust justice of the peace were each held on $5,000 bond. Laura Biggar also would have been arrested as part of the surprise roundup, but, by chance, she had skipped court that day, presumably still stricken over the death of her imaginary son.

With its tangled strands of greed, intrigue, and a whiff of sex, the story was bannered on front pages across the country with headlines like the *Boston Globe*'s "ACTRESS FOILED IN PLOT FOR A MILLION." For all her notoriety, Laura Biggar was as hard to find as the Invisible Man in H. G. Wells's recently published science-fiction tale. The artful actress took refuge with theatrical friends in Manhattan at a secret location known only to her aptly named lawyer, Samuel Frankenstein. In unctuous tones, Frankenstein insisted that Biggar was so eager to prove her innocence that she craved nothing so much as surrendering to New Jersey authorities. But the lawyer was too much of a gentleman to allow the actress to jeopardize her blushing beauty in a New Jersey jail cell awaiting trial. As he explained to the *New York Times*, "I told her to remember that Dr. Hendrick, though a well-known man, had not found anyone to go on a five-thousand-dollar bond for him, so how was she certain to get a bondsman? 'Don't give yourself up,' I said to her, 'until you've got the bail.'"

That bail wail was answered on Thursday afternoon, September 30, when a messenger boy arrived unannounced at Frankenstein's law offices on West 134th Street. His message: Gentleman Jim Corbett, in a gesture of solidarity with a fellow performer, had agreed to stand behind the $5,000 bail money for Laura Biggar.

And standing in Corbett's corner—eager to make the financial arrangements—was none other than his close friend Freeman Bernstein, the noted theatrical producer from Bayonne, New Jersey. After a telephone conference with Biggar's attorney, Freeman confided to the *Evening World* that the actress had been whisked out the back door of a house on East 110th Street and was now en route to New Jersey to turn herself in. But the ever-modest Freeman convinced the newspaper that "he was desirous . . . of little publicity in the matter."

Despite shying away from the spotlight and feeling embarrassed by the publicity, Freeman held court for reporters at his theater Tuesday night as he promised that there would be "lots doing" over the next few hours. He spent most of the evening sitting on a bench on the front porch of the small hotel at Bergen Point, the exact spot where Corbett was spied chatting with Laura Biggar several times during his week playing the Washington Park Amphitheater. Now, as the rain performed a ragtime rhapsody on the porch roof, Freeman offered to provide the newspaper boys with play-by-play updates on his talks with Frankenstein. The account in the Jersey City *Evening Journal* captured Freeman's flimflam flair and his corner-of-his-mouth confiding style ("I'll let you in on the scheme") that would sustain him for the next four decades. "I felt sorry for the woman and it did not take me long to find a man willing to furnish the $5,000 bond," Freeman said with the bravado of a recent bankrupt. "Who is he? Well, now I can't tell you just yet. He is a well known New York businessman and has a fine home in Staten Island."

As the evening wore on, Freeman alternated between exasperation that Frankenstein had not called him to confirm that Laura Biggar was finally in transit (she was still in Manhattan at a new refuge on West 134th Street) and creativity in inventing elaborate escape routes for her worthy of Arthur Conan Doyle. "As soon as Frankenstein calls me up and gives the word," Freeman explained, ". . . I will place Miss Biggar in the closed coach, and with her bondsman will go to Staten Island, where we will remain tonight. And in the morning, we will drive to some quiet station where we can get the Long Branch train without Miss Biggar being recognized."

At midnight, as a dejected Freeman retired for the night, he was close to suggesting that attorney Frankenstein had behaved monstrously. By then reporters had figured out, after some broad hints from Freeman, that his motivations were not (brace yourself) entirely altruistic. His hustle was to put Laura Biggar back on the vaudeville stage, calculating that she could earn back her entire $5,000 bail money in a month because of public curiosity.

Throughout his life, Freeman's indomitable approach to setbacks suggested that—before he had dropped out of school—he had learned the story of John Paul Jones ("I have not yet begun to fight"). But Wednesday morning, his dreams of managing Laura Biggar's return to show business in tatters, Freeman hoisted the white flag. He had run out of time, since the High Holy Days were beginning that evening. The show-business baronet of Bayonne told the gentleman from the press, "It's all off, so far as I'm concerned. I have given them every opportunity of accepting my plan, but I'm tired of waiting for them and will withdraw my offer to provide a bondsman for Laura Biggar."

So what went wrong?

Corbett, then playing an independent theater in Milwaukee with other blacklisted performers, confirmed that he had wanted to guarantee Laura Biggar's bail. So while Freeman could be inventive in hitching himself to the highfalutin (he would later claim a friendship with the Prince of Wales), Gentleman Jim had become a gilt-edged connection. Freeman's shadowy bondsman from Staten Island, who turned out to be Colonel Bob Ammon, possessed the cash, since he had just slithered away from the Franklin Syndicate stock fraud with a reported $140,000. (A year later, Ammon would be in residence at Sing Sing, but I digress.)

The most plausible explanation was that, despite the pieties mouthed by her attorney, Laura Biggar was in no rush to surrender to the police. She remained in Manhattan for another month before reluctantly returning to New Jersey to stand trial in November. Her acting skills—including a dramatic fainting spell—dazzled the jury. In an incoherent verdict, the jurors acquitted Biggar while convicting the bribable justice of the peace and the lovesick Dr. Hendrick, who acted on her behalf. Now for the happy ending: Even though Laura Biggar never received her share of the Bennett fortune despite thirteen years of futile litigation, she did marry Dr. Hendrick shortly before he died.

With the summer vaudeville season over at Bergen Point, Freeman plotted his next move. He picked up a part-time job arranging Sunday concerts (musical performances that were exempt from the blue laws) at the Bijou Theater in Paterson, New Jersey. Billed as "the prince of vaudeville" by the *Paterson Morning Call*, Freeman put on concerts featuring performers like the aging "wench," Harry Le Clair, as well as John West warbling his new song, "On a Pay Night Evening."

But mostly Freeman sat in his tiny New York office at 1440 Broadway plotting his next payday or pay night. He shared the building near Longacre Square with small-time vaudeville agents like the all-woman team of (Emily) Fernandez and (Matilda) Paine. More relevant to a promoter like Freeman—who had transformed himself into an accomplished publicity hound—1440 Broadway housed the New York offices of the *Billboard*, a leading show-business weekly. What passed for business for Freeman that fall primarily was appearing before federal district court judge George Adams to put the final signatures on the documents certifying his bankruptcy. No legal phrase ever thrilled Freeman more than the boilerplate line declaring that he and his brother Sam had earned "full discharge from all their debts in bankruptcy."

For Freeman, there was one remaining debt that was about to discharge with the bang of a stage revolver. Charles Kanter, no stud in the cousin department, wanted his diamond tie tack back. The item in question, unfortunately for all concerned, was residing at a pawnshop with Freeman's name on the ticket. With lack of family feeling—especially for a man who was out on bail after his own misadventures in the pants trade—Kanter issued a complaint that prompted a New Jersey grand jury in November to investigate whether to indict Freeman for grand larceny.

But the fix was in for Freeman.

With his lifelong gift for making fast friends, Freeman reaped the bounty of his six months in Bayonne. Bail was immediately provided by James W. Shannon, a glad-handing Democratic Party stalwart who reigned as the Exalted Ruler of the Bayonne Lodge of the Elks, the fraternal organization that, since May, counted Freeman Bernstein among its exalted members. The grand jury decided that the diamond stud affair was a dud. Freeman beat the rap on his first grand larceny charge.

Kanter wasn't so lucky, since he soon would be sentenced to five years in Sing Sing for bankruptcy fraud. But before he went up the river, Cousin Charlie got his revenge. An article in the January 24, 1903, *Bayonne Herald* announced that the Washington Park Amphitheater would be under new management for the coming summer season: "Mr. J.J. Frank, the proprietor, assisted by Mr. Charles Kanter, will give the enterprise his personal attention." For Kanter, the drop deck headlines on the story must have sparkled like his missing diamond stud: "To Reopen April 6 Under New Business Management—Only First-Class Vaudeville Talent to Be Engaged—Freeman Bernstein Out."

5

In the photograph on the cover of the 1899 sheet music, May Ward exudes sultry innocence with her blond ringlets, bow-shaped mouth, and peaches-and-cream complexion. The eighteen-year-old is billed as "the dainty little comedienne," but even a high-necked white blouse cannot mask her curves.

By rights, the song she was plugging, "I'd Leave Ma Happy Home for You," belonged to Blanche Ring, who had introduced it at Tony Pastor's Music Hall and turned its signature "Oo-oo-oo-oo" chorus into a national sensation. But the dark-haired, doughy-faced Blanche Ring lacked the oomph and oompah to sell the sheet music, especially since her photograph had to be paired with a caricature of a woman in blackface to signal that the tune by Harry Von Tilzer was sung in dialect: "I'd leave ma happy home for you— oo, oo, oo, oo / You're de nicest man I ever know—oo, oo, oo, oo." So the music publishers rotated fetching young singers on the cover of the sheet music, including the precocious May Ward.

This was how careers were launched in the waning days of the nineteenth century.

May Ward was born as May Southward in New York in 1881. She was the daughter of James Southward (an iron molder who had emigrated from England) and the Irish-born Mary Southward, who hailed from County Cork. May was just ten years old when her mother died from pneumonia in 1891—which explains why she was on the stage at age thirteen without anyone resembling a chaperone. In late 1897, she won her first minor press notices while gracing the stage with burlesque troupes at the Savoy Theatre in Chicago. She appeared in a show called *Fun in a Railway Station* with the Parisian Burlesque Company—and then two months later, she was back performing with the London Gaiety Girls Burlesque Company, pleasuring the audience in a pastiche called "King for a Day."

Burlesque in those days was part minstrel show, part parody of highbrow culture like opera, and part display of female pulchritude. Chicago had been a mecca for burlesque ever since Little Egypt electrified the 1893 Columbian Exposition with her hootchy-kootchy version of a belly dance. Shows had become increasingly risqué as they attracted an all-male, mostly lower-class audience. But the featured performers also got to step into the gaslit spotlight for solo specialty numbers, which for May Ward meant a mixture of singing and light comedy.

Fresh on the heels of her sheet-music star turn in 1899—and vaudeville performances as a singer in theaters like Egbert's Music Hall in Newark—May Ward left her happy home in penny-ante burlesque troupes to join the elite Rentz-Santley company for a forty-week tour in 1899. With elaborate costumes and sets, Rentz-Santley featured send-ups of the classics, transforming *Romeo and Juliet* into "A Hot Time with Shakespeare." When the tour hit Washington in October with the eighteen-year-old receiving fourth billing, the *Washington Post* declared that Rentz-Santley "bears the reputation for being the leader in the field of burlesque" with its "high-class vaudeville and extravaganza." Five months later, May Ward had moved up to second billing as the Rentz-Santley company played to packed houses in Baltimore with its parody of the play *Sappho*, which was then facing an indecency trial in New York.

After the burlesque season was over, May Ward spent most of the summer of 1900 singing atop the Hudson River pleasure boat, *Grand Republic*, in a club called the Floating Roof Garden. Much of her material consisted of so-called coon songs—ragtime tunes performed with exaggerated black accents—like "You Can't Fool Me No More." Her photograph adorned the 1900 cover of the sheet music of this song by Nathan Bivins, along with a cartoonish drawing of an African American couple angrily glaring at each other.

But the blue-eyed May Ward aspired to be more than merely a "coon shouter," as she was billed during a 1902 return to Baltimore with the Rentz-Santley troupe. Which was a fortunate career move since this musical craze lasted only a few more years before it was abandoned—even in those segregationist days—as too demeaning to blacks. Instead, May Ward's picture now adorned sheet music for romantic tunes as well as comic ditties performed in dialect. In a sheet music photograph that embodied the song's title, "Oh, the Girls, the Lovely Girls," she coyly peers out from behind an ornamental wooden screen, her curly shoulder-length hair barely constrained by a bow and her smile barely constrained by secret amusement. The same fetching snapshot graced the cover of the 1902 sheet music for Harry Von Tilzer's "In the Sweet Bye and Bye."

Instead of touring during the fall of 1902 with the Rentz-Santley company—which offered a wisp of glamour and the stability of lengthy bookings in major cities—May Ward entered the grease-paint world of one-night stands by joining the cast of a melodrama called *A Jolly American Tramp*. As soon as the curtain went down to the cheers of provincials at theaters like the Kasson Opera House in Gloversville, New York, the cast searched for an open saloon and often had to settle for drinking hooch out of a paper sack. A few hours in a flea-bag hotel and then on to the train for a long jump in shabby railroad coaches, the stink of traveling salesmen's cigars embedded in the upholstery, and only a faint breeze making it through the begrimed open windows. Rome wasn't built in a day, but Rome, New York, was played in a day (August 27). Then it was on to Benton Harbor (August 30), Fort Wayne (September 2), Lima (September 3), Kokomo (September 8), Ottumwa (September 15), Omaha (September 21), Cedar Rapids (September 25), Iowa City (September 26), and Rock Island (September 28).

Part of the turn-of-the-century fad for hobo dramas, *A Jolly American Tramp* promised audiences "Pathos, Comedy, Sentiment and Realism." The plot, which was about as realistic as President Teddy Roosevelt playing the ukulele in a tutu, revolved around a fiendish husband who chloroformed his beautiful wife in order to collect the insurance on her life. A hobo with a heart of gold finds the unconscious woman locked in the attic of a haunted house— and, without asking for anything more in return than a good meal, exposes the dastardly scheme. May Ward starred as the soubrette, the saucy maid whose knowing wisecracks suggested that she was smarter than anyone else onstage. The publicity handout for the melodrama burbled, "This lady is chuck full of magnetism and introduces a number of clever and charming specialties in her role."

Most of the local reviews of *A Jolly American Tramp* were plot summaries or press releases. But May Ward's career got a boost when the theatrical weekly, the *Billboard*, described her performance as "very clever." In fact, May Ward's entire career was built on cleverness. The *Morning Telegraph*, a New York show-business and sporting daily, offered a trenchant appraisal of her assets when she played Miner's Bowery Theater in an earlier production: "May Ward [is] an attractive young woman with a not very beautiful voice. . . . Her dancing is unconvincing, but she smiles brightly at the audience and her amiability covers her other shortcomings."

That was May Ward in a nutshell—her charm, her youthful good looks, and her adroit sense of how to please an audience elevated her far beyond her modest abilities onstage. As a result, she blossomed into a minor star in vaudeville and later in silent movies. No blushing coquette, no stagestruck innocent from the provinces, she received most of her education backstage. Smart, tough, and hungry, she figured out from an early age how the world worked and how to use her natural endowments to exploit it. And that was why, even though she didn't know it yet, May Ward was the ideal companion for Freeman Bernstein.

As 1902 glided into 1903, Freeman should have had every reason to feel depressed. He was bankrupt. His financial backer, Charles Kanter, had tried to stick it to him for stealing a diamond stickpin. He had been bounced from his theater in Bayonne. A lesser man—or, at least, one with less moxie—might have retreated to Hyman and Yetta's tenement apartment on River Street in Troy and settled for a life running a sideshow concession in a low-rent Hudson River amusement park. But Freeman still rented a small theatrical office in the Rossmore Hotel on the west side of Broadway between Forty-First and Forty-Second Streets. He also had a scheme for making his mark on Manhattan. And more than that, he had somehow found a mark to pay for it.

With typical flamboyance, Freeman unveiled his plans with a display ad in the show-business section of the Sunday, January 18, 1903, edition of the *Morning Telegraph*. It shared the page with a promo for Lambert and Pierce ("The English Coon and His Valet"), an announcement that the Faust Sisters ("The Australian extraordinary graceful contortionists") were available for bookings, and a bit of bragging about a new act that had just conquered Boston—the 3 Keatons, featuring seven-year-old Buster ("The most amusing, grotesque and acrobatic act ever seen in Boston").

Just as necessity had inspired him to become the Barnum of Bayonne, now desperation again made him an entertainment pioneer, a Buffalo Bill of the boondocks. This time Freeman was ballyhooing a new summer vaudeville theater in Fort George at the narrow northern tip of Manhattan—a panoramic, yet still partly rustic, area perched on a cliff one thousand feet above the Harlem River. Since 1895, a rough-and-tumble amusement area had survived here, but it was a disorganized hodgepodge of penny arcades, shooting galleries, small-scale rides, and sideshows. The leading attraction in the area was the Fort George Hotel and Casino, which catered to affluent German Americans seeking a weekend getaway complete with Bavarian music and military band concerts.

Freeman always boasted a keen eye and an intuitive sense of possibilities. Fort George was the terminus for three Manhattan streetcars: the Third Avenue, the Sixth Avenue, and the Amsterdam Avenue lines. Freeman grasped that sweltering immigrants from the Lower East Side and elsewhere could be transported to the gates of his new theater at the corner of Amsterdam Avenue and 191st Street for a five-cent fare. And stay for the vaudeville and the five-cent beer. For Freeman, it always was about the nickel.

Lacking capital as always, Freeman set as his goal to present the best vaudeville that money could buy—as long as the acts were willing to work cheap. His initial ad, which also appeared in the *New York Dramatic Mirror*, urged, "All High Class Vaudeville Acts Write Immediately for Open Time." But the money sentence came next, a line that Freeman could have emblazoned on his business cards: "State Lowest Salary in First Letter."

Named the Trocadero Music Hall after a popular theater in London, Freeman's twelve-hundred-seat summer showplace opened for business on Monday, May 4. A renovated theater with the sides covered by flimsy weatherproofing, the Trocadero allowed smoking during performances and vendors roamed the aisles selling liquor. The opening week headliners were Jones, Grant, and Jones, who had appeared on a bill for Freeman in Bayonne the prior August. They were three African American singers who, in the grotesque fashion of the day, performed tunes like "Give Me Back Dem Clothes" in blackface. (Throughout his career, Freeman enthusiastically booked black acts—less because he was a crusader for equal opportunity and more because the performers were more apt to accept his low-ball salary offers.) Also on the Trocadero's opening-night bill of fare: the Oriskany Troupe ("the premier acrobats in the universe"), comedian Eddie Leslie ("the greatest of all mimics"), the singing Browning Sisters, and the banjo-strumming duo of Claudius and Corbin.

One week after Freeman opened the Trocadero, he was felled by a calamity on par with Carrie Nation showing up in an ax-wielding mood: The Trocadero was raided. Not because any of the performers were working blue, for family vaudeville in those days—unlike burlesque—shunned double entendres as too suggestive for women and children. Freeman was also too smart to cross Tammany Hall, so all the liquor licenses were in order. But while Freeman could buy off the local ward-heelers, he could do little against the blue-nosed patrician reformers from Fifth Avenue. Someone had tipped off the Society for the Prevention of Cruelty to Children that the Two Pucks, the singing and dancing Eva and Harry, were slightly underage.

Freeman had every right to feel pucked.

The brother-and-sister act, now in their teens, had performed everywhere: The 1902 sheet music for the song "Eva" showed an old photograph of the little girl in a ruffled dress with her arm around Harry, who was wearing a miniature tuxedo. As the high-minded SPCC complained in its report: "Officers of the Society visited the Trocadero Music Hall at Fort George, in which a vaudeville entertainment was being given, and where they found two well-known children of the stage—the 'Two Little Pucks,' who are known in real life as Harry and Eva Salmon—engaged in singing and dancing, both of which acts are prohibited by statute. Aside from the improper surroundings in which the children were found, that of a low-class music hall, in which drinking and smoking are indulged, it was known that they were severely taxed by late hours and over-exertion."

Oh, the horror of it all.

Freeman and the stage-door parents (Abram and Lena Salmon) were promptly convicted of violating Section 289 of the Penal Code covering the employment of minors in theatrical performances. In pronouncing sentence, the judge declared, "We cannot resist the conviction that these parents have been living largely upon the earnings of these children, which amount from $125 to $150 per month." Defendant Bernstein was fined $50 for employing them. The Two Pucks prudently avoided New York City for the next few years on their touring schedule. Eva Puck grew up to be a musical-comedy star of the 1920s, taking the title role in *The Girl Friend* and having a song written especially for her by Oscar Hammerstein for the inaugural production of *Show Boat*. Aptly enough for a performer who got her start working for Freeman Bernstein, it was "Life Upon the Wicked Stage."

Fearful of being arrested again, Freeman tried to ingratiate himself with Tammany Hall in July by hosting an afternoon theater party at the Trocadero (featuring two thousand gallons of ice cream and several barrels of lemonade) on behalf of John J. Dooley. Unfortunately for Freeman, Mr. Dooley was defeated for Democratic district leader.

The next time the Trocadero was raided, it had nothing to do with politics, patrician reformers, or underage performers. When the sophomore class at Columbia held a "smoker" at the Trocadero, they brought along twenty-five freshmen as their prisoners. This Ivy League kidnapping invited retaliation—so 150 Columbia freshmen stormed the Trocadero to rescue their imperiled classmates. Needless to say, it was a great night for Freeman to be in the liquor business at the Trocadero.

Every August, since his formative years, Freeman heard a siren song: the racetrack bugler announcing the "Call to Post" at Saratoga. With the Trocadero flourishing . . . or, at least, breaking even . . . or, at minimum, staying one step ahead of the bill collectors, Freeman had a Winner's Circle Idea for Saratoga. With all the horseplayers in town, with the hotels bursting, with little to do other than sit in a rocking chair between dinner and late-night gambling, he would bring a vaudeville bill to town. Not name-your-lowest-price performers, but something he could plausibly bill as "Bernstein's Vaudeville Stars—The Greatest Aggregation of Vaudeville Talent ever brought together."

A lesser dreamer might have hedged his bets by booking Bernstein's Vaudeville Stars into Saratoga's twelve-hundred-seat Broadway Theater. But Freeman never did anything halfway: Only the five-thousand-seat Convention Center in the heart of town on Broadway was good enough for him. This was his triumphal homecoming. Every sporting man, railbird, and tout at Saratoga would know that Freeman Bernstein—that loud, crude, brash wise-guy kid with the head for numbers—had made it big in vaudeville.

The newspaper ads heralding the coming of Bernstein's Vaudeville Stars to the Convention Center on Tuesday, August 12, and Wednesday, August 13, began running in the *Daily Saratogian* more than a week in advance. Impulsively, Freeman wired Moses Reis, who owned a chain of legitimate upstate theaters, and added a Monday night date at the thirteen-hundred-seat Griswold Opera House in Troy. This time to save a little money, he didn't even bother with ads in the *Troy Times*. If Freeman Bernstein couldn't fill a house in his hometown through word of mouth—if he couldn't sell out the theater on Third Street less than a half mile from the tenements where he grew up—then he ought to go back to the Klondike or help Carrie Nation sell hatchets.

When Freeman came up the weekend before the shows for the running of the Travers and the Saratoga Special, all his old pals at the track (plus a bunch of freeloaders) were hitting him up for Annie Oakleys to see the show from the best seats for nothing. Whether he was in the chips or down with the chumps, Freeman was a notorious soft touch—so most of the seats down front at the Convention Center were spoken for without a penny changing hands.

But the true Saratoga Special was Bernstein's Vaudeville Stars. The headliner was veteran monologuist Marshall P. Wilder ("The Prince of Entertainers and Entertainer of Princes"), who specialized in the kind of jokes best described as rib-ticklers. A sample: "My little niece loves going to church. So I asked her if she could remember the minister's sermons. 'Oh, yes,' she said. 'Jacob died last Sunday, and Joseph died today. But I don't know who'll die next Sunday.'"

Wilder's delivery must have been something to behold, since the jokes themselves would have gotten him laughed out of any railway smoking car in America.

The other headliner, Amelia Summerville, was pitch-perfect for the pretensions of Saratoga in August. With deft mimicry, she mocked a high-society afternoon tea in which the well-bred women tried to impress Summerville with their limited theatrical and musical gifts. This conceit allowed her to sing such crowd-pleasing tunes as "My Rainbow Coon" and "Under the Bamboo Tree" without breaking character.

The performances should have been Freeman's stirring charge up San Juan Hill.

As Freeman expected, the Monday night show at the Griswold in Troy was a raucous success with every seat filled. In fact, the *New York Dramatic Mirror* called Bernstein's Vaudeville Stars "a great gathering of artists, who pleased enthusiastic audiences."

Instead, Saratoga turned into Freeman's Valley Forge.

The newspaper ads, the rental of the Convention Center, the salaries, train fare, and hotel bills for the performers, plus enough Annie Oakleys to shoot a hole in anyone's budget, added up to financial disaster. Without anything to pawn other than his good name, Freeman began writing salary checks to his vaudeville stars with the hope . . . the dream . . . the fantasy . . . that money would somehow materialize from somewhere to cover them.

Freeman favored obscure banks in out-of-the-way places, so it would often take weeks for the checks to bounce their way to his account. But Freeman always wrote a rubber check with a grand flourish—there never were trembling hands, nervous tics, or other evidence of psychic discomfort. There was only hope.

The checks, despite Freeman's air castles of dreams, eventually returned marked "N.G." for "No Good." But Freeman happily discovered that when an actress or a comedian sued him for nonpayment, they were more likely to win laughter than justice. A normal commercial dispute with, say, a carpenter who put the finishing touches on the Trocadero would end with Freeman being ordered to pay up—or else. But when Marshall P. Wilder got his day in court over Freeman's worthless check for $293.50, the judge could barely contain his own hilarity as he asked the plaintiff, "Well, do you want a good check for bad jokes?"

Amelia Summerville made the mistake of using a bogus $200 check from Freeman to settle her overdue bill at the Vendome Hotel in Manhattan, where she had been living for seven years. The result: no more afternoon teas at the Vendome for her. Not only was the actress evicted, but the hotel also brought her to court over $218.41. Trying to find hidden assets, the lawyer for the Vendome questioned her on the witness stand about whether she was receiving any payments from her former husband. As the newspapers reported the next day with glee, Summerville responded in a voice thick with theatrical incredulity, "What? Receive alimony from an actor?"

(In fact, when Freeman declared bankruptcy for the second time in 1911, Amelia Summerville was listed as one of his creditors, still struggling to be paid eight years after she trusted a check signed by Freeman Bernstein.)

After his Saratoga Salary Shortfall, Freeman and his brother Sam hit the road in the fall of 1903 with performers who never begged the Bernstein Brothers for an advance on their salary—and who were willing to work for little more than meat scraps and dog food. With a city kid's lifelong weakness for four-legged friends (plus a few fierce carnivores), Freeman concocted a touring show grandiosely billed as the Winter Circus and London Hippodrome. The circus was built around Mlle. Adgie (born Adelaide Castillo in New Mexico), who was hailed as the greatest woman lion tamer of the era. Fearlessly she cavorted with her three lions in a twenty-minute show, riding a big cat one moment and putting her head in its mouth the next. The bill was rounded out with the usual minor-league circus attractions: Professor Wincheman and his dancing bears, Girard Leon's trained donkeys, five Japanese jugglers, Professor Shedman's performing dogs, and what were advertised as "seven swarthy Hindoostan dancers."

Freeman and Sam opened for a week in Troy—fulfilling the fantasy of every small boy in America to come back to his hometown with a circus and a dark-eyed woman lion tamer. By the time they got to Schenectady, Freeman was demonstrating his flair for bunkum and ballyhoo. He spread the word that one of Mlle. Adgie's lions had gotten loose backstage and almost swallowed one of Professor Shedman's dogs, who was miraculously unharmed. Then there was the performance in which one of Professor Wincheman's trained bears wandered off the stage (probably by design). "The children screamed, women shrieked, some fainted and others became hysterical," reported the *Schenectady Evening Star*. "Bruin trotted down the aisle while the spectators scrambled to get out of the way. The screams and shrieks of the latter frightened the poor bear, which is as harmless as a baby and as playful as a kitten." The kittenish Bruin was quickly captured, but the ursine escape added a whiff of danger to every ticket sold in Schenectady.

Unfortunately, the following week at the Armory in Utica was all circus but no bread.

Mlle. Adgie was willing to face the lions every day, but she refused to accept the biggest danger of all when performing for the Bernstein Brothers—not being paid. When she was offered Freeman's patented promises instead of back salary in Utica, Mlle. Adgie cracked her whip, grabbed her chair, and escorted her three lions back to Manhattan. Freeman and Sam were left with a big top but not a big act. Nothing worked during the long week in Utica as the two would-be Barnums faced the horrible realization that if Bruin the Bear got loose again, there would be alarmingly few spectators to menace. The reviews of the Winter Circus and London Hippodrome were good: "There wasn't a poor act in it and there were several excellent ones," declared the *Utica Sunday Journal.* But try feeding the bears and performing donkeys with newspaper clips.

Facing the kind of animal (and performer) mutiny that would have caused Noah to scuttle his ship, Freeman and Sam bailed out in the middle of the night. The final verdict in the local paper was harsh: "Such unpleasant notoriety as the first managers, Bernstein Brothers, gained in police court is not of the kind that is good advertising in a Puritan city like Utica." But, especially in 1903, what happened in Utica stayed in Utica.

B ack in New York—and on the lookout for five angry Samurai sword–wielding Japanese jugglers and seven snarling, swarthy Hindoostan dancers from his Winter Circus—Freeman could enjoy the comforts of home sweet home at the Trocadero. Despite his checkered check-bouncing career on the road, Freeman still had a theater in upper Manhattan. And the Trocadero was on its way to becoming the signature theatrical success of his career.

Okay, Freeman was laying it on a bit thick late in life when he called the Trocadero "the rendezvous of practically all the sporting element of New York." But running a warm-weather theater in Fort George encouraged his instinct for innovation with such novelties as Amateur Night every Friday. During the summer of 1904, Freeman began to attract the kind of glowing notices in the theatrical press that he had fantasized about on the other side of the Hudson in Bayonne. "Under the management of Freeman Bernstein the Trocadero Music Hall, Fort George, has attained a prominent position in amusements this season," declared the New York *Sunday Telegraph*. "Each evening the capacity of the auditorium is tested: mostly families and ladies with escort. The players behind the bright lights are engaged with a degree of nicety that shows men of experience are at the helm." Reviewing a show at the Trocadero the following week—built around black-faced ragtime minstrel Tascott singing tunes like "You Must Think I'm Santa Claus" (which he later recorded for Edison phonographs)—the *Sunday Telegraph* predicted that "if Manager Bernstein keeps up the good work he will have to build an addition to his house."

The Trocadero gave Manager Bernstein the cachet and, more important, the cash to achieve what in a Jewish immigrant family was the greatest symbol of worldly success—he rented a permanent home in Manhattan for his parents, Hyman and Yetta.

No more worrying about the landlord. No more moving every May 1 to another run-down building on River Street in Troy to save $3 a month on the rent. No more working as a peddler lugging a heavy sack for Hyman, who was approaching his sixty-fifth birthday. Now they were living with Freeman in an old-fashioned farmhouse on a large lot on Audubon Avenue and 190th Street, right around the corner from the Trocadero. The rocking chairs on the rambling front porch were so comfortable—and the house so secluded and far from the street—that the Irish cop on beat, Officer Packey, used to take long naps on them in the middle of the night when his flat feet got tired.

I grew up hearing about this fabled ancestral home from my father, who loved to brag, "I was born in a farmhouse on Manhattan Island." By 1909, when my father came along, Freeman had turned the house over to his younger sister, my grandmother Rose, her husband, Alexander Shapiro, and their four sons. Hyman, now retired, and Yetta lived with them, presumably supported by Freeman.

In 1904, as the dominant figure in the family, Freeman installed his brother Sam as the assistant manager of the Trocadero. This cemented a lifelong pattern in which Sam—occasionally grudgingly—played second banana to his younger brother. Sometimes, though, bit players get to portray the hero. A fierce thunderstorm hit Manhattan early in the evening on Decoration Day. With fifteen hundred holiday-makers crammed into the Trocadero, including storm refugees who had been attending auto races nearby, a lightning bolt scored a direct hit on the theater, sparking a small fire in a corner of the wooden structure. The accompanying thunderclap overhead triggered a panicked rush for the exits. Sam jumped onto the stage, quieted the music, and in a loud voice calmed the crowd, explaining that there was no danger and that the fire was already being extinguished by the pelting rain. Tragedy was averted, reported the *New York Times* in a front-page article, "by the coolness shown by Samuel Bernstein, the manager."

Every career has a turning point when a few impulsive choices determine the direction of a lifetime. For Wyatt Earp, it was the decision to mosey on over to the O.K. Corral. For Harry Houdini, it was the moment that he spied his first pair of handcuffs. For Freeman, it was the middle-of-the-night fantasy that he could create his own vaudeville circuit.

Had he been content to patiently build upon the initial success of the Trocadero Music Hall, Freeman might have had a conventional show-business career that led to his owning a year-round theater farther downtown. But vaudeville—as Gentleman Jim Corbett and the rest of the White Rats learned to their dismay—was fast becoming a rigged game. Promoters like Keith and his partner Albee in the East and Martin Beck in the West had leased the grandest theaters in major cities from Boston to Los Angeles, from New Orleans to Toronto, to offer performers like W. C. Fields and Eva Tanguay a seamless web of top-drawer bookings.

Freeman—just a year after marooning a menagerie in Utica—was never going to challenge the Keith or Orpheum circuits. But just as every great con man believes his own con, Freeman boasted the confidence that, with a few breaks, he could soon be playing with the big boys. He had the instincts of an impresario, he had a genius for the mass entertainment market, he had an audacious resilience in the face of adversity, but he never had the capital. Late in his career, Freeman lamented to *Variety*, "My misfortune has been that whenever I thought up a good coin-getter I never had any coin to go through with it."

Freeman's good coin-getter, after the Trocadero closed for the season in 1904, was a creative notion to bring year-round vaudeville to Greenpoint, a working-class immigrant neighborhood on the East River in Brooklyn. Unable to afford to build a winter-proof theater from scratch, Freeman announced in early October that he had found a way for the Lord to provide. Well, not exactly Jehovah from the Old Testament, but rather an abandoned Presbyterian church that—with a little finagling with altars, crosses, and stained glass—could be transformed into a vaudeville theater in just six weeks. Freeman even hired an architect to transform the church into an eleven-hundred-seat showplace for saints and sinners alike.

"The house will be the only one in a densely populated district," observed the Brooklyn *Daily Standard Union*, "and there is no reason why it shouldn't be a go." Freeman's partner in the venture, Louis Leavitt, a paint manufacturer and a local under-sheriff, was wired into Tammany Hall as a crony of party boss Big Tim Sullivan. With that kind of political pull, the city building department shouldn't have presented a problem. But just ten days later, Freeman announced that the choir-to-chorus-line conversion failed to pass muster with the city inspectors. The real reason? Probably Freeman was once again short of coin ("Just give me a day or two. Bunch of checks are coming in tomorrow and my brother Sam owes me four hundred simoleons") and Leavitt wouldn't bankroll the de-churching by himself.

If Freeman couldn't bring his stars to Brooklyn, then he could add their glittering presence to life in the provinces. Vaudeville in 1904 was still a big-city novelty like elevator buildings and elevated trains. As the *Harrisburg Telegraph* put it in an article heralding the arrival of Freeman's touring company, "A great deal of curiosity has been aroused in this city by . . . our first real glimpse of polite vaudeville so deservedly popular in all the large cities of the world."

Freeman's fall 1904 tour was headlined by veteran trouper Mattie Keene, who got her start in show business touring the Oklahoma territory in a Conestoga wagon in the 1880s. This time, she was portraying a woman lawyer (get the smelling salts) in a comic piffle

titled "Her First Divorce Case." Burnt-cork comedian Will Dockray, who specialized in mossy nineteenth-century minstrel routines,
was available after flopping at Proctor's Theatre on Twenty-Third
Street: "He is a brave man," said the *Morning Telegraph* about his
perseverance in the face of outdated material, "but unamusing."
Then there was the singing duo of (Mabel) Carew and (Gertie)
Hayes, who had somehow concocted a musical reenactment of the
running of the Kentucky Derby. Freeman brought back the aging
child star, La Petite Mignon, now pushing eleven, who had graced
his bill in Bayonne. Freeman's audience-pleasing secret weapon was
one-legged acrobat Paul Stevens, who balanced himself on a pole on
a slack wire and then began bouncing. And for the public spirited,
the show closed with Marconi moving pictures from the Russo-
Japanese War.

Everything was so hastily arranged that Freeman couldn't even
decide what to call his touring ensemble. He billed them as "Bernstein's Big Vaudeville Company" when they opened at Poughkeepsie Opera House on October 20, but a day later, on a quick foray
over the Massachusetts border to North Adams, he renamed them
"Freeman Bernstein's Cosmopolitan Vaudeville Company." Maybe
Freeman couldn't fake being cosmopolitan in his hometown, so it
was back to "Bernstein's Big Vaudeville Company" for two days at
the Griswold Opera House in Troy. But that label was ditched for
good in Syracuse when the troupe appeared for four performances
at the Wieting Opera House under the moniker "Bernstein's High
Class Vaudeville Stars." (Freeman gloried in the phrase "high class,"
as if proclaiming it often and loudly enough would transform the
boy from a Troy tenement into an American aristocrat.)

By the time Bernstein's cosmopolitan and high-class performers
had crammed into their dressing rooms backstage at the Wieting,

this had become more than a vaudeville tour, more than a way for Freeman to wait out the long months until the Trocadero reopened in the spring. What the world was witnessing was the birth of a new year-round vaudeville circuit—the Bernstein Circuit.

Freeman sensed opportunities in cities like Troy, places large enough to theoretically support sophisticated vaudeville (rather than, say, just touring companies still performing chestnuts like *Old Tom's Cabin*), but small enough not to have already been gobbled up by Keith and Albee. Initially, Freeman promised to supply rotating weekly shows to theaters owned by Moses Reis in Syracuse, Troy, Utica, Oswego, Scranton, and Wilkes-Barre. The jumps by train would be short since all six cities were within two hundred miles of one another. For a theater owner like Reis, often forced to cope with darkened houses midweek, these promised vaudeville shows appeared to be a godsend. As the *Scranton Republican* reported, "The management of the Grand opera house announces that by special arrangement with Freeman Bernstein, the well-known vaudeville manager, we are to have at least two first class vaudeville companies each month."

Ah, the joys of self-creation: Two years after he was booted from a summer theater on the wrong side of the Hudson, Freeman now was routinely described as a "well-known vaudeville manager."

The obvious circuit-breaking problem with the Bernstein Circuit was that its manager was broke. Freeman always lived off box-office receipts and promises. When the cash wasn't in the till, the bell began to toll. The tour started out well, since Troy was once again a safe haven for Freeman with the *New York Dramatic Mirror* succinctly reporting that the show "pleased, fine audience." But the Wieting Opera House in Syracuse presented a particular challenge since the audiences that normally filled its elegant pale-green-and-gold interior were used to symphonic concerts and stage plays star-ring Ethel Barrymore. Needless to say, Freeman's personal definition of "high class" did not ascend to these exalted realms. The *Syracuse Journal* sniffed in its review of Bernstein's High Class Vaudeville Stars, "We can imagine a bill at the Wieting that would really and truly boom vaudeville, but this isn't it." The only performer who impressed the newspaper's unnamed critic was "one-legged man Paul Stevens . . . [who] showed not only that he can make a two-legged man look pale in acrobatics, but he is a veritable triumph of man over balance."

Since Freeman's traveling vaudeville troupe had only a single leg to stand on, he should have known that there would be box-office troubles ahead. The *Dramatic Mirror*, which offered weekly capsule reports on theater attendance, noted that "business fair" at the Wie-ting and "small attendance." That was followed by Freeman's brave return to Utica, which produced the terse assessment: "small atten-dances; poor performances." Scranton, which was slated to be the linchpin of the Bernstein circuit, was friendlier on October 29 with the local paper reporting "good sized houses" and "liberal applause." But playing Harrisburg was akin to following Buffalo Bill's Wild West Show with an act built around rubber-tipped arrows. Bern-stein's vaudeville stars, such as they were, came into the Lyceum immediately after the most incandescent performer in the galaxy—George M. Cohan touring in *Little Johnny Jones*. Then on to Leba-non, Pennsylvania, where Freeman's ragtag band of players was booked into the Academy of Music one day ahead of a real attrac-tion: May Ward on the road in a melodrama titled *Queen of the White Slaves*.

Even as Freeman boldly talked about expanding his circuit as far west as Akron to the twenty-one cities where Reis owned theaters, he and his perpetual sidekick Sam had to deal with vaude-ville's voracious appetite for novelty. Bernstein's High Class Vaude-ville Stars were slated to return to Troy and Scranton—and that required an entirely fresh lineup. No more Mattie Keene hamming up the notion of a woman divorce lawyer, no more dance numbers by the precocious La Petite Mignon, and, most of all, no more one-legged acrobats. Short of scratch, Freeman had to quickly come up with new acts from scratch.

Luckily, Francesca Redding, a star of the 1880s with her own small ensemble of players, was at liberty after playing at Hurtig and Seamon's 125th Street theater in Manhattan. Her problem was that she had been performing the same comic playlet (*The Man from Texas*) for three years and its age and hers were beginning to show. Also on the bill were monologuist James B. Donovan ("the King of Ireland") and Albene and La Brant, a team of mentalists. With his eye for the cheap, Freeman also booked (presumably for small change) Robinson and Grant, dwarf comedians known for their crude onstage antics. In truth, Freeman had hit the bottom of the barrel.

When Freeman discovered that he couldn't go home again to Troy ("medium houses," according to the *Dramatic Mirror*), he began to sense the intimations of disaster. Utica once again offered no relief: "poor performances." Carbondale was the kind of tough Pennsylvania coal town that expected all traveling shows to feature a free downtown parade, as was the custom with nineteenth-century circuses and Wild West extravaganzas. If Syracuse believed that Freeman wasn't classy enough for the Wieting Opera House, then Carbondale, in contrast, recoiled from Bernstein's high-class vaude-ville as if it were the Ring Cycle sung in Urdu. Barely able to muster the train fare to transport his company the twenty miles from Carbondale to Scranton, Freeman still hoped for a reprieve. He had done well in Scranton in late October—and the *Scranton Republican*, undoubtedly grateful for Freeman's advertising business, predicted that Bernstein's Vaudeville Stars "will undoubtedly be greeted by a crowded house."

Instead, the Lyceum was crowded with echoes as the threadbare jokes bounced off empty seats. Albene and La Brant could barely find a mind to read in the mostly vacant house. After counting up the meager gate receipts from two shows—a computational task that barely involved three digits—Freeman and Sam quickly calculated that there was just enough cash to cover two train tickets back to Manhattan. Their own.

Stranded in Scranton, with neither salaries nor train fare home, were nearly twenty members of Bernstein's Vaudeville Stars, including Francesca Redding. With their hotel bills unpaid after they were abandoned by the Bernstein Brothers, the performers suffered the further indignity of having their luggage impounded overnight. "Sam and Freeman Bernstein were the ostensible managers, but they have not stuck to the ship," the New York *Morning Telegraph* scornfully reported. "When it sprang a leak and started to go down they struck out for shore." The *Syracuse Journal*, recalling earlier performances by Bernstein's High Class Vaudeville Stars, sniffed, "The wonder was that the company didn't strand sooner."

Freeman's Scranton Scramble—following on the heels of his earlier circus vanishing act—established a lifetime pattern. Over the years, Freeman would abandon vaudeville troupes from Hartford to the Dominican Republic. Whenever Freeman entered a theater, the first thing he looked for was the Exit sign.

His lack of sympathy for performers and their signed contracts probably flowed from the belief that everyone should share in his grief. Why should he (Freeman Bernstein, the prince of vaudeville) suffer alone from sparse audiences in two-bit towns? So he was unembarrassed about elbowing his way into a lifeboat as soon as the band struck up "Nearer My God to Thee."

There is no way to sugarcoat this: My great-uncle could be a schmuck.

True, his callous instinct for self-preservation was probably fueled by the blazing desperation of a showman who could remember the tenement fires of Troy. Freeman was the John Henry of vaudeville—a lone, undercapitalized, hard-hammering dreamer competing with the mighty engines of the Keith and Orpheum circuits.

Throughout it all, Freeman remained convinced of his own rectitude. He had a code and, in his own mind, he stuck to it. Even when fleecing the gullible, he did it with such infectious high spirits that he believed that the marks didn't really mind the marked cards and the losers the loaded dice. No one in show business worked harder than Freeman . . . to borrow money. And when he had a bankroll, he was to generosity what that dime-tipper John D. Rockefeller was to thrift. As Freeman wrote to a friend in the late 1930s, "I have paid every man I owed, a dollar in the world when I had the money—as when I get money I pay. It may take a little while, but I don't owe my friends anything."

As they said in other contexts, Freeman was developing a reputation. Al Jolson's brother Harry tells the story in his 1951 autobiography, *Mistah Jolson*, of the pair being so down on their luck that they were forced to work for Freeman in a turkey (vaudeville lingo for an independent) burlesque show. The Joelson Brothers, as the act was spelled in those days, begged and pleaded with Freeman's partner Henry Dixon for an advance on their paltry salary. Rebuffed, they went twenty-four hours without eating before they mustered the courage to appeal to Freeman's good nature. As Harry Jolson tells it, Freeman raised their hopes by telling them to wait until after that night's show. After the curtain went down, he came to their dressing room, locked the door, and, instead of reaching for his wallet, snarled, "If you two kids ever ask me for money again, I'm going to kick the living hell out of you. Remember that."

For all his verbal ferocity, Freeman was not built like a brawler: His World War I draft registration card describes him as "short" and "stout." So any threat of penalty kicks were empty epithets. Al Jolson's most assiduous biographer, Herbert G. Goldman, puts the incident in 1904, but uncharacteristically fails in his attempt to find a record of the performance. My guess is that Harry Jolson, writing nearly half a century later, mangled the details in his memory. The theater was probably the Trocadero, since Freeman proudly lists Al Jolson as having played there. The story illustrates the way that the name Freeman Bernstein became synonymous with tightwad vaudeville managers. In fact, I am surprised that *bernstein* didn't enter the show-business lexicon as a verb meaning "not being paid": "Two lousy weeks on the road and then they bernsteined me."

But there was another I'm-juggling-as-fast-as-I-can side to Freeman—for he always believed that if he had enough balls in the air, one of them would turn to gold before it landed in his pocket. Stepping up in class in early 1905, Freeman found a deep-pocketed backer for his vaudeville theater in Greenpoint. Charles E. Blaney, the author of a successful series of Broadway melodramas including

A Run on the Bank, had developed a yen to become a producer. That was all Freeman needed to run to the bank after he convinced Blaney to spend $14,000 (about $360,000 today) to arrange for a hasty religious conversion of the vacant Baptist church, including erecting a stage over the baptismal font.

The renamed Garden Theatre opened February 13 featuring Flo Irwin, an actress who had been around so long that she and her sister May had taught Lillian Russell how to apply stage makeup back in 1880. The early bills in Greenpoint demonstrated Freeman's persuasive charms (or the desperation of bit players in vaudeville), since he was able to book a series of performers who were alumni of Bernstein's Unpaid Vaudeville Stars—the loyal, if under-talented, La Petite Mignon; Will Dockray, whose black-faced minstrel routines were as tattered as a Civil War sleeping bag; and James B. Donovan, whose crown as the King of Ireland had been dented during the hasty retreat from Scranton.

In mid-April, Freeman and his associates pulled off a coup by booking May Yohe and her current husband, Captain Putnam Bradlee Strong, into the Garden Theatre to try out their new vaudeville act.

May Yohe, who always fascinated my father, built her international reputation in 1894 when, as an eighteen-year-old American-born music hall performer in London, she managed to bedazzle Lord Francis Hope into marriage. Lord Hope was not only poised to become the eighth Duke of Newcastle, but he was also the owner of a forty-four-carat bauble known as the Hope Diamond. The jewels, the title, and a lush London life that included the friendship of the Prince of Wales (soon to be Edward VII) failed to prevent Madcap May from running off in 1901 with Captain Strong, the son of a former mayor of New York.

But passion came with a price—the need to earn a living. The former Lady Hope and her strong-armed captain were scheduled to open in Boston on April 16 in a playlet called *The Actress and the Detective*. So a practice performance two days in advance, far from the bustle of Manhattan, made sense. Or, at least, it did until May Yohe saw the theater. Arriving late on a rainy Friday afternoon, accompanied by her Japanese maid, she was appalled by the crudeness of a bedsheet sign in place of a formal marquee: TO-NIGHT! MAY YOHE AND CAPTAIN BRADLEE STRONG WILL APPEAR AT THE GARDEN THEATRE. Equally troubling was the discovery that the theater had only a single piano instead of an orchestra. "I shan't get out," the actress declared from inside her hansom cab in an imperious tone that she may have learned from the Prince of Wales. "The idea—to dare bill me at this place." After berating the hapless house manager, she headed back to the Manhattan ferry in the driving rain.

If May Yohe had truly craved seclusion to rehearse *The Actress and the Detective*, Greenpoint would have provided the needed privacy. The owner of the Garden Theatre couldn't have filled the house even if he had booked Edward VII. At the end of the month, after one money-losing week after another, Charles E. Blaney hoisted the white flag. As the Brooklyn *Standard Union* put it in its epitaph for the theater, "The attractions were the same as those seen in the best vaudeville houses in Brooklyn and Manhattan . . . [but] Greenpoint evidently didn't want amusements brought to their door."

As a showman, Freeman grasped the power of illusion, whether it was created by a borrowed diamond stickpin or May Yohe's hauteur. Which is why he understood the desperation with which the former Lady Hope had lured her decorative major onto the stage in the rickety playlet *The Actress and the Detective*. Major Strong was headed straight to bankruptcy court—and their only income came from stumbling around onstage for twenty minutes as a novelty act.

But even the novelty of seeing a former duchess onstage wasn't working. Back at another theater in Brooklyn, after an unsuccessful foray into Boston, the critic for the *New York Sun* sniped, "It is positively Mr. Strong's first appearance on any stage, but the bill only calls him a celebrity, which nobody can deny. His wife is similarly titled, but is billed, not as Mrs. Strong, but as Miss May Yohe, the 'Star of Two Continents.' Why the management didn't make it three, by including Asia, is not apparent." The *Sun's* poison-pen man on the aisle went on to say that Strong "bowed nervously at the scattered applause and occasionally Yohe smiled encouragingly at him. She wore no valuable diamonds."

A few days after this mocking review appeared, Freeman proudly announced that he was now in charge of booking May Yohe and her captain for a spring vaudeville tour.

It was, in effect, an alliance between Freeman's hopes and the Hope Diamond. By the end of May—even though no one would ever confuse Captain Strong with Nat Goodwin playing Shylock—the couple was earning $1,000 a week playing major vaudeville houses like Oscar Hammerstein's Victoria Theatre. During the run at Hammerstein's, Freeman stopped by the suite rented by the two lovebirds at the Hotel Astor. May Yohe, her captain, and Freeman decided to have an early supper—only to discover when the bill for $32 arrived that the net worth of the three of them was precisely $9.20. Freeman's solution: Sign an IOU on behalf of Hammerstein's. Another IOU was needed after Hotel Astor tried to evict the former Lady Hope from her suite. Freeman's IOUs rained down like the confetti that showered Admiral Dewey during his victory parade after the Spanish-American War. At the end of May

Yohe's week at Hammerstein's, she was presented with a check for what was left of her $1,000 salary . . . $75.

Freeman learned a lucrative lesson from May Yohe: Celebrity sells, especially celebrities who had just been in the headlines. "Freaks," as they were called in vaudeville in those days, became Freeman's specialty. Especially appealing to Freeman—an operator who would never win the imprimatur of the Better Business Bureau—was that headliners from outside show business tended not to be picky about who represented them. They didn't know vaudeville agents from secret agents. The trick was to get there "firstest with the mostest." Freeman became the agent who met the ocean liners with contract in hand and raced to sign up anyone who had just appeared as a spicy witness in a murder trial.

Even though Freeman fancied himself an international vaudeville agent, booking circuses in Berlin one day and former duchesses into Hammerstein's the next, the Trocadero remained the only solid thing in his would-be empire, the Rock of Fort George. Freeman's initial gamble on the outlying neighborhood was paying off, even if he benefited only indirectly. Joseph Schenck, who three decades later would help Freeman pay his legal bills, also recognized the potential of a scenic area where three streetcar lines converged. With capital from Marcus Loew, a well-coined penny-arcade operator, Schenck opened Paradise Park in 1905, complete with a Ferris wheel, a roller coaster, and a dance hall. The goal—and Schenck and Loew almost achieved it for a few years—was to turn Fort George into a rival of Coney Island. As the show-business weekly *Billboard* put it, "Paradise Park is admirably well managed and the excellency of the trolley facilities, with a five-cent fare to and from any point in Manhattan, makes it truly the mecca of the workingman and his family."

What about our old friend May Ward?

Everything had been coming up roses for the dainty comedi-enne ever since her picture had appeared in the *Police Gazette* while she was showing off her pulchritude with the Fay Foster Burlesque Company. Alternating between burlesque and vaudeville—the lines were still blurry in those days—she toured in everything with a provocative title, from *The Devil's Daughter* to *Queen of the White Slaves*. But the true measure of her success (beyond appearing on the cover of sheet music for Harry Von Tilzer songs like "In Vaca-tion Time") came during the summer of 1905 when her decision to change vaudeville companies became major show-business news. Under the headline "Hurtig & Seamon Get Even," the *Morning Telegraph* reported that May Ward had abandoned Al Woods (the impresario behind *White Slaves*) to sign a three-year contract with rival producers. A few days later Jules Hurtig and Harry Seamon announced she would be singing "What Are You Goin' to Do When the Rent Comes Around" in their new musical spectacular called *In New York Town*.

On a Sunday afternoon in early August, Jules Hurtig was stroll-ing the midway on Amsterdam Avenue in Fort George when he chanced on Freeman playing a customary role—berating an actor with colorful threats and the crude language of a refugee from grade school. "As all the esthetic theatergoers of the Fort George District are aware," wrote the *Sunday Telegraph* in recounting the incident, "Bernstein is the somewhat unconventional manager of the Tro-cadero Music Hall. He possesses an individuality worth thousands of dollars to him and dialect which David Warburg has often envied."

(A major comic performer of the era, Warburg was famous for his heavy-handed Jewish-peddler vaudeville routine in which he came onstage wearing baggy pants and an ancient frock coat shiny with the years. Freeman may have fit many Yiddish stereotypes, but he spoke unaccented straight-from-the-streets English.)

Hurtig was so impressed by the volcanic exuberance of Freeman's eruptions that he announced on the spot that he wanted to add a new character to *In New York Town*. There was only one condition: Freeman Bernstein was the only actor who could play Freeman Bernstein. While there is no record that Actor Bernstein actually made it onstage in the Hurtig and Seamon show, Manager Bernstein had achieved what he had always dreamed of—he was a show-business character in New York town. With his parents enjoying the big farmhouse in Fort George and his name in the papers, Freeman had everything he needed. Except for the girl.

Two weeks later, May Ward topped the bill at the Trocadero.

6

Back in the days when a young Damon Runyon was brushing up on his drinking skills while working for newspapers in Denver, Sime Silverman was popularizing the kind of Broadway characters who would later be called Runyonesque. And while Freeman Bernstein would have stood out as colorful even if he had worked in a paint factory, Sime Silverman made him a theater-district legend with the help of his new showbiz rag called *Variety*.

Both Freeman and Sime (which is how he signed his articles) were born within months of each other in 1873 to Jewish families in upstate New York. But while Hyman Bernstein was a peddler, Sime's father was a prosperous moneylender in Syracuse who later moved to Manhattan. After a decade chafing as his father's book-keeper, Sime wangled his dream job in 1903 as a vaudeville critic for the *Morning Telegraph*. That lasted until Sime made the mistake of panning an act that had heavily advertised in the *Telegraph*, and was fired.

With bravado that Freeman might have envied, Sime parlayed a discounted $2,500 note from his father-in-law into enough cash to launch *Variety* on December 16, 1905. Reflecting Sime's personality, *Variety* lavished attention on vaudeville and scorned anything highbrow. But three months after he stumbled out of the starting gate with an inaugural issue that sold only 320 copies, Sime was broke. An unpaid printer attached all of *Variety*'s tangible assets: three chairs, two typewriters, and a table. Acting on behalf of *Variety*'s many other creditors, cops stood guard to make sure there were no secret stashes of cash. As Sime later recalled, "Two deputy sheriffs occupied *Variety*'s office for 62 days. . . . The deputies were with us so long people thought they were part of the staff."

But Sime kept publishing, and the fledgling weekly caught on. By early 1907, *Variety* was outselling stodgy rivals like the *Billboard* and the *New York Clipper*. But the newspaper's finances remained shaky for years. As Dayton Stoddart wrote in his 1941 biography, *Lord Broadway: Variety's Sime*, "The greatest headliner act . . . [was] Sime himself—Sime juggling discounts, overdrawn bank balances, printers' threats, actors' squawks, weekly payrolls."

The hard-drinking, late-night-gambling-and-rambling proprietor of *Variety* was precisely the kind of press lord who could appreciate the artistry of Freeman's unorthodox business practices.

It helped that Sime remembered that Bernstein-Levitt-Toube purchased the top banner advertisement under "Vaudeville Agents" in the first issue of *Variety* and advertised weekly after that. The new hyphenated firm—which had incorporated in August 1905 with $3,000 in capital (obviously not from the Bernstein branch of the operation)—represented Freeman's latest attempt to move beyond merely managing the Trocadero. Ira Toube handled bookings for carnivals, while Victor Levitt offered connections to East Coast vaudeville theaters in small cities like Poughkeepsie and Passaic. Like all of Freeman's enterprises, Bernstein-Levitt-Toube was launched with a blare of trumpets as the firm claimed to handle international bookings for the Chang Su Ho Gardens in Shanghai and Luna Park in Berlin. About the only amphitheater not under the sway of Bernstein-Levitt-Toube was the Colosseum in Rome.

But Freeman's partnerships tended to be about as permanent as May Yohe's marriages. In February 1906, Sime broke the news that Bernstein-Levitt-Taube had dissolved with Freeman buying out his partners. (It's a safe bet that Freeman settled the deal with promissory notes rather than cash.) Six weeks later, *Variety* plugged Freeman's move to an office in the Sheridan Building, a two-story beehive of theatrical activity that covered the entire Broadway block between Thirty-Sixth and Thirty-Seventh Streets.

The true honor came when Freeman provided the news peg for *Variety*'s coverage of the San Francisco earthquake. In those days, Sime stubbornly refused to write about anything (war, pestilence, giant holes in the earth) unless it had a show-business connection. So *Variety* reported, "Freeman Bernstein, one of the New York representatives of the Sullivan-Considine circuit, received a wire from the Western headquarters a day or two ago, saying that the circuit's house, the Lyceum in San Francisco, is the only theatre left standing in the city." Without Freeman sharing his newsworthy telegram, readers of *Variety* would never have known that the largest city in California had been reduced to rubble.

Pretty soon Sime began to see the comic possibilities of . . . well . . . Freeman being Freeman.

An early *Variety* story began, "The inner workings of the Freeman Bernstein office in the Sheridan building have always been chaotic and the perilous way from the outer gate to the inner portal fraught with terror to the visitor by reason of a multiplicity of office boys and other functionaries." The un-bylined *Variety* correspondent (presumably Sime himself) recounted trying to work his way through the entourage to reach Freeman's lair only to be told by a particularly officious office boy, "I told you not to go in there. When I tell you to wait, you wait." *Variety* noted that Boss Bernstein himself "did not seem nearly so sure of his position as did the shirt-sleeved young man."

That was the only moment in Freeman's long career in the pages of *Variety* when he was overshadowed by anybody.

From the moment that he made May Ward his headliner at the Trocadero in August 1905, Freeman was smitten on top of the world. Just as Louis XVI built a new pleasure palace on the grounds of Versailles for Marie Antoinette, Freeman gave May Ward the most glittering prize in his realm—he arranged for her to play the Palace, where he was the manager.

Huh?

Was Freeman in 1905 running the most hallowed theater in vaudeville, the glittering diadem of the Keith-Albee Empire? No, that particular Times Square theater didn't open until 1913. But for a while in 1905, Freeman was the manager of the *other* Palace Theatre—the one in the middle of a Jewish neighborhood at 130th Street and Third Avenue. The one where the best seat in the house cost twenty cents.

Even without Freeman's love-struck patronage, May Ward's career was thriving. The music columns repeatedly mentioned that she was singing Harry Von Tilzer's hits—and she felt flush enough to place a promotional ad in the *New York Clipper* billing herself as "the Dainty Little Comedienne." (In that well-rounded era, the dainty May Ward weighed in at 130 pounds.) A week playing the

Family Theater on 125th Street in mid-September inspired a rapturous review in the *Sunday Telegraph*: "She combines good looks, handsome wardrobe, with an artistic blending of character work, which is a delight to witness."

Hitting the road with the out-of-town tour of *In New York Town*—the show in which Freeman had been promised a cameo—May Ward got good billing and friendly notices: The Syracuse *Post-Standard* called her a "spritely soubrette." The show itself was an attempt to bring a vaudeville sensibility to the legitimate theater with scenes set in a Bowery music hall and at a hotel roof garden so that performers could do their acts without totally abandoning the flimsy plot. When Hurtig and Seamon's musical spectacle arrived at the West End Theatre in Manhattan, May Ward's publicity photograph graced the *Sunday Telegraph*. The press-agent copy was pure gush: "Her 'chic,' neat and talented manner in portraying the various parts assigned to her care have made her services in demand by managers standing high in the theatrical firmament."

Not all the reviews were rapturous. An anonymous critic for the *Morning Telegraph* clucked, "May Ward's dancing reminded me of the queer actions of mother's pet hens early in the morning." But one vaudeville manager named Bernstein either liked pet hens or was not deterred by queer dancing.

Most of the details of the courtship between Freeman and the spritely soubrette have to be left to the imagination. But I like to fancy that Freeman won May Ward's heart with flamboyant gestures after she almost died from appendicitis in late December 1905. In fact, he may have been the one who arranged for her to spend her long convalescence at Mount Sinai, the preeminent Jewish hospital in Manhattan, which had just moved to a new 450-bed facility at Fifth Avenue and 100th Street. I can see Freeman arriving at the hospital with enough roses to equip every Stage Door Johnny in New York. The candy boxes would have been stacked so high in his arms that there was an international shortage of Swiss chocolate. Okay, Freeman probably put the get-well gifts on the cuff, but it's the thought that counts. Freeman's style would have been to ingratiate himself with May Ward's doctors by giving them tickets down front to Hammerstein's Victoria and passing along you-can-trust-me-on-this racing and stock-market tips. And no nurse could resist his flattery, even if Freeman was simultaneously dripping cigar ashes on her white uniform.

May Ward returned to the stage in late February 1906, gracing the bill at the Harlem Music Hall on 125th Street, Hurtig and Seamon's New York vaudeville house. By mid-March, she was at the Crystal Theatre in Detroit as a featured attraction behind a world-renowned genius: Bonner, "the horse with a human brain." Watching Bonner show off his mastery of arithmetic, May Ward figured out a way to multiply her own fans. As the reviewer for the *Detroit Free Press* put it, "Miss May Ward, a singing comedienne, is the hit of the show. Her voice is of average quality as variety shows go, but she knows how to catch the house by direct appeal and her song 'Did You See My Henry Brown' gives her a chance to talk to the men and women in the front row. This of course delighted the house."

With her limited vocal range and awkward dance steps, May Ward was learning the enduring truth of show business—you gotta have a gimmick.

Increasingly, her musical numbers turned to parodies. When she returned to the Harlem Music Hall in May, *Variety* reported, "May Ward sang two songs and finished with a burlesque imitation of Vesta Victoria singing the new popular 'Waiting at the Church' selection. She gained many encores through it." (Vesta Victoria—not to be confused with the queen with the same last name—was a British music hall star who had come to America in 1904. Her hit, "Waiting at the Church," was built around the would-be groom writing, "Can't get away to marry you today / My wife won't let me.")

By November, when May Ward made it to Hammerstein's Victoria—the best venue in vaudeville—she was experimenting with novel ways to put over her songs. One scheme was to fiddle with the lighting. "Miss May Ward should be congratulated and ought to feel greatly satisfied at the success she made this week at Hammerstein's," declared the *Evening Telegram*. "Of course, she has two things in her favor—beauty and talent, which is half the battle nowadays." The rave review went on to point out that she won major laughs by singing personally to men picked at random from the front rows "while the theatre is dark and the man with the spotlight flashes the rays upon the man she sings to." *Variety* also praised this trick of light in its own review, noting, "She did very well with her audience."

Freeman himself was a dervish throughout 1906, doing business deals with such whirlwind frenzy that you might think he was trying to raise money for a dowry. He was booking vaudeville acts at the Palace (his royal domain on 130th Street) while managing New Jersey theaters in Passaic and Paterson. Practicing his legerdemain at a distance, Freeman even briefly revived his amusement park on Cuyler Island in the Hudson River near Troy. After the Trocadero (now mostly run by his brother Sam) kicked off its season in April, Freeman leased an open-air theater on the Jersey Shore in Pleasure Bay. Somehow Freeman arranged for a popular singer-comedienne named May Ward to headline the opening vaudeville program over Decoration Day weekend.

But the big deal for Freeman was allying himself with John Considine, who owned a chain of West Coast theaters stretching from

Vancouver to San Francisco. With a shock of white hair and a reputation as a handyman with a gun, Considine was a bighearted sporting man who got his start in Seattle running box houses (whorehouses
that featured vaudeville acts instead of a piano player doing the best
he can). In early 1906, Considine came to New York for a convention
of the Fraternal Order of Eagles. While soaring with the Eagles in
Manhattan, Considine flew into a partnership with Tammany boss
Big Tim Sullivan. They created the Sullivan-Considine circuit—the
largest independent vaudeville operation outside the clutches of the
Keith and Orpheum circuits—with Sullivan as the gilt-edged front
man and Considine handling the details.

Needing a New York booking agent for the circuit, Considine
found a kindred spirit (they both had been caught up in the Klondike gold rush) in Freeman Bernstein. In September 1906, *Variety*
gently mocked Freeman ("generally listed as a vaudeville agent") for
his vocal insistence that he and only he represented the Sullivan-
Considine circuit in New York. Describing Freeman brandishing
checks and promissory notes to prove his Sullivan-Considine bona
fides, *Variety* noted archly, "When Mr. Bernstein receives the cash
for the negotiable paper he may pass some of it around."

Considine returned to New York that fall, offering prime acts
as much as $500 a week to go west. *Variety* contrasted his negotiat-
ing style with Freeman's by printing an overheard dialogue with
an actor:

Bernstein: How much?
Artist: A hundred a week.
Bernstein: Where did you ever get a hundred?
Considine: What's that got to do with it? Is it worth a
   hundred to us?

Over the next three decades, John Considine was worth thousands to Freeman—especially in bail money.

Elevated by his Considine connection and basking in the Broadway fame that came with his frequent cameos in *Variety*, Freeman was taking on an uncharacteristic patina of dress-circle respectability. In October, this fifth-grade dropout with a booming voice and a lifelong indifference to proper English grammar formed a new firm with Robert Grau, a leading agent for opera singers. The brother of the former director of the Metropolitan Opera, Grau had managed the 1904 American farewell tour of Italian soprano Adelina Patti, whose voice is praised in both *Anna Karenina* and *The Picture of Dorian Gray*. Even though Madame Patti made an estimated $250,000 from her farewell tour, Grau testified in court, "I did not make one cent out of the tour of Patti, and, in fact, I lost all I had."

Hounded by money problems, Grau had recently abandoned a vaudeville troupe in Springfield, Massachusetts. For Freeman, that was more of a rite of passage for a potential partner than a disqualification. The new Bernstein and Grau booking agency claimed an initial valuation of $100,000, but the Park Row attorney who handled the deal had to advance the two penniless principals $25 to pay for the incorporation papers.

But Freeman paid cash for one vital document—ponying up a dollar for a marriage license.

So what did the fetching May Ward see in Freeman, a man charitably described as short and stout? Beyond his charms, his chancer's dreams, and his choice to live the good life without paying for it, May Ward also sensed that Freeman was a man who she could count on. God knows, it wasn't that she detected middle-class virtues like dependability and stability beneath his show-business bluster. But from the beginning she had his number, responding to his hustles by laughing and saying, "Freeman, I always get you before you start." Also, May Ward—a performer who calculated every angle—figured out that never again would she have to pay an agent's fee.

The Freeman Bernstein–May Southward (her real name) wedding was held on Thursday, December 6, 1906, in the Fort George farmhouse at 500 Audubon Avenue.* The state of New York marriage certificate (no. 30115) contains a few oddities. Both the bride and the groom lied about their ages. Like an actress in any era, May Ward trimmed four years off her age by claiming to be twenty-one. Freeman—who lived by his wits rather than his youthful beauty—boldly sliced five years off the calendar by declaring himself to be twenty-eight, perhaps to cover earlier exaggerations.

The ceremony was performed by Orthodox rabbi Harris Orliansky. Since the rebbe was born in Russia and had lived in Glasgow, I like to imagine that Orliansky spoke English with an Eastern European accent cut with a Scottish burr. The choice of the rabbi may have been a bow to tradition and a way of honoring Hyman and Yetta, who were at the wedding. An equally plausible explanation—knowing Freeman—was that Orliansky was willing to work cheap, since he had been in America for less than two years and lacked a congregation. A down-on-his-luck rebbe was also more likely to find a Talmudic rationale for performing an interfaith marriage. By all accounts, Orliansky was charismatic and long-winded, favoring lengthy sermons on how Jewish survival through the ages was built on the altar of enterprise and thrift. Presumably, Freeman's

---

* In researching this book, nothing has given me as much pleasure as the discovery that Freeman was married in the same house where my father would be born two and a half years later.

enterprising approach of never paying his bills was not what Orlian-sky meant by Jewish thrift.

It was a short—or, at least, a thrifty—honeymoon. Three days after the wedding, May Ward was performing two-a-day shows at the Metropolis, the leading vaudeville house in the Bronx. Topping the bill were the comics Monroe, Mack, and Lawrence, famed for their sketch "How to Get Rid of Your Mother-in-Law." After just seventy-two hours of marriage, May Ward probably did not need to resort to any of the trio's tricks to discard her mother-in-law, even though Yetta Bernstein would be living in her marital home at 500 Audubon Avenue. But over the holidays, just to be on the safe side, May Ward ("New York's most popular comedienne") hit the road headlining a Christmas show at the Majestic Theatre in Plymouth, Pennsylvania.

On an icy afternoon a few days before Christmas, Robert Grau got up from his small desk in Freeman's chaotic office and—without grabbing his overcoat from the rack or saying a word—stormed out of the Sheridan Building. He then vanished into the city that O. Henry was calling "Baghdad-on-the-subway." Unable to pay the rent on their apartment on East Eighty-Second Street, Grau's wife turned to Freeman for help. Freeman arranged to move Mable Grau and her two daughters to an inexpensive apartment on East 153rd Street, putting an exclamation point on the family's fast downward slide from the days when they lived in a mansion in New Rochelle.

With no clues about Grau's disappearance, Freeman called upon the press-agent skills that had served him so well during that business with Laura Biggar. The newsboys on the afternoon of

January 3 shouted out the front-page headline "ROBERT GRAU MISSING. FOUL PLAY IS FEARED." The next day an actress reported that she had seen Grau slumped against the pillar of an elevated train platform in Manhattan with his clothes filthy and tattered. When she tried to speak to him, Grau fled.

(The impecunious impresario's condition may have been related to drug addiction in an era when opiates were the opium of the masses. Grau was to die in 1916 from an overdose of morphine that he was supposedly taking to treat his insomnia.)

Hours later, Freeman—with his customary flair for publicity—summoned reporters to read them a letter that he had just received from a distraught Grau: "I'm still in New York and alive. You don't know what I have suffered during the last two weeks. I have wandered in every section of the city looking for friends, but found none. . . . The result of it all left me a miserable wretch, penniless, without even enough to pay for a meal. I sent all I had—$8.65—to my dear wife for Christmas. I will telephone tomorrow and arrange to meet you."

Grau materialized as promised, clutching a letter from Ellen Terry in which the greatest British actress of the era promised to let him manage her next North American tour. Or, at least, that was what Grau claimed in an effort to put a fig leaf of good fortune on his return from oblivion.

Even though his brief partnership with Grau was drawing to a close, Freeman showed his generous side by taking the lead in organizing a benefit for him six weeks later. Held at the Majestic Theatre on Columbus Circle, the tribute featured a star-spangled array of theatrical and vaudeville talent, most of whom Grau had managed in more prosperous times. The entertainment ranged from the theatrical matinee idol Robert Hilliard, known for his impeccable dress and diction, to the elderly comedian Henry Clay Barnabee, famed for parodying a man with a wooden leg. As Grau himself would later write, "Barnabee was the greatest individual impersonator of all time." Also onstage that night were, yes, the dainty May Ward and the rough-and-tumble vaudeville star Maggie Cline, whose repertoire featured such songs as "Nothing's Too Good for the Irish" and "How McNulty Carved the Duck." Cline had a number of patented moves that defined her stage persona. Whenever she headed toward the wings at the end of her act, she would audibly ask a stagehand for a drink. When the Irish singer was handed a glass of water, Cline would loudly complain with theatrical ferocity, "This is what they give me when I'm dying for a glass of beer."

Watching veteran performers like Maggie Cline reminded May Ward that it took more than a fetching gap-toothed smile, an alluring shape, and a few popular songs to create a headliner. Calling herself the "Dainty Little Comedienne" was not going to cut it. Fame in vaudeville demanded a signature number that made you stand out from everyone else onstage—an act so big that it would define a career.

And in the spring of 1907 May Ward found it. Or, to be precise, she swiped it, stealing the idea for "May Ward and Her 10 Dresden Dolls."

Dresden china dolls with hand-painted faces and exquisite costumes had become a symbol of feminine beauty. During the summer of 1898, Mrs. Stuyvesant Fish gave a dress ball at her seaside mansion in Newport that featured chorus girls dressed as Dresden dolls handing out cotillion favors. That same summer singing star Bonnie Thornton was touring in vaudeville as "the Dresden doll." When the glamorous Adele Ritchie returned to the vaudeville stage from legitimate theater in 1905, she billed herself as the "Dresden

China Comedienne." That description was apt since Ritchie's costumes and hats were so elaborate that she vied with Lillian Russell in what the newspapers called the "Battle of the Prima Donnas . . . for the sartorial championship of vaudeville."

But no vaudeville performer had the idea of actually depicting Dresden dolls onstage until . . . well . . . Laura Howe.

Never a headliner, Howe was an attractive and clever young singer whose career later vanished into the mists of small-time vaudeville without ever getting that big break. Probably the closest she came was with an act called "Laura Howe's Four Dresden Dolls." As described in the local papers when she played the Family Theatre in Scranton in May 1906, the curtain rose to depict a mantelpiece shelf dominated by a huge German clock and four life-size Dresden figurines of young women. Magically, the four Dresden dolls came to life and, as they began daintily singing and dancing, Laura Howe joined them onstage for the solo parts. The problem with the act was not its visually lush opening tableau but what came next. As the critic for *Goodwin's Weekly* ("A thinking paper for thinking people") put it when the troupe hit Salt Lake City, "Laura Howe and her Dresden dolls had more the appearance of old crockery, without even a sunny crack to enliven their inane exhibition."

Theft of vaudeville acts was so common during this period that in 1913 the theatrical weekly the *New York Clipper* established a script registry system, and a few years later *Variety* followed suit. But in 1907, when May Ward hit the road with *her* Dresden Dolls, all Laura Howe could do was fume as she played dinky towns like Sioux City, Iowa.

May Ward previewed her new act at the Family Theatre in Scranton on June 3, almost a year to the day after Laura Howe's company played the same theater. (Scranton must have been a helluva town for sales of German-made china figurines.) No expense—or, more likely, no amount of credit—was spared for these Dresden Dolls. May Ward traveled with a stage manager, an electrician, three costume changes for each of the eleven performers, and three separate painted sets designed by the leading theatrical house, Lee Lash Studios.

If May Ward couldn't really sing and certainly couldn't dance, she could still overwhelm vaudeville audiences with the sheer exuberance of her spectacle. As she learned in burlesque, nothing succeeds like excess. So the publicity handouts gushed about the "double quintet of comely and shapely young misses."

In place of Laura Howe's mantelpiece shelf, May Ward offered a Dresden toy shop filled with giant boxes. As the curtain rose in Scranton, a stagehand gently took each box down from the shelf— and out jumped a flesh-and-blood replica of a Dresden doll. The ten dolls arrayed themselves around the stage before breaking into the opening number, joined by May Ward. Two scene changes, featuring the painted sets, rounded out the seventeen-minute act—a trip to Narragansett beach in Rhode Island to show off the dolls in seaside finery and a glittering palace ballroom somewhere in Europe dripping with ersatz elegance. Nothing in the show made logical sense other than the enduring reality that beauty sells. The critic for the *Scranton Republican* reported, "Yesterday's audiences were delighted with the efforts of Miss Ward and her company and called them out again and again at every performance."

Unlike burlesque, this was not a show designed for leering trolley-car motormen and sex-starved office boys. Instead, May Ward and her Dresden Dolls catered to the clothing fantasies of mature women and little girls. At matinee performances, every child was handed a commemorative doll and, once a week, a genuine

$20 Dresden doll was given away to a lucky theatergoer with a marked program.

This inspired salesmanship, which may have been influenced by Freeman, became May Ward's trademark. The doll matinees, which continued through 1913, gave her cachet as one of the rare vaudeville performers who could sell out afternoon performances as well as evening shows. Deprived of a traditional childhood and thrust on the burlesque stage at thirteen, May Ward found that her biggest fans were little girls caught up in the frilly fantasies of a life that she never had.

Laura Howe couldn't compete. A small notice in *Variety* in mid-1908 announced, "Laura Howe and her 'Dresden Dolls' believe there are too many 'Dresden Doll' acts to retain distinction for offering any longer, and [have] decided to be known hereafter as 'Laura Howe and Co.'"

The reviews of May Ward and her Dresden Dolls (soon slimmed down to eight) during the summer of 1907 described a rocky launch. The *Philadelphia Inquirer* sniffed, "Miss Ward's voice is of only fair quality, but the act would have gone well had it not been for poor stage management, which resulted in the absence of necessary borders, poor lighting and other marring defects." When the troupe played a summer theater at Brighton Beach, the *Variety* critic (not Sime) noted, "The costumes now worn by the girls are badly soiled and evidently not new." *Variety*'s man on the aisle also complained, "A semi-patriotic finale behind a transparent screen upon which pictures are thrown is useless."

Throughout their careers, May Ward and Freeman displayed a weakness for red-white-and-blue excess. Even though they were both born in New York State, they had an immigrant's appreciation for America—a land where the uneducated son of a Jewish peddler could become a theatrical impresario and a refugee from the back rows of burlesque could become a vaudeville star. They believed in the self-created life as passionately as any farmer plowing a homestead in Oklahoma. Freeman and his new wife understood that wrapping themselves in the flag offered crowd-pleasing theatrics. But they were never cynical about it—any more than Irving Berlin was a decade later when he wrote "God Bless America."

Despite his complaints about the Brighten Beach show, the *Variety* critic also saw the brightening potential of the Dresden Dolls: "With entirely new costumes, two different selections and a better arrangement of lights, Miss Ward will have a 'girl act' capable of standing comparison with the best. . . . Miss Ward can carry a dainty costume, and should get all possible from her prepossessing appearance."

May Ward undoubtedly enjoyed being called a looker in the reviews and everywhere else. But what mattered to her, like every vaudeville performer, were bookings. And thanks to her girl act, the Dresden Dolls were suddenly traveling in classy company. May Ward signed a lucrative twenty-five-week contract with the new Klaw and Erlanger circuit, which was backed by Lee and Jacob Shubert with William Morris doing the booking. Klaw-Erlanger was a bold attempt to challenge the Keith and the Orpheum circuits for supremacy of high-class vaudeville. This latest outbreak of the Vaudeville Wars, which raged intermittently during the first two decades of the twentieth century, was the best thing that happened to in-demand performers since the installation of running water in dressing rooms.

Starting her Klaw and Erlanger tour in Philadelphia and Pittsburgh in late June, May Ward found herself sharing a vaudeville stage with an up-and-coming lariat tosser and joke teller named

Will Rogers and his pony, Teddy. Also on the bill was singer Louise Dresser, who would later costar with Rogers in seven movies. At the Nixon Theater in Pittsburgh, as Dresser recounted in her autobiography, the house manager was loudly grumbling backstage about the bum cowboy act foisted on him by the circuit's booking office in New York. "The gentleman was displeased with Will at the start of his act," Dresser wrote, "but when the audience caught the humor of the man and the act finished with them clamoring for more, we all realized that a new star had dawned."

That week Pittsburgh was awash in stardust, since the critic for the *Pittsburgh Press* was equally ensnared by May Ward and her Dresden Dolls: "We were taken captive last night by the despotism of the dancing feet."

When Klaw and Erlanger expanded their vaudeville invasion to St. Louis and Kansas City in September, "May Ward and Her 8 Dresden Dolls" were headliners along with Hardeen ("the handcuff king"). Farther down the program were the Original Keatons, featuring nearly twelve-year-old Buster and his parents, Joe and Myra. This was a knockabout acrobatic act in which Buster was the major target of flying arms and feet. To make it easier for his parents to hurl him across the stage like a piece of luggage, Buster's costume featured a suitcase handle mounted on his shoulders.

Back at a Klaw and Erlanger house in New York in November, May Ward was on the bill when the Scottish raconteur and singer Harry Lauder made his American debut. Actually, she and the Dresden Dolls spent most of the evening watching from the wings as Lauder played to a rapturous audience for more than an hour. Wearing kilts that showed off his bandy legs and speaking with an accent so thick you could smell the peat, Lauder laughed his way through stories about his ragamuffin childhood as the "simplest member of his family," his travels with a chum named Mackie, and songs like "Stop Your Ticklin' Jock."

As Harry Lauder was tickling the fancy of New York vaudeville audiences, the clock was ticking down on what was probably the most successful phase of May Ward's career. Battered by the unrelenting competition from the Keith circuit, bruised by a financial panic that dried up lines of credit, bothered by a lack of theaters, and bound by a foolhardy decision to offer twenty-five-week contracts to two hundred performers, the Klaw and Erlanger circuit sued for surrender in November. As a result, the Shuberts scampered back to legitimate theater, never again attempting to enter vaudeville.

For performers, the white flags of surrender flying over the sixteen Klaw and Erlanger theaters symbolized disaster. No longer would there be an independent wheel offering high-class vaudeville in the East and Midwest, since the Orpheum circuit (under Martin Beck) was in cahoots with the Keith operation, which was run by Edward Albee. In classic monopoly fashion, this meant that major acts had to accept much lower weekly salaries and intermittent bookings or consign themselves to small-time vaudeville.

May Ward and her Dresden Dolls scrambled to replace their lost Klaw-Erlanger bookings. They played the Forrest Theatre in Philadelphia, an independent house that offered both straight plays and vaudeville. The local critic for *Variety*, George M. Young, reported, "The musical act of May Ward and her 'Dresden Dolls' is in much better working shape than when it was seen here during the summer. . . . [But] the patriotic finale, which is the weakest part of the act, is still retained." While some big-name Klaw and Erlanger performers were blacklisted, May Ward and her Dresden Dolls were lucky enough to be booked for a brief tour on the Orpheum circuit. They played Minneapolis ("Singing and dancing excellent, beauti-

fully staged and costumed," declared the *New York Clipper*); headlined the opening of the new Orpheum house in Memphis; and returned east for a booking at the Orpheum Music Hall in Boston.

But May Ward's days as a queen of the road were fading. Her
picture still adorned the cover of sheet music like the animal ditty
"Down in Jungle Town." By April 1908, with eight Dresden Dolls
to feed (plus Freeman), May Ward was reduced to simultaneously
playing two different New Jersey theaters, fourteen miles apart.
Twice a day, under the direction of Freeman, two open cars ferried
the girls from the Majestic Theatre in Perth Amboy (2:15 and 8:15
shows) to the New Plainfield in Plainfield (3:20 and 9:20 shows).
Crowds gathered to watch the Dresden Dolls in their scanty stage
costumes race over bumpy roads from stage to stage. On chilly
spring evenings, May Ward and her troupe sang their first song in
Plainfield with chattering teeth from the open-air journey. According to *Variety*, "Freeman claims a million dollars or so might induce
him to repeat the experience, but even so, he would insist then that
the cash be deposited in plain sight."

Freeman was born with a divining rod that gravitated toward
rogues and reprobates. And as a booking agent, he loved putting them on the stage, especially if there was some coin in it.
Which is how Freeman first got involved with booking tours to the
Caribbean and Latin America.

His client was the male equivalent of May Yohe—Hungarian
violinist Rigo Jancsi, famed for luring an American-born Belgian
princess away from her titled husband. But after nine years with
Rigo, the former princess Chimay (the daughter of a Detroit shipping magnate) felt that the music had gone out of her marriage. She

jilted the violinist in 1905 to run off with another man. No longer playing the palace, Rigo had no choice but to seek his fortune in New York. Forming a gypsy orchestra, Rigo quickly became a sensation at the Harlem Casino.

When Rigo was playing, two waiters had the full-time jobs of ferrying perfumed notes from swooning women in the audience to the bandstand. Rigo's schmaltzy violin solos became so frequent that the rest of the orchestra felt that they were just chopped liver. An uprising was organized in early 1907 by Antonio, who played the Hungarian cymbals. Frederico, the cellist, bluntly told Rigo, "You are not the only soloist in this place. We want to play once in a while and get a little piece of this popularity." And, presumably, a little piece of the women—although, in Antonio's case, it's hard to see how the Hungarian cymbals offered a route to a robust love life.

But Rigo refused to listen, not always the best attribute in a musician. Before long, the rest of the gypsy orchestra had landed a lucrative gig at a Second Avenue café and the unemployed Rigo was so broke that he was bounced from his apartment in a palatial building called the Sans Souci because he owed $300 in back rent. A reporter from the *New York Press* tracked down Rigo and his latest wife (yes, he had one) at the shabby Hotel Breslin. Forced to explain their reduced circumstances, Mrs. Rigo brazenly claimed, "We left the Sans Souci because we were troubled at all hours of the day by newspaper men."

When Rigo came to him for help, Freeman had an inspiration. An American concert tour was out of the question, since Rigo's prior agent had failed to arrange enough bookings to support a prima donna violinist and a backup orchestra on the road. Freeman's eureka moment was the realization that anyone who had been in the headlines in America—no matter how tarnished their halo or tangled their romantic life—could pile on the pesos south of Miami. He booked Rigo at $500 per week (about $12,000 today) to tour Cuba, Puerto Rico, Venezuela, and Brazil. By Easter, Rigo was serenading the senoritas from a small balcony overlooking the dining room of the Miramar Hotel in Havana.

As a new husband, Freeman was falling short in the good-provider department (the commissions from Rigo aside). He had been suddenly stricken with the Con Man's Curse and sent off to Grifter's Gulch. His name kept popping up in the papers, but for the wrong reasons.

Anyone who believes that there's no such thing as bad publicity should consider the sneering opening of this February 1907 *Variety* story: "The ways of cheap agents are ofttimes funny, but Freeman Bernstein, who is advertised as the New York booking agent for the Sullivan-Considine circuit, is entitled to the blue ribbon."

It turned out that Freeman had booked comedians Frank Martin and Charles Buckley to do an Irish-brogue skit for $100 a week at the Family Theater in Harlem, which he was overseeing for the Sullivan-Considine circuit. But when Martin and Buckley showed up for their opening night, the house manager told them that they weren't on the bill and that, in order to perform, they'd have to cut their salary. Instead, they called their lawyer and quickly won a judgment against Freeman, which they were under no illusions that they'd ever collect. At the end of the *Variety* article, vaudeville performers were warned "to be extremely careful what sort of contract is signed in any business transaction in which Freeman Bernstein is concerned."

Magician Henry Clive wasn't careful enough. Clive, who made his living from card tricks and sleight of hand, learned to appreciate the amazing feats of prestidigitation that Freeman could perform with a standard vaudeville contract. In a letter to *Variety* in June 1907, Clive explained that he had signed a contract for a fourteen-week tour on the Sullivan-Considine circuit with Freeman and Chris Brown, who ran the operation's Chicago office. But the booking was canceled with no warning and no compensation, leaving him stuck in Detroit with his marked cards and his coat with capacious sleeves. As Clive put it in his letter, "I would like you to publish this to warn artists not to place too much confidence in 'contracts' signed by these parties."

Then there was the odd business, reported in cryptic terms by *Variety*, that Freeman had made derogatory comments about a rival vaudeville circuit in order to book performers for Sullivan-Considine. The tone of the article hinted at the peculiar unwritten rules of vaudeville: It was permissible to blacklist performers but taboo to snipe at the competition.

With even *Variety* turning against him, Freeman's downfall was swift.

John Considine—who had a reputation as a straight shooter even when he wasn't gunning down ex-sheriffs—felt compelled to do something about his rapscallion representative in New York. In July, *Variety* reported that Chris Brown would be heading east to take the reins of the circuit's New York office. While pointedly praising Brown's "conscientious, businesslike and intelligent manner," the newspaper twisted the shiv by noting that Freeman was being demoted to assistant.

Freeman fought back with the only weapons at his disposal: blarney, ballyhoo, and bunk. He spread the rumor along the Great White Way that as soon as Brown arrived in New York, they would be forming a partnership of equals to handle the Sullivan-Considine bookings. That face-saving gambit lasted until *Variety*'s Chicago correspondent weighed in: "The rumor of a partnership . . . is not verified here. The report came from New York. Mr. Brown knows nothing of it."

Desperate to save his job, Freeman headed west pretending that his destination was St. Louis, where May Ward and her Dresden Dolls were playing the Garrick. In truth, he went all the way to Seattle to plead with John Considine for another chance. No dice. Freeman's most respectable job was coming to an end. Right after Thanksgiving, *Variety* ran a small item with a familiar headline from Freeman's days in Bayonne: "BERNSTEIN OUT."

But Freeman had grown as a grifter in those five years since he was booted from Bayonne. Those late nights on Broadway with May after her shows, those years using the lobby at Hammerstein's as a second office, and those after-midnight poker games punctuated with wild yarns had given Freeman a rascal's roster of high-roller friends: flashy men like West Virginia coal baron J. M. Richards, famous for handing $51,000 in cash to a hotel desk clerk in Atlantic City with the offhand remark, "Here, keep my spending money until I come out of the bath."

Just when it looked like Freeman was headed toward the rocks, Richards offered him some Kentucky bourbon to go with it. In February 1908, Freeman was brought in as the general sales manager for a group that had purchased the Old Tub Fowler Distillery in Falmouth for $300,000. The lasting consequences of Freeman's brief adventure along the Bourbon Trail had nothing to do with booze and everything to do with highfalutin titles. The vice president of the distillery was R. W. Nelson, the former mayor of Newport, Kentucky, known everywhere by the local honorific of Colonel Nelson. For in Kentucky, there were more colonels than kernels of corn. So after being a promoter for a Kentucky distillery,

Freeman (a man who was off shooting craps when God gave out physiques with a military bearing) felt entitled for the rest of his life to call himself "Colonel Bernstein."

Even if Freeman had started calling himself Czar Nicholas, it would not cover the awkward reality that he was fast becoming penniless.

His brother Sam was busy running the Trocadero . . . into the ground. A season of dwindling gate receipts prompted Sam, in desperation, to hire a scantily clothed performer to reenact the Dance of the Seven Veils. This was part of the Salome craze sweeping show business, originally inspired by Oscar Wilde's play about the daughter of Herod who danced provocatively in exchange for the head of John the Baptist.

In 1908, Salome dancing, with its barely veiled sexuality, was shocking public morality. Gertrude Hoffman danced at Hammerstein's with what *Variety* called "a most perceptible wiggle," creating little doubt that she was wearing nothing but short white pants underneath the filmy wrappings. Eva Tanguay went even further with a costume that she described as "strings of rhinestones and pearls . . . but not much else." Tanguay's version was so risqué that it threatened to replace "cooch" dancing in burlesque. (A 1908 *Variety* headline: "COOCHERS vs. SALOMERS.")

But the Trocadero, in the midst of a small but growing Jewish neighborhood in Fort George, was not ready for anything this brazen, especially from a copycat Salome. All it took was a single Monday night performance at the Trocadero and Salome was salami. Sam caved after protesting Fort George mothers threatened to shut down the vaudeville house. Things became so bleak that Sam announced to *Variety* that he could either rent the Trocadero to the teetotaling Methodists for a conference or try to lure back the scandalized Jewish mothers by offering free fifty-cent table d'hôte dinners with every twenty-five-cent admission ticket.

Freeman, at the same time, was arousing the ire of a different Jewish neighborhood. With nothing working from booze (the bourbon business) to broads (May Ward was so broke that she had to ditch the Dresden Dolls), he was reduced to returning to his carnival roots. In partnership with his father, Hyman, who had grown bored in the big house in Fort George, Freeman leased a block on Fifth Avenue—at the wrong end. Envious of the money that Joseph Schenck was coining by running Paradise Park just outside the gates of the Trocadero, Freeman decided to create his own summer arcade called Midway Park at the corner of 110th Street and Fifth in Harlem.

But Freeman forgot that Paradise Park was surrounded by open land on the cliffs of Fort George. In contrast, Harlem in those days was a thriving middle-class Jewish neighborhood—and Mrs. Leopold Oppenheim, Mrs. Josephine Klau, and Mrs. Clara Glauber, who all lived on 111th Street, had no interest in seeing the hurly-burly of Coney Island arrive on their corner. Their attorney, Ira Ettinger, sued Freeman for creating a public nuisance.

"Bernstein maintains here an exhibition of trapeze performance by female athletes in scant costume," Ettinger told a sympathetic judge. "There is a merry-go-round making alleged music at all hours. There is a blatant brass band. . . . The show collects noisy, boisterous, unruly crowds who block traffic in the streets." Mrs. Glauber, whose nose was out of joint, complained that the reek and roars from the ill-smelling lions, tigers, and hyenas gave her a nervous condition. She was also incensed that, in the middle of the afternoon, schoolboys could see underdressed aerialists performing on the high wire fifty feet above Fifth Avenue. Oddly enough, none of the impressionable schoolboys offered affidavits to support Mrs. Glauber.

Freeman might have survived the Morality Police of 111th Street if only the winds of fate had cooperated. But everything collapsed on a Wednesday afternoon in late June when Midway Park was crammed with more than two thousand women and children. The attraction was free admission as Freeman struggled to find gimmicks to keep his merry-go-round whirling and his brass band booming. But nobody was prepared when a thunderstorm hit with a vengeance with winds gusting as high as thirty-five miles an hour. As lightning flashed in the skies above Little Coney Island, women with their children in tow took refuge against the wall of a building under construction designed to house Freeman's movie palace. A derrick collapsed in the wind and steel girders tumbled toward the crowd. Miraculously, no one was seriously injured, but more than fifty patrons of Midway Park were treated for cuts from the flying debris. The ground at 110th Street was littered with frankfurters that went flying and popcorn scattered by the wind. They served as a memorial for Freeman's storm-tossed dreams.

If Freeman had been content to run failing carnivals, he might as well have stayed in Troy. And with the Klaw and Erlanger circuit kaput, May Ward's career was moving closer to has-been than headliner. When she toured, it was toward the bottom of the bill (promoted as a "well-known soubrette") with a show organized by Charles Robinson, famed for his routine "The Tramp and the Hebrew."

Things were getting so bad that Freeman could imagine that in the next go-round, he could play both the tramp and the Hebrew. He had schemes and scams, but most of them involved his wife, May, literally breaking a leg onstage. "No one on the stage carries anything like the amount of insurance maintained by little May

Ward," declared the *Trenton Evening Times* in October 1908. With at least a dozen policies, she was covered to the hilt for every calamity (burglary, fire, injury to her pet dogs) except being hog-tied by Will Rogers's lariat. She even told her life insurance agent, "From what I read, my continued existence is a great deal more certain than that of your company. But I'll tell you what I will do. I'll insure my life with you if you will get some other corporation to insure my insurance."

But even Lloyd's of London couldn't insure a fading vaudeville star against bad bookings. Freeman knew just what his wife needed: a show that would be bigger than just May Ward and Her Dresden Dolls. It was time to go legitimate . . . if only Freeman could find the coin to pull it off.

7

John Reisler started out as a fighter, even though he was built like a fireplug. But pretty soon John the Boxer gave way to John the Barber. By 1903, the *Police Gazette*, the Baedeker of barbershops, was reporting that Reisler "is patronized by more sporting men than any tonsorialist in the country." His devoted shave-and-a-haircut crowd included producer Sam Harris, boxers Jim Corbett and Tom Sharkey, plus the usual gaggle of gamblers, gangsters, and Broadway go-getters.

With the best-looking manicurists in Manhattan, high-stakes pinochle played amid the shaving straps, and the smell of bay rum cut with cigar smoke, the barbershop on West Thirty-Eighth Street was Freeman's idea of heaven. And Reisler—who was socking it away from card games and stock tips—was Freeman's idea of a theatrical angel. The trick was to convince John the Barber to become John the Producer. Freeman lured him with the vision of being able to surprise customers like Sam Harris: "You can quit in the middle of a shave and say: 'I'm a big producer too, so I'm giving up my business.'"

An agate type item on the stock pages of the September 4, 1908, *New York Times* announced the incorporation of the John J. Reisler Amusement Company with $10,000 in capital and Freeman Bernstein as one of the three directors. A week later came the news that the company's first production would be a musical comedy heading for Broadway that fall called *The Cash Girl* starring May Ward.

In putting together a vehicle for his wife, Freeman demonstrated an eye for identifying promising talent. The twenty-two-year-old composer George Meyer later wrote "For Me and My Gal" and lyricist Earle Jones went on to scribble the words for "That Old Girl of Mine" and "On Mobile Bay." May Ward's costars included old-time minstrel Tim Cronin and actor Snitz Edwards, who would later achieve fame in silent movies playing opposite Douglas Fairbanks in *The Thief of Baghdad* and Lon Chaney Sr. in *The Phantom of the Opera*. Freeman could be cheap about paying actors, a champ at kiting checks, and a churl when presented with overdue bills, but he never stinted on his wife's career.

Featuring songs like "The Tale of an Old Rag Doll" and "I'm a Detective," the three-act musical revolved around disguised heiress Mary Day (May Ward), who proves her mettle by working in a department store as a cash girl ferrying money from the customers to the cashiers. By the second act, Mary has transformed herself into a New York vaudeville headliner courted by every Stage Door Johnny in town. Taken up by the aristocratic De Puysters in the third act, everything is revealed and made right at their mansion in the Catskills. By the standards of early twentieth-century musicals, whose books were famously slapdash, *The Cash Girl* made as much sense as anything else headed to Broadway.

With three sets and a cast of sixty, including seventeen featured players, *The Cash Girl* opened on October 10 to a nearly sold-out house at the Baker Theatre in Dover, New Jersey. But then, according to the *New York Dramatic Mirror*, the musical "failed to please, poor business" at the Burlington (New Jersey) Auditorium. Worcester was worse ("fair business") as the show limped into Boston's Globe Theatre for its final pre-Broadway tryout. For John Reisler, the show had become *The Cash Hole*. With his initial $10,000 (about $250,000 today) long gone, Reisler took out a mortgage on his barbershop to raise another $5,000. He should have remembered that the vaudeville house created onstage for the musical's second act was called the Folly Theater.

The Beantown critics were friendly. "'The Cash Girl' has a chic young star—Miss May Ward. Her manner is ingenious and she sings clearly," declared the *Boston Journal*. Even more enthusiastic was the *Boston Globe*'s man on the aisle: "The new piece is built on conventional lines, but it is one of the brightest and most tuneful entertainments that has been presented at this theater for many a day. Miss Ward is happily fitted with a role that displays her versatility and charm of personality."

The charitable reviews turned out to be akin to praising the verve and zest of a patient as he lay on his deathbed. By the week's end, it was John the Broke Barber as *The Cash Girl* lowered its final curtain amid a flurry of lawsuits. The stage manager seized the scenery and costumes, while May Ward ($800) and Tim Cronin ($350) sued Reisler for back pay. A Chicago printing company claimed that Reisler personally owed them $20,000, which was more than the cost of the entire ill-fated production. Even Freeman filed court papers arguing that he was due $610 from the John J. Reisler Amusement Company.

A few days after *The Cash Girl* slammed its empty cash drawer shut in Boston, Reisler was back trimming whiskers on West Thirty-

Eighth Street. Expecting a shave and a laugh, Sime Silverman slipped into the familiar elevated chair only to find the most morose barber in Manhattan. "What's the matter, John?" Sime asked. "Your wife come back?" Reisler, who had been downplaying his involvement in the failed musical on the advice of Freeman, told the whole sad story to the owner of *Variety*, even explaining that he was unable to cover the mortgage on the barbershop.

At just that moment, George M. Cohan, the jauntiest man on Broadway, wandered in for a trim, only to discover that his favorite barber had been trimmed. Within days, Cohan, his partner Sam Harris, Sime, Sam Scribner (the biggest producer in burlesque), and a few others had raised $1,500 to buy Reisler a new barbershop on West Forty-Fifth Street, a few steps from Broadway. There was a limit to their altruism, however, since they insisted on free haircuts and shaves from John the Sadder But Wiser Barber. (Reisler, by the way, remained a Broadway institution for years, even going on to manage a fighter named Jack Dempsey for a while.)

In February 1909, May Ward, wearing a three-quarter-length fur coat and a large gray hat, appeared before a judge in Boston to successfully plead for the release of the sets from *The Cash Girl* so she could tour with the show in the fall. As for Freeman, *Variety* reported, "Bernstein usually goes to Brooklyn when he requires a shave."

My father, Salem Shapiro, was born in the family's farmhouse in Fort George on April 23, 1909. I can imagine Freeman's booming voice dominating the clatter of relatives, all three generations of the family in America, as he told jokes about palsied mohels and handed out celebratory Corona Corona cigars. He'd be explaining how much May wanted to be there—how much she loved children as well as her dogs—but she was on the West Coast touring again with her Dresden Dolls. While Freeman talked sentimentally about his sister Rose (upstairs with her fourth son, my father), he would also be complaining with volcanic theatricality about how Sam was ruining the Trocadero around the corner. "If you want to see vaudeville, real vaudeville," Freeman might be saying, "come to my new place. It's opening next month. You'll have the time of your life. Show them this and they'll give you a seat down front." Only when a relative or a neighbor looked closely at the free pass, signed by Freeman with a flourish, would they notice that the theater was on the wrong side of the Hudson River . . . in Bayonne.

Nothing symbolized Freeman's dashed dreams like his forced return to the Washington Park Amphitheater. Sure, he put the best face on it as the *Bayonne Herald* wrote, "Manager Freeman Bernstein announces a gala [opening] night. . . . The local theatergoers will greet this announcement with pleasure when they learn that the management is the same that introduced high-class vaudeville in Bayonne in the year 1902." The paper went on to recall that Freeman had brought to Bayonne singer Nora Bayes (who soon went on to become a star of Ziegfeld Follies) and Gentleman Jim Corbett. This time around, Freeman kicked off the 1909 season with May Ward ("the Dresden Doll Comedienne late star of the 'Cash Girl'") followed a week later by another former heavyweight champion, Jim Jeffries, at $2,500 a week. He even tried Sunday night movies, only to be arrested and fined a symbolic $1 for violating Bayonne's blue laws. But no matter who was on the bill, Freeman knew he was in exile. Instead of spending his nights roaming Broadway, Freeman was in Bayonne glad-handing visiting Elks clubs from Staten Island and Jersey City.

Bookings for Washington Park were handled by William Morris, who was mounting a comeback after being blacklisted following the collapse of the Klaw-Erlanger circuit. There was a natural affinity between Morris and Freeman—both Eastern European Jews of the same age, short on book learning and long on street smarts, who found themselves as vaudeville outlaws, consigned to independent circuits and theaters. They worked in tandem for several years and shared late-night card games with the likes of Sime Silverman. Morris always understood that while Freeman would cut corners and everything else when he was broke, he would try to make things right when he hit the jackpot. As a result, according to Freeman's obituary in *Variety*, "He could always borrow up to $500 in any branch of the William Morris agency."

By September 1909, Freeman was willing to do anything to avoid being buried in Bayonne. Which is why he agreed to serve as vaudeville agent for one of the greatest charlatans of the early twentieth century—the spurious spiritualist known as Madame Diss Debar. Harry Houdini would later write about her in *A Magician Among the Spirits*, "Were I permitted to go into detail I could tell tales of Diss Debar that would shock even the worst roué of the Montmartre. . . . Better far had she died at birth than to have lived and spread the evil she did."

Freeman knew what he was getting—in fact, almost everyone in America knew her notorious history. Claiming to be the daughter of King Louis of Bavaria and the dancer Lola Montez, the Kentucky-born swindler had served a year in prison in the 1880s for hoodwinking an elderly lawyer out of his Madison Avenue mansion. Moving her act abroad, she convinced a wealthy South African contractor to fund a free-love community called the College of Occult Sciences. In London in 1901, she was sentenced to penal servitude for operating what was described as an "immoral cult" known as Theocratic Unity. After serving five years at the king's pleasure in England, she popped up in Detroit masquerading as Mother Elinor, the self-crowned Queen of the House of Israel. When Mother Elinor vanished, so did $10,000 in jewels. Just as Freeman was arranging to set up Madame Diss Debar for a week at Hammerstein's Victoria, the newspapers reported that her long-time assistant, David Livingston Mackay (known as David the Prophet), was being deported to Canada based on an undisclosed prior conviction for selling pornography.

One detail, though, proved irresistible to Freeman: Hammer-stein's would pay $1,000 to put her onstage for a week. As Freeman told *Variety*, "The old gal has buncoed some of the best of 'em. I'll show her a few things she overlooked." But on opening night, singer Louise Dresser refused to go on when she discovered that Madame Diss Debar was on the program—with top billing. Things went downhill from there with the spiritualist's performances fast becoming the greatest show-business disaster since *Our American Cousin* played Ford's Theatre in Washington. When Madame Diss Debar was onstage, the silence at Hammerstein's was so total that a real estate agent named Jerome Wilson was arrested for the crime of applauding too loudly. Presumably, Wilson woke up too many sleeping patrons—and they complained to the police.

Sime Silverman couldn't resist reviewing the act (billed as a lecture) for *Variety* himself: "She said nothing of interest, excepting to claim that she is immortal." The oft-arrested spiritualist (about sixty and looking older) came onstage wearing flowing white robes, ready to challenge all the accusations made against her by the "venal press." She insisted, for example, that she had been arrested in England simply for holding meetings. But, as Sime noted archly, "If the Madame had told the real reason why she was arrested, convicted and sentenced to prison on the other side, Hammerstein's would not be able to hold the mobs that would want to hear her." But mobs were the least of Madame Diss Debar's problems at Hammerstein's. At the end of her disastrous one-week booking, Freeman showed up at Hammerstein's with an oversize doll (left over from May Ward's act) as a peace offering. According to *Variety*, Willie Hammerstein, Oscar's son and the manager of the Victoria Theatre, laughed the whole thing off, saying that the "featured flop" was nothing compared to his poker losses.

A lesser man than Freeman would have been disconsolate over the Diss Debar Disaster. But throughout his life, Freeman shamelessly confronted adversity with good-humored bravado. Rather than rail against the fates, he would be back at the rail the next day with a guaranteed tip straight from the jockey's brother. Sure, Freeman didn't always get the breaks, especially in the stretch. But he always followed the credo: Play enough long shots—and, sooner or later, one will come galloping home.

Less than two weeks later, Freeman's deal-making compass was pointing due north. Like everyone else in America, Freeman was caught up in the biggest furor over the North Pole since the publication of *The Night Before Christmas* in 1823. Two rival American explorers—Captain Frederick Cook and Commodore Robert Peary—returned to civilization in September 1909, each claiming to have been the first to reach the Pole. With competing newspapers taking sides (the *Times* was a Peary paper while the *Herald* was campaigning for Cook), there was a hunger to hear every detail of the dueling dogsled sagas. As Lincoln Steffens wrote at the time,

"Whatever the truth is, the situation is as wonderful as the Pole. And whatever they found there, those explorers, they have left there a story as great as a continent."

Cook, a medical doctor who claimed to have reached the Pole in April 1908, became the initial favorite, since he had the good sense to head straight for New York. Everyone in show business wanted to see Captain Cook on the stage. The Shuberts offered him $10,000 for just two lectures at the Hippodrome. A William Morris agent approached him about a short vaudeville tour. But nothing compared to Freeman's frontal assault, which must have made the explorer long for the tranquility of life among the polar bears.

The day after Cook landed in New York, Freeman bearded him at the offices of the Arctic Club. Bursting through the crowd, Freeman boomed, "Howdy, Doc. I've got a little proposition here that's going to get you some easy money if you go about it right." Seeing puzzlement on the faces of the patrician sportsmen swirling around Cook, Freeman went right into his sales pitch: "All you have got to do is to play in vaudeville for 25 weeks and there's $100,000 waiting for you at the end of the run. How about it, kid? That's some money, eh? And that's not all, Doc. Just to show you how far we will go for you, you have only to start at Hammerstein's, talk for eighteen minutes every afternoon and evening, and go on about your business. Any softer graft than that, eh? You can't pick up stuff like this at the Pole."

Afterward, Freeman was puzzled about why he got a cold shoulder from the Arctic explorer. "I offered that guy, Cook, $100,000 for twenty-five weeks, and he's thinking it over," Freeman marveled. "Can you beat that?"

That season Freeman was getting the freeze-out everywhere. About the only act that he was booking was his wife's tour in *The*

Cash Girl. Where once the show was headed to Broadway, now it was stuck in the purgatory of one-night stands in upstate New York and Canada. Auburn (October 30), Cortland (November 1), Binghamton (November 2), Waverly (November 3). The towns and the local opera houses blurred into a grease-paint fog. But throughout the ordeal, May Ward, at least publicly, exuded high spirits. Meeting with local reporters, the star of *The Cash Girl* conjured up the clichés of show business before they were even clichés, blithely calling the thirty-five-member company "one big happy family." During a publicity interview with the *Rome Daily Sentinel*, the Dresden Doll comedienne coyly revealed, "This afternoon we are going to the skating rink. I guess the roller skating craze has returned, as far as *The Cash Girl* company is concerned, for on an afternoon when there is no matinee, we almost always patronize a rink."

Such were the joys of rinky-dink towns and a rickety show. From the bleak winter landscapes of the Pennsylvania coal country (Pittston, Hazleton, and Honesdale) to small southern cities like Chattanooga, the *Cash Girl* company chugged on one step ahead of the bill collectors. Finally, after thirty weeks, Freeman gave up the ghost. But not before he got the entire cast to sign a receipt saying that they were paid in full—and couldn't sue him for back wages. "I gave the bunch some stuff from the show to work home and pick up a little easy money on the way," Freeman explained to *Variety*. Translation: Instead of following the normal show-business practice of giving the cast of *The Cash Girl* train fare back to New York, Freeman saved cash by pawning off costumes and bits of scenery on the performers in hopes that they might use these discards onstage as they worked themselves home.

Back in New York, Freeman had other problems—and they looked suspiciously like his brother Sam. Frustrated with the way that Sam was running the Trocadero, Freeman decided that family feeling ended at the ticket booth window. At the start of the 1910 summer season, Freeman announced that he would be opening up his own Moulin Rouge music hall right down the street from the Trocadero. That decision brought with it a few brotherly complications since, according to the 1910 census, Sam was living with Freeman and May in a house on West 178th Street. The Moulin Rouge—which never was more than a building with a rough stage and tables and chairs—made as small an impression on vaudeville as it did on relations between the Bernstein brothers. "Sure, we speak," Freeman told *Variety*. "What made you think we didn't? It's brotherly opposition."

Even after *The Cash Girl* crashed, May Ward could still bring in the coin. But just not enough of it to keep her in minks and to give Freeman a fat bankroll that wasn't padded with cutup newspaper.

Back working solo in vaudeville, May developed a new comic act built around ethnic parodies. When she unveiled it at the independent Plaza Music Hall (booked by William Morris), the critic for the *New York Clipper* praised her for embracing "a wide range of dialect numbers—Hebrew, negro and Italian—and in each one she showed a skill that made her work keenly enjoyable. The 'dago,' which came at the conclusion of her act, was probably the best of the lot." May Ward mocked an accent of an immigrant from old Napoli by adding a final "a" to almost every word ("I got-a what you call-a dis-a nice-a sweetheart") in songs like "That Dreamy Italian Waltz," a tune that also featured her face on the cover of the sheet music.

New act or old (with or without the Dresden Dolls), May Ward was facing the reality that she would never be a headliner in New York. Instead, she was too often listed in the newspaper write-ups as "among the others on the bill." When she appeared at the Winter

Garden (owned by the Shuberts) for a Sunday night concert, *Variety* noted sympathetically, "May Ward had an impossible spot, 'No. 17,' but sang three songs holding the house very well." There was a whiff of desperation about her efforts: She flooded Broadway with cards urging everyone to vote for her as the Mardi Gras Queen of Coney Island. And then in a crowning setback, she finished second in the only New York election in which Tammany Hall didn't rig the votes.

In November 1910, *Variety* reported that Freeman was back in business as a full-time vaudeville agent and "will do naught else but hustle for headliners, he says."

Freeman's first target was British actor John Lawson, a shimmering figure on the London stage who was obsessed with battling anti-Semitism. Lawson's most famous production, *Humanity*, turned the stereotypes in *King Lear* on their head with a saintly Jewish banker and a greedy Christian who abuses his hospitality.

Lawson had brought that same Star-of-David sensibility to New York in October with a new thirty-minute playlet called *The Open Door*. The British actor must have been surprised by the ferocity of the reaction from prosperous Jews in show business like Sime Silverman, who gloried in being an assimilated American. Sime's signed review in *Variety* attacked Lawson's "declamatory defense of the Jew." He also wrote, "Mr. Lawson may accept the silent reception of the American audience as conclusively indicative that in America the Jew does not care to be upheld or any defense of him attempted on the stage."

After the hostile reaction to *The Open* Door, a disheartened Lawson slammed the door on his New York engagement and was about to head back to Europe aboard the *Oceanic* when Freeman caught up with him. The sailors on the ship were shouting "All Ashore" and getting ready to raise the gangplank in New York as

Freeman worked out the final details of a fourteen-week touring contract. Freeman probably would have stowed away if that's what it took to get Lawson to agree to promptly return to America. During the hurried shipboard negotiations, it is easy to picture Freeman presenting himself as the most devout Jew on Broadway, a friend of learned rabbis, a pillar of Temple Emanu-El, and a man who would be studying the Talmud if it were not for the sordid business of making a living.

Freeman was as good as his word—with a bit of mischief thrown in.

As soon as he booked Lawson, he began running weekly ads in *Variety* heralding the upcoming tour featuring *Humanity*. Freeman even mocked Sime Silverman's exaggerated sensitivities by featuring a quote from his critique of Lawson's performance: "It has unpleasant features. . . . Lawson's declamatory defense of 'The Jew.'" But Freeman's ad also featured a money review from the New York *Evening Mail* declaring, "John Lawson is one of the best actors in New York. You forget he is acting."

Meanwhile, Freeman had not lost sight of his polar star. His thinking: If I can't get Captain Cook, I'll get someone *like* Captain Cook. Airborne adventurer Walter Wellman certainly fit the bill. Not only had Wellman repeatedly tried to reach the North Pole by land, but he also twice attempted to fly over it in a dirigible. Convinced that he had been beaten to the Pole, Wellman turned his attention to a wetter and wider obstacle—the Atlantic Ocean. In mid-October 1910, Wellman took off from Atlantic City for London with a crew of five in his dirigible *America*, attempting to be the first to cross the ocean, seventeen years before Lindbergh. Fighting high winds and dense fog, the *America* stayed aloft for nearly seventy-two hours before safely descending near a steamship

375 miles east of Cape Hatteras. Even in failure, the *America* made history since its wireless operator, Jack Irwin, became the first dot-dash man in history to communicate with land from an airship.

Working in tandem with William Morris, Freeman arranged a lecture tour for Wellman. Unfortunately, the balloonist had given so many newspaper interviews and told his story so often that by the time he was booked into Carnegie Hall in mid-November, Wellman was offering little other than hot air. With ticket sales moving at the pace of a polar expedition, Freeman announced a few hours before curtain time that Wellman had been tragically felled by the sudden onset of laryngitis. But the *New-York Tribune* puckishly wrote, "It was reported in other quarters that the box office was attacked with a severe hoarseness and could not speak above a whisper." As for Freeman, the *Tribune* described him as looking "as though he had been bounced over several waves and lost half a dozen tanks of gasoline when he was found and called upon to explain why there was no lecture."

Wellman's tour never got airborne: The next night he confessed to a small crowd in New Haven that he'd rather make another try at crossing the Atlantic than give a lecture. Freeman had better luck with Jack Irwin, whom he booked for twenty weeks on the Sullivan-Considine circuit.

Back in good graces with John Considine, Freeman was doing surprisingly well as a vaudeville agent in early 1911—so well that he bought nearly a full-page ad in *Variety* to trumpet the fifty-eight acts that he now represented. Freeman had all the trappings of Broadway prosperity: an office above the Knickerbocker Theatre (where *The Foolish Virgin* had been playing), a telephone (Murray Hill 5147), and a cable address (Freebern: New York). As always, he displayed a distinctive hand with the advertising copy, wooing would-be clients with ransom-note capitalization and random font sizes. "CALL ON US if you want work. . . . WE FIND IT FOR YOU. . . . PLENTY OF WORK FOR EVERYBODY. . . . ALWAYS ON THE JOB. . . . DON'T LOAF if you have the act. . . . WE PROMOTE, MANAGE AND ATTEND TO YOUR PRESS MATTER. . . . You don't have to hang around hallways or offices. . . . OPEN DAY AND NIGHT. . . . Phone any old time. . . . NO ACT TOO BIG."

Or too small. A wheel at the center of the *Variety* advertisement was designed to show that Freeman was a big wheel by offering a circular listing of all the acts that he had out on the circuit. Most of the clients of the agent with the cable address Freebern were small-timers—the sort who hung around the anterooms of Broadway offices praying for a booking. Performers like comedian Eddie Foyer (not to be confused with Eddie Foy), the Five Juggling Jordans (masters of the flying Indian clubs), Probst (unequaled as a birdcall imitator), Gennaro's Venetian Gondolier Band (canals not included), the Four Jones (Freeman tastelessly billed them as "The Komikal Koons"), and Tim McMahon's Watermelon Girls (the mind reels trying to imagine the act).

In a tribute to Freeman's persuasiveness, there were a few headliners who listed Murray Hill 5147 as their manager's telephone number. Beyond May Ward, Freeman's all-star list included John Lawson, Harry Jolson (Al's older brother), minstrel man Tim Cronin (a star of the original version of *The Cash Girl*), and Jewish dialect comedian Joe Welch (famed for his signature line as he schlumped onto the stage, "You t'ink I'm heppy?").

At a standard rate of $500 per week, Welch was paid better than Will Rogers or almost anyone in vaudeville aside from female impersonator Julian Eltinge ($1,500) and sex symbol Eva Tanguay ($2,500). So when Welch was booked for twenty weeks on the

Sullivan-Considine circuit, his agent was very heppy. Freeman celebrated with one of the most extravagant gestures of his career: He actually bought his own ticket to see vaudeville at the American Music Hall. But Freeman quickly realized the error of his free-spending ways when he discovered that his seat number was M-113, complaining, "I knew there was hoodoo around here somewhere—and they had to slip a '13' besides."

The voodoo that hoodoo so well promptly arrived in the form of May Ward's first bankruptcy petition. The *New York World* ran a fetching two-column picture of the vaudeville star wearing a bonnet on its front page above the headline "DRESDEN DOLL SEEKS REFUGE IN BANKRUPTCY: May Ward Owes $2,300, But Says She Hasn't a Dollar to Settle." Her debts (about $57,000 in modern dollars) included $220 to a prominent Harlem florist, $150 to the Bloomingdale Brothers for furniture, and $15 to Madam Bertha, the milliner who presumably fashioned her bonnet. Other obligations included $568 to a lithographer for theatrical posters and $170 to the *Morning Telegraph* for advertising. About all that were missing were jewelers' bills—but that was Freeman's responsibility.

Unlike the stereotypical husband in the Sunday funnies enraged by his wife's extravagance, Freeman was puffed up with pride over the legal filing. And why shouldn't he be? It wasn't his money. As *Variety* told it, "Freeman is happy, as usual. Even the bankruptcy failed to disturb his wonted equanimity—and besides, didn't 'The Dresden Doll' have her picture in three papers through it. Freeman boosted [her] salary as each picture appeared." Less than a week later, May Ward topped the bill at the Grand Opera House in Brooklyn.

Not all of Freeman's clients had the headline-happy help of a bankruptcy petition. About this time, Freeman wangled a Sunday night booking at Miner's Bowery Theatre for a young comic trio called Goldie, Fields and Glide. They were rough around the edges—Fields came on as a Jewish immigrant with a bushy stage beard, and Glide, playing his brother, was made up in blackface so exaggerated that all the audience could see were his oversize white-painted lips. Backstage after the show, Freeman paid them for their one-night stand and begged them to break up the act. "That was the end of Goldie, Fields and Glide," recalled the soon-to-be-famous comic who had billed himself as Glide. "Goldie went back to the laundry and Goldberg. I went back to umbrellas and Burns."

And that was how George Burns credited Freeman for helping make his career in his 1955 autobiography, *I Love Her, That's Why!*

Despite the woeful Wellman and the disgraced Diss Debar, Freeman continued to have his eye out for "freaks" who could compel the curious to pony up at the box office. Nothing onstage beat a beautiful woman tangled up in a murder case—something that Freeman pioneered years earlier with Florence Burns. She was a Brooklyn woman, widely suspected of shooting her gentleman friend Walter Brooks, who wiggled off the hook when the grand jury returned with a surprise finding of suicide. Freeman immediately put her onstage at Proctor's 23rd Street Theatre at $750 a week. One night early in the run, the femme fatale disappeared just before showtime. Faced with panic over a lost leading lady, Freeman brazenly told the stage manager, "They don't know out there what they're going to see. Send on anybody." So a chorus girl played Florence Burns for a night.

In September 1911, Freeman snared the most famous other woman in America—seventeen-year-old Beulah Binford. Her rakish lover, Richmond merchant Henry Clay Beattie Jr., had everything, including the encumbrance of marriage. But not for long. One night Beattie invited his young wife (descended from one of the First Families of Virginia) to take a late-night car ride in the countryside. Their romantic idyll was interrupted by a shadowy rifle-toting highwayman who fatally shot Mrs. Beattie. As for Henry Beattie, he bravely fought off the elusive robber and returned to Richmond with the lifeless body of his wife and the highwayman's rifle. Oddly enough, this rifle was identical to one that Beattie himself had purchased just three days earlier.

The trial dominated front pages across the country. Even though there were no witnesses to the murder, the rural Virginia jury of twelve farmers deliberated for less than an hour before sentencing Beattie to the electric chair. Beulah Binford—described in the papers as a woman who "sowed wild oats that produced a whirlwind of sordid romance"—was jailed as a material witness in the case, but she was never asked to testify. Hundreds of concerned citizens, many with strong opinions about her morals, surrounded the jail as Beulah was released following Beattie's conviction. She announced that she was headed to New York where she had offers to appear in moving pictures and to grace the vaudeville stage at $1,000 per week.

Freeman was only involved with the vaudeville side of Beulah's new career, having booked her for a six-week tour starting at the Liberty Theatre in Philadelphia. He suggested to reporters that she might sing a few songs. But Freeman added—reflecting his cynical attitude about booking freaks—"It really doesn't matter what she does as long as people have a chance to look at her."

But what Freeman didn't consider was that people would also have a chance to think about what she did before seeing her perform. Within hours, everyone on the East Coast was boycotting Beulah. The rector of St. John the Evangelist Episcopal Church in Philadelphia thundered, "Under no circumstances should our city authorities allow Beulah Binford to appear. Such a woman brings sin close to our doors." Mrs. Belle de Rivera, a prominent Manhattan clubwoman, told the *New York World*, "To me, the announcement of the possibility of the appearance of this Binford girl on stage is disgusting." The Woman's Christian Temperance Union promised to picket any appearance by Beulah in vaudeville—and leading suffragettes also expressed outrage at this affront to public morals.

Freeman, who had abandoned failing vaudeville troupes and circuses, knew how to fold a losing hand. As he told the *New York Call*, "I've had a lot of freaks in my time—Florence Burns and May Yohe. But I've decided that I can't stand for Beulah. New York doesn't want her kind." During other interviews, Freeman confessed to being puzzled why Beulah was being shunned while other shady ladies had done well in vaudeville. "I don't know just why New York has gotten on its hindmost moral legs at this late date," he said. "Now I am not saying that Beulah Binford is a saint—we all know she is not. I speak as a practical theatrical man, not as a publicist or a moralist. But I do stand for consistency."

Freeman was the soul of consistency—when it came to not paying bills, when it came to living well without cash, and when it came to remaining unflappable in the face of show-business disasters. A week after he bailed out on Beulah, Freeman was at his office blithely waving off lawsuits from angry actors who did not get promised bookings and from credulous creditors who thought they had acquired exclusive rights to *The Cash Girl* in return for voiding their debts. Marveling at Freeman's equanimity in the face of the parade of process servers, *Variety* memorably described him as "the small time agent with the big time nerve."

Even though his finances were fast resembling Marie Antoinette's *after* the French Revolution, Freeman decided that his stature on Broadway required not only an automobile but also a uniformed chauffeur. Commandeering a $4,500 automobile was easy, but Freeman's stroke of genius was equipping his new driver, a Russian émigré, with a fur-lined coat with the oversize initials "FB" on each shoulder. Freeman bought the coat from an usher at the Folies Bergère.

But the day of financial reckoning comes, as it must, to all men. On November 21, 1911, Freeman was featured in the *New York Times* in the section called "Business Troubles" that might as well have run his photograph on a daily basis. Identified as a "music hall manager," Freeman filed a petition for bankruptcy listing debts of $19,304 (nearly a half million dollars today) and no assets. Now Freeman and May Ward were a matched set: the Bankrupts. But insolvency only carries a social stigma if it's mixed with a sense of shame for failing in John D. Rockefeller's America. And no one would ever call Mr. and Mrs. Freeman Bernstein embarrassed about anything.

In fact, shortly after his second court filing as a deadbeat in less than a decade, Freeman would brag to *Variety* about his ability to still buy items on credit. "They trust me," he explained, as though everyone else were financial simpletons. "Why not? Since I went through bankruptcy, I don't owe a dollar in the world."

8

Two weeks later, the jolliest bankrupt in New York was sharing a cigar with a visitor from *Variety* in his new office on the fourth floor of the Heidelberg Building overlooking Times Square. Freeman was always a talker (how do you think he won May Ward?), but on this day he even surpassed Billy Sunday at a temperance rally. As the man from *Variety* took notes, Freeman sketched out a vision that was so ahead of its time—so prescient— that he should have been known as OkCupid Bernstein. Freeman's line of patter went like this:

> Now, with nothing to worry me beyond a few old debts, I have thought out a new department in connection with my managerial direction of vaudeville features. I am going to start a Bureau for the Lonesome. . . .
>
> In the summer, New York is alive with transients, men and women from all over. Then there are the men and women who live here the year round, all alone.

They don't know anybody, and they are lonesome, especially in the evenings. Well, I am going to be First Aid.

I shall circularize the principal hotels, apartments and boarding houses. I will tell them that no one in New York need be lonesome for little Freeman Bernstein is here. . . .

I expect a fellow might come in and say, "I feel so lonesome. Can you introduce me to an amiable young woman, about twenty-six, who won't talk about home and mother, nor tell me how much she knows about cooking." . . .

Then I refer to my card system, and two lonesome people are thrown together to while away what would have been a dreary evening for both.

I shall charge a registration fee of $2, which covers everything. . . . It looks like a good scheme to me. I understand there are always 92,000 lonesome men and 163,874 lonesome women in New York City. I expect to be famous all over the world as "The Lonesome Man."

All this dialogue appeared in *Variety*, one of more than fifty of Freeman's soliloquies transcribed over the next fifteen years by the Lonesome Man's personal Boswell . . . Sime Silverman. Even allowing for comic embellishment by his amanuensis, the diction and the argot fit with the few surviving examples of Freeman's writings (and the transcripts of his interviews with prosecutors).

So we know what Freeman sounded like.

That is the gift that Sime gave posterity—re-creating the chatter of a Broadway character from the days before World War I and the talkies. Aside from presidents giving formal addresses and singers on Edison recordings, we so rarely get spoken words from that era. But Freeman's distinctive phrasing and vocabulary endure in the pages of *Variety* from a century ago.

Back in those days, however, everyone in show business knew what Freeman sounded like since his kettledrum voice rattled the rafters whenever he joined a conversation or picked up the phone. In fact, comedian Johnny Stanley was doing his act in a theater on Union Square when a heavy piece of scenery loudly crashed backstage, ruining his joke. Without missing a beat, the comedian ad-libbed, "That was Freeman Bernstein booking an act."

Sime's columns featuring the free-associating Freeman were the equivalent of a vaudeville routine in which human frailties are exaggerated for laughs. In the pages of *Variety*, Freeman played a perpetually broke Broadway agent hounded by bill collectors. Oh, the tyranny of type casting. While some of Freeman's schemes were air castles (like his dating service for the lonely), the reality was that he was indeed desperate for cash as process servers perched outside his office like pigeons on a windowsill. So the *Variety* columns actually were art imitating life as performed by Freeman Bernstein.

"I'm no person. I'm a corporation," Freeman proudly announced to Sime in mid-1912, two months after the *Titanic* sank. (In truth, Freeman had paid the $5 fee to New York State to incorporate himself.) "Somebody told me," he said, "that to place 'Inc.' after my name would make people believe I had been given a degree by Princeton and would impress the actors more than 'Mgr.' does."

To test this proposition, Freeman stopped off in a saloon one afternoon with no ready cash other than a $100 money order (of dubious origins) made out to "Freeman Bernstein, Inc." As Freeman told it, "The bartender gave me a nice glass of beer. It looked so good I asked him if he wouldn't have one—and to show him I could spend if I wanted to, I asked another fellow in the place to have a drink too." This is how friendships were forged, especially as Freeman "got the bartender coming my way with a story about a couple of dames." After another round or two, the bar tab was up to forty-five cents.

Freeman confidently placed his money order on the bar top and said, "Take it out of that. And give it to me in big bills." Maybe the story about the two dames wasn't the icebreaker that Freeman thought it was, since the barkeep snarled to a mug standing nearby, "Go through this guy and if you don't find any coin on him, use the mallet." Fearing that his next stop would be Bellevue, Freeman prudently remembered that he had a dollar in his shoe. The whole experience left Freeman baffled: "So I haven't been able to find out yet what this corporation thing is all about."

Years later, *Variety* editor Abel Green ridiculed Freeman as "Sime's pet journalistic stooge." That is flat-out wrong. Freeman understood precisely what he was doing as he played the sap for Sime. For Freeman, the choice was obvious between taking the free advertising offered by Sime's columns or actually having to pay for it.

Remember how Freeman jacked up his wife's salary demands as soon as her picture appeared on the front page of the *New York World* after her bankruptcy. And dating back to his quest to find bail money for Laura Biggar, Freeman understood the cash value of having his name in the papers. He loved it when, in the middle of Teddy Roosevelt's 1912 third-party campaign for the White House, *Variety* called Freeman "the guy who put the 'Bull' in Bull-Moose." In an early Sime column, Freeman got away with this shameless bit of puffery in the form of a quote: "Just say that this office will book the

Sunday concerts at Miner's Bronx. . . . And don't forget to mention that M.W. Taylor will open the greatest small time theatre in the world next Monday. It's the Keystone [in] Philadelphia. . . . And, say, while you are about it, just tell 'em I have so much business [I] had to engage a special lawyer in Chicago to collect some of my bills."

Freeman wasn't entirely blowing smoke rings: He had established a niche as a leading agent for small-time vaudeville. The *Billboard*, which in those days covered show business for the bill-posting and outdoor advertising trades, called Freeman "perhaps the largest ten percent agent outside the United fold." (The United referred to the United Booking Office, the in-house agents for the big-time Keith and Orpheum circuits.) He was handling the bookings for three-show-a-day theaters like the Keystone, a new house in downtown Philadelphia, which put on quality vaudeville (minus big stars) for just twenty cents. Freeman had also worked out an arrangement with Frank Keeney, a notoriously cheap operator who ran split-week theaters (offering three-day bookings) in small cities like Schenectady, Binghamton, Bridgeport, and New Britain. Never losing sight of his origins, Freeman installed his brother Sam as the manager of the Lyceum in Troy. But Sam—never losing sight of self-preservation— fled Troy early in 1912 when there wasn't enough cash in the box- office till to pay the performers.

Like a carpetbagger heading south in the years after the Civil War, Freeman grasped the opportunities created by America's victory in the Spanish-American War. With the sugar industry booming, the Caribbean seemed ripe for vaudeville. Freeman's first visit to the liberated islands came during the 1911 Christmas season when he booked May Ward as a special attraction at a circus playing in San Juan. As patrons walked through the gates, they immediately saw the Flea Circus and the Monkey Music Hall direct from Luna Park at Coney Island, plus the midget Princess Wee-Wee and the Dresden Dolls in midperformance. The show was such a success that Freeman took out, yes, a full-page paid ad in *Variety* to proclaim that May Ward had been extended, ultimately playing for eighteen nights. Freeman always found rubes with money irresistible, which is why he immediately called Puerto Rico his "dream of an ideal country."

Put Freeman on an ice floe off Antarctica for eighteen nights—and the penguins would consider him a chum for life. During his time in Puerto Rico, Freeman became boon companions with the millionaire director of the San Juan Opera House and the local secretary of the American Tobacco Company. Probably after boasting that he made annual pilgrimages to La Scala and that Puccini was the best man at his wedding, Freeman convinced them that he was just the promoter to bring the leading sopranos and tenors in the world to the San Juan Opera House. Suddenly blessed with an unlimited budget, Freeman confided to *Variety* that while he would continue "his agency business in New York, he will arrange to give the southern proposition full attention."

Freeman was entrepreneur enough to hire a forty-five-member opera troupe and dispatch them to San Juan on the steamer *Carolina* for a successful tour of Puerto Rico. But Freeman soon decided to high-hat high culture and send the island what it really needed—vaudeville.

Bringing in Frank Keeney as a partner and sending Sam (who couldn't go back to Troy) along as a manager, Freeman announced the creation of the Puerto Rico circuit. It was such virgin territory that even silent movies were a novelty. When the troupe arrived in San Juan, Keeney cabled Freeman in New York that vaudeville was so popular that two thousand customers had to be turned away on opening night. Freeman responded by wailing to *Variety* that it was just his bad luck to bring in a partner on such a sure thing.

Actually, Freeman's southern proposition was shakier than it looked. The *Player*, the union newspaper of the reinvigorated White Rats, reported that while Freeman came through with the promised round-trip steamship passage and prepaid hotel rooms for the performers, salaries were a luxury. A dispensable luxury. The only money that acts like Four Yankee Girls and Moric & Scoric ever received were piddling advances wangled out of a reluctant Keeney.

Heading back to New York after the Puerto Rican tour ended a week earlier than planned, Sam wired Freeman that he was bringing with him a future circus sideshow performer called the Spanish Giant. Summoning *Variety* to the Heidelberg Building, Freeman channeled his inner P. T. Barnum (never far from the surface) as he boasted that the giant was so tall that there was no way to measure his height. As an illustration, Freeman explained that the giant had difficulty eating, since the food always got cold during the long trip up from the table to his mouth.

That journey from the cup to the lip was always Freeman's undoing.

He would start with high hopes of profits, only to see them vanish in midair like dollar bills with wings attached. His next vaudeville tour was headlined by May Yohe—pushing fifty, divorced, and reduced to living in a rooming house with her memories of the Hope Diamond long gone. Under Sam's management (Freeman had moved on to Venezuela), the fancifully named Bernstein Opera Company set off for Puerto Rico as the jumping-off spot for a six-month ramble through Latin America. But this time, they couldn't get up San Juan Hill. (Okay, the famous one is in Cuba, but San Juan must have one somewhere.) As chorus girl Evelyn Davis complained about theatergoers in Puerto Rico, "They don't know if 'Florodora' is an opera or a new brand of canned goods."

Opening night on Sunday attracted a decent crowd, but the Bernstein Opera Company's pastiche of a Broadway musical was greeted with stony silence. Part of the problem was linguistic since the patrons only spoke Spanish aside from a small clump of extremely quiet Americans down front. Monday night, fueled by bilingual word of mouth, the audience had dwindled to fifty. When fewer than two dozen tickets were sold for Tuesday night, Sam knew exactly what to do—he took the next boat to join Freeman in Venezuela.

A marooned vaudeville troupe in America could hitchhike, hop a freight train, or call upon friends for rescue. But getting home from Puerto Rico was wet work. "We sure were in some fix," Evelyn Davis told the *New York Herald*. "No money, big hotel bills, no friends, nothing to eat and none of us wore steamboats in place of shoes." Eventually twenty-two desperate vaudevillians put on a benefit that raised enough to get them back to New York. Freeman told the *Herald* that he had generously guaranteed steamship fare for everyone as soon as he learned of the plight of the Bernstein Opera Company. But by the time his wire reached San Juan, the performers were already on the high seas. So Freeman did what any honorable impresario would do in similar circumstances—he asked for his money back.

The combustible marriage of Freeman and May Ward, especially as portrayed in the pages of *Variety*, boasted all the hallmarks of a popular newspaper comic strip—maybe *Jiggs & Maggie*—transported to vaudeville. The Bernsteins' battles (warning: shocking revelation ahead) were mostly over money. Usually, it was Freeman who invented artful schemes to wheedle ready cash out of his wife, but sometimes it was the free-spending May who rummaged through her husband's pockets late at night, searching for a hidden bankroll.

Sime spotted Freeman and May Ward dining on Hammerstein's Roof on a warm Monday night. "They were speaking to each other," he marveled, "although Mr. Bernstein had neglected to adorn his 5½ x 2¾ person with evening dress." Asked about this fashion faux pas, Freeman responded, "Oh, I have the Tuxedo, kid, all right. But I didn't dare wear the tux."

The happy couple invited Sime to join their merry twosome. Within seconds, Freeman resumed telling the tuxedo story, which turned into a tale as circuitous as the route of Walter Wellman's dirigible. "May here and I are great pals," Freeman said, "and she's the best in the world, even if I do say so in front of her and it will cost me another ring tomorrow. But she's a great gal for hanging onto the coin, and that's how it happened."

It all started on Saturday night when May asked in a voice as sweet as the glaze atop a Danish pastry, "Freeman, how's business?" Sensing that she was putting the touch on him, Freeman responded cautiously, "Fair, kid, fair." The evasive action didn't work because May had already heard that Freeman had collected $100 on an old debt. "Don't you try to hold that, you've been standing me off for two weeks." So Freeman reluctantly handed over the $30 that he hoped would bankroll him for the coming week.

That night Freeman, always an insomniac, stayed up until nearly dawn playing Canfield solitaire and trying to figure out how to get that $30 back. Around noon Sunday, he suddenly suggested to May that they take an automobile ride out to Long Island. Engaging a Packard, they were driven around until nearly sunset, with May saying as they arrived home, "This is the nicest day I ever spent." That moment of marital bliss ended abruptly when Freeman pointed out that he had no money and they owed the driver the $30 that he had given May the night before.

So what does any of this have to do with Freeman being out on the town at Hammerstein's sans tuxedo? "I haven't had my clothes off since because May will go through them sure," Freeman said, proud that he had managed to hold on to the rest of the $100. "And that's why I didn't dare taking a chance going into a Tux."

Even Sime's columns on things like Freeman acquiring a Dictaphone on approval ("I think it will take me about six months to give it a good try") would suddenly veer off for an update on the state of the Bernstein marriage. "I'm a great man for regularity in business," Freeman said. "Why, it's only the other day I started a bank account. That was fine, too. But I told May, and May made me give her a check, just to flash, she said. So I wrote it for $500. The very same day she had the butcher cash it."

When Freeman wasn't trying to outwit May (about all that was missing was her coming after him with a rolling pin), his monologues often revolved around staying one step ahead of the landlord. His ad in *Variety* heralding his move to the Fitzgerald Building at Forty-Third and Broadway blared: "MUST MOVE TO LARGER QUARTERS. Quarters too small in Heidelberg Building." But as he confided to Sime in August 1912, "Paying twice as much rent here as I did across the street, but I don't have to pay for September. They gave me the month free." For Freeman, what always mattered was not the notional amount of the rent but how many months he could go without paying.

When *Variety* caught up with Freeman moving into his new offices above George M. Cohan's theater, he was uncharacteristically euphoric. He already had printed up IOU forms with his new office address on paper so fancy that the IOUs resembled stock certificates. Freeman sent an office boy out to the Park & Tilford cigar shop to get a box of twenty-five-cent Cubans and another box of phonies that he could pass off to the unsuspecting. The flowers that he received from the landlord and grateful clients (yes, he had a few) were rerouted to May, who was enjoying the summer at the Jersey Shore. "I just told May she could start that flower garden down at Long Beach now if she wants to," Freeman said. "I'll stake her to these fancy bouquets and they cost a lot of coin, too." Two weeks later, one of those fancy bouquets, a now-wilted horseshoe display, showed up in the offices of the new Consolidated Booking Office with the compliments of Freeman Bernstein.

As he escorted Sime on a tour of his "quiet and dignified" offices (or as quiet as Freeman's booming voice would allow and as dignified as a refugee from grammar school could get), Freeman explained the reason for his optimism. "The way they have vaudeville framed up now the small time is all to the goodsky," he said. "Everybody wants acts, and there's going to be more big stuff playing the small time than the big time. . . . I'm going to book all over. Freeman Bernstein has more telephone calls in a day than any agent in the world. Just between you and I, most of them are for touches, but they count just the same. I've got a bunch of coin out with actors. Say, ain't this a great business when you land? Here I am loaning money instead of borrowing it. I never thought I would be able to do that."

Of course, it didn't last. But it was fun while the money flowed—and Freeman could square himself with everyone. In February 1913, Freeman took May on a real vacation and paid (yes, paid) for first-class tickets aboard the *Bermudian*, the finest luxury liner steaming between New York and Hamilton, plus $16 a night for a hotel suite. When he returned to New York, he tried and failed to interest vaudeville managers in a line of trained fish that he saw at an aquarium there.

But it was Freeman himself who played the fish. With the weather in New York unseasonably warm, May convinced him that she could get a sealskin coat cheap because everyone thought winter was over. When the coat arrived at Freeman's office COD with a bill for $450 attached, Freeman fainted dead away. (Or so *Variety* claimed.) But May explained everything with a dizzy wife's line that was probably already mossy in 1913: She had really saved Freeman $550 because one of the sealskin coats was listed at $1,000.

Whenever Freeman had some cash to spread around (and May hadn't gotten hold of it), he was a sucker for get-rich-quick schemes, but not the obvious hokum that he used on out-of-towners: "I'll sell the Metropolitan opera house for anything they have got. . . . If they don't want the Metropolitan, we will sell them a collar factory in Troy, and throw in the gals."

But a certain type of investment would prove irresistible to Freeman—a bourbon distillery in Kentucky, a high-class suit factory on Canal Street, or his own vaudeville theater. Freeman knew a thing or two about cooked books: "Read this report and see how my shows go," he told Sime. "Every one a hit, ain't they? Well that's for managers. Here read the other one—that's on the level." His financial shenanigans convinced him that he knew all the angles. No one was ever going to pull a fast one on Little Freeman Bernstein.

So Freeman conned himself into spending $2,500 to pick up a ten-year lease to operate the Bender Theatre in Utica, a city of seventy thousand between Albany and Syracuse. May Ward had recently played the eighteen-hundred-seat theater under the prior management, giving away more than one thousand dolls. The *Utica Herald-Dispatch* trilled that she was "dubbed the 'Dresden Doll Comedienne' because she is so delicate, so pink and white and pearly-teethed."

The Bender was losing money when Freeman took it over—and the cash demands quickly bent him out of shape. After Freeman tried to cut an actress's wages when it was time to settle up at the end of the week, the *Player* went to the barricades against the Union Buster in Utica. "Again we warn performers against doing business with Freeman Bernstein," the White Rat rag roared. "Remember Bernstein stops at nothing and plays no favorites."

But it wasn't just the White Rats who were coming out of the woodwork to demand that Freeman pay up. Joe Quinn, an eighteen-year-old who owned and operated the motion-picture projector at the Bender Theatre, tried to remove it when Freeman was late on the payments. In May, A. W. Bender, who owned the theater, sued Freeman for nonpayment of the lease. That seemed an ideal moment for May Ward (who once again was the headliner) and Sam Bernstein (whom Freeman installed as manager) to get in a car at the end of a Saturday night performance and flee back to New York.

All through 1913, the White Rats treated Freeman like he was the biggest threat to unions since Andrew Carnegie ordered the Pinkertons to break up the Homestead steel strike. "ALL ACTS ARE FORBIDDEN TO DO BUSINESS WITH BERNSTEIN AS HE HAS NOT AS YET SETTLED WITH THOSE HE OWES," the *Player* declared in a typically soft-spoken editorial. "UNTIL HE MAKES GOOD, YOU MUST KEEP AWAY FROM HIM."

When capital letters failed to change Freeman's methods, the

White Rats went with scabrous invective: "No decent manager does business with Bernstein. No good act goes near his office. Those acts that are seen in his office represent the fringe of the theatrical profession: they belong to the 'down and out' class. This parasite, Bernstein lives off these poor creatures. Bernstein typifies the distinct character of the 'Panderer' of the Underworld. He boasts to those who meet him how he trimmed such-and-such a performer. All decent men and women should shun him as they would a leper."

Stung by the ferocity of the White Rats, Freeman veered between vague offers to settle with any shortchanged performers and threats to sue the actors' union for libel. When Freeman went to the district attorney to instigate a libel action, the White Rats countered with forty complaints of contract violations. "Bernstein says when he saw the army appear, it looked more like he was on trial for murder than he wanted to have someone indicted," *Variety* reported. "The season started off very well for Freeman, but what he got early has been taken way from him since someone told him Utica was a regular city."

Normally, Freeman economizing was like William Howard Taft going on a diet. But necessity can teach almost anyone thrift, which is why Freeman tried selling at a profit the luxurious Rainier touring car ("The Pullman of Automobiles") that he bought when he was feeling flush. The car had become so easily recognizable on Broadway that Freeman would never dare leave it with the top down for fear that a creditor might drop a brick on it. "I can't afford in these hot times to keep both a car and myself," he told *Variety*. "One of us most go, and it must be the car. It cost me $900. I have spent $800 in repairs and gasoline, and another $60,000 used up worrying over what I could have done with the first $900. But I will sell cheap. For $1,100 cash and notes, or anything you say."

But Freeman refused to dispose of the one luxury item that was draining his wallet like an oil leak—even at a tidy profit.

When you're a rotund forty-year-old Broadway agent married to a showgirl famed for her pink-and-white complexion and pearly teeth, you're never going to get off cheap. May Ward could spend money faster than the United States Mint could coin it. As a performer, she commanded a minimum of $300 a week—and she blew through every penny of it, along with a good chunk of the change that Freeman brought in.

With Freeman lying awake nights trying to figure out how to finance his car, May decided it was just the moment for them to start sleeping someplace else. Despite her recent bankruptcy, she found a starstruck real estate firm willing to front her a $21,500 mortgage. So she impulsively bought a sixteen-room house on nearly an acre lot at 164 Elm Avenue in the Chester Hill Park neighborhood of Mount Vernon, north of the Bronx.

After growing up backstage in burlesque troupes, May loved this suburban version of the country with the fervor of Marie Antoinette playing a milkmaid. Give Mrs. Bernstein a piece of property and she would populate it with a menagerie worthy of Mother Goose. Before long, her brood included six dogs (shared with Freeman), two tomcats, two horses, two canaries, a parrot, and a flock of hens. In fact, Freeman confided to Sime that he was entranced with the notion of the hens laying eggs with the monogram "F.B." but couldn't figure out how to pull it off.

Even though May immediately took off on a West Coast tour on the Sullivan-Considine circuit, Freeman claimed to have immediately adjusted to the move to the country. "Mount Vernon thinks I'm a banker," Freeman proudly told *Variety*. "I ain't told nobody

I'm in the show business, for I'm building up a credit that when I blow the town ought to be good for a lot of money."

The night before his wife blew town for her vaudeville tour, Freeman cooed, "May, I don't want you to go on this long trip with any bad feelings between us. So if you will let me have $500, it will be all right." When that didn't work, Freeman tried and failed to get her to round off his current $600 loan to $1,000.

Ever the devoted husband, Freeman was standing beneath the soaring steel arches of the new Pennsylvania Station to see May off to Seattle the next afternoon. Even though he had been plotting for twenty-four hours, Freeman still hadn't come up with a scheme to get his wife to part with the desperately needed cash. But then as the conductor was shouting "All aboard," May came through on her own. She handed him a fat packet with a $20 gold certificate on top as she purred, "Freeman, here's some coin. I don't want to go and have you sore."

Taking a gander at the thickness of the bankroll with a practiced eye, Freeman figured that there had to be $800 in there, enough to keep him going for a month or two. When Freeman got back to his office, he eagerly took the rubber band off the thick wad of cash—only to discover that the only thing under the $20 gold certificate was a long letter from May telling him to save his money.

Throughout his life, Freeman believed that clothes made the man—or, more precisely, that a flashy appearance made a man look like he deserved credit. That was the theory behind the diamond stickpin that he had lifted back in Bayonne to keep the bill collectors at bay. Whenever he thought about hitting it big, Freeman's fantasies revolved around shirts and ties from Sulka, bespoke suits, and hand-cobbled shoes.

But in the winter of 1914, Freeman's wardrobe was becoming more Salvation Army than Savile Row. Unable to afford a personal tailor (or to find one willing to cut cloth on credit), Freeman tried an indirect approach to snag English tailoring. He convinced a hansom-cab driver to abandon life behind a horse and become a taxicab driver instead ("a night hawk behind the wheel"). As a reward for this motorized advice, the nighthawk bequeathed Freeman his no-longer-needed English walking suit with a frock coat and his silk top hat that was shiny on one side. As Freeman bragged to Sime, "Did you get the braid on the coat and vest? Say, do you know that this is the best money getter I ever hit upon. I have already borrowed $108 today on the strength of the scenery—and from people, too, who know me. I'm all swollen up over myself. Wait until May gets a flash. Bet she will fall for me again."

By springtime, though, Freeman the clotheshorse had become the clothes hearse. His entire wardrobe had taken on a funereal pallor. The final indignity came when Freeman was spotted rubbing lemon peel over last summer's straw hat in a desperate effort to make it look presentable. "Ain't it tough," he wailed, "when I've got to dig out my old bonnet and make it look like new myself?"

Freeman's straw hat was not the only accessory that had faded with the years—so had his wife's career. Although May didn't know it at the time, her western swing on the Sullivan-Considine circuit would be her last major vaudeville tour. She still won favorable reviews: "Miss Ward is just 130 pounds of good humor of the most spontaneous sort," declared the *Salt Lake Tribune*. Her weekly ads in *Variety* announcing that she was "HEADLINING ON

THE S-C TIME" appeared on the same page as the promos for a young comic quartet called the "4 MARX BROS."

But there were hints that pep alone couldn't keep the Dresden Doll Comedienne, now over thirty, going as a headliner. She embraced a new gimmick—inviting dozens of men in the audience to come up onstage to waltz with her. But even the vaudeville version of taxi dancing could not give wing to her career. When she returned to Mount Vernon, Freeman had to scramble to get May weekly bookings at minor vaudeville houses like Frank Keeney's in Newark and the Miner theater in the Bronx, where she was billed as an "added attraction."

Like many married couples facing the high cost of living with diminished earnings, Freeman and May would discuss money during their quiet moments together. "Freeman, listen," May said one evening as they read the papers together in Mount Vernon. "Here's a guy that copped three hundred thousand dollars and he only got 19 years." Freeman quickly calculated that he would be the guy in the clink for nineteen years and May the one rolling in dough. So he suggested, between puffs on his cigar, that the guy was a chump to get nailed in the first place. That set May off as she shouted that Freeman wouldn't let her work, that he knew nothing about money, and that he had never made more than $100 on his own in his life.

After this mature financial discussion, Freeman returned to his traditional fiscal methods—locking his office door for half a day because his brother Sam had impetuously promised the telephone company that the phone bill would be paid if they came right over. Freeman would sign checks with his left hand knowing the bank would return them—after a week or two—because it didn't recognize his signature. Every morning, Freeman would race to his office before eight o'clock to make sure that he could pocket any checks that came in the morning mail before the bill collectors spotted him.

"You know my rep," Freeman told Sime. "I can dodge more summonses than any man in the world. Have held the record for 15 years—and dodged as many as three a day without stopping business, but it's getting so now I can't walk on the main streets. They're everywhere." His outer office had become so overrun with angry creditors that paying clients couldn't make it to Freeman's inner sanctum.

Things got so bad that Freeman needed a human sacrifice. So he dispatched his personal Sancho Panza—his brother Sam—to joust with the windmills of bill collectors. On Freeman's instructions, Sam strode into the outer office flashing a fat wad of stage money and loudly asking if anyone had a $500 bill to exchange for all this cash. Rather than convincing the army of process servers that Freeman was suddenly flush, Sam was nearly trampled as all the creditors grabbed for his bankroll before discovering—with disgust—that it was counterfeit.

Freeman kept scheming, but vaudeville was reeling from the popularity of silent movies. As Freeman complained to *Variety*, "No easy money in sight, all the houses closed up and nothing but pictures." But the Boy from Troy didn't give up easily. Despite his stripped-down financial condition, Freeman arranged summer leases on three burlesque houses to present inexpensive vaudeville shows. But he soon abandoned that venture when his losses hit $1,000 per week. Even his efforts to cash in on the motion-picture craze left him floundering in the dark. Freeman took over a Second Avenue theater with the plan to offer movies and a few singers for a top price of a dime. But when long-unpaid stagehands grabbed his first-night box-office receipts of $53, Freeman decided that prudence ruled out a second night.

Things got so bad that Freeman ended up stiffing the Boy Scouts. Handling the bookings for cheapskate Frank Keeney in New Britain, Freeman instructed the house manager to cut the agreed-upon wages for the Boy Scout Band when it was time to settle up after a week of performances. Even though the Scout's motto is "Be Prepared," bandleader Paul Doti was unprepared to be shortchanged. An enraged Doti made such a racket outside the hotel where the house manager was residing that the leader of the Boy Scout Band was arrested for disturbing the peace.

Even in failure, Freeman boasted a visionary streak. He instinctively grasped that the real money in motion pictures was not likely to end up in the pockets of theater owners. "Those picture actors, they tell me, work steady all the time and get good money," Freeman mused aloud to Sime. "Who books them? Wonder if they wouldn't want a cute, little guy like myself to boost their salaries? I would go 60-40 and give them the big end at that."

Back in the spring of 1914, Freeman's idea of a big end weighed 226 pounds and smelled of liniment. More than a decade after he put Gentleman Jim Corbett on the vaudeville stage, Freeman finally got around to managing a fighter in the ring. He took on the career of Battling Jim Johnson—one of a half-dozen African American boxers who so dominated the sport that fight promoters were forever searching for the Great White Hope. Battling Jim's claim to ringside fame was that in late 1913 he had fought out-of-shape heavyweight champion Jack Johnson to a draw in Paris in the first title match between two black boxers.

Despite his lucky break in the pre-Freeman Paris fight (the champ broke his left arm in the third round), Battling Jim was less a master of the Sweet Science than a pug whose primary skill was his ability to absorb punishment and stay on his feet. The *New York Times* derisively described him after he lost a bout that Freeman had arranged: "Johnson is a burlesque fighter. He roams around the ring with all the grace of a hippopotamus, but with not as much speed."

The reigning champ Jack Johnson refused to fight a fellow black man for the title and was unable to return to America because of a racially motivated Mann Act conviction. So the top black heavyweights were reduced to sparring with each other in a round-robin series of bouts as they dreamed of a shot at the crown. Battling Jim, for example, squared off against Joe Jeannette four times in 1914 and took on Sam Langford in three other fights. The often-languid bouts (many of them held on West Sixty-Sixth Street in the new four-thousand-seat Stadium Athletic Club) became so predictable that the *New York Times* called them a "weekly punch argument."

Throughout his career, Freeman was color-blind: He treated his black performers and boxers exactly like his white clients. That is, sometimes badly.

But Freeman probably never expected to make much money from managing Battling Jim. As a sporting gentleman schooled at Saratoga, he loved the atmosphere at ringside. The stench of cigar smoke and sweat, the boasting and the bravado, the side bets, the sharp dressers and their bimbos. For Freeman Bernstein—the self-educated refugee from up the Hudson River—a fight crowd was home, a club where he knew all the secret handshakes.

Freeman exploded like a veteran fight manager in December when he heard rumors that black heavyweight Sam McVey would get a shot at the title if he defeated Battling Jim in their upcoming bout. "My man whipped Jack Johnson a year ago and should have the preference," Freeman told the *New York Evening Telegram*. "But I am perfectly willing that the clash tomorrow night should decide who is going to get the match. We haven't any doubt concerning the outcome. . . . McVey with all his known cleverness cannot stand off a man as strong and as fast as my man."

Freeman was pretty fast himself when a familiar nemesis showed up as Battling Jim was strapping on his gloves to face McVey. A deputy sheriff was waiting at ringside to attach the gate receipts to cover an old bill that Freeman had somehow neglected to pay. With fancy footwork and a dizzying flurry of promises, Freeman shushed the sheriff and arranged for Battling Jim to be paid for the ten-rounder.

Freeman's fisticuffs with the deputy sheriff proved more vigorous than any of the punches thrown in the slow-moving fight, which was won by McVey. The *New York Sun* called it "as sad a bout as the fans ever looked upon. For ten rounds they mauled, clinched, backheeled and did everything but fight." Battling Jim never got another shot at the title—and the closest McVey came was a six-round exhibition bout with Jack Johnson in Havana.

Like a rummy who craves respectability during his brief moments of sobriety or a Casanova temporarily smitten with fantasies of hearth and home, Freeman had his moments when he dreamed of a life of rectitude. "So I am going to square everybody," he promised *Variety*. "What do they call it? Reform? No, not that exactly, for you know how I do business. But it's what they say is the Christian spirit. That's a funny one, ain't it? Me and the Christian spirit."

Even though Freeman lapsed more often than a minister having an affair in the choir loft, Honest Bernstein always maintained his standards. He was never, in his own mind, a thief. "I wouldn't stand to see anyone gyped," Freeman told Sime. "But you know my stuff—the easy work that brings out the sugar without any hard words and no bad feelings."

Freeman's goal was always to leave his marks with a smile on their faces and their pockets grinning but empty. He figured out more angles than Willie Hoppe. As Freeman put it on another occasion, "When I die, no matter where I go, you can go gamble that I will pick up a little coin on the jump."

But the jumps that mostly were worrying Freeman involved getting his wife back on the road at $300 a week. When even John Considine couldn't come up with a return West Coast engagement for May, things looked bleak. The Bernsteins faced a financial crisis so severe that all the rubber in the Amazon wouldn't cover their bouncing checks. But the enduring strength of Freeman and May was that—no matter what their finances—they never had pretensions to lace-curtain gentility. Given a choice between pride and a fall, they would jettison pride in an instant.

Which is why in the summer of 1914—like a fighter stepping down in class to get bouts—May Ward announced her return to burlesque. In the seventeen years since she got her start with the Gayety Girls Company in Chicago, burlesque had become bawdier than before and dedicated to double entendres. As Freeman put it succinctly, "The idea of a burlesque show is girls and gross receipts. I have paid some attention to both in my time, but now my watchful eye is on the gross only." Still, the striptease was a rarity in burlesque (peelers only became common in the 1920s) and any discreet disrobing took place behind translucent screens.

Vaudeville, on the other hand, was built around a wholesome appeal to family audiences. Even star performers like Sophie Tucker faced strict censorship when they performed on the leading Keith and Orpheum circuits. The Last of the Red Hot Mamas was told, for instance, to strike sacrilegious phrases like "hope to God" and "oh, you old devil" from her act. As Tucker explained, "There was no arguing about the orders. . . . You obeyed them or you quit. And if you quit, you got a black mark against your name in the head office and you didn't work the Keith circuit anymore."

Burlesque, which had its own theaters and managers, never achieved bourgeois acceptance. The Ziegfeld Follies were the toast of Broadway with their displays of female pulchritude and costumes worthy of Cleopatra on a dressy Saturday night. But even though a burlesque show in 1914 might not show any more female skin than a Ziegfeld performance, it carried the stigma of leering working-class male audiences.

The highest-paid acts in burlesque performed on the Columbia Wheel, a circuit of more than forty theaters stretching from New York to Kansas City. The Columbia Wheel tried to maintain a veneer of respectability by claiming that it offered something anatomically impossible—clean burlesque. The Columbia Wheel even occasionally sent censors on the road to make sure that the performers were true blue but not working too blue.

That same naughty-but-nice approach was adopted by the opposition Progressive Wheel. As the publicity handouts in papers like the *Troy Times* declared, "The policy of the new circuit is to present clean and meritorious performances without resorting to the filth that has so long been associated with the term 'burlesque.'" The Progressive Wheel covered much the same territory as the Columbia circuit (including the Rand Opera House in Troy). But with shakier finances, the Progressive Wheel struggled with the threat of performers and local theater owners defecting to the Columbia.

May Ward, as a former vaudeville headliner, was the perfect recruit to flesh out the thirty-week 1914–1915 burlesque season on the Progressive Wheel. Her new show (put together at a cost of $25,000, mostly for costumes) stole from every aspect of her career. The opening segment was called "Kinkelstein's Department Store," a necessary renaming since Freeman had already sold the touring rights to *The Cash Girl* several times over. The ads billed the production as "MAY WARD and her Eight Original Dresden Dolls, supported by Cast of 40—mostly girls—in The Garden of Love."

When the tour launched in August in upstate New York (Glens Falls, Troy, and Schenectady), newspaper stories credited May Ward as the designer of the costumes and the overall supervisor of the production, even dabbling in rewriting the musical lyrics and the book of the show. "It may be this fact which accounts for the smoothness of the performance offered by her company," the *Buffalo Daily Courier* wrote as *The Garden of Love* hit town.

War erupted in Europe just as *The Garden of Love* was heading out on the road. And Freeman—that apostle of global peace—took the news personally.

"I think it's rotten, pulling this war just as everything looked all right for me," he told Sime, trying to find the show-business angle in the wrenching carnage in Europe. "I had May out for the season and was commencing to wear my jewelry again. Then this guy [Kaiser] Wilhelm started something. I hope Wilhelm will put that Kingdom business in Europe on the bum. Killing 7,000 Germans in a day. It's a dirty shame, says I, for I bet that among them were at least three good acts."

Even though Canada, as part of the British Empire, was at war with Germany and Austria-Hungary, May Ward's next stop on the Progressive Wheel was the Star Theatre in Toronto. These were strange days with ads for burlesque shows appearing in the *Toronto Star* just above an official governmental notice reminding citizens "that in the hurry of mobilization articles of uniform and equipment have been left [at] . . . homes or boarding houses."

Despite the war (or because of it), Toronto proved to be the Garden of Coin for May and the Dresden Dolls. The show grossed more than $1,000 on its first day (including a ladies' matinee). *Variety* reported, "The Star's showing has been talked about, considered exceptional these war days."

Freeman certainly had no complaints about burlesque, as he was preparing a tour on the Progressive circuit for the comedians Solly and Nat Fields (late of "Fields & Fields in Paris"). Okay, Freeman had one complaint: May would no longer let him go on the road with her show. "Wise girl, May," Freeman admitted to Sime. "I had piped off three blondes, two brunettes and a red head, but [I] must have been working coarse for May to get on me so quick."

Life was sweet and the sugar bowls were overflowing as May was getting ready to open at the Cadillac Theatre in Detroit in late September. Then—and you could just hear Freeman cursing his rotten luck—the Progressive Wheel went bust amid a flurry of lawsuits. Freeman was so upset when *Variety* caught up with him that he absentmindedly put his cigar (a good Cuban) into the inkwell on his desk. "Nothing is breaking for me lately," he said. "I had a run there for a while when I could get away with murder, but now it's going the other way. Nothing stands up."

May and the Dresden Dolls tried to stick to their original schedule, moving on to the Englewood Theatre in Chicago. But after a dismal week on the South Side, they limped back to New York grateful for train fare.

No stranger to desperation, Freeman began booking the remnants of *The Garden of Love* wherever he could find a little affection. Wildcatting brought with it a new problem: Independent burlesque houses had none of the pretentions of the Columbia Wheel. Shows were expected to be cruder and earthier with the emphasis on girls, girls, girls.

Even a stripped-down version of the $25,000 production needed costumes and scenery. But the local sheriff in Worcester, Massachusetts, seized every trunk and flat to cover unpaid bills. This was a moment that Freeman had been preparing for like a schoolboy memorizing the Gettysburg Address for an oratorical contest. Freeman convinced the sheriff that closing down the show would mean that no one would get paid. But if May Ward and the Dresden Dolls could continue on to Bridgeport and Boston, everyone (and this was a Freeman Bernstein guarantee) would get one hundred cents on the dollar. And there might be a little bit left over as a gesture of appreciation for the sheriff.

Freeman may have been known throughout his career more as a jail man than a Yale man, but in Boston he was banking on the Ivy League. May Ward and the Dresden Dolls were playing the Howard Athenaeum the weekend of the Harvard-Yale game—and they were the only show with girls in town. Okay, to be technical, female impersonator Julian Eltinge was also starring in *The Crinoline Girl*.

Speculators, hoping to make a killing on burlesque, gobbled up many of the seats for May Ward's Saturday night performance and started reselling them for as much as $4 a ticket. But the Yale alums in town for the game were in no mood to linger in Boston after Harvard's 36–0 rout. Instead of celebrating with their bosom buddies, the Yalies slunk out of town, stopping only at the box office of the Howard Athenaeum to try to return their tickets.

Hartford, the next stop on *The Garden of Love* desperation tour, offered scant insurance against failure. The scathing opening-night review in the *Hartford Courant* read like it had been dictated by the president of the local Anti-Vice League: "May Ward's play, or whatever it may be called, is of a burlesque type that is several shades cruder and stupider than what is expected. . . . It is not with any intention of urging others to go that we record the fact that the same thing will be repeated this evening and twice tomorrow."

With just seventy-five tickets sold (and another few rows of burlesque buffs watched on free passes) the opening-night take from "The Garden of Losses" was $51.80. Freeman canceled the next performance, using the flimsy excuse that May Ward was ill with appendicitis, which would have been a medical miracle since hers had been removed in 1905.

Over the next twenty-four hours, as he tried to find an escape hatch, Freeman displayed a wider range of emotion than Sarah Bernhardt in her prime. He ridiculed Hartford: "Some town when a real theater can get out only 200 people for the opening performance and when 125 of these are Annie Oakleys." He played Freeman the Honorable when he announced that all bills would be paid and the cast would get train fare back to New York. And he sounded the kind of defiant note reminiscent of Napoleon on Elba, promising that he would replant *The Garden of Love* on the burlesque circuit. "And this time," Freeman thundered, "I'll win."

The *Hartford Courant* overheard a plucky Dresden Doll trying to offer encouragement to a disconsolate chorus boy. Sipping a beer, she said in an accent that can only be imagined, "Cheer up, dearie. This here ain't the only bloomin' tank on the map."

Show business was changing—and Freeman and May knew they had to change with it. Playing bloomin' tank towns in burlesque and vaudeville wasn't the only way to keep a career going. May Ward had been a headliner, a star on the Klaw-Erlanger and Sullivan-Considine circuits. She and Freeman could get back on top as winners. They just had to find a way.

9

Twentieth-century show business was born on the evening of March 3, 1915. The delivery room was the Liberty Theatre on West Forty-Second Street, where ushers wearing Confederate gray and Union blue uniforms escorted the first-night throngs to their seats.

Under its original name, *The Clansman*, the production was already playing in Los Angeles and had been shown at the White House to the evident pleasure of Virginia-born President Woodrow Wilson. But New York was the true test: Could a show like this sell out while charging $2 ticket prices comparable to the best live theater and vaudeville?

Anticipation had risen so high that the New York newspapers sent their first-string theater critics. The audience rendered its own verdict shortly after the curtain went up: Every scene in the tightly paced story of North and South was greeted with sustained applause. The cheers would have drowned out the spoken dialogue—if there had been any.

The morning-after press reaction was equally rapturous. In

what may have been the original "I laughed, I cried" review in history, the critic for the *New York Evening Journal* gushed, "[It] will thrill you, startle you, make you hold on to your seats. It will make you laugh. It will make you cry. It will make you angry. It will make you glad. It will make you hate. It will make you love."

During the quiet moments at the Liberty Theatre, you could hear the first faint death rattles of vaudeville. An evening of variety could not compete with the spectacle of D. W. Griffith's battle scenes or the star power of anguished close-ups of Lillian Gish. Broadway audiences—weaned on Nickelodeons and hastily produced one-reelers—had never seen a story of this dramatic complexity as it hurtled from Pennsylvania to Washington to South Carolina. Or imagined that the silent screen could hold their rapt attention for the three-hour running time of *The Birth of a Nation*.

Freeman—normally blessed with a divining rod for big occasions—somehow managed to be in Cuba looking after his boxing interests on opening night. But like every showman in North America, he soon heard that *The Birth of a Nation* was selling out every performance at the Liberty Theatre, with its profits running $14,000 a week.

It had been a tough year for the Bernsteins. And it was only March.

In mid-January, May had declared bankruptcy for the second time—listing the house in Mount Vernon as her only asset, with debts ranging from a $12,500 mortgage to a $3,000 bill for theatrical printing and an additional $1,571 for costumes.

What was galling for Freeman was not his wife's insolvency. That was, after all, a family tradition. But the lack of publicity symbolized the waning of her career. Instead of May's picture appearing on the front page of the *New York World*, as it did after her first bankruptcy in 1911, now her financial problems were dealt with in a few lines, as if she were a failed furrier.

A trouper to the last, May returned to vaudeville after her bankruptcy. When she appeared at the Broadway Theater in early 1915, *Variety* wrote encouragingly, "Full of personality, life and pep and with a good voice and 'some shape,' May measures up just as strong as ever." But her bookings remained episodic. She brought a cash-poor, stripped-down version of *The Cash Girl* to Philadelphia and then returned to New York with a piffle called *The Garden of Mirth*. This, by the way, was a reworking of her burlesque act (*The Garden of Love*) rather than an homage to Edith Wharton's *The House of Mirth*.

To escape the winter gusts blowing through the holes in his bankroll, Freeman sailed south in quest of a little sugar. Havana, with more than three hundred thousand people, offered the louche landscape that Freeman craved—shows, gambling, girls, a whiff of corruption, and the New York sporting crowd. Heavyweight champion Jack Johnson had fled to Cuba from Paris after the outbreak of the Great War. And now fight buffs were waiting for him to take on Jess Willard, the latest Great White Hope.

Freeman's own heavyweight meal ticket, Battling Jim Johnson, was also in Cuba under the temporary management of his brother Sam. Putting his brother in charge was a risky move since Sam (who lacked Freeman's fast-talking charm) had an incendiary record that dated back to his starting a tenement fire in Troy by smoking in bed.

While still in New York, Freeman had arranged for Battling Jim to take on his longtime nemesis Sam McVey in a twenty-round bout with a $10,000 purse in Havana. It seemed a pretty risk-free proposition since Freeman had been paying off the American referee Sam Lewis for the past year and had fronted his passage to Cuba. But with his brother Sam running the show, anything could happen.

The outdoor fight was so lethargic, without a real punch being thrown, that the large crowd began throwing their seat cushions at the boxers. "When they finished," said a newspaper account, "the ring was so deep with pillows that the men couldn't move about, which they showed little inclination to do anyways." The referee—forgetting that he was in Freeman's pocket—grew so disgusted with the fake fisticuffs that he demanded that the fighters go an additional five rounds. But, at that moment, Battling Jim became Bailing Jim as he refused to leave his stool for the twenty-first round. The suddenly honest referee declared McVey the winner—and the whole incident jeopardized Battling Jim's reputation for toughness. More alarming was that Battling Jim ended up being shortchanged $1,000 from his promised purse—including part of Freeman's fee.

In Cuba, Freeman also met with the latest fighter to join his stable, Ted "Kid" Lewis, the British lightweight champion. Born Gershon Mendeloff (yes, Kid Lewis was Jewish Lewis), he was one of the greatest British boxers in history, immortalized in *Ring* magazine's Boxing Hall of Fame. A smart fighter in all matters aside from his choice of Freeman as a manager, Lewis announced from Cuba that he would soon be establishing his American training headquarters in Mount Vernon. That put him conveniently near the house that Freeman and May still called home despite her bankruptcy.

Kid Lewis's brief career under Freeman's tutelage was marred by . . . *I don't even know why I bother to finish this sentence because the predicate is so predictable* . . . disputes over money. Two months after he arrived in Mount Vernon, the British champion was arrested for welching on a $44.23 boardinghouse bill. According to Lewis, he had given the money to Freeman, who had, oddly enough, neglected to settle the account. By September, the welterweight thought that he had wiggled out of Freeman's control. But when Lewis arrived in Boston for a major bout, he was greeted by a threat of another arrest over legal claims that he owed Freeman $2,000 in management fees. The moral would have been obvious to the Marquess of Queensberry: If you have Freeman in your corner at ringside, a process server is probably sitting on the stool next to him.

For all their financial fandangos and bankruptcy bunkum, May Ward and Freeman spent their careers on the cusp of lasting success. With a few more breaks, they could have been sashaying down Broadway every night, dressed to the hilt, wearing jewelry that they never needed to pawn. Or even living in Beverly Hills, a few mansions down from Douglas Fairbanks and Mary Pickford. Powered by pluck and desperation (plus a healthy dose of inspiration), Freeman's best schemes were too early or too underfunded or too unlucky. In a show-business world filled with the never-was's and never-will-be's, Freeman and May were the Almosts.

By spring 1915, though, Freeman and May were the Almost Finisheds. Sitting in his dingy office in the Putnam Building at Broadway and Forty-Third, the sometime vaudeville agent and fight manager moaned to himself, "Freeman, you're through. You ain't seen a dollar in a week, the landlord is trying to get in and the phone people are annoying you."

What added poignancy to the lament was that Freeman had

exhausted his credit and was down to one good cigar. With only $8 in his pocket (thanks to the last trusting check-cashing joint on Broadway), Freeman had reached his "In Emergency, Break Glass" moment. Calling May in Mount Vernon on the phone (and being thankful the line still worked), Freeman announced that it was time for them to blow town. But they had to go separately so no one would suspect that they had vamoosed.

After calculating the geographic limits of their finances, the Bernsteins agreed to rendezvous in Philadelphia—a city where brotherly love extended to Freeman not having any creditors. As his train left Pennsylvania Station, he gave himself a pep talk: "Freeman, you ain't flopped yet, though you have been broke half your life. Take a chance, kid. There must be somebody in the world with money. And where would they hide? Philadelphia."

Unfamiliar with life on the lam, Freeman accidentally got off the train in Germantown, a well-heeled suburban neighborhood filled with Revolutionary-era homes six miles northwest of Central City. Instantly befriending a prosperous older gentleman also getting off the New York train, Freeman was soon being escorted on a tour of Germantown. As they walked, Freeman casually mentioned to this fine chap that he was looking for a furnished residence to rent (price was no object). Not only was the house next door to his tour guide available, but his new friend was also eager to introduce him to the family renting it out. A few handshakes, a few funny stories, and a few cigars later, Freeman was signing a lease without the need for the first month's rent or even a deposit.

With May joining him in Germantown (and already making plans for her menagerie), Freeman began taking long walks. It was such a luxury to stroll along the street without having to constantly duck in doorways because people he owed money to were heading his way. One day Freeman noticed a long-empty building down-town that used to be a photographic studio. And suddenly the shutter in Freeman's brain clicked. He had seen the future—and it was the motion-picture business in Germantown.

Freeman already had his star in May Ward. The stately homes of Germantown provided an ideal backdrop for a historical drama, since the setting could easily masquerade as the Revolutionary War, the Civil War, or any time in between. With the sinking of the *Lusitania* by a German U-boat that spring, jingoism was rising, even though the United States was still officially neutral in the Great War. Freeman—grateful to be living by his wits in America rather than dodging Cossacks in the Old Country—was always eager to drape himself in red, white, and blue. Beyond Freeman's personal patriotism, *The Birth of a Nation* (and its $14,000 in profits each week) demonstrated that glorifying American history was smart business—the sort of star-spangled proposition that would appeal to Freeman's new friends. In fact, the gentry of Germantown ended up helping him raise the money to launch the Continental Photo-Play Corporation.

Freeman had lucked into everything—aside from minor omis-sions like a script and a director.

Pining for the bright lights of Broadway, Freeman devoured old copies of *Variety* like a castaway rereading the few pages from Dick-ens that had survived the shipwreck. Even the advertisements in eight-point type made Freeman nostalgic. He read everything from a promotion for $295 waterfront lots in Far Rockaway to an anguished plea to "Anyone knowing the whereabouts of HARRY HOLT (Har-vard Trio Cyclists) please write his mother immediately."

Wedged between these two advertisements at the back of the May 7 issue, Freeman found his own D. W. Griffith. The line that piqued his interest read: "DO YOU WANT A DRAMATIC SKETCH WITH A PUNCH AND A GO?" Joseph Adelman (a sometimes actor, drama teacher, and author of playlets for the stage) announced to *Variety* readers, "I can write something for you."

As he had done in putting together *The Cash Girl* for his wife, Freeman was drawn to hiring talent. He just wanted to guarantee that the talent would work cheap. Although Adelman had probably spent as much time behind a camel as behind a camera, he came equipped with the one essential skill for a movie director: the ability to order actors around with confidence. A longtime faculty member at the American Academy of Dramatic Arts, Adelman had taught students like William Powell (Class of '12). Equally important, Adelman had in his trunk an unproduced four-act play about the Battle of Saratoga in 1777 called *A Continental Girl*.

Freeman was not a Revolutionary War buff. Sure, he knew about the Declaration of Independence (Freeman had put his John Hancock on enough rubber checks) and may have nurtured a sneaking admiration for Benedict Arnold for getting away with it. That was about the extent of his eighteenth-century knowledge with one exception—the Battle of Saratoga, which had been fought just twenty miles from where he grew up.

Aware that he remained as popular in Manhattan as a vice raid, Freeman donned a cloak of invisibility for the next few months. Adelman turned his play into 180 movie scenes—building the story around the beautiful Flossie Burgett (May Ward), who was simultaneously courted by an American patriot and a British officer. Ever frugal with performers, Freeman called upon the invisible army of itinerant actors to play his wife's suitors. For Captain Staunton, the staunch redcoat, Freeman chose Norwegian-born Olaf Skavlan, who had mastered theatrical swordplay by playing anonymous Shakespearean parts on Broadway like "A Knight" in *King John*. His red-blooded American rival was portrayed by William Sorelle, who had already spent fifteen years in the movies appearing in as many as twenty short features a year for the Edison Manufacturing Company. As Sorelle liked to joke, "I was playing leads when D.W. Griffith was dancing in the chorus."

Despite their inexperience, Freeman and Adelman were inspired by the visual excitement of *The Birth of a Nation*. The apprentice moviemakers took over a 250-acre farm on the outskirts of Germantown as the setting for the outdoor scenes in *A Continental Girl*. The farm even boasted a flooded quarry that, filmed from the right angle, could look like Lake George. Flush with other people's money, they rented forty-two nitrogen-filled lamps to film after dark and to add intensity to the illumination of indoor scenes. Their reenactment of the Battle of Saratoga included a realistic-looking scaling of a cliff by local lads in Continental uniforms. Freeman somehow wangled the use of diving horses that had been part of an act at the Hippodrome in New York—and Adelman deployed this equine talent in a watery escape scene. May Ward did her own stunts (a tribute both to her fearlessness and to Freeman's finances), including clambering up a forty-foot flagpole to rouse the Continentals by flying the stars and stripes.

Only in mid-July, with the filming of the five-reeler well under way, did Freeman reveal the Revolution that he had been fomenting in Germantown. He orchestrated an article in the Philadelphia *Evening Ledger* announcing that May Ward would be starring in the first production of the Continental Photo-Play Corporation. An accompanying news photograph showed a cameraman filming bewigged redcoats in full uniform and young women in bonnets with an imposing colonial mansion in the background. But even though the headline in the *Evening Ledger* played up the German-town connection ("New Local Producing Company Is Taking 'A Colonial Girl' Against Backgrounds of House in Suburbs"), Freeman's intended audience extended far beyond Philadelphia.

Freeman knew that he was not merely promoting a photoplay. This was his last chance to sell May Ward's star power at a time when she needed nitrogen-filled lamps to brighten her career prospects onstage. But motion pictures weren't vaudeville or even burlesque—and Freeman figured out a strategy to exploit the difference.

Even after *The Birth of a Nation*, Freeman sensed that movies still suffered from an inferiority complex compared to live entertainment. Sure, motion pictures had their own twinkling array of leading performers like Francis X. Bushman, Mary Pickford, Charlie Chaplin, and Theda Bara. But they still belonged to a lesser galaxy than stars like George M. Cohan and Eva Tanguay, who were taking bows onstage on Broadway and in vaudeville. That insight provided the key to May Ward's unique status. It was not who she currently was as the star of *A Continental Girl*—but who she had been.

"Miss Ward Deserts Stage" was the breathless headline in the *Altoona Tribune*. Her transition was treated as the equivalent of George Bellows giving up his easel and brushes for finger painting. As the *Photo-Play Review* put it, "Miss Ward is probably the most admired actress that ever deserted the speaking stage for motion pictures."

Most of the publicity for *A Continental Girl* revolved around May Ward as a soapbox preacher—proselytizing for the superiority of motion pictures over the stage. "When May Ward gave up vaudeville for the movies, the 'Dresden doll comedienne' discovered one tremendous compensation," declared the *Evening Ledger* in an item syndicated nationally and picked up by newspapers like the *Chicago Tribune*. That compensation was that the star of *A Continental Girl* suddenly had the time to lavish attention on her pets—seven dogs, two canaries, one parrot, two tomcats, and a horse. (Her other pet, named Freeman, was not mentioned.)

Another syndicated feature from the *Evening Ledger* that popped up in a paper in Ogden, Utah, stated, "Miss Ward votes for the photo-play as a road to health, as well as wealth and happiness. As a vaudeville headliner, she used to finish work by eleven, get to bed at twelve or one, and never be up again before noon. All the while it was stuffy theaters, dusty dressing rooms and the Pullmans." (You can just picture the matrons of Ogden recoiling in horror at this portrayal of life upon the wicked stage.) But now—atingle and aglow with the healthful elixir of motion pictures—"She lives in an old colonial house in Germantown, Pa., gets up every morning at six [and] rides off into the country." Presumably, on a horse.

When May wasn't galloping into the misty morn, the former burlesque headliner was busy composing aphorisms about her new life in motion pictures. She was quoted in the *New York Herald* saying, "Film and the world films with you. Act and you act alone." Or as she knowingly told the *Photo-Play Review*, "Many a split-reel man imagines he's a five-part feature." She even claimed to be writing an *Old Movie Goose Book*, although this children's classic never seems to have gotten beyond this bit of doggerel that would have embarrassed Edgar Guest:

Old Mother Hubbard
She went to the cupboard
To get her poor dog a bone.
But when she got there

The cupboard was bare.

And all she could give him was a trading stamp ticket to a movie show.

In promoting *A Continental Girl*, Freeman discovered the press agent's best friend—movie fan magazines. A back-page advertisement in the *Photo-Play Review* rewarded May Ward with her first magazine cover. The head shot featured her smiling Cupid's-bow mouth and her cascading golden hair held back by a lace headband. And the caption called her "one of the most popular young ladies to step into the camera's eye." It also insisted that the supposedly twenty-six-year-old May Ward was born in 1889 (a theatrical fib that would have put her onstage in burlesque as an eight-year-old) and that "one could easily judge her to be a half dozen years younger."

The *Photo-Play Review* also conducted a full-page interview with May Ward that made her seem like the Clara Barton of the animal kingdom. Visiting the borrowed farm (now called "Ward Manor"), the interviewer described her loving care of a crippled canary and a cat with ocular problems. "The canary which has but a single leg is a good singer," said the chatelaine of Ward Manor. "The cross-eyed cat I regard as an omen of good fortune." The credulous reporter gushed over her other animals, especially her poodles, "regarded as the finest in America." Her domesticity was also praised: "It is doubtful if there appears a more carefully kept home than the quaint Germantown mansion over which 'The Continental Girl' reigns as queen."

Freeman probably didn't mind being airbrushed out of the domestic perfection that was his wife's life. Especially since the *Photo-Play Review* folded before he had to pay for the back-page advertisement. Anyway, his secret hideout had not lasted long.

Variety had promptly tracked him down in Philadelphia: "The outward indications are that Bernstein likes this berg. He has taken a summer residence in exclusive Germantown on one of the very spots where the Battle of Germantown was fought in the Revolution. At night Freeman sits on his rented front porch and tells his wealthy neighbors of the many interesting battles he has had while in show business."

A Continental Girl premiered in Philadelphia in early September—daring to go up against *The Birth of a Nation*, which was starting a lengthy local run as part of its national tour. The review in the *Evening Ledger* suggested that Freeman's creation had held its own. "May Ward makes an effective and vivacious Colonial girl," said Philadelphia's dominant newspaper. "Her support is excellent, with the exception of the stagey villainy of Olaf Skavlan." The anonymous newspaper critic lavished praise on the reenactment of the Battle of Saratoga: "Though the aim of the producer was not to stage a scene which might be called into comparison with such big special films as 'The Birth of a Nation' . . . it is remarkably effective."

Motion Picture News, a leading trade weekly aimed at theater owners, was also laudatory. "With a clean story full of love, romance and patriotism, capable actors, fine direction, clear photography and many thrills for the spectator—this first picture of the Continental should win much popularity," wrote Irene Page Solomon, the paper's Philadelphia correspondent. She had kind words for May Ward, who "with her blonde curls, pleasant smile [and] petite figure . . . makes an attractive Flossie Burgett." But the reviewer tempered her verdict by noting, "The part does not require any great depth of emotion."

So how good, in fact, was *A Continental Girl*?

Alas, none of May Ward's silent movie work survives. And

despite the nationwide publicity campaign for *A Continental Girl*, there were only a handful of reviews, since the picture had been released by an unknown studio. So we have to depend on the verdicts of the *Evening Ledger* and the *Motion Picture News*. Their critics portrayed *A Continental Girl* as a credible production, ably acted, and more ambitious than many successful motion pictures released in 1915.

Freeman confronted a familiar problem in trying to distribute *A Continental Girl*—the movie business in 1915 wasn't any more welcoming to small-timers than vaudeville.

With all of his continentals tied up in one picture, the cash for promotion was flowing out faster than any profits were trickling in. To save money on expensive prints, a single copy of *A Continental Girl* bounced from theater to theater in Philadelphia, playing in sequence the Great Northern, the Globe, the Wayne-Palace, and the Victoria. Freeman tried to sell exclusive statewide distribution rights to the movie. "Your Opportunity for Big, Quick Returns Is Right Here and Now. Get One of the Strongest State Right Features Ever Offered," blared his ad in *Variety*. But the only 1915 showing of *A Continental Girl* outside the state of Pennsylvania was at the Royal Theatre in Wilmington. Not even Delaware, but the port city in North Carolina.

While Freeman was mesmerized with *The Birth of a Nation*, he missed another motion-picture milestone that occurred just two days after D. W. Griffith's masterpiece opened in New York. With two hundred cheering employees seeing him off, Carl Laemmle boarded the Lake Shore Limited at Grand Central Station en route to Los Angeles by way of Chicago. Laemmle, who headed the Universal Film Manufacturing Company, was abandoning his office at 1600 Broadway for a former 230-acre ranch just outside L.A. The opening of Universal City symbolized the westward-ho migration of the motion-picture industry and the rise of the studio system. Little Freeman Bernstein—making underfinanced movies one at a time in Germantown—was like a monk slaving over an illuminated manuscript who was invited to a book party for Gutenberg.

Now that he was past forty and had been broke for half his life, Freeman probably realized that he'd never be rich unless fifty-to-one horses started galloping home and wealthy strangers remembered him in their wills. What Freeman craved more than anything was not wealth but to stay in the game.

A Continental Girl made it possible. Even though the motion picture had barely been shown beyond the Main Line, Philadelphia considered it a rousing success—particularly Philadelphia Jews eager to get into the movie business before it was too late. The October 29, 1915, Philadelphia *Evening Ledger* announced the formation of the Franklin Film Manufacturing Corporation with $200,000 in capitalization. Freeman was, of course, the president. But the money men were two local real estate developers (Jacob Edelstein and Alexander Weidenfeld) and a lawyer (Maurice Rose). "The Franklin Film Manufacturing Corporation has five scenarios ready," the *Ledger* reported, "and expect to produce one feature every four weeks."

Joseph Adelman's bottomless trunk of unproduced plays yielded a searing social melodrama called *Virtue*, which became Franklin Film's first production. May Ward played Rose, a beautiful girl from the provinces ensnared into white slavery and then rescued in the final reel by her long-ago true love. To demonstrate her virtue before she was chloroformed and abducted, the script called for Rose to rush into a fire at a girl's seminary to rescue a crippled classmate. With Freeman so popular in Germantown that they might have inducted him into the Daughters of the American Revolution, the movie mogul convinced the town to lend him a recently abandoned high school building for his adventures in pyromania. Freeman then invited the Philadelphia newspapers to witness the filming as the reporters marveled at the fiery cinematic illusion that could be created by half a dozen smoke pots and a few artificial flames in the windows. In another publicity stunt, Freeman announced that he was trying to get heavyweight champion Jess Willard to tutor May Ward for her numerous fight scenes—including the climactic battle atop a table at a wild party in New York.

However, for Freeman, *Virtue* was not its own reward. A patriotic spectacular like *A Continental Girl* did not offend anyone with the possible exception of Revolutionary War purists. But now Freeman was confronted with the two most frightening words in a filmmaker's vocabulary—The Censors.

The Supreme Court in early 1915 had upheld Ohio's right to prevent *The Birth of a Nation* from being shown in the state without draconian cuts. The high court's unanimous opinion stated, "The exhibition of motion pictures is a business pure and simple . . . not to be regarded . . . as part of the press of the country or as organs of public opinion." This meant that, despite the First Amendment, movie censors reigned supreme, subject only to their aesthetic whims, sanctimonious prejudices, and state laws. And, just Freeman's luck, the Pennsylvania State Board of Censors was so prudish that it made Cotton Mather look like a free-love advocate.

The Pennsylvania Blue-Nose Brigade decreed in early December that the only way to take the vice out of *Virtue* was to snip two reels from the five-reeler. Not only did the state censors need smelling salts after filmed scenes of May Ward struggling to escape a brothel in New York, but they also felt faint during footage of a cross-country race at the girl's seminary when the young ladies were shown running in one-piece tracksuits. "The parts they have cut out are not immoral or objectionable," Freeman told the *Evening Ledger*. "The censors have put an evil interpretation upon certain scenes that a minister would not object to. It will ruin the whole film if their decision is allowed to stand."

Reeling from the threat to its five-reeler, the film company announced in a black-boarded ad in the *Evening Ledger* that it was appealing the decision in state courts. "The Censors have given their decision against the great moral picture VIRTUE with MAY WARD," the advertisement began. "They have decreed in their arbitrary manner that two complete reels shall be eliminated, thus destroying the story and the moral influence which the picture in its entirety conveys." Everything in the nearly full-page public notice was formal. Even the typeface looked like something that Strawbridge & Clothier would use to announce an exclusive offering of gentlemen's evening wear.

Freeman seized upon the obvious rebuke to these small-minded guardians of Philadelphia's public morality: He would bring *Virtue* to a city that appreciated the subtle nuances of cinematic art.

With a full-page ad in New York's Sunday newspapers, Freeman ballyhooed the exclusive engagement of *Virtue* at Daly's Theatre at Broadway and Thirtieth Street: "The Most Striking, Realistic and Sensational Film Ever Presented to the Public. A Thrill in Every Scene. In the End Virtue Overcomes All Obstacles and Vice Is Driven to Its Lair." Five film stills accompanied the display copy, including a nefarious Lothario in a top hat lifting an unconscious May Ward into his limousine with the help of a uniformed chauffeur. Philadelphia-style dignity was abandoned as the advertisement urged moviegoers to see "The Startling Stairway Fight between the Rich Man and His Mistress" and to watch "The

Famous Seeley Dinner Outdone." (Topping the Seeley Dinner would have been quite a challenge since the 1896 celebration of Clinton Seeley's wedding at Sherry's restaurant climaxed with Little Egypt emerging from a cake nude.)

Freeman's problem was that what happened in Philadelphia didn't stay in Philadelphia. Because of the notoriety of *Virtue*, George Bell, the New York City commissioner of licenses, insisted on approving the photoplay before its December 13 premiere. Too busy to screen the motion picture himself, Bell accepted the critical judgment of his deputy, Ephraim Kaufman, and declared that *Virtue* was "indecent, immoral and contrary to the public welfare and therefore shall not be shown."

Kaufman was dispatched to Daly's Theatre to close down the movie before its inaugural 1:30 p.m. showing. The afternoon had been marked by the first blizzard of the season to hit New York—and the several hundred shivering moviegoers waiting to see the scandalous motion picture had little patience for a punctilious Pecksniffian like Kaufman. Unable to buy tickets, the patrons rushed by the ushers and filled the orchestra seats. Urged to leave, the snowstorm survivors shouted that they had spent carfare to make it to Daly's Theatre and they were entitled to a reward of *Virtue*. "At this point," reported the *New York Herald*, "the fire hoses were manned and the cold Croton was turned upon the 'movie' enthusiasts already wet from the storm. This was too much, and the theater was quickly cleared."

Even Freeman—who knew something about luck running so cold that it froze—never imagined that fire hoses would dampen the public's enthusiasm for *Virtue*. But, at least in New York, the motion picture won a brief legal reprieve. A judge permitted *Virtue* to be shown as the legal wrangling continued. He needn't have bothered. The small crowd at Daly's Theatre on December 13 immediately began grumbling when they discovered that the advertised symphony orchestra consisted of two violinists and a piano player. When the curtain went up on the main feature, the Bronx cheers could be heard as far away as the Bronx. According to the *New York Times*, "Some of the audience expressed their disapproval by voicing adverse sentiments from their seats and others asked for a refund at the box office."

Two days later, *Virtue* was permanently banned in the City of Vice.

By early 1916, the primary business of the Franklin Film Manufacturing Corporation had become shelling out Ben Franklins to pay legal fees. The firm's Pennsylvania lawsuit established the precedent that decisions of the board of censors could be appealed to state courts. But that legal victory turned out to be worth as much as two tickets down front for the Broadway run of *Virtue*. The Court of Common Pleas ruled that while the demands of the censors were "minute and far-fetched," they did not violate the statute.

So now Philadelphia, too, was permanently off-limits for *Virtue*. In fact, the motion picture's next showing would not be until April 1916 when it debuted in that American metropolis known for its sophistication and tolerance—Bismarck, North Dakota. The promotional ad in the *Bismarck Daily Tribune* heralded May Ward as "BROADWAY'S LEADING ACTRESS" and called the photoplay the "Most Sensational and Daring Moral Lesson Ever Presented to the Public."

But Freeman plugged on—trying to imagine who might pay for a new movie starring May Ward, directed by Joseph Adelman, and shot at the film works in Germantown. Freeman still had one powerful friend whom he had never touched for a loan. When he was struggling to bust out of Bayonne, Freeman had gotten to know an up-and-coming Jersey City politician named Joe Tumulty. Now Tumulty, who remembered the free passes from Freeman, was personal secretary to Woodrow Wilson. And Freeman kept struggling to figure out how to make a buck off the Tumulty connection—especially since he sensed that the president didn't have the time or talent to star with May Ward in a motion picture.

But what about a photoplay *about* Wilson?

The president was preparing for a second term—and he needed the kind of promotion that a feature-length movie could provide. With the economy roaring down the track like a runaway locomotive, the film would be called *Prosperity*, filled with visual evidence of the good times that had accompanied Wilson's first three years in office. Tumulty agreed to raise Freeman's novel idea with the Democratic National Committee, which would be handling the publicity for Wilson's reelection campaign. Freeman, making sure that he got publicity of his own, planted an item in *Variety* headlined "DEMOCRATIC 'PROSPERITY' FILM."

Prosperity once again proved elusive for Freeman. His Woodrow Wilson movie idea died—and Tumulty steadily lost influence at the White House. But, in what may have been the most visionary moment of his life, *Freeman Bernstein invented the campaign commercial*. And never made a penny from his genius. Not until the 1940 presidential campaign, nearly a quarter century later, did anyone try to use a movie to sell a candidate. And the first "I Like Ike" television ads only appeared in 1952.

Genius may be its own reward, but it doesn't pay the bills for a motion-picture studio. In late March 1916, the Franklin Film Manufacturing Corporation declared bankruptcy. A week later—in a stunning coincidence known to beleaguered Jewish businessmen everywhere—a devastating $125,000 fire swept through the movie lot in Germantown. As the *Philadelphia Evening Ledger* reported, "Six explosions of chemicals at the height of the spectacular fire made rescue work dangerous. Thousands of dollars worth of aniline dyes, rare because of the war, were destroyed." But a vault containing $25,000 in movie negatives somehow survived the fire unharmed.

Freeman, by chance, was in New York when the fire erupted. Sime Silverman visited Freeman the next morning as the burned-out movie mogul was sorting through a pile of insurance policies. "See, I told you there was money in pictures," Freeman said. "I have had a fire . . . [and] what an intelligent fire this one was. It missed some negatives. Of course, I didn't have many and I didn't have many studios, but give me credit for having one dandy fire."

But despite the insurance payout, Freeman's film empire was little more than sooty debris. And as Freeman would soon learn, his nine-year-old marriage to May Ward was also being reduced to ashes.

10

The man with more aliases than an entire wall of post office "Wanted" posters was born as Herman Krueger to German and French parents in Europe in the late 1870s. Or maybe not. He claimed to have bedded 2,002 women. Or maybe not. He did marry dozens of them without worrying about laws against bigamy or trigamy. Along the way, police estimated, he lifted from his brides and lovers jewelry worth more than $1 million.

Only a few inches over five feet tall with a dark brown mustache, he would never be mistaken for a matinee idol. But—and this was the one thing about him that was certain—he could beguile women. "I gave the women something worth more to them than all the money they had or ever will have," he boasted late in life. "I gave them romance. . . . I typify romance. I came into women's lives with the promise of love, money, fame and success—social, theatrical or in whatever field they may have wanted all their lives."

He was using the name Brooks in Salt Lake City in late 1915 when, through a charming case of mistaken identity, he met the recently widowed Laura Milam. Over a very proper cup of tea at the Newhouse Hotel, Brooks learned of the untimely death of prosperous shopkeeper Harvey Milam and the starstruck dreams of the couple's nineteen-year-old daughter, Cora. By chance, Brooks happened to be a theatrical man himself and thought that he might help Cora break out of the chorus of provincial vaudeville troupes.

Before long, mother and daughter were having dinner almost every evening with the engaging Mr. Brooks, who was lingering in Salt Lake City because of unexplained business interests. When Laura Milam confided her intention to sell the store and their two homes because Cora needed a more sophisticated stage than Utah, Brooks arranged to broker the $12,500 deal. But mostly he spent his time prepping Cora for the big time—rehearsing an act with her for eight weeks. As she later recalled, "[He] posed as a theatrical manager and said that he would make an Ellen Terry out of me."

Dreaming of a Broadway debut, the fledgling actress and her stage-door mother left Salt Lake City with Brooks en route to New York. They took a circuitous route at Brooks's suggestion, stopping first in Butte, Montana, and then tarrying at the Savoy Hotel in Denver. Not trusting banks, Laura Milam decided that the safest place for her $12,500 nest egg (worth about $275,000 today) was in a chamois purse that she wore around her neck.

Cora had no idea about her mother's unorthodox financial arrangements with her cash. But Brooks had learned the secret of the chamois purse. One afternoon as Laura was luxuriating in her bath at the Savoy, she heard footsteps in her dressing room. She thought nothing of it until Brooks failed to appear for dinner. As his puzzling disappearance continued beyond midnight, Laura Milam (just to be cautious) looked inside her chamois purse. And found cutup newspapers—and nothing else.

Seven months later, May Ward met Brooks in New York. He was now using Siegfried (Sig) Wallace as his nom de fraude.

T he Great Germantown Film Fire—the towering inferno of Freeman's cinematic dreams—left the burned-out movie mogul in the ash can. For all of his initial bravado, the movie studio had been underinsured with just enough money left over to pay the mortgage. Back in New York, his finances remained the butt of jokes. A minor comedy act (Fenton and Green) showed off in *Variety* by advertising its version of the Seven Wonders of the World. Wonder Number Six: "Freeman Bernstein paying his debts."

In the fall of 1916, as Woodrow Wilson ("He Kept Us Out of War") was being reelected to a second term, Freeman was as cheerful as a Republican ward heeler. About all of Freeman's operating capital came from a single source—pawning his wife's jewelry. "When it goes against you, kid, how it does come," Freeman moaned to Sime Silverman. "Certainly that gloom tornado picked me out and just hung around me for three months. It's still hanging too. I can't chase it away."

The same gloom tornado was hanging over May Ward's career. With money from Joseph Goldstein (another Jewish theater owner caught up in the fantasy of becoming a movie producer), she starred in another movie, *Where Is My Father?* Joseph Adelman lifted the story from Alexandre Dumas, but the production ended up more as French farce than continental classic. "It is not an artistically produced film," sniffed the *Moving Picture World* in a June 1916 review. "There is not one of the players who consistently holds to a character with convincing ability."

After leaving Germantown, the Bernsteins rented a house (with

May's money) in Leonia, New Jersey, not far from the future site of the George Washington Bridge. Even with plentiful Hudson River ferries, Freeman had a long trip each morning to beat the mailman to his office at Broadway and Forty-Third Street. But the house in Leonia gave May what she craved more than anything other than stardom—a place for her animals. She lavished her love on seven dogs, five cats, two parrots, and a fast-multiplying colony of rabbits. (Her one-legged canary had flown off somewhere along the way.)

Now thirty-five, May almost certainly had no illusions that she would ever have children. Maybe her infertility dated back to her emergency appendectomy in 1905 and turn-of-the-century surgical techniques. Maybe Freeman was responsible for her failure to conceive. Or, more likely, their careers kept getting in the way. "No, I ain't never been a father," Freeman said in 1927. "May was on the Sullivan-Considine circuit. I booked the S-C time then and I thought May might just as well be cut in while it lasted."

But whatever the cause of her childless state, May faced constant comparisons with Freeman's three fruitful sisters. The eldest, Jennie Feinberg, had eleven children, ranging in age from nine to twenty-nine. My grandmother Rose Shapiro had six children at home. And Becky Potofsky, the baby of the family, already had a baby son and daughter. At least, Sam Bernstein was not yet married.

One of the rare scraps of family lore that has come down to me is the conviction that May's infatuation with all animals and Freeman's love of dogs were compensation for not having children. As Sylvia Potofsky, Becky's daughter, wrote in a brief family memoir, "The only interesting member of our family was my mother's brother, my Uncle Freeman. . . . He was married, but had no children. Instead they had dogs."

And strong family ties. May's father, James Southward, died

in 1913, but afterward her older brother (Charles, a ne'er-do-well carpenter's helper) and her younger sister (Elizabeth, an actress) lived with her and Freeman for a time. Freeman—no matter how threadbare his finances, no matter how exasperated he became with Sam—remained devoted to his parents (especially his father, Hyman) and smitten with his many nieces and nephews.

With her movie career silenced by the censors and the critics, May Ward plotted her return to vaudeville. In her view, the biggest obstacle she faced in getting back onstage was her ill-considered choice of an agent. And she had a point. The way Freeman's career was going, he would have been hard-pressed to book Queen Marie of Romania for a split week doing burlesque in Ottumwa. But one of the most wrenching moments in the marriage came when May broke the news to Freeman that his professional services were no longer required. "I told my husband three months ago that I intended to get a new manager—that has been his job," May said in September 1916. "We've been quarreling all the time lately. He left me once—for three nights."

But Freeman came back and, in his fashion, never deviated from his devotion to May. That September, he asked May to accompany him on a business trip to a city that has always symbolized moonlight and romance—Syracuse, New York. Sam Bernstein was managing the Bastable Theatre (the Bowery Burlesquers were a recent attraction) and, as usual, he needed help. Freeman had expected to meet May at the 125th Street Station for the trip upstate. But when she failed to show up on the train platform, Freeman began to sense the full dimensions of marital disaster. In Syracuse, Freeman appeared worried and distracted, displaying his emotions in a way that he never had while dodging process servers and bill collectors.

Reality was even worse than Freeman imagined: May had left him for Siegfried Wallace.

The charming stranger with continental manners boasted about important theatrical connections—and promised to get her twenty weeks of vaudeville bookings at $700 per week. May Ward was not an impressionable girl from the sticks like Cora Milam. Nor was she a naïf in the wiles of theatrical agents after being tutored by Freeman for a decade. So why did she fall for Sig Wallace's line of patter? Maybe it was the mustache and the middle European accent. Maybe it was irresistible sexual attraction. Or maybe in her desperation, she actually believed that Wallace could resurrect her moribund career.

Shortly after Freeman returned from Syracuse to a wifeless house, May telephoned the housekeeper to say that she would soon be returning to Leonia with her lawyer to pick up her clothes. Freeman did what any abandoned husband would do—he called the cops. Telephoning the Bergen County police headquarters in Hackensack, Freeman tearfully explained that his beloved wife, May, had been abducted by white slavers. The famed actress—now addled by cocaine and other drugs—had lost any ability to elude her captors.

It was a dramatic story that no police dispatcher could resist. And Freeman had lifted it, reel by reel, from the plot of *Virtue*. He correctly assumed that no one would recognize the tale's cinematic origins since the nearest theater where *Virtue* was playing was in Anaconda, Montana.

Aroused by the discovery of a white slavery ring, the Bergen County sheriff sent his best man to Leonia—Constance Kopp, the lady sheriff with her gold-plated handcuffs. Accompanied by a junior male officer, Kopp the Cop hid in the Bernstein parlor and waited. When the returning May Ward paused to turn on the lights, Kopp cuffed the actress while her partner arrested May's attorney,

Arthur Basch. Unsure of the charges against May (unlike the elusive white slaver Sig Wallace), the Hackensack police held her for five hours as the Bernsteins argued their way toward a temporary reconciliation. Basch was also released as part of the general amnesty.

Then, two days later, May Ward disappeared again. Freeman, with the help of the lady sheriff, immediately obtained fresh New Jersey warrants against Basch and Siegfried Wallace. But May and her artistic mentor had fled the state—and were spending the last weekend of summer hiding out at a Long Island resort hotel in Long Beach.

Don't smirk knowingly. Arranged by Basch's law partner, Henry Neuwirth, the hotel accommodations would have won the approval of the Pennsylvania Board of Censors. As May Ward later recalled in a legal deposition, "Neuwirth told me that he was doing this for the purpose of keeping me away from my husband, because he knew the authorities were looking for me. He registered Mr. Wallace and myself as Mr. and Mrs. Neuwirth. . . . Of course, I did not occupy the same room with Wallace, but an adjoining room."

So forget those leering insinuations. The lady said that they occupied adjoining rooms. Nobody but a cad would disbelieve her.

On Monday, the fake Mr. and Mrs. Neuwirth (Sig Wallace and May Ward) met with the real Neuwirth at his law offices near Wall Street. Constance Kopp—a brave and determined police officer who later went on to run a detective agency—received a tip revealing where the fugitives were convening. When the Jersey Kopp arrived at 120 Broadway with a New York City cop in tow, they arrested Sig Wallace for white slavery.

Enraged that her paramour was being trucked off to the Tombs, May Ward railed against the injustice of it all to reporters. She mocked Freeman's accusations: "He's been charging that I use 'coke' and other narcotics and that I'm practically an insane person, wrested from his charge. I'm ready to submit to a medical examination here and now as to use of drugs of any sort." And she went on to ridicule the notion that she had been abducted: "I'm a woman more than thirty-five years old, if I have to admit it, have traveled many times from coast to coast, and any person trying to kidnap me or make me a white slave would have the liveliest 138 pounds of fighting woman to handle that ever was tackled."

(Like Freeman, May treated her age as a detail best shaped to the circumstances. In the 1910 census, she was a dewy twenty-three years old. On another census form, in 1915, she admitted to being thirty-one, which was three years younger than her real age. When promoting *A Continental Girl* that same year, she told movie magazines that she was a precocious twenty-six. Now a year later, she had aged a decade. Belatedly admitting her real age was an unusual ploy for an actress—especially one who was described in the newspapers as a "good looking, blonde woman"—but it helped convince reporters that her entanglement with Sig Wallace was solely based on career considerations.)

One-thousand-dollar bail was set for Wallace, who had not yet been connected with Cora Milam. After her years with Freeman, May Ward didn't find it suspicious that her Sig—this supposedly powerful figure in show business—couldn't raise a dime to pay for his freedom. When Henry Neuwirth pressed her for help in finding someone who would stand bail for Wallace, May reluctantly admitted that she had one tangible asset—a $3,000 necklace that Freeman had pawned for $925. May handed over the pawn ticket after Neuwirth assured her, "It is only security until he is either discharged or surrendered."

After Sig Wallace walked out of the Tombs the next day,

Freeman dropped the charges, saying that—on reflection—his wife had been absent on business matters rather than kidnapped. It was a magnanimous gesture by Freeman, motivated in part by his sense that, for once, the publicity was not helping anyone's career. With Wallace no longer facing trial, May asked his lawyer, Neuwirth, to return her pawn ticket. But, as she discovered, "Neuwirth [had] without my consent or knowledge redeemed my necklace, and as I am informed, he paid $1,002.75 principal and interest." And, despite months of personal appeals that spilled over into the law courts, she never got her necklace back.

Determined to live apart from Freeman, May still had enough money to move into Room 510 at the Hotel Marseilles at 103rd Street and Broadway. By chance . . . and, oh, what coincidences can occur in a city of nearly six million . . . Sig Wallace also took accommodations amid the Beaux-Arts splendor of the Upper West Side apartment-hotel.

Dorothy Rothschild, a pixieish twenty-three-year-old working for *Vogue*, lived in the only other large building on the block, a rooming house across the street from the Hotel Marseilles. May undoubtedly passed her on the street or sat near her in a restaurant. The young writer had just published a poem in *Vanity Fair* titled "Women: A Hate Song." The types of women who enraged Rothschild included:

And then there are those who are always in Trouble.
Always.
Usually they have Husband-trouble.
They are Wronged.

May Ward and the fledgling poet, who later became known as Dorothy Parker, were not destined to become friends.

In late October, *Variety* ran a two-sentence item with the headline "BERNSTEINS SEPARATED." But even as the show-business weekly was confirming the obvious, May Ward was belatedly beginning to question her romantic choices. Sig Wallace, for all his pitchman's promises, had failed to deliver a single vaudeville booking. And it looked to her like the signed contracts that he brandished were forgeries.

But she still trusted Wallace enough to invite him to visit her in Room 510 on Wednesday morning, November 1. For . . . err . . . business consultations. Without May Ward noticing, the slick-fingered theatrical agent lifted a heart-shaped diamond brooch (valued at $1,000) and a diamond princess ring ($400) from her pocketbook atop her dresser. Wallace left her room a short time later—only pausing afterward to pawn the jewelry at two midtown shops before disappearing from New York.

May had too much pride to immediately go running back to Freeman. He sounded resigned when he told *Variety* in November, "You heard about May blowing. But I ain't kicking on that or saying a word. We stuck for 13 years and she was all right all the time, so if she wanted to blow that was up to her." A gentleman like Freeman had his code—especially since he was slowly moving toward a partial reconciliation with May. Before too long, the Bernsteins would be living together at the Hotel Marseilles.

On October 27, 1916, Les Darcy—the greatest boxer in Australian history—stowed away on the departing tramp steamer *Hattie Luckenbach*. The route was from Newcastle, north of Sydney, to Antofagasta, Chile. But what mattered to Darcy, the Australian middleweight champion who had never earned more than $5,000 for a bout, was his final destination: America, the Land of the Big Fight Purses.

As part of the British Empire, Australia had loyally declared war on Germany and Austria-Hungary in 1914. But enacting a military draft remained a different matter. Working-class opposition to conscription forced Australia to fulfill its promised troop commitment through volunteers. To spur recruitment and to eliminate exit routes for slackers, Australia in 1916 refused to issue passports to men of military age. So unlike lesser Australian fighters already in America, Darcy was trapped. He wanted to go to the States for the money and the challenge (after winning forty-six of fifty bouts, Australia had become too small a canvas). But even before his illicit departure, Darcy was attacked in the sporting press as deserving the white feather of cowardice.

By the time Darcy hopped aboard the *Cushing*, a Standard Oil tanker, in Chile, the fight world was hailing the coming arrival of the twenty-one-year-old Australian champ as the biggest event since the invention of lace-on boxing gloves. When the *Cushing* arrived in New York harbor on December 23, the *New-York Tribune* reported, "The bay was cluttered with tugs and launches bearing promoters who wanted to handle Darcy and managers ready to volunteer their services at any amount from 10 per cent up. No visiting member of royalty ever had a bigger reception committee than the one which greeted Les Darcy."

Promoters concocted outlandish schemes to reach Darcy, such as masquerading as a doctor examining the passengers on the *Cushing* in quarantine. But Tex Rickard trusted his reputation as the manager of heavyweight champion Jess Willard. When the tug that Rickard chartered (filled with sportswriters and out-of-town fight figures who were already hitting the whiskey as dawn broke on the twenty-third) pulled aside the *Cushing*, the impresario was invited aboard. Soon Rickard returned with his prize—the smiling Darcy in a blue serge suit who regarded the whole spectacle "as funny as a circus."

Once Darcy was ashore, Rickard set up headquarters at the Brotzell Hotel on East Twenty-Seventh Street in a suite that soon became as clamorous as ringside at a heavyweight championship. "I didn't leave Australia to get out of fighting," Darcy told the *New York Evening World*. "I intend to go to war before very long. As soon as I have had three or four fights here." It was part of a set speech that Darcy repeated as he shadowboxed his way through the crowd of sportswriters enjoying Rickard's booze. Darcy's promise that he would head for Canada or London to enlist at the earliest opportunity didn't convince everybody. The pro-British *New-York Tribune*, angling for America to enter the Great War, sniffed that Darcy's patriotic remarks seemed as authentic as "a schoolboy reeling off 'The Boy Stood on the Burning Deck' for the first time."

When reporters asked him who he wanted to fight first, Darcy said, "Anyone, particularly Jess Willard." Rickard gave a loud laugh as he pointed out that Willard was nearly a foot taller than the Australian and outweighed him by eighty pounds. Darcy, who bristled with self-confidence when the topic turned to boxing, insisted that he could take down Willard. "Well, if he's that big I think there's all the more chance of finding a soft spot on him somewhere."

But Rickard had other ideas. "I'd rather match you with Georges Carpentier, the Frenchman they're making into such a war hero," the promoter said. "You'd draw better with the Frenchmen, son, and he's just about your size."

Rickard served as Darcy's generous host—buying him a new wardrobe, escorting him on sightseeing tours of New York, and fending off other promoters. But Rickard didn't have a signed contract. The lack of a piece of paper seemed like a minor detail. "Darcy's plans will depend entirely upon Rickard," the sports editor of the *World*, Robert Edgren, wrote in his December 26 column. "It is likely that he will wait for Carpentier to come to this country." To underscore the point, Edgren headlined the column, "Les Darcy Is Lucky to Have Such a Great Sportsman as Tex Rickard to Advise Him Here."

Edgren, as much a double threat as any college football star dominating on offense and defense in a leather helmet, had made his reputation as a sports cartoonist. Accompanying his column were a series of drawings titled "Seeing New York With Les Darcy."

The images ranged from the Australian's wide-eyed wonder at his first glimpse of snow to a cartoon of a frustrated Jess Willard running after a sleigh containing Darcy and Carpentier. Edgren's caption: "Santa Tex Didn't Leave Anything In That Little Willard Boy's Stocking." The last drawing in the sequence showed Darcy in a dinner jacket as the legend read "The Australian Champion Will Do A Little Stage Work Before He Fights . . . Probably A Little Turn in 'Refined Vaudeville.'"

But Rickard didn't have a signed contract for Refined Vaudeville—or anything else.

Four days later, the *World* featured a front-page interview with Georges Carpentier from Paris in which the European champion admitted, "I am in a very bad condition." A military pilot, Carpentier had injured himself in a fall from his observation plane at the front. He estimated that he would need at least four months before he could fight again—assuming the French air force would give him leave to come to America for the bout.

The news from Paris left Darcy disheartened. If he followed Rickard's advice and waited for Carpentier, it would be spring before Darcy got his first American fight purse. In that case, where would he get the money that he had promised to send home to his mother and to his nine brothers and sisters?

A few hours later, Freeman Bernstein miraculously materialized like an overweight fairy godmother with a big cigar and bigger plans.

The downcast Darcy was sitting in his suite at the Brotzell Hotel chatting with Rickard and a few newspapermen when Freeman burst into Room 702 uninvited. Rather than fawning over Darcy like other promoters, Freeman politely asked the fighter to accompany him into a side room to discuss a proposition. Freeman then whipped out a contract promising to pay Darcy $37,500 for fifteen weeks on the stage and in the ring. To seal the bargain, Freeman flashed a fat roll of borrowed money and handed Darcy some bills off the top for his immediate needs. Within ten minutes, Freeman became the first promoter in America to snag Darcy's signature on a contract.

Back at the Hotel Astor in Times Square (where he was living as he worked toward a reconciliation with May), Freeman summoned the newspaper boys for an announcement: "Darcy signed with me this afternoon. The contract calls for him to box or perform for me for the period of 15 weeks. . . . The contract is absolutely binding."

Turning his attention to the most famous promoter in America— the great sportsman who had taken Darcy under his wing—Freeman suggested that he would have to come begging. "You understand that Darcy and Rickard had no written agreement," Freeman said. "I may agree to let Darcy box under Rickard's promotion, provided Rickard offers inducements that appeal to me." Reveling in triumph, Freeman couldn't resist going on about how "I put one over on the other promoters" and boasting that he "was going to make a sackful of money."

Who could blame Freeman for chortling?

Eighteen months earlier, he was so tapped out that he had to blow town. In late September, just three months ago, he was portrayed in the newspapers as a cuckold, reduced to claiming that his wife had been abducted by white slavers. His vaudeville career had collapsed, his film career was in embers, and he no longer had any boxers (not even pugs with glass jaws) in his stable. But little Freeman Bernstein—the Boy from Troy with more brass than the longest bar rail in New York—had shocked the entire fight crowd by snaring Les Darcy. And everyone was talking about it. "The whole town is giving Rickard . . . the big laugh," said Tommy Walsh, a fight manager who didn't even know Freeman. "It's the richest bit of smart stuff pulled in an age."

After the news broke, Rickard angrily denied to reporters that he had been played the sucker by Freeman. "I don't believe that Darcy has done anything of the kind," Rickard insisted when asked about Freeman's signed contract. "[Darcy] came to me today and told me of this man's scheme. . . . He said he would bring the contract to me before it was signed—and I believe he will keep his word." Darcy, who disliked confrontation outside the boxing ring, added to the confusion over the contract by disappearing from the Brotzell Hotel for the evening, preferring to sightsee without Rickard playing tour guide.

Whenever he pulled off his smart stuff, Freeman had a habit of improving the truth. Talking to reporters, he had initially doubled the size of Darcy's contract to $75,000, which would have been $5,000 per week. Freeman also neglected to mention that Darcy had negotiated himself an escape clause: He could leave the vaudeville stage for the boxing ring whenever he needed to go into training for a bout.

As a result, Freeman retained only partial control over Darcy's boxing career. Even as Tex Rickard clung to the fantasy that he could bring Georges Carpentier to America, Freeman was haggling over alternate bouts with a promoter who was none other than John the Barber (the hair clipper who got clipped in 1908 playing moneybags for *The Cash Girl*). But as the negotiations dragged on—partly because of the chaos over who actually represented the Australian fighter—vaudeville was beginning to look like a shrewd short-term bet for Darcy.

Freeman planned to launch Darcy onstage in Hartford at the Parsons Theatre, where two years earlier May Ward's ragtag tour in *The Garden of Love* ended after a single calamitous performance. This time, Darcy was slated to go through his paces for a few rounds as part of an athletic carnival. Darcy would also, the *Hartford Courant* explained, "appear in an exhibition of training methods as used in Australia, illustrating how he developed his gigantic shoulder muscles."

The management of the Parsons Theatre undoubtedly remembered Freeman, which explains why he couldn't work out the tour arrangements in Hartford. So instead Darcy opened on January 10 in Bridgeport, which—coincidentally, of course—was the home of P. T. Barnum.

In anticipation, the *Courant* gushed, "Never in the history of the sport of boxing from the days of the ancient Greeks and Romans . . . has there been as much interest in an exponent of the fistic art as there is in Darcy." The hoopla helped. The one-night stand in Bridgeport, which featured Darcy sparring for three vigorous rounds with Freddie Gilmore, the welterweight champion of the Midwest, was a roaring success. Darcy pocketed $800 from the Bridgeport gate receipts, and Freeman assumed that he would have no problem meeting his $2,500-a-week nut and start making a sackful of money.

But for Freeman, life on the road always provided a lesson in humility.

With America moving toward war in response to aggressive German U-boat attacks on Atlantic shipping, the euphoria surrounding Darcy's arrival soon gave way to sniping over his absence without leave from Australia. Sportswriters began referring to him as Les Slacker. The *New-York Tribune* archly noted "the incongruity of a professional fighter travelling fifteen thousand miles to avoid being dragged into the greatest of all fights." In his syndicated column, Grantland Rice utilized a recent headline to crack, "'Kaiser favors an early peace,' in which respect he has nothing on Les Darcy." And Darcy himself sounded like a war resistor when he said in an interview, "In Australia, they have come to learn that war is nothing but a grim, merciless battle where you must kill—or be killed."

Things got so bad that the *Trenton Times* promoted the mid-January arrival of Freeman's athletic carnival with the defensive headline: "DECLARES DARCY IS NOT 'SLACKER.'" But business was slack with only $60 coming in at the box office. Bookings in Reading ($64) and Baltimore ($66) represented more defeats along the eastern front. After Freeman paired Darcy with a local favorite as his sparring partner, Allentown ($450) allowed the tour to fortify its rickety finances. Responding to rumors that he was about to give up on his vaudeville career, Darcy said, "I intend to stand by Bernstein, who has lived up to his agreement with me. . . . Until I go into training I shall continue on the stage under Mr. Bernstein's management, and I will fight for him, too. The finances of our show are in good condition."

Not for long. An appearance at the Olympia Athletic Club in Philadelphia only brought in $127, although the *Inquirer* did acknowledge, "The crowd took kindly to Darcy, for he appeared willing to oblige them, grinning at every opportunity." For Freeman, it was not a smiling matter, since he had to oblige Darcy with $1,000 that night to cover the remainder of the contract for the week. And he didn't have the coin.

All through his career, Freeman had stiffed performers when gate receipts were sparse. But Darcy—the biggest celebrity whom Freeman had ever managed—was his ticket to permanent ringside seats in the sporting world. If Freeman broke the contract, another promoter would sign Darcy up before the first rays of morning sunlight hit the Liberty Bell.

Nobody knew the dangers of a broken contract better than Ben Rosenthal, who was traveling with the tour to handle the newspaper boys and to serve as ringside announcer when Darcy sparred. After three decades in the fight game, Rosenthal had managed to sock away something that Freeman always craved: ready cash. When Darcy came to collect the rest of his salary for the week, Rosenthal produced $1,500 on the spot—and instantly became Freeman's partner.

With the newspapers filled with speculation about whom Darcy would fight first (Battling Levinsky or American middleweight champion Al McCoy), the tour limped its way across Pennsylvania. At every stop, the athletic carnival accompanying Darcy grew smaller. Acts like the Terrible Turk and the boxing Weston Sisters drifted away fearing for their next paychecks as rumors of unpaid hotel bills followed Freeman like a pack of bloodhounds.

When things looked bleakest—that is, when Ben Rosenthal could no longer afford the burdens of partnership—Freeman tried a trick that had worked for May Ward: stepping down in class to burlesque.

Abandoning vaudeville freed Freeman to jettison the tatters of his athletic carnival (axing everyone except sparring partner Freddie Gilmore). Playing to a raucous male crowd (attracted by the girls, girls, girls as much as the Aussie fighter) also allowed Darcy to spar for a few rounds without having to pretend that he was a stage performer.

Darcy, a teetotaler, initially balked at the bawdy atmosphere of burlesque. But he lost all inhibitions about the earthy side of show business when the first week's gross receipts in Pittsburgh hit $5,900. Buffalo (where Darcy welcomed the arrival of his Australian trainer, Mick Hawkins) was equally lucrative. And despite blustery winter weather, Darcy's week at the Haymarket Theatre in Chicago brought in $6,350.

For Freeman, this was the best payout he could ever have imagined: The tour broke even. Ben Rosenthal became that rare Freeman partner to be paid back in full, the show-business equivalent of a unicorn.

Adding to the euphoria: Les Darcy had been booked for a $30,000 March 5 title bout against Al McCoy at Madison Square Garden. And there was talk about a $50,000 purse for a fight in Milwaukee later in the month. With Freeman getting a piece of the ring action (and making plans to put Darcy back onstage between bouts), his personal gloom tornado had finally taken a powder. That's the way luck works—when Les Darcy slipped onto a freighter leaving Australia in October, who could have imagined that the middleweight with the uppercut from Down Under would be the salvation of long-suffering Freeman Bernstein?

On February 12, at the end of his Chicago booking, Darcy

returned to New York to begin training for his first fight on American soil. How I wish I could have witnessed the scene at Grand Central Station: a proud-as-punch Freeman stepping off the Twentieth Century Limited escorting the most famous fighter in the world, who was resplendent in a new wardrobe featuring spats and a silk hat. But in my imagination it is Freeman who became the center of attention, gabbing and glad-handing his way down the platform, sprinkling cigar ash as he went, his voice booming through the underground cavern, the embodiment of the happiest man in show business.

Not for long, since Woodrow Wilson was training for war. The president broke off diplomatic relations with Germany and asked Congress to move to the brink of active hostilities by allowing the arming of merchant ships. Three days before Darcy's American debut at Madison Square Garden, New York Governor Charles Whitman delivered a sucker punch—the fight was canceled. "The Governor believes," said the chairman of the state athletic commission, "that as this country is on the verge of war, it would be both unpatriotic and unseemly to place upon a pedestal a man who has virtually deserted the military service of a nation that will be our ally."

Darcy became a ghost ship, a boxer without a country. Ohio and Louisiana also banned planned bouts. After America declared war on April 6, 1917, Darcy announced that he was preparing to become a naturalized citizen, telling reporters, "I like the United States, although I can't say that the United States has shown any great liking for me." He then enlisted in the Army Air Corps—and Sergeant James Leslie Darcy was granted two weeks' leave to prepare for a bout in Memphis. The moment the Australian-born fighter signed his American military papers, the public mood shifted. Even

Governor Whitman commented, "I am very gratified that Les Darcy has enlisted, and I hope that others of the profession will follow his example."

In late April, Darcy suddenly collapsed walking down the steps of Memphis City Hall. At the hospital, doctors discovered that the stumps of two of Darcy's teeth, which had been knocked out during a fight in Australia, had become perilously abscessed. On May 24, just five months after he arrived in New York harbor like visiting royalty, the twenty-two-year-old fighter succumbed to raging infection. The headline in the *Memphis Press* read "LES DARCY DIES OF A BROKEN HEART."

The only money that Les Darcy ever earned in America was on the vaudeville and burlesque stage under the management of Freeman Bernstein.

When America enlisted in the Great War, the doughy Freeman was too old to go overseas as a Doughboy. Just to be on the safe side, though, he backdated his birth date to 1872 on his draft registration card, which, by the way, described his military bearing as "short" and "stout." Ever patriotic, Freeman remained eager to do anything to aid the war effort—especially anything that would also aid him on the home front.

Realizing that he had a star-spangled asset in the surviving prints of May Ward's first five-reeler, *A Continental Girl*, Freeman sold them to the Mutual Film Corporation. The deal (for a lot less than the $670,000 that Mutual was paying Charlie Chaplin yearly) required the Revolutionary War photoplay to be reborn under a new name. Calling it *A Daughter of War* meant that it would be treated as a new movie—and Freeman wouldn't have to share the proceeds with creditors or former partners.

The movie weekly *Motography* played along by announcing, "The Mutual Film Corporation, to answer the demand for war pictures and aid in arousing the patriotism of the recruits, has issued a special picture, 'A Daughter of War.'" The reenactment of the Battle of Saratoga—along with May Ward's heroics cheering on the Continental troops from atop a flagpole—was mostly shown in small towns like Bemidji, Minnesota, and Kane, Pennsylvania. To drum up business in Kane, the promoters ran an inflammatory newspaper ad that began, "MEN! Are You Cowards?" Scattering exclamation points like confetti, the display copy in the *Kane Republican* screamed, "Don't Scoff! It's Not Impossible! If Men Won't Fight, Women Must! SEE MAY WARD in 'A Daughter of War.'"

Freeman—a man who concocted schemes the way a small boy invents excuses—would never limit himself to fighting on one front in his struggle to profit from the Great War.

On May 5, just a month after Congress declared war, Freeman sent a warning about an espionage ring to his old friend in the White House, Joe Tumulty, the president's personal secretary. According to Freeman's letter, enemy agents were embedding coded messages in movie films that were then exported to neutral Holland where German agents picked them up. Freeman was vague about the source of his secret intelligence. But since movie reels in those days contained several hundred feet of blank film, the story was plausible enough to prompt an investigation by the Justice Department's Bureau of Investigation, the predecessor to the FBI.

Agent H. W. Grunewald took time off from his vital war work (helping build the case that sent anarchist Emma Goldman to prison for sedition) to visit Freeman's chaotic Times Square office. Freeman was in Canada on business, but his assistant, J. L. Costello, eagerly passed on the details of the plot. Well, Costello would have passed them along if he had known the details. But, like Freeman, all he had to go on were nebulous rumors.

Costello (and Freeman on a later visit by Grunewald) sketched out plans to thwart the Mata Hari of the movie reels. With government money, they could set up an office in Manhattan to promote the export of films to Europe. Then, by running each reel through a projector, Freeman and the team under his command could check for the handiwork of German spies passing along military secrets. And it would be Freeman's selfless contribution to the war effort, freeing customs officials up for more pressing duties.

Maybe listening to Emma Goldman's fiery antiwar speeches clouded Grunewald's judgment, because the federal agent stated in an August 8 report to his superiors, "From interview with Bernstein I am not inclined to rely on his statements and think he desires to secure a position with the Government."

Never a man to let a good war go to waste, Freeman instead decided to become a military contractor: not a small-timer making boots and belts for the soldiers, but a commodore of commerce, a shipbuilder ruling the waves.

Freeman Bernstein—whose nautical adventures had mostly been limited to the Staten Island ferry—was preparing to give the Electric Boat Company a run for its money. Freeman filed the papers in Delaware to set up the American U-Boat and Arms Corporation with a claimed capitalization of $3 million. To show that he was serious, Freeman leased a shipbuilding plant on City Island in the Bronx with seven hundred feet of waterfront footage where J. P. Morgan had constructed his yacht, the *Corsair*.

(Yes, this is the only time in American history when the House of Morgan and the House of Bernstein will be mentioned in the same sentence.)

For some reason, the notion of Freeman's armada aroused skepticism along the Great White Way. A story in *Variety* about the delivery of the embossed stock certificates for the American U-Boat Company was headlined "BERNSTEIN'S WAR WEALTH." The *New York Clipper* described Freeman standing in the middle of Broadway conspicuously inspecting the plans for his shipyard. The show-business paper suggested that he might as well build it in Times Square.

The headline on the *Clipper* story turned out to be prophetic: "LIKE THE SWISS NAVY." But while his U-boat plans went *glub-glub*, Freeman recovered his sunk costs by selling the City Island lease to the Sound Shipbuilding Company. Thus ended Freeman's wartime adventures in unsound shipbuilding.

For most of 1917, May Ward's show-business career was in dry dock. In mid-October, she accepted diminished billing ("Extra Added Attraction") to appear in Philadelphia in a comic piffle (*Forward March*) that spoofed military life. The former headliner was rewarded with a single line in the Philadelphia *Evening Ledger*'s review: "May Ward, billed as the Dresden China Doll, pleased with her songs and chatter."

But May Ward's most pleasing performance of the year came in a courtroom rather than on a vaudeville stage. Her old friend Sig Wallace had materialized with a few new names (Dr. Carl Edwards, Karl von Edwards), a new wife (off performing in vaudeville with her three daughters on the Pantages circuit), and a once-merry widow from Buffalo who accused him of being a jewel thief.

Von Edwards, now a German baron, had met his latest love interest—Minnie Strangman, a tall blonde in her midthirties who had inherited a beer empire—in Buffalo. The hopped-up baron was posing as a potential buyer for the late Carl Strangman's brewery and adjoining beer garden. Soon von Edwards gallantly offered to accompany Mrs. Strangman to New York on a shopping spree. While touring down Fifth Avenue in her chauffeured limousine, the Buffalo blonde spied a dress shop that intrigued her. Bursting out of the car, she asked von Edwards to wait with her purse containing $35,000 in assorted baubles. The bogus baron waited with the jewels all right—for six months, until he was arrested in Detroit and brought back to New York for trial.

Police quickly deciphered the diamond-encrusted link connecting Cora Milam, May Ward, and Minnie Strangman. Testifying at the late October trial that was to send von Edwards to Sing Sing, Freeman's wife recalled, "He said he had made many actresses and would make me." All true, all true. "First of all," she continued, "he would write a play for me. Second, he would take care of my jewels for me. Third, he disappeared."

May Ward's most satisfying moment of revenge came earlier when she was asked to identify the man she knew as Sig Wallace in a police lineup. A dozen men were arrayed before her as she was asked to place her hand on the shoulder of the thief who had stolen her brooch and ring. The Dresden Doll walked slowly down the row of men until she recognized the light-fingered Lothario. Her reaction: She raised her right hand and—*whap!*—slapped the bogus baron in the face.

11

Panic ruled the waves along the Eastern Seaboard during the late spring of 1918. On June 2, a single German U-boat attacked nine unarmed passenger ships and freighters off the coast of New Jersey. Among the boats sunk by the U-151 was the *Carolina*, carrying 218 passengers and 117 crew members from San Juan to New York. The Germans fired on the *Carolina* and then used signal flags to order everyone aboard into lifeboats before torpedoing the steamship. In heavy seas, one of the *Carolina*'s lifeboats capsized, drowning eight crew members and five passengers—the first deaths from a U-boat attack in Atlantic coastal waters.

Four days later, Freeman sailed from San Juan to New York aboard the *Coamo*. He understood the danger lurking beneath the water, since he had arrived in Puerto Rico in mid-May aboard the ill-fated *Carolina*. When the *Coamo*'s wireless operator received reports of nearby U-boats as they steamed north of Cape Hatteras, many passengers erupted in "Oh god, we're going to be torpedoed" hysteria. But not Freeman—or so he later claimed. He remained an island of calm as the *Coamo* pumped up its boilers and outran the U-boat.

Back in New York, Freeman exuded bravado as he told and retold the story of how the German underwater navy didn't scare him. He was fearless, he explained to *Variety*, because "they have been trying to submarine me around Broadway for the last ten years."

In truth, Freeman was willing to swim through shark-infested waters if there was money at stake. Puerto Rico, which he had been repeatedly visiting since February, was about to put a healthy suntan on his bankroll. Freeman had finally mapped out the road to war wealth—providing entertainment for the troops. Taking advantage of the twenty-five thousand soldiers and sailors stationed on the island with little to do but grouse about KP duty, Freeman had returned to his roots as a canny carny operator.

"Phenomenal success attended all my efforts. . . . Business being done is beyond all expectations," Freeman boasted in a June ad in the *Billboard*, the journal of record for the carnival trade. He went on to offer the proven allure of a Bernstein partnership: "Will furnish 50 per cent of the capital and will go in on a 50-50 basis with any showman that can produce the goods and knows what getting big money means."

Freeman booked return passage to Puerto Rico aboard the *Coamo* on July 8 with his latest show. It combined the feminine side of vaudeville (Louise Cook's Models, the Five Violin Beauties, and the Gifford Sisters) with a circus (animal acts and sideshow attractions) and carnival games (the honest and . . . well . . . the challenging to win). But just as the *Coamo* was about to sail from Pier 35 in Brooklyn, the captain panicked over the presence of Freeman's biggest attraction—a five-hundred-pound man—aboard his ship. The jittery captain offered a deal: He would transport the sideshow star only if the bulging behemoth would agree not to get into a lifeboat if the *Coamo* were torpedoed.

Calculating the risks of a U-boat attack and the risks of not being paid by Freeman if he landed in Puerto Rico, the fat man prudently decided to stay on dry land. So at the last minute before lifting anchor, deckhands hurriedly retrieved the oversize man's oversize luggage from the bowels of the *Coamo*.

On the seven-day voyage from New York, the chorus girls compared notes on their contracts, only to discover that Freeman had promised every single act 50 percent of the profits. While a few dumb blondes may have been daunted by the math, there were enough brainy brunettes to figure out that Freeman's generous division of the profits defied every rule of third-grade arithmetic.

But these phantom profits vanished in a mystery that could be called *The Revenge of the Fat Man*.

When Freeman's traveling show arrived in San Juan, the trunks containing the costumes and street clothes for the showgirls had disappeared. Most likely, the trunks had been removed from the *Coamo* along with the five-hundred-pound man's luggage amid the chaos of departing from Pier 35 in Brooklyn. Or else the baggage had been mistakenly impounded in Puerto Rico. (Freeman was always meticulous in paying the bills for outbound passage, since he needed the performers and their luggage. Return passage was a different story.)

No trunks meant that the chorines had nothing to put on other than the filmy summer clothes that they had been wearing on the deck of the *Coamo*. No trunks meant that Freeman had nothing to put on the stage. And most alarming of all for Freeman, no shows meant no cash.

The local government—dominated by the Catholic Church and just twenty years removed from control by the Spanish monarchy— was troubled by the arrival of a boatload of young women from

New York, none of whom seemed to have been schooled in a nunnery. Pretty soon, detectives were following Freeman and the chorus girls. And it didn't take long for the gumshoes to report that the out-of-towners were, as they put it euphemistically, "distracting" soldiers and civilians alike.

As far as Freeman was concerned, what his performers did on their own time to cover (or, more accurately, uncover) their lack of a paycheck was their own business. Freeman spent his time screaming at the steamship company (and eventually collecting $3,100 in damages) until they finally delivered the missing trunks after a week's delay.

Despite the reappearance of the costumes, the show did not go on for long. After little more than a week of performances in San Juan and Ponce, the Puerto Rican government shut down Freeman's troupe in the most permanent way possible—they banned all women from performing on the island. (Freeman promptly announced that he would soon be returning with an all-male circus.)

The no-girls-allowed decision, motivated by a need to uphold public morality, undoubtedly deflated the morale of the bored soldiers and sailors stationed in Puerto Rico. But the real morale problems were with the performers who had trusted a Bernstein promise. Wangling their own passage back to New York (and, in some cases, having to depend on the kindness of strangers), they hit Broadway in a state of rage.

Babe and Charlotte Anderson, two-fifths of the Five Violin Beauties, were ready to string Freeman up. In *Variety*, they claimed that he had hit all the wrong notes in Puerto Rico by encouraging the chorus girls to dance with local men at $1 a turn after every performance. And the Gifford Sisters (Jane and Teddy) wrote to the *Billboard* to complain that their reputations had been tarnished by a "scandal" they had nothing to do with. Their bank accounts had also been tarnished, since Freeman owed them one week's salary for the canceled shows.

In the prior three years, Freeman had made a movie about white slavery and had charged that his wife had fallen into the clutches of white slavers. Now, in a turnabout, Freeman himself was accused of violating the Mann Act.

The United States Customs Service tipped off the Justice Department about alleged hanky-panky and hootchy-kootchy in Puerto Rico. Customs agents claimed that Freeman's theatrical troupe— according to the Bureau of Investigation's files—"was only a cover to conceal his real purpose which was to take the young women to Porto Rico for immoral purposes. It was stated . . . that subject would drive them about in an automobile and introduce them to wealthy men and wanted to divide money received in this manner with him."

Special Agent E. R. Jentzer from the Justice Department had the honor of becoming the first American law enforcement officer to open up a criminal file on Freeman.

Jentzer's first interview in New York was with eighteen-year-old showgirl Hattie Rand, who lived with her mother in Greenwich Village. Summarizing her responses in a report, Jentzer wrote, "She had been through an awful deal; that Bernstein had taken all their money and he got into trouble with the authorities and was arrested; that if it had not been for the kindness of the citizens and the police they would have starved to death; that the police arranged with the steamship company to take all the troupe back to New York."

But Hattie Rand was also Freeman's ace character witness. As Jentzer put it, "Miss Rand told her mother that Bernstein never attempted to induce her to commit an immoral act, but only spoke of him as a thief and a swindler." Jentzer abandoned the investigation after other performers confirmed Miss Rand's crooked-but-clean story.

Had he known about the federal investigation, Freeman might have had special business cards printed up to celebrate his exoneration: FREEMAN BERNSTEIN, THEATRICAL AGENT, PUTNAM BUILDING, NEW YORK. THIEF. SWINDLER. BUT NEVER A PIMP.

Even though he had to take a brief powder from Puerto Rico, the Caribbean proved to be a source of sugar for Freeman's finances. With May resuming her vaudeville career as a single, the Bernsteins suddenly were prosperous enough to think about the stiff income taxes that Woodrow Wilson had enacted to pay for the Great War. Make no mistake: Freeman was never thinking about *paying* his taxes. He was just mulling over the Talmudic question of what was income to a financier like himself who specialized in off-the-books enterprises.

"How do they know if I made any money last year?" Freeman asked Sime Silverman. "If I've got to give up to the Government every time I get a fresh stake, I am going to keep on making touches. Do you have to pay tax for borrowed money? Well, it's income ain't it? To me it's just the same as money made."

Anyway, Freeman explained to *Variety*, every bit of cash that came in vanished when the nags were running: "I don't give it back to the people I got it from. I give it back to the books. . . . I wonder if the Government would stand to have me put down these Saratoga markers? If they come after me, I think I'll take a chance on that."

In fact, if the government wanted him to make a declaration about his income, Freeman was already prepared with a script. "Up in Mount Vernon once," he recalled, "I tried to put a quick touch of the bank there and they asked me for a statement. I said: 'I'm known as an honest man.'"

Honest Freeman Bernstein soon was busy finding out that the secret to war wealth was . . . the end of the war.

The signing of the Armistice on November 11, 1918, was even more lucrative for Freeman than palming an extra ace in an all-night poker game. After fifteen years of bravado and bluster as he faked his way along Broadway, Freeman finally had stumbled onto a working coin factory. And it was so legal, it was government-certified.

Freeman became the vaudeville impresario that he always fantasized about and he reinvigorated May's career, turning her into a record-breaking headliner. And Freeman owed it all to the slow-moving machinery of the United States Army.

At the moment when the soldiers came surging out of the trenches in celebration of peace, America had two million Doughboys in France. But getting them home for Christmas or even Valentine's Day 1919 was impossible. The United States initially had only enough serviceable troop ships to ferry one hundred thousand men per month across the Atlantic.

Even when they returned to the States, members of the victorious American Expeditionary Forces spent long weeks waiting for their discharge in disembarkation camps. Back pay from their time in the trenches had to be calculated by hand from hard-to-locate records, and soldiers had to be examined by military doctors to see if they qualified for disability payments. All the Doughboys felt flush, since between back pay and a bonus voted by Congress, they were owed at least $100 (about $1,300 today). And stuck in camps, they had almost nothing to spend it on.

The situation couldn't have been better if Secretary of War Newton Baker had personally written a contract with Freeman's name on it. As far as Freeman was concerned, nothing could beat a captive audience of Doughboys with dough.

Somewhere along the way, Freeman had befriended J. R. Banta, a vaudeville small-timer whose major claim to fame before the war was disappearing with the box-office receipts from a theater that he managed in Logansport, Indiana. Banta, in short, was a kindred spirit.

Through his well-placed brother, a colonel in the peacetime army, Banta wangled a commission running the entertainment programs at Camp Merritt in northern New Jersey, the largest debarkation camp in the country. Banta (who was given the honorary rank of major) also had thumb-on-the-scales influence at the other two large camps in the New York City area: Camp Mills, ten miles east of Queens, and Camp Upton in the middle of Long Island. All these camps boasted huge Liberty Theatres (average size: twenty-five-hundred seats), constructed during the war by the government to provide uplifting entertainment to soldiers.

But uplift soon deflated. As an army report put it, "The average soldier would not patronize the more cultured forms of entertainment." Instead, and this should have been a shock to the War Department, the young men in uniform desired to see "beautiful girls, beautifully costumed, clever girls, with good voices and who could dance."

Sounds like somebody had been sitting in the front row taking notes during May Ward's career, from her early days in burlesque to the Dresden Dolls. Freeman—always a man to give the average soldier what he really wanted—put his wife on the road in early 1919 touring Liberty Theatres. As Freeman bragged in a March ad stripped across the top of the page in *Variety*, "ALL RECORDS BROKEN by MAY WARD, 'THE DRESDEN DOLL,' IN ALL LIBERTY THEATRES . . . PLAYED TO A MILLION DOUGHBOYS."

As always, Freeman's arithmetic veered toward the creative, since he was claiming that May Ward had in a few short months entertained nearly one-quarter of all the American men who ever put on a uniform during the Great War. But make no mistake: She was a record-breaking Liberty Theatre attraction at Camp Merritt and Camp Upton. Since Freeman couldn't duplicate May with carbon paper, he did the next best thing by hiring other girl acts like Dolly Le Roy and the Pullman Palace Girls. By mid-April, Freeman had four separate vaudeville shows on the road touring the camps. *Variety* called him "the acceded champ camp show-er of the Liberty cantonments."

But success could not change Freeman Bernstein.

Whatever the size of his bankroll, his shortchanging of performers remained the same. Maybe—to put the best face on it—he was too wedded to his hustles and hijinks to ever reform. Maybe his debts from playing the nags were too risky to ignore or he was badly in hock from buying May a new fur coat and expensive jewelry. But more likely (and, as his relative, embarrassing to admit), he scorned performers so desperate that they signed on with Freeman Bernstein as their booking agent.

The duo of James and Parsons, who billed themselves as "colored comedians," contended that Freeman had cheated them out of half a week's salary. When they objected publicly, Freeman retaliated by telling the army that they had been illegally selling liquor at Camp

Upton. The *New York Age*, a leading black weekly, complained, "Bernstein is accused of going around the Putnam Building calling James and Parsons snitchers to other agents, vowing they would never get a day's work in the building and making other threats unbecoming a booking agent of principle or good standing."

In truth, Freeman was color-blind when it came to chiseling actors. The comedy duo of Fletcher and Smith complained to the White Rats, the vaudeville union, that Freeman after a week had canceled their three-week contract to play Liberty Theatres because they refused to pay him a kickback. Harry Mountford, a leader of the White Rats and a longtime foe of Freeman, gleefully passed these accusations on to the War Department.

The army began posting closing notices on most Liberty Theatres in June 1919 because most Doughboys had received their discharge papers. By this time, though, a whiff of corruption surrounded the booking practices of the operation. Freeman, in particular, was singled out because he was pocketing a higher percentage of the gross than most other vaudeville agents. "I got mine, kid, and I'm going to keep it," an unapologetic Freeman told the *New York Clipper*. "They can yell their heads off. It's all over now. In two weeks, I'll be on my way to South America to put out a show. And I'll get mine there, too, see. That's me."

Okay, this was not Freeman's most likable moment. But it had been a tough four years for him: his rapid departure from New York when he was broke, his misadventures in the movie business, and May's public fling with another man. And every once in a while, the hunger and the desperation that drove him forward became nakedly obvious. If Freeman managed to be charmingly roguish in tough times, he turned hungrily grasping on those rare occasions when the chips were piling up on his side of the table.

Instead of heading to South America, Freeman realized that as long as the last Doughboys were hanging around the military camps, money was still hanging around for the taking. With most Liberty Theatres shut, Freeman plunged back into the carnival business. Since Doughboys were immediately disinfected as soon as they got off the boat from France, Freeman headlined an ad in the *Billboard* for a carnival at Camp Mills: "WHEN A SHIP COMES IN, HERE IS WHERE THEY LOSE THEIR COOTIES AND SPEND THEIR MONEY."

In addition to the usual sideshow attractions (palmistry, rides, baseball games, fish ponds, glassblowers, and freaks), Freeman always tried to add a patriotic motif. For a show at Camp Upton, Freeman even purchased a bobtailed water spaniel known as Belgian Jack. Discovered on a battlefield in France after being gassed, the dog had become the mascot of the army's fabled Rainbow Division, commanded by Douglas MacArthur. But, as Freeman soon discovered, it's hard to keep them down in the kennel after they've seen Broadway. Belgian Jack escaped from Freeman's office in the Putnam Building and disappeared, presumably going on to build his own career in show business as a solo. All Freeman was left with was a khaki blanket with the insignia of the Rainbow Division—and his memories.

Freeman had grown so cozy with Major Banta—now in charge of entertainment at all remaining Liberty Theatres—that in late June he offered the army's booking agent free office space in the Putnam Building. Freeman greased the friendship by promising Banta a piece of the action from his certain-to-be-a-gusher investments in the Kentucky oil boom. These connections paid off when the War Department canceled a carnival that Freeman was about to open at Camp Mills because the bunko games were too crooked and the midway entertainment was too tawdry for the delicate sensibilities of soldiers returning from France. Rather than leaving Freeman in the lurch (a place where he normally spent even more time than at the Putnam Building), the army bought the carnival from him for $6,500. The military brass cleaned up the operation and allowed soldiers to attend for free. Freeman also cleaned up by peddling to the government a second carnival he had planned for Camp Upton.

Thanks to Uncle Sam, Freeman was so flush that, according to *Variety*, he tossed a lamb chop from his $1 breakfast at Shanley's grille to the restaurant's cat. "You know how much I care for money," Freeman said. "I have credit accounts all over and don't need any. You saw me throw that chop to the cat? Well, that's what money means to me."

Of course, a little coin allowed Freeman to do things he really cared about: He secretly bought a racehorse named Kalatan that he touted all over the Putnam Building as a sure thing until the nag came up short at Saratoga. And accompanied by his old friend, vaudeville promoter John Considine, Freeman joined the fight mob in Toledo on the Fourth of July to see Jess Willard defend his heavyweight crown against newcomer Jack Dempsey.

They took a chartered train from New York (the Theatrical Business Men's Special) along with show-business luminaries like George M. Cohan, Sam Harris, and Eddie Foy. For $90 plus standard train fare, they had ringside seats to gape as the smaller Dempsey pummeled an out-of-shape Willard before forty-five thousand fans. As Grantland Rice wrote (actually, overwrote) from ringside, "Squatted on his stool in his corner, a bleeding, trembling, helpless hulk, Jess Willard, the Kansas giant, this afternoon relinquished his title of heavyweight champion of the world, just as the bell was about to toss him into the fourth round of a mangling at the paws of Jack Dempsey, the young mountain lion in human form."

While Freeman was enjoying the sporting life, his brother Sam and his nephew Abe Feinberg (the son of his oldest sister, Jennie) remained back in the Putnam Building bantering with Major Banta. The budgets had been slashed for vaudeville at the remaining Liberty Theatres, so Sam and Abe Feinberg had to scramble for tank-town talent to put on entire shows for $6 or $7 a night. Banta took a shine to Sam, calling him a "more reliable man than his brother Freeman." Of course, that compliment was like calling czarist war bonds a better investment than Confederate money.

Enraged by Freeman's shortchanging of acts, Harry Mountford, the White Rat official, finally got the War Department to look into his complaints about the booking practices for the Liberty Theatres. In addition to kickbacks, Mountford charged that Freeman and Sam had demanded that performers appear for free at New York theaters on Sundays as the price for being booked into army camps during the week. Mountford, who made Inspector Javert look like a slacker, even expected the government to investigate rumors about "poker games in the Putnam Building with the Bernsteins and Feinberg where raises to $20 were frequent."

After a preliminary inquiry, army inspectors in New York informed the director of Military Intelligence in Washington, "There is considerable graft going on in Liberty Theatres. . . . A man wishing employment would first have to see Major Banta, who would then fix a salary and then turn him over to Mr. [Freeman] Bernstein, who then employed him. In a case of a friend of the Inspectors, arrangements were made for a salary of $300.00 a week, but this had to be split fifty-fifty with the Major."

The War Department summoned Banta to Washington where

he was questioned by six army officers. Colonel Jason Joy—a man who, despite his name, displayed a limited sense of fun—sternly told Banta, "I believe that all along, unwittingly or not, you have let [the Bernsteins] get away with something that you should not have."

Following a lifelong pattern dating back to his first arrest in Troy for stealing $10, Freeman wriggled off the hook because, as a civilian, he was beyond the jurisdiction of the War Department. But Major Banta was fair game. And he freely admitted to the War Department investigators that the pickings had been lush. "When Freeman Bernstein was booking for the Liberty Theatres before July 1st," Banta said in his testimony, "there was a lot of money made, and he did practically all the booking of these shows."

But the War Department's probe into the Liberty Theatres soon went as dry as the saloons after Prohibition. The Doughboys were back in civilian life and the army was fast being whittled down to isolationist size. Despite the suspicions raised by Free-man's generosity with oil stocks, Banta remained a bantamweight target. So the War Department investigators shrugged their shoulders, shoved the paperwork into a file cabinet, and forgot about Banta and Freeman.

This bureaucratic lassitude fit the celebratory mood of the times when the loudest fireworks went off with the sale of Babe Ruth to the Yankees on December 26, 1919. The War to End All Wars was over and the Roaring Twenties were about to get revved up.

Freeman had his share of partners over the years—and all of them could be described with one word: trusting.

But now, thanks to his war profiteering, Freeman was finally in a position to step up in class. He was going into business with Jack

Curley, the biggest fight promoter this side of Tex Rickard and the man who had turned wrestling into a major New York sport. Freeman had originally met him in Cuba in 1915 when Curley was managing Jess Willard for his heavyweight championship fight against Jim Johnson. At the time, Freeman was awed, which was about as rare for him as Mae West blushing. "Jack Curley is the king of Cuba," Freeman gushed to reporters. "He's got the whole island hypnotized."

Even before the Bambino slugged his first home run as a Yankee—and even before Man o' War won the Triple Crown at Belmont—New York had gone sports mad. Attractions like six-day bicycle races were selling out Madison Square Garden. Freeman's scheme was to rent the Garden for a winter week to put on the biggest indoor event that the city had ever seen—boxers and wrestlers (that was Curley's department), circus acts and carnival sideshows all under one roof. As Freeman blared in a mid-January ad in the *Billboard*, "WANTED—CONCESSIONS OF EVERY DESCRIPTION. Rides of all kinds. . . . Freaks of all kinds, Diving Show, Hawaiian, Plantation. In short, live entertainment and concessions that will get the money."

The concessions were designed to sop up the gravy since the promoters could pick up a lot more cash from games with spinning wheels than from the door receipts from spinning turnstiles. But Freeman ran up against another longtime nemesis: the city's Bureau of Licenses, the same killjoys who had shut down his morally uplifting movie, *Virtue*, four years earlier. This time around, the city censors took the side money out of the sideshow by banning certain challenging games testing both luck and skill on the outlandish theory that they could be rigged. (Could you imagine Freeman Bernstein tolerating such an affront to fair play?)

With Jack Curley ponying up the $5,000 needed to rent the Garden, the World's Greatest Athletic Carnival and Circus opened on Groundhog Day 1920. Once Freeman saw the opening day's gate receipts, he predicted a long winter for his bank account.

The problem was not the talent. Freeman—who had loved the big top since he toured with his Winter Circus in 1903—had rediscovered his inner Ringling. He borrowed the elephant act from the Walter L. Main Circus, hired Charles Weir's Performing Bengal Tigers, and featured Gordon's Boxing Kangaroo. Curley handled the wrestling by building matches around such ring kings as Joe Stecher, Waldek Zbyszko, and, of course, Strangler Lewis. But Freeman and Curley were soon grappling with the harsh reality that they didn't have the money to pay the promised full week's salaries— and anyone who had been around show business understood the risks that came with crossing a man who trains Bengal tigers.

Then the weather turned cruel.

The worst winter storm in fifteen years hit the city on February 5, combining eight inches of snow with sleet and gale-force winds. Streets were impassable, the elevated trains shut down, and walking was treacherous. Freeman's parents—Yetta and Hyman—were living with their youngest daughter, Becky Potofsky, her husband, Sam, and their two children at Broadway and West 180th Street in Fort George. Somehow during the storm, seventy-five-year-old Yetta slipped and then died from the injuries from the fall, unable to get to a hospital.

Yetta had been in America for half a century. She and Hyman had become naturalized citizens in 1885. Yetta had celebrated the marriages of all five children—and had eighteen grandchildren from her three daughters. The only obituary appeared in *Variety*:

"The mother of Freeman and Sam Bernstein died at her home in New York Feb. 5. . . . Death resulted from a fall."

Freeman was afflicted with too many pressing business problems to properly mourn. The World's Greatest Athletic Carnival and Circus closed on February 8 with the promoters losing more than $20,000. On paper. Freeman, who brought a lifetime of experience to these matters, negotiated reduced salaries with all the performers, although the elephant act played big foot by demanding a 90 percent payment.

Then Freeman—like all Jewish sons reeling from the death of their mothers—headed to New Orleans where the ponies were running.

Before he left, Freeman promised to square things with his creditors in the Putnam Building by sending them the inside dope from Jefferson Park according to the railbirds, touts, and the occasional jockey's brother-in-law. But, as *Variety* reported, "Out of nine 'sure thing' tips sent north by him, only one returned a winner. That may have been an error."

No matter how much Freeman lost through his turf investments, he always had a strategy. "I'm out for a record," he announced. "I'm going to have every bookmaker in these dry States tell each other how much I got into them for before I'm finished. I haven't many to make before the record will be complete."

Back in New York, Freeman had a moment when he displayed the raw emotions about his mother and his aging father that he normally kept hidden in a cloud of cigar smoke. Even though Freeman and Sam were both pushing fifty, they got into a street brawl with a group of cabdrivers that landed everyone in Night Court, although all the charges were soon dropped.

The Bernstein Brothers had taken Hyman home to Fort George after a night on the town—a father and his two sons trying to distract themselves from their month-old grief over Yetta's sudden death. While Freeman helped the frail seventy-eight-year-old Hyman up the stoop and inside, Sam stayed with his official New York black-and-white taxi, which would then take the brothers back downtown. As Sam waited, a group of independent nighthawk drivers, who thought that Fort George was their exclusive territory, got into a loud argument with the downtown cabbie.

Sam, always quick with his fists, came to the rescue of his driver by knocking one of the nighthawks to the ground. That was enough to make Sam the new target. Freeman stepped back outside to see his brother encircled by flying fists. Throughout his life, Freeman was more of a flighter than a fighter. But this had been a tough month—and Sam was in trouble—so Freeman the Fireplug reluctantly joined the fracas, punching wildly, until the police arrived.

The next day, according to *Variety*, "The Bernsteins seemed all right, excepting Sam could move his fingers with difficulty. Freeman said the only blow he received Sam handed him in the excitement. . . . Freeman added it was his first test of endurance in some time. It rather surprised him as the uptown melee lasted about eight minutes. Freeman said his previous record for fast work, since he left the maiden class, was but three minutes."

That was how Freeman and Sam's last night out with their father ended.

Four days later, on March 12, Hyman died after an operation for a bladder problem at the Philanthropic Hospital in Harlem. This time a paid death notice ran for two days in the *New York Sun*. The funeral was held on Sunday morning in Sam's apartment on West 114th Street near Columbia University. And, I presume, my father, then ten years old, was judged old enough to attend the ceremonies honoring the Peddler turned Patriarch who had brought the family to America.

D espite losing both his parents within a month, Freeman still had to make a living. Or, more accurately, he still had to flash a big enough roll so that there were always suckers . . . sorry, lenders . . . to cover his expenses. In Freeman's perpetual quest for cold cash, it seemed inevitable that he would eventually head north to Toronto.

The Grand Army of United Veterans of Canada announced in April that the organization would be holding the biggest outdoor carnival in the history of the Dominion at the end of May. The planned boxing matches, circus, and vaudeville performances in Exhibition Park were all designed to raise money for Canadian veterans of the Great War. And Freeman convinced Richard Greer—a Toronto politician and veterans' leader—that he had the connections, the sporting flair, business acumen, and the philanthropic streak to pull it off.

Freeman offered the Grand Army veterans a seemingly irresistible deal: He would cover all the expenses himself and split the profits fifty-fifty with the organization. The proposal sounded so alluring that Greer and his colleagues ignored reports from Bradstreet, the leading credit-rating agency in New York, that Freeman's business reputation was—to put it euphemistically—unorthodox.

Two championship boxing matches were slated as the high points of the exposition, bringing in evening crowds that would profitably linger among the games and concessions along the midway. In the most ballyhooed bout, Jimmy Wilde, the Welsh-born flyweight champ, would defend his world crown against Patsy Wallace, the top-rated American. And Cleveland's Johnny Kilbane, the world featherweight title holder, would take on Canadian challenger Frankie Fleming.

In advance of the bouts, Freeman spent his time ingratiating himself as a big spender with the sporting crowd in Toronto. Every day, he would escort Charlie Hallat, a leading local fight promoter, to an exclusive tobacco shop, where Freeman would expansively urge his new Canadian friend to take a handful of $1 cigars as a gift. Freeman would also pick up a few Cuban Coronas for himself—and put the whole thing on his tab. Of course, as Freeman headed back to New York, he instructed the cigar store to send the bill to . . . c'mon, you can guess . . . Hallat.

In Toronto, Freeman did find congenial companions who understood that sometimes being Jewish required a certain flexibility in business ethics. He gravitated to Meyer Brenner, a twenty-nine-year-old scrap-metals dealer with a shady reputation, who owned a string of racehorses and included Freeman in card games at his Jewish social club. As Freeman later recalled, "He was a very sporty boy, a play boy."

Even when everything was on the up-and-up, Freeman couldn't catch a break. The circus was canceled at the last minute after Freeman discovered that the city of Toronto intended to tax him $1,000 a day for holding it. Johnny Kilbane, managed by Hallat, arrived in Toronto only to find out that Frankie Fleming wouldn't fight because he couldn't get down to 126 pounds, the top weight allowed in the featherweight division.

A bunch of schemes were floated to find a palooka to take on Kilbane. But Freeman—when it came to boxing, at least—was a man of principle. "Not on your Mary Ann," he told the *Toronto*

Star. "If we can't give them Kilbane and Fleming, we will not bunk them with a substitute bout. This is a 'show-me' town, and the boys will not stand for a raspberry."

The only thing that Freeman still had going for him was the outdoor Jimmy Wilde–Patsy Wallace bout at Exhibition Park, which attracted the biggest fight crowd in Canadian history. The *Toronto Star* called the fight a "sensational . . . battle between a wizard with the gloves [Wilde] and a game, hard-punching opponent [Wallace] who relied entirely on haymakers to bring victory." Wallace almost succeeded, dominating through the early rounds and forcing the champ to his knees in the seventh round. But the judges declared Wilde the winner on points, under the theory that a champion shouldn't lose his crown without a knockout. The American press was livid, with the *Detroit Free Press* headlining its story "PATSY WALLACE ROBBED IN BOUT."

Many of the Grand Army veterans felt robbed as well. To prevent an accurate count of the crowd, Freeman refused to use the turnstiles at Exhibition Park, claiming that the keys couldn't be found. He grabbed $9,000 from the gate receipts, announcing that he needed the cash immediately to pay the fighters. And, oddly enough, when Freeman sold the movie rights to the fight for $1,000, the money vamoosed before it made it to the Grand Army's bank account. Like many visionaries, Freeman regarded green-eyeshade bookkeeping as the stuff of lesser men.

Despite the doubters, Richard Greer, who brought Freeman to Toronto, continued to trust him. (Greer would become Freeman's Canadian solicitor and lifelong friend.) Also rallying to Freeman's defense was the most colorful boxing writer in New York—Bat Masterson, the former sheriff of Dodge City, who had traded in his six-gun for a battered typewriter at the New York *Morning*

Telegraph. Masterson was a regular at Shanley's grille in Times Square where Freeman often joined him for a $3 steak at a side table.

When Greer came to New York in July to drum up support for a Jack Dempsey–Georges Carpentier title fight in Toronto, the Bat man built his column around the virtues of the Canadian connection. Masterson had a reputation for hating fixed fights and crooked managers, so his endorsement came with a silver-bullet guarantee. "When Mr. Greer arrived in the city," Masterson wrote, "he called on Freeman Bernstein, the theatrical impresario . . . and solicited Mr. Bernstein's assistance in the event that Dempsey and Carpentier signed for Toronto. He made Mr. Bernstein a very liberal offer for his services, which it is understood, Mr. Bernstein accepted. Mr. Greer was very favorably impressed with the way Mr. Bernstein handled the Wilde-Wallace battle last May."

Despite Masterson's imprimatur (his column also ran in the *Toronto Star*), the Canadian veterans were unconvinced by the old gunfighter. They held their own investigation in August into Freeman's handling of the fight and the money from it. "The Grand Army of United Veterans desired to have Mr. Bernstein held or brought back from New York to give a full accounting," reported the *Toronto World*, "but are informed by the detective bureau that no definitely proven charge can be laid against him. The board decided that it looks as if anyone guilty have well covered their tracks."

Once again, Freeman beat the rap.

These were flush times for Freeman as he (briefly) replaced his Michigan roll with a real one featuring a genuine $500 bill on top. His Canadian coin harvest even allowed him to start buying May dinner every night at Shanley's without hitting her up for a touch. Taking a few weeks off from what passed for work, Freeman set out to play the ponies full-time. That, of course, required him to square things with all the bookies who were holding his markers. As he told Sime Silverman of *Variety*, "Some of these books are showing big profits now, but I bet there would be a loss if they took my account out."

Even as Freeman talked boldly about making so much at Saratoga in August that he'd quit show business, he also had a sense of how quickly his roll could go blouie. "I must leave for Saratoga in a couple of days," he said. "If you don't see me after the Saratoga meet is over, have someone look in the Erie Canal at Albany. I will be there, on the right side, near the bottom."

Freeman convinced his brother to join him at Saratoga—partly because Sam was willing to spring for their passage on a Hudson River liner and partly because both Bernstein Boys wanted to stop off in Troy on the way. Freeman explained to *Variety* that the side trip had been his brother's idea: "Sam said he felt like riding once through his own hometown and not be afraid of the sheriff."

Two weeks into the Saratoga racing season, Freeman was signing letters to his friends at *Variety*, "Yours as ever broke." Hard-pressed to raise train fare to get back to New York (Sam had already bailed when he was tapped out), Freeman joked, "I am looking around for a warm spot over the winter. They tell me there's nothing to eat up here then but snow and nothing to sleep on but ice. Looks good for me this winter."

But you can't keep a good con man down for long.

A month later *Variety* headlined "Times Sq.'s Greatest Manipulator Now Living at Plaza." Rather than debunking the story, Freeman explained how he had come to be bunking at the ritzy hotel: "They took me cleanly in Saratoga. . . . But I got mixed up with a money guy there and you know me when I smell coin. I told the guy a few things and he wanted me to go into partnership with him. I told him . . . I would direct the investing of his money. So I am with that guy over at the Plaza telling how to shoot his money into larger lots."

From his ninth-floor suite overlooking Central Park, Freeman contemplated the business propositions coming his way. There was the Hollywood thing. Tired of making marzipan movies, Marshall Neilan (who had directed Mary Pickford in *Rebecca of Sunnybrook Farm*) wanted Freeman to come out to the West Coast to appear in a film called *The Promoter*. Not only was this a role that Neilan sensed would not be an artistic stretch for the actor, but Freeman could also offer the production technical expertise in such matters as cashing bogus checks in New York drawn on London banks.

But Freeman was enjoying life too much at the Plaza to be seduced by the siren song of Hollywood. "Ain't that a great dump," Freeman said, still marveling over his new digs. "The only hotel I've ever got into that had six exits. Yes, of course, they are entrances, too, but I only think of exits. Hey, can you imagine what I can pull with six different ways of getting in and out of a hotel?"

Unlike most hotels where Freeman had stayed over the years (usually just once), the Plaza would not run a tab for first-time guests with unusual credit histories who were not listed in the *Social Register*. As Freeman said about the hotel, "They do charge. I'm paying $12 a day to sleep in a room with a bath. You know me, paying $12 to sleep in a room with anything. I never believed I could do it. I asked them about a room without a bath and they almost gave me the bum's rush. Well, the bankroll is skidding, kid, and the twelves are commencing to look larger and larger."

About the time that Freeman started fantasizing about raising money to pay his hotel bill by selling the oil-drilling rights to Central Park, he reluctantly checked out of the Plaza.

Freeman—in case you hadn't noticed—had always been guided by a life philosophy. As he explained it to *Variety* editor Sime Silverman, "The difference between you and me is that you work hard all the time and are always broke; I work once in a while and I am broke now and then."

After his Plaza suite failed to yield any sugar, Freeman was forced to work up a little Staten Island sweat. When the wheel of fortune turned against him, Freeman placed his faith in games with wheels. He put together a carnival on Staten Island not too far from the ferry to Bayonne. But a police raid on opening night shut down some of the more, well, lucrative games of chance. Then it rained for three days. Plagued with bad luck, Freeman was probably expecting hail or locusts next. Instead, the tail end of a tropical storm delivered him a tornado. The high winds blew the concessions halfway to Bayonne, and, in the confusion, a trained dog act escaped to explore the fleshpots of Staten Island on its own.

It was enough to prompt Freeman to announce to *Variety*, "I'm blowing out! New York's too tough." For a man who had never crossed an ocean and had just acquired a passport, Freeman had picked up a bad case of wanderlust. "Say, kid, did you ever hear of a joint called China?" Freeman asked Sime. "It's near Java somewhere and they tell me it is the biggest layout around there. I'm just nuts about this China."

Instead, after a quick cram course on the British peerage ("How do you talk to those Lords over there? Do you say, 'My Lord' or 'My Pal'?"), Freeman sailed to England on the Cunard liner, the RMS *Aquitania*. Beneath the oak-beamed ceilings of the seventy-six-foot-long First Class Smoking Lounge, Freeman puffed his

Coronas, plied new friends with show-business stories, and plotted his triumphant entry into London. As Freeman reported back to New York, "I knew it when I got off at Southampton. Nobody shied away from me as I walked to the train, and I says to myself: 'Freeman, this is the place.'"

Inspired by his stay at the Plaza in New York, Freeman didn't stint on a London hotel. He booked himself into the Carlton in Haymarket, although Freeman's palate was probably not sensitive enough to realize that it was Auguste Escoffier who presided over the hotel's acclaimed kitchen. Freeman's mind, in fact, was on more elevated topics than food.

Burlesque, to be precise.

As he announced to the London correspondents of both the *Billboard* and *Variety*, he was in heavy negotiations to set up an American-style burlesque wheel in London and other British cities. But even as he concocted his burlesque scheme, Freeman was discovering that travel was broadening. "I must have been stale," he said in a letter. "A guy like me should travel. There are so many saps around I don't know which one to tap first."

The day before the *Aquitania* sailed from New York, Man o' War had whipped Sir Barton by seven lengths in a match race in Windsor, Ontario. And that got Freeman's mind racing. Even though he didn't have any racing connections in England (though Freeman would have blended in perfectly at Ascot), he did know a thing or two about publicity. It didn't take much to impress the newspaper boys—and get his name in the headlines along the way.

On November 3, just two weeks after Freeman first set foot in England, the *Daily Mail* reported, "Efforts are being made by Mr. Freeman Bernstein, the American sportsman and racehorse owner, who is in London, to bring the famous American racehorse, Man o' War, to England to run next spring." How that sentence must have tickled Freeman: "American sportsman and racehorse owner" made him sound like a Vanderbilt or a Whitney.

The gullible *Daily Mail* reporter went on to quote Freeman's claim: "I cabled to Mr. Samuel Riddle, the owner of Man o' War, at Philadelphia last night guaranteeing him £20,000 to bring Man o' War over. . . . I think Mr. Riddle will accept. If so, I intend, if possible, to arrange a match at weight for age over 10 furlongs. Then I shall take the horse to run in France."

The story was picked up around the world. Even the *New-York Tribune*, which should have known better about a local boy, described Freeman as a "New York Sportsman" in its front-page headline. As Freeman gleefully wrote Sime Silverman, "Have you been reading my press stuff about Man o' War and the theatres. I even made the guy you have over here fall for me. Of course I took a chance that you didn't write him about me, and thanks for that."

The whole incident made Freeman feel like a stud. As for Man o' War, he retired to stud.

12

Not since Captain Ahab had there been a man more at home on the high seas than Freeman Bernstein. In place of the Great White Whale, Freeman was out to harpoon the Great Rich Sucker. Freeman made four transatlantic round-trips during a nine-month period beginning in December 1920. While he favored the *Aquitania*, Freeman also happily settled for a first-class stateroom aboard the RMS *Olympic*, the surviving sister ship of the *Titanic*.

Not bad for the Boy from Troy whose parents had arrived in steerage.

These six- and seven-day crossings offered Freeman something even better than salt air, ocean views, and invigorating walks on the Promenade Deck. "This traveling over the ocean gets you in right with a lot of nice people," he cabled *Variety* from the *Aquitania*. "I have met people on this boat I never met anywhere else. They can't take the air on me here unless they sew themselves up in the stateroom."

Freeman pointed to Vincent Astor as the sort of nice person he was unlikely to meet in the elevator of the Putnam Building. Astor, who had become one of the world's richest men when his father went down on the *Titanic*, was Freeman's fellow first-class passenger on the *Olympic* during a mid-March 1921 crossing from Southampton. "It doesn't do any harm to run across that kind does it," Freeman wrote, "but it hasn't done me any good either. But you can't tell. I may use him yet. What a backer he would make for a carnival to travel around the world? And he would never miss the coin."

But Freeman couldn't just buttonhole Astor with a friendly "Hey, Vinnie" on the *Olympic*'s Grand Staircase or jab him in the ribs in the middle of a massage in the ship's Turkish Bath. Freeman needed an icebreaker, although that probably was not a word to be used around a man whose father's last memory was hearing a shipboard band play "Nearer, My God, to Thee."

Without that icebreaker, Freeman might have had to content himself with only his cigar for company under the stained-glass windows of the Smoke Room on the *Olympic*. Luckily, he had an accomplice who helped him make friends more easily than Dale Carnegie. Aboard the *Olympic*, Freeman announced that May Ward, the acclaimed star of vaudeville and the screen, would be giving an impromptu concert in the first-class lounge. When Freeman, serving as stage manager, accidentally mangled the title of one of May's songs, his new friend Vincent Astor immediately corrected him. On the same voyage, Freeman applied his personal magnetism to magnates like Charles Schwab, the semiretired founder of United States Steel.

Working with the teamwork of Fred and Adele Astaire, Freeman and May soon perfected a lucrative transatlantic racket that they called the Anniversary Gag. On the first night out from port, Freeman and May would stroll arm in arm into the first-class salon to gaily announce, "It's our wedding anniversary. And we want you all to celebrate with us. Champagne for the house."

After corks were popped and flutes were raised filled with Moët & Chandon Imperial, Freeman and May, the happy couple, suddenly had enough new chums to last them the voyage. The next day, Freeman suggested to some of these Champagne Charlies that—just to pass the time—a friendly game of cards would do the trick. Maybe, he would hint, a few small wagers might make things interesting. Nothing heavy-handed was needed, since these were friends who had helped Freeman celebrate his wedding anniversary on the high seas. And whether the game was gin rummy, pinochle, auction bridge, or poker, Freeman was rightly confident that, after a few days on the Atlantic, his cardsharp skills would pay him many times over for the cost of the anniversary champagne.

The swag from crossing the Atlantic went beyond Freeman's card-table winnings. Whenever Freeman reached dry land, his luggage acquired a new heft and about the only thing left in his stateroom was the bare mattress. As Freeman's niece, Sylvia Potofsky, recalled from her 1920s childhood, "We always had fine linen napkins and towels from the White Star Line."

Freeman believed that getting there was half the fun and twice as lucrative. But he also had serious business on the other side of the Atlantic. In London, Freeman managed to get within the presence of the Prince of Wales (later Edward VIII, who had that fling with Wallis Simpson). "I just addressed him as Your Worship," Freeman recounted. "It seemed to make a hit with the kid. He asked a couple of people who I was and, as they didn't know, I told him myself. He said I was charming, so I blushed to make good on his remark. If the Prince behaves himself I may let him in on anything I put over at the track."

But the real action for Freeman revolved around reviving May's flagging vaudeville career. He booked her as a solo act in early 1921

Freeman Bernstein was already an apprentice gambler when this
picture of his hometown—Troy, New York—was taken around 1890.
He and his family lived in a tenement (not visible in this photograph)
in a Jewish neighborhood, at the far end of River Street.

Freeman's Trocadero Music Hall—the one glittering business success
of his career—is behind the buildings at the far left. This postcard
view of Paradise Park amusement area is from around 1910.

May Ward was featured on the burlesque stage in 1897, when she was sixteen. By 1899, she was a big enough star to adorn the cover of the sheet music of one of her songs.

On the lam from creditors, Freeman set himself up in 1915 as a silent-movie mogul with his wife as his star. *A Continental Girl*, set in the Revolutionary War, was inspired by *The Birth of a Nation*.

Shortly after she married Freeman in 1906, May Ward stole the idea for a new musical act set in a toy store, featuring her surrounded by eight Dresden Dolls.

When the New Yorker Hotel opened in 1930, it claimed to be the tallest in the world. All Freeman needed was one gullible desk clerk to believe his tall tale so he could cash $4,000 in rubber checks to cover his losses from running a sports book.

Above: Sime Silverman, who launched *Variety* in 1905, lovingly chronicled Freeman's antics, published his monologues, and promoted him as "the Pet of Broadway."

Left: Les Darcy, the greatest Australian boxer of his era, just before he stowed away to come to America in 1916. Darcy died tragically before his first American fight—and the only money he earned was in vaudeville, managed by Freeman.

After Freeman was arrested for jumping bail in 1935, the New York City Police Department commemorated the occasion by taking his photograph—catching his scowl in both front and side views.

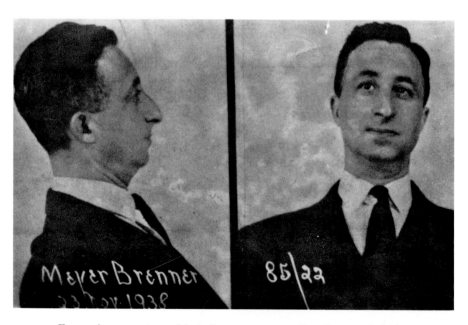

Freeman's co-conspirator Meyer Brenner, a corrupt Canadian metals dealer, after he was jailed in Toronto in late 1938 prior to extradition to America.

The Nazis contracted for scarce Canadian nickel in 1936, but instead—thanks to Freeman—they got rusted auto bodies and tin cans. Otto Reich was hired to take this photo of the bogus cargo on the docks in Hamburg as evidence that Freeman had defrauded them.

Freeman and his lawyer, Greg Bautzer, in court fighting extradition to New York in 1938 on bum-check charges. When he wasn't battling to keep Freeman in Los Angeles, Bautzer was bedding seventeen-year-old Lana Turner.

In April 1937, Freeman was the happiest man in California after the governor refused to extradite him for nicking the Nazis. A triumphant Freeman chortled at a jailhouse press conference, "Hitler ain't got a thing on me."

Freeman, a born showman, mugged for the flashbulbs by giving a mock Hitler salute as he celebrated his release two months after his 1937 arrest.

In early 1937, Mae West invited Freeman to come up and see her sometime. Here she is on the set of the 1936 movie *Go West, Young Man*.

Fresh out of the slammer for bilking the Nazis, Freeman decided to try to make a buck (okay, four bits) by peddling his story. Most of the surviving copies of his booklet were bought by the New York DA's office.

WAS HITLER'S NICKEL HI-JACKED?

By
FREEMAN BERNSTEIN
AS TOLD TO
Maurice B. Haas
The STORY of the CENTURY

PRICE 50 CENTS

My parents, Salem and Edith Shapiro, in 1980. My father's outlandish
but true tales of his uncle Freeman inspired this book.

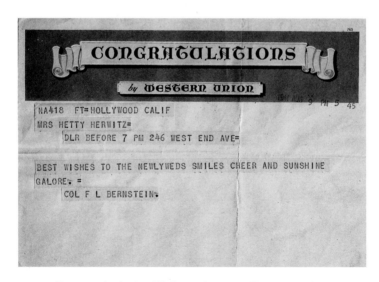

Down on his luck in Hollywood in 1941, Freeman wished
my parents "sunshine galore" in a wedding telegram—
and gave himself the unearned title of "Colonel."

playing such leading British music halls as the Empire Theatre in Nottingham and the Holborn Empire in London. She was billed, as always, as the Dresden Doll until Freeman remembered that Germany was on the wrong side in the Great War. So Freeman switched to something that seemed militarily safer, calling her the China Doll.

A few hours before his wife opened at the Holborn Empire, Freeman was standing on the sidewalk in front of the London music hall admiring the marquee that read MAY WARD, THE CHINA DOLL. Several passing Brits started chuckling over the billing of her as a China Doll. One of the men cracked, "I wonder if she will break?" Freeman stepped forward. "Gentlemen," he said, "she broke me."

Freeman should have left it there. But he made the mistake of telling his wife the story in a restaurant after her successful opening night. "Break you," May shouted. "You poor nut, I never seen you often enough to make a touch, for when you came home you were broke." With that, May stormed out of the restaurant, leaving Freeman with only one option—signing his wife's name to the check.

As he told this story to *Variety*, Freeman allowed himself a burst of husbandly pride. "They tell me over in Paris they are nuts over blondes so that's where we hike from here," he said. "And if I figure they are nuts in Paris about blondes they must be crazy in Africa so it looks as though I will have to take May around the world, just to show how good looking she is and what a good single act she does."

In Paris, they mostly ogled the Eiffel and leered at the Louvre. But afterward, Freeman took May on a side trip that Baedeker did not recommend as part of the Grand Tour. In the depths of winter, they went to Poland and Lithuania. The Bernsteins arrived in the aftermath of brutal post–Russian Revolution fighting among Polish forces, Lithuanian nationalists, and the Red Army. The Jews, of course, had been caught in the middle with pogroms in Vilna and elsewhere.

Just a year after both his parents died in America, Freeman made the pilgrimage to visit the relatives who had stayed behind. One of his stops was Stutchin (or Szczuczyn), a half-Jewish town (population: 4,500) about ten miles off the railroad line in the northeastern Polish province of Lomza Gubernia. This was the area that contains my family's roots—and I undoubtedly have ancestors buried in the Jewish cemetery whose gravestones were leveled by the Nazis.

Freeman's emotional journey remains shrouded in uncertainty, since even the names of the Polish relatives were lost to the Holocaust. In 1939, Joe Shapiro, my father's prosperous older brother, managed to pay enough bribes to book passage for some of these relatives to escape Poland. Their boat was supposed to sail from Danzig in mid-September. On September 1, the Nazis invaded Poland. My Polish relatives were never heard from again.

Freeman, while observing the High Holy Days, was never a religious Jew. He had, after all, married outside the faith. And his entire business career was based on a loose interpretation of the Eighth Commandment ("Thou shalt not steal"). But his visit to the land of his fathers touched something deep in him. Returning to New York in mid-March 1921, Freeman spoke passionately about the Jews of Vilna—suffering from food shortages, anti-Semitism, and political uncertainty, yet uniting to support one another and their religious patrimony.

Freeman expressed these sentiments in an unusual gangplank interview as he and May stepped off the *Olympic*. A reporter from a leading Yiddish daily, *Der Tog* (*The Day*), was greeting the ship, since there were seven hundred Jewish immigrants in steerage. Steered to Freeman (or noticing a Jewish name among the first-class passengers), the dockside correspondent from *Der Tog* asked in English about conditions in Europe.

That was all the prompting that Freeman needed to reply at length. Referring to his visits to Warsaw, Vilna, Kaunas, and Stutchin, Freeman had a message for the generous Jews of New York: Beware of con men.

The problem, Freeman explained (and, remember, he had devoted a lifetime to the study of financial irregularities), was that Americans were naively trusting unscrupulous messengers to deliver funds to their needy relatives. Too often the money was waylaid before it reached Poland. Equally serious, Freeman said, was the plight of Jews waiting in the ports of Europe for passage to America. According to a translation of the front-page article in *Der Tog*, Freeman described the trouble that immigrants "endure at the hands of various swindlers, and the manner in which they are treated even after boarding ship."

Then, Freeman gestured dramatically in the direction of Charles Schwab, who was just coming down the gangplank. A Catholic, Schwab had no identification with Jewish causes. But Freeman insisted to *Der Tog* that he and the business titan had spent the crossing from England jointly lamenting the treatment of immigrants from Eastern Europe. Cornered, Schwab had no choice but to provide the obligatory quote to the Yiddish press: "The Jewish immigrant is the most welcome in the United States. . . This type of element builds a nation, and I wish them much luck and success."

At a time when industrialists like Henry Ford were reprinting the anti-Semitic forgery, *The Protocols of the Elders of Zion*, this was a scoop for *Der Tog*. Thanks to Freeman, the Yiddish daily ran in the middle of the front page a story headlined (in translation):

"THE JEWISH IMMIGRANT HELPS BUILD OUR AMERICA, SAYS STEEL MAGNATE SCHWAB."

Five days after the *Olympic* docked in New York, Freeman and May were again celebrating their wedding anniversary on the high seas, this time heading to Southampton aboard the *Aquitania*. Freeman's working theory was that Europeans were slow on the uptake, although he reluctantly admitted, "Some of these English are smarter than you might think." But the Brits were not that much smarter, since Freeman was convinced that schemes that wouldn't fool the rubes in Rock Island would rake in the pounds, francs, and marks on the Continent.

So Freeman sailed with a repertory troupe of twenty-two actors who would theoretically . . . very theoretically . . . beguile audiences in the Land of Shakespeare with leftover American nineteenth-century melodramas and theatrical chestnuts. As a keen judge of horseflesh (most of his mounts later fleshed out the population at the glue factory), Freeman also brought along a string of sixteen yearlings that he intended to sell in Austria. Mostly, though, Freeman longed to gamble on a continent famed for its gilded casinos and corner betting parlors.

But wagering can be the curse of the sporting class. In June 1921, Freeman was either foolish or unlucky—or a mixture of both. Of all the pool halls in all the towns in all of Europe, Freeman walked into the wrong one.

It all began, as Freeman later explained, because he needed to see a man about a horse. While his countrymen in Europe flocked to American Express, Freeman preferred a hangout where the bookmakers spoke his kind of English. In Brussels, he hung his chapeau at a poolroom managed by his friend Dave Lion, whom Freeman had hired back in 1913 to run the Bender Theatre in Utica. Lion had later learned the bookmaking trade working as a Tattersall Man in London. Now Lion was making book amid the clatter of billiard balls, taking horserace bets only from foreigners. Lion's theory was that the Belgian bookmaking monopoly wouldn't object as long as he stayed off their turf.

But Lion gambled wrong.

Just as Freeman was putting down his francs to back up his frank opinion of the day's racing card, the police raided the joint. It turned out that the local bookmakers didn't appreciate the competition— and, as a result, the gendarmes applied a harsh lesson to the Americans. Along with Freeman and Lion, the police also nabbed Harold H. Swift, a Florida underwater-real-estate man who claimed without evidence to be an heir to the Swift meatpacking fortune.

After being moved from jail to jail, the prisoners were marched through the center of the city in handcuffs, jeered by rowdy crowds, and eventually deposited in a dungeon known locally as the Tunnel. (*Guide Michelin* rated the food and the accommodations at the Tunnel as even worse than at the Bastille.) For the first time in his life, Freeman heard the prison doors slam shut behind him as he braced himself for a night behind bars in his solitary cell.

His jailers neglected a few niceties over the next twenty-four hours, such as notifying the American embassy of his detention and allowing Freeman to communicate with May, who was waiting for him in Ostend. But, more ominous, they forgot to feed Freeman. *Variety* later noted sympathetically, "As Bernstein when in New York ate regularly either at Shanley's or the Hotel Astor and developed an eating habit, that made him particularly displeased."

Even hungry, unshaven, and tortured by the *drip-drip-drip* of a leaky dungeon roof, Freeman was not without resources to wiggle out of the Tunnel. He still had his checkbook. On the second day of his Belgian Captivity, Freeman found an avaricious prison guard who was impressed by a check signed with a flourish for $1,000. That dubious piece of paper was enough to get word to the Paris edition of the *New York Herald,* which then alerted the world and the American embassy of Freeman's predicament. Once released, Freeman couldn't decide whether to sue the Belgian government, complain to Secretary of State Charles Evans Hughes, appeal to the League of Nations, or just fume because the *Herald* story gave the shifty Swift top billing.

If life reflected the tidy patterns of a Victorian novel, this arrest would have been the symbol- and cymbal-clashing moment when everything changed.

For Freeman, the Roaring Twenties slowly descended into the Rap Sheet Twenties. As Freeman approached his fiftieth birthday, the world was beginning to pass him by. Movies and then radio turned vaudeville into a Fabulous Invalid. After a few trips to Europe trying to revive her Dresden Doll days, May quietly retired after a quarter century on the stage. Without her income or the ability to put the touch on his wife, Freeman was left with his seedy carnivals, his gambling, his hustles, and his rackets. And it soon wasn't enough.

Broadway treated the Belgian arrest as another comic install-ment in the Freeman Follies rather than as a blot on his already dubious reputation. In fact, amid the parched days of Pro-hibition, the only law-abiding folks in Times Square were in a Sal-vation Army band.

A few days after Freeman got his newspaper ink for being in the clink, he and May sailed back to New York aboard the *Berengaria*, the crown jewel of the Cunard Line. The crossing was congenial, since the boat was carrying the European fight crowd flocking to Jersey City for the long-awaited Jack Dempsey–Georges Carpentier bout. When the *Berengaria* docked in New York, May and Freeman posed for the dockside photographers, looking like a couple of swells in the haze of flashbulbs. Even though it was midsummer, May was wearing a full-length evening cape and a broad-brimmed hat. Freeman, with his double chin thrust confidently toward the camera, was dressed in black tie and sporting a dress cane. He was loosely holding a brown-and-white dog on a leash. Underwood & Underwood, a leading photographic syndicate, sent the picture of the Happy Threesome (May, Freeman, dog) to newspaper Sunday rotogravure sections with the cutline "Mr. and Mrs. Freeman Bernstein, well-known in New York theatrical circles, who arrived recently from Europe."

The esteemed Mr. Bernstein returned to Europe a few weeks later. In his haste to leave Belgium, Freeman had abandoned a string of horses that were feeling their oats at the Hippodrome Wellington racetrack in Ostend. Fearing that these nags, originally destined for Vienna, would prove his personal Waterloo, Freeman teamed up with his favorite jailbird, Dave Lion, to sell them. The two men returned to New York together in early September aboard the flagship of the Bernstein Fleet, the *Aquitania*.

For a man who had ventured no farther than Bermuda in his first forty years on the planet, Freeman was beginning to appreciate the wide world beyond Broadway. Part of it was that foreigners tended to believe that Americans were innocents abroad rather than masters of hype and hokum like Freeman. Exotic lands also allowed Freeman to display the skills that he had perfected in vaudeville—fearlessness and the unshakable confidence that he could talk himself out of any scrape.

Testing that proposition, Freeman announced to *Variety* in March 1922, "If you see May and she doesn't know where I am, tell her . . . that I was going to Russia." This was not a gag to hide from his wife. Freeman did visit Moscow a few months later, although the details, alas, are sketchy. As the *Morning Telegraph* reported, "Freeman Bernstein, a theatrical manager, went to Russia to sign a leading actor, but had to return without him."

Moscow in 1922 was a frightening place, even though an American passport did cloak Freeman with a warming layer of safety. After brutal mismanagement by the Communists caused the worst famine in Russian history, the only food anywhere came from American relief efforts directed by Herbert Hoover. But Red paranoia meant that the Cheka (the secret police) suspected all foreigners, including American aid workers, of being enemy agents. Vladimir Lenin, in the last healthy year of his life, launched a campaign to destroy organized religion—targeting the Jews along with the Russian Orthodox Church. And the purges began as Lenin went after party dissidents who believed that ordinary workers should have a voice in a workers' regime.

I imagine Freeman, his coat collar turned up against the chill, gawking at the onion domes of Red Square, wondering whether he could sell the deed to the Kremlin to a sucker back in New York. I can also picture him, speaking not a word of Russian, loudly negotiating with an implacable Red bureaucrat in an office with no heat and peeling paint over whether an actor would be allowed to tour capitalist America. Mostly, I see Freeman calculating the angles as he tried to decide whether a $100 bribe would seal the deal or land him in Lubyanka prison. Whatever he tried, the unnamed actor remained trapped in Moscow.

Ultimately, Moscow was not Freeman's kind of town. The Bolshoi was fine, but Ziegfeld would have done so much more with the costumes and the staging. In a city where human existence was a gamble, the bookies wouldn't even take bets on the latest show trial. And the rigid Marxist ideology must have puzzled Freeman. I can almost hear him asking, "Where's the coin in Communism?"

In contrast to this Mission to Moscow, Freeman's foreign travels usually pointed him toward warmer and more forgiving climes. Like the West Indies—the land of rum and Coca-Cola where the Yankee dollar reigned supreme.

With May not working but still spending, Freeman felt the pressure to play the Cash Guy. But running carnivals through Puerto Rico, Haiti, and the Dominican Republic was no easy way to fatten his bankroll. As Freeman admitted to *Variety*, "Those carnival guys are too tough for me, and you know, kid, when I say that they must be some tough."

So he tried to go back to the softer stuff, booking the kind of performers that he loved: circus folk and all-girl acts. "In those southern countries they are just nuts about blondes," Freeman explained. "Get me a troupe of blondes . . . [and] it's a mint, kid, I'm telling you."

Freeman had only one problem—his wife. "I tried it out on May, knowing what a pipe it would be," Freeman told Sime. "But May didn't seem to care much about my scheme. She just said, 'You big bum, you try to pull that one over and you have to hire a new pair of eyes to find your way home.' And so that queered that."

Once again, a gloom tornado had taken up permanent residence over Freeman's head.

When Freeman advertised in the *Billboard* for sideshows and concessionaires for a July 1922 trip to the Dominican Republic and Haiti, he listed the Criterion Cigar Store on Forty-Second Street as his office address. Yes, Freeman Bernstein—the famed international sportsman and Broadway impresario—was reduced to doing business out of a cigar-store phone booth. Freeman's ad copy in the *Billboard* gave off a whiff of desperation: "I will be at the above address each day from 9:00 A.M. to 6:00 P.M. to see you in person until the day the boat sails."

Just to cover his bets and without telling his wife, Freeman also traveled with a bevy of girl acts. And in avuncular fashion, he laid out the facts of life for these comely performers on the boat to Santo Domingo. "Girls, now, behave yourself down here," said wise old Freeman. "This is a fine country and you can get anything by holding out. Stick to me and the show, take care of yourself, don't do anything without talking it over with me first and I'll send you home looking like a branch of Tiffany's."

Aimee Semple McPherson couldn't have said it better in a sermon at her International Church of the Foursquare Gospel.

Freeman's morality ploy worked like a charm in the Dominican Republic, especially since he spiced it up with lectures about the local men. Freeman warned his female charges "about Spaniards being handy with the knife, how jealous they are, and how easy they toss you once they get you."

The opening-night performance in Haiti was so pure that it was easy to assume that all the girls in the show had been convent educated. "Nobody had made a squawk," Freeman recalled. "Everything had been on the up and up the first day, not a wrong dollar so early."

After the show, Freeman's blond protégées asked permission to go swimming, since the temperature was steamy. Freeman said sure, only vaguely noticing that next door was a large white house with manicured grounds. Thirty minutes later, the chief of police of Port-au-Prince appeared at Freeman's door asking if the girls from the show were in the water.

Freeman fessed up since he figured he had nothing to hide, calling them "the best from the United States, all blondes and all nice dames." The police chief responded with a derisive laugh. "Nice girls, yes," he said. "They are swimming off the lawn of that white house and they have nothing on and a priest lives there and he phoned us."

That was the abrupt end of Freeman's Haitian holiday. But Freeman had learned his lesson. Or so he told Sime Silverman: "No more women, no more gals, no more dames. I'm going back with only dumb acts, all male."

Freeman might give up dames, but never diamonds. Or the three other suits in a deck of cards.

A few weeks later, Freeman was working his way to Europe, playing poker in first class on the *Berengaria* with his pal Dave Lion and Gus Dreyer, a theatrical attorney and Times Square regular. And they had found a live one: Walter Candler, a son of the founder of the Coca-Cola Company.

A playboy, Candler was separated from his second wife and traveling to Europe with (and fronting the bills for) friends from Atlanta, car dealer Clyde Byfield and his alluring wife, Sarah. After dinner on the last night at sea, Freeman announced that he would be treating Candler and the Byfields to a champagne party. It was Freeman's patented Anniversary Gag minus May Ward. As they lounged in wicker chairs in the Palm Court, celebrating a festive crossing, Freeman suggested that the gentlemen might play a little poker. Sarah Byfield—who later won a beauty contest judged by Rudolph Valentino—looked on, enjoying her champagne. With a lone piano tinkling in the background, Mrs. Byfield from time to time danced with all the men in the party except for Freeman.

The stakes in the poker game were sky's the limit, but for a change the cards were running with the heir to the Coca-Cola fortune. "If Candler calls me a gambler, let him say I trimmed him," Freeman said later. "I admit I played cards with him, but I lost." But by late in the evening, Freeman had figured out a way to square the books and to become a square guy with one of the richest men in Atlanta.

With a tipsy laugh, Sarah Byfield returned to her stateroom around two thirty in the morning, claiming to be suffering from mal de mer. A yawning Candler, who had shared a few private words with Freeman, left the Palm Court a few minutes later. But the New Yorkers (Freeman, Dave Lion, and Gus Dreyer) kept urging Clyde Byfield to help them keep the party going. Another drink, another hand of cards, a few stories about show business, anything to get the car dealer to stay. But Byfield—who may have been worried about engines racing elsewhere on the ship—abruptly called it a night.

When Byfield opened his stateroom door (and I shudder in horror at what I'm about to type), he found his wife in bed and Candler partly undressed. Candler tried to mutter something about ministering to Mrs. Byfield's seasickness, but his bedside manner was not up to medical standards. Byfield then slugged Candler before turning his fists on his wife—punching Sarah about ten times, leaving her face and eyes bruised and bloodied.

The ugly scene only ended when Candler offered to write a $25,000 check on the spot. Money talked as Mrs. Byfield wept. As for her husband, he shouted at Candler after pocketing his check,

"You can have her. I'm through with her." But a few minutes later, the two men—the pride of the Atlanta *Social Register*—agreed to try to work things out in a civilized fashion after the *Berengaria* docked in France.

Even before Freeman learned of Sarah Byfield's ordeal, his sympathies were all with Candler. Not only was Freeman a man of the world when it came to sexual indiscretion, he was also a man of the world when it came to somebody else paying the check. Just before the boat docked in Le Havre, Candler volunteered to pick up the champagne bill from the night before.

At the Hotel Carlton in Paris, Freeman, Dave Lion, and attorney Gus Dreyer negotiated with Byfield on Candler's behalf. (It is safe to assume that Freeman and Company were motivated by a reward more tangible than simple gratitude.) The New Yorkers explained to Byfield that the Coca-Cola heir's $25,000 check would bounce like it had been written by Freeman himself. Instead, they offered the Wife Beater $4,500 cash and Candler's note for $20,500. Byfield—who was broke and worried about passage back to America—happily accepted the cash and the IOU. But he balked when Dreyer brandished a letter for his signature exonerating Candler of untoward behavior toward his wife.

That was, at least, what Byfield later claimed during a trial in which he tried to get $100,000 in damages from Candler. Byfield insisted that he only signed Dreyer's letter under duress. And what did this pressure consist of? According to Byfield, Lion and Freeman were "preparing, I thought, to leap at me." Unless he feared Lion's roar or Freeman landing on him with a thud, the threat did not appear credible. Or so an Atlanta jury felt in dismissing Byfield's suit.

Back in New York, momentarily fortified by Candler cash, Freeman again tried his hand at boxing promotion. All the talk among the fight crowd was that Harry Wills (who earned the title of World Colored Heavyweight Champion) had to be Jack Dempsey's next opponent, since the champ was running out of white mugs. Freeman didn't have a contract with either fighter, but he had something even better—a vision of a new stadium seating 125,000 fight fans arising just over the New York City border in Yonkers.

"I am a promoter for an arena to hold the Dempsey-Wills fight," Freeman told *Variety*. "Get that? Ain't that the pickings? It looks, kid, as though they framed that one for me. A heavyweight championship fight a year from now. Bo, I'll build that arena on paper, sell stock . . . and before the year is up I can be in Japan on another racket."

Freeman was prescient in his plans for paying for the outdoor stadium. On the spot, he invented naming rights and seat licenses.

He envisioned a lumber company painting the name of a national company and its logo on every seat—and then charging the company for the advertising. Freeman would promise ticket brokers exclusive access to the box ($100) and ringside ($50) seats for an advance fee of a sawbuck—$10—for each ticket. Flashing that wad of cash, Freeman would then sell stock in the entire venture, cleaning up before a single punch was thrown.

Like most of Freeman's dreams, this one ended with the alarm clock going off. Dempsey's manager, Tex Rickard, refused to allow the champion to fight a black man, so Harry Wills never got his shot at the crown. And Yonkers never got a shot at Bernstein Arena.

For all his schemes and gags, for all the ways that he reveled in *Variety* calling him "the sage of Times Square," Freeman was fast becoming the Pauper of the Great White Way. He managed to wangle office space for a few months from his lawyer Robert Morgan

McGauley, but that ended with Freeman owing his mouthpiece two months' rent and $300 for long-distance phone calls.

The only way Freeman financed another carnival tour of the West Indies was by selling the same set of concessions (dice, red and black, and other games of, well, chance) several times, collecting a cash advance with each bogus transaction. Not only did Freeman leave one of the unlucky concessionaires, Louis Candee, on the dock in Brooklyn when the steamer sailed for the Dominican Republic, but he also stuck the unwary Candee Man with a check for $500 (stamped "Insufficient Funds") drawn on the Chatham & Phoenix National Bank. Needless to say, the phoenix did not rise again and Candee was left holding the bird.

Even by Freeman's standards, this was the worst tour since Napoleon played Moscow. Freeman departed Santo Domingo the only way he was traveling these days—one step ahead of a mob of creditors. He fled aboard the *Iroquois*, the pride of the Clyde Line, owing $4,000 and leaving behind most of the thirty-one carnival operators and chorus girls who had accompanied him south.

But this time, Freeman also had Joseph Moran, the American vice consul in the Dominican Republic, on his tail.

While Freeman was on the high seas, Moran cabled Secretary of State Charles Evans Hughes, urging the government to detain Freeman as soon as the *Iroquois* docked in New York. As Moran put it, "Earnestly advise that the Department immediately consider . . . returning him to Santo Domingo or taking other appropriate action looking to vindication of American good name nor suffering on account of anti-American propaganda."

Federal agent Harry Leslie from the Bureau of Investigation met Freeman on board when the *Iroquois* docked at Pier 34 in

Brooklyn on December 14. According to Leslie's FBI report, Freeman was an honest man going through a bad patch: "He stated he is in the show business and also operates roulette wheels, as well as owning several jumping horses. He states that he had a bad break because he was 'double crossed.' . . . He further advised that he made as high as $68,000 in 12 days and that $1,200 was to him a small amount. . . . Subject assured agent that he would meet his obligations as soon as possible."

This was just what Vice Consul Moran feared when he sent his initial cable to the State Department. In words that were the diplomatic equivalent of a warning from the Better Business Bureau, Moran wrote about Freeman: "Caution Shipping Board not to allow him to escape on any suave story he may tell to any Department of Justice agent."

During the isolationist 1920s, diplomats were often ridiculed as striped-pants dilettantes drinking tea with their pinkies raised. But Joseph Moran, stuck in a backwater like Santo Domingo, fingered Freeman Bernstein with dead-on accuracy: "He has a gift for making black look white."

13

All through the nineteenth century and into the early decades of the twentieth, America had a cavalier attitude toward crooks who fled abroad to avoid prosecution. The official U.S. policy could be roughly summarized as "Don't let the Golden Door hit you on your way out of the country."

Not until 1842 did the United States even get around to signing its first permanent extradition treaty. Although America eventually signed accords with the leading nations of Europe and Latin America, most of the early extradition cases involved sailors on a spree and cattle rustlers working both sides of the Rio Grande. By the 1920s, the United States had more extradition treaties than actual criminals that it tried to bring back in leg irons (rarely more than forty a year). So unless you stole a necklace from a senator's daughter or held up FBI Director William Burns at gunpoint, the government wasn't going to go to the trouble of bringing you back.

While it is hard to picture Freeman Bernstein sitting in a law library poring over the text of the 1842 extradition treaty with Britain, he understood that the best way to be safe as a lamb was to be on the lam in another country. As Freeman told *Variety*, "I have been studying up extradition rather than Prohibition."

His immediate problem was Louis Candee's sour mood after getting none of the promised sweets from Freeman's ill-fated Dominican Republic carnival. Candee, active in the Showmen's League of America, obtained a warrant for Freeman's arrest rather than laughing off the latest installment of the Bernstein Legend.

For Freeman, with vivid memories of the Tunnel in Brussels, "arrest warrant" constituted fleeing words. He took the train to Boston, where he hopped a boat to Halifax, Nova Scotia. No innocent abroad, Freeman then financed his escape by playing cards on a liner from Canada to Southampton. Once word reached New York that Freeman was in Europe, the warrant was dropped.

Freeman's wanderlust was also fueled by the reality that there was less and less to glue him to Times Square other than the sticky hands of his creditors. Instead of an office, Freeman was camping uneasily with Sam (who had taken over the vaudeville business) in the Putnam Building, even though the two brothers were barely speaking.

Freeman didn't even have a hat rack to call his own in Manhattan. May, after retiring from the stage, had insisted that they move from West 128th Street (Harlem was changing) to a rented house in Cedarhurst, Long Island, just over the line from Queens. Here May had space to indulge her true passion—lavishing her love on what grew to be a pack of fifteen dogs, including her favorite, a one-eyed Pomeranian. Small wonder that Freeman, even when at home in Cedarhurst, had one eye on the schedule of luxury liners sailing from New York.

Always a sartorial peacock even when forced to use a lemon to refresh last year's Panama hat, Freeman treated his temporary exile in London as a moment to refurbish his wardrobe. Where would such a fashion plate go other than to Peacock & Co. at 35 Albemarle Street in Mayfair, right next to Brown's Hotel? Freeman had three bespoke suits made and then, after the final fitting, wired the gentlemen's tailor to ship the clothes to him in Paris immediately. Assuming that a pillar of the New York theater world like Mr. Bernstein had pressing business on the Continent, Peacock & Co. rushed the suits onto the Channel ferry without requiring payment. That may have been the biggest mistake in British clothing history since Beau Brummell accidentally donned a brown cravat with a blue suit.

Puzzled by Mr. Bernstein's failure to respond to their letters requesting payment (impecunious English gentlemen write back immediately offering hollow promises), Peacock & Co. in desperation asked *Variety* for assistance in locating the clotheshorse thief. As Sime Silverman recounted in an editor's note, "*Variety* assured Peacock & Co. they had company among Freeman's creditors. . . . Those who knew Freeman well feared for King George when Bernstein sailed for London, but the King may have been saved through being busy the day Freeman called. Freeman with a Peacock suit on will probably become so vain he will reduce and then the suit won't fit him—that's Peacock's only chance for evens."

With this credit history, Honest Bernstein had a natural affinity with Honest Abe Lincoln. Which may explain why Freeman, briefly back in America, ended up running the amusements for an Abraham Lincoln Celebration and Jubilee in Philadelphia in the summer of 1923.

The profit motive also raised its tousled head: Freeman saw the potential to pick up a little coin operating the concessions and putting on a small circus at the Lincoln jubilee. And—unlike many in an era of casual racism and KKK marches—Freeman was untroubled that the event was sponsored by a group of local African Methodist Episcopal (AME) congregations. When Freeman heard that five hundred Sunday-school students from black churches would act out a tableau of Lincoln's life, he figured that their proud parents would be in the mood to spend money at the games and booths.

In short, Freeman could be a scapegrace about almost everything except race.

Shortly after he celebrated his fiftieth birthday in August, Freeman was jolted by the specter of his wife's mortality. May had tumbled down a flight of cellar steps in Cedarhurst, hitting her jaw when she landed. She ignored the injury until she became alarmed by the swelling of her jaw. Her doctor's diagnosis: a broken jaw and, more ominously, septic poisoning, which could be fatal in the days before penicillin. She convalesced for nearly a month at St. Joseph's, a Catholic hospital in nearby Far Rockaway.

In a testament to either the shaky state of his marriage or his faith in the medical care provided by the nuns at St. Joseph's, Freeman blew town before May was released from the hospital. Tired of Europe and having worn out his welcome in the West Indies, Freeman's new destination was south of the border.

Senor Bernstein popped up in Mexico City in late September, claiming to a major newspaper, *Excélsior*, that everything was greased for Jack Dempsey to fight a four-round exhibition bout in their fair city. Freeman didn't care that he lacked a commitment from the heavyweight champ, an opponent, or the $25,000 appearance fee he supposedly promised Dempsey. As Freeman discovered when he promoted a fictitious match race in London for Man o' War, the importance of a gag like this was to get your name in the papers as the kind of sportsman who could get the Manassa Mauler to come to Mexico City.

Freeman appreciated the way that the boxing ethics of Mexico City appealed to his sense of fair play. He was at ringside in early October for a bout that cemented future middleweight champion Tiger Flowers's reputation as the best black boxer since Jim Johnson. Flowers's opponent, Fireman Jim Flynn, was cruising on his reputation as a lug who had once knocked out Jack Dempsey in the first round. But according to rumors, Dempsey had taken a dive for $500 in that 1917 fight—and, anyway, Flynn was now forty-four years old.

Outweighed by more than fifty pounds but heavily favored in the betting, Flowers pummeled Fireman Flynn at will. With about a minute left in the second round, Flowers knocked out Flynn with a vicious left hook. But the referee—who apparently was just learning to count in Spanish—took so long to get to ten that Flynn was saved by the bell. Flynn stumbled through the next two rounds barely throwing a punch. After a stinging left uppercut from Flowers at the beginning of the fifth round sent Flynn bouncing off the ropes, the lights in the indoor arena suddenly went out and the electricity didn't come back on.

While the boxers waited in their corners in darkness, Flowers's right hand began to swell up—having been broken in a collision with Flynn's jaw. A doctor examined the black fighter's injury and then escorted Flowers from the arena to have the broken hand set. The moment that Flowers left, the referee leaped to his feet to declare the barely conscious Fireman Jim Flynn the winner.

Never a patsy when the fix was in, Freeman probably had money on Flynn at long odds. Afterward, he certainly had a fat enough bankroll to promote a fight on his own. Billed as the "Battle of the

Ages," this bout pitted the geriatric Flynn against forty-year-old Sam Langford, known in the papers as the "Boston Tar Baby." But it was Flynn who was fast acquiring a new nickname—Canvas Back. The man who KO'd Dempsey was knocked down by Langford four times in the first round and twice in the second before staying down for good in the third.

Freeman—sensing he had a good thing with the Old Lords of the Ring—arranged a January 1924 rematch in Juarez, just over the border from El Paso. Langford won this eight-round bout on points. But Juarez proved a tough town for Freeman to crack. The locals didn't appreciate a fast-talking American muscling in on their rackets. And with guns everywhere, Juarez and the surrounding state of Chihuahua were in active rebellion against Mexican President Álvaro Obregón.

The fear of bullets in the boxing ring was enough to send Freeman temporarily scurrying back to Broadway. As the *New York Clipper* put it, "Freeman knows enough to assume without debate that he can't break in on the short end of a shotgun promotion in a strange country—especially Mexico."

But Mexico City still beckoned by offering a different proposition combining a lack of gunfire with new opportunities for graft. Stymied by the oily nature of boxing, Freeman decided to go for the real thing. As he later explained to Sime Silverman, "Don't you remember that oil well I nearly discovered in Kentucky? Well, bo, I discovered it all over again in Mexico. Yes, they can say what they want about Mex, but I say it's a great country."

In truth, Freeman didn't limit himself to oil wells but instead offered the entire mineral wealth of Mexico to lucky investors. It was a swindle older than the Pony Express: immediate riches as soon as your money order for $50 or more arrives in the mail.

Writing from Mexico City and using nom-de-mail aliases like "Harmon Beggs" and the transparent "Freeman Berns," the get-rich-quick huckster promised everyone on his sucker's list: "2000% in six months **** is my goal—my guarantee. REMEMBER—A DIVIDEND EVERY THIRTY DAYS—NEXT DIVIDEND . . . WILL NOT BE LESS THAN 90%. It will probably be 200%. DO NOT WAIT. SEND YOUR REMITTANCE TODAY."

An investment prospectus like this soon won the attention of the newspapers—and not on the financial pages. "Charles Ponzi, the 'boy wizard' of Boston, was the veriest 'piker' in promises, compared with Harmon Beggs of Mexico City," the *Brooklyn Eagle* wrote. "Ponzi offered only 50 percent on your money in 90 days, sometimes anticipating interest payments in half that time, 45 days. Beggs assures you of 2,000 percent on your money within six months."

The Post Office Department—which deciphered Freeman's identity as fast as you could lick a two-cent stamp—honored his ingenuity by issuing a fraud order on March 18, 1924. The postmaster in El Paso, Texas, was instructed not to forward any sealed envelopes to Freeman's address in Mexico City. The State Department and the Justice Department chimed in by pressuring the shaky Mexican government to arrest swindlers like Freeman for fraud. Sensing that the Federales were closing in on him, Freeman grabbed his hat and danced out of Mexico. "I am never going back there," he told *Variety*. "Left $68,000 behind in cash, too, but the bank wasn't open that early the morning I left."

Despite the haste of his departure, Freeman did not leave empty-handed or, to be precise, empty-leashed. A few weeks earlier in Mexico City, as family legend has it, Freeman was strolling over to visit the archbishop. (Yes, this unlikely pairing suggests that had Freeman popped up in ancient India he would have been sharing a rice bowl with Buddha.) En route to the cathedral, Freeman fell into a deep excavation pit and couldn't climb out. Only the frantic barking of a large stray dog brought help. For years afterward, Freeman would take the dog (so rambunctious that it scared small children) with him everywhere, introducing the oversize mutt, "This is Mugsy who saved my life in Mexico."

Freeman (and Mugsy) returned to New York in time for the unruly bedlam of the Democratic convention that began amid sweltering heat on June 24 in Madison Square Garden. Helping inspire a Will Rogers wisecrack ("I am not a member of any organized party—I am a Democrat"), the convention delegates dithered for two weeks before nominating on the 103rd ballot John W. Davis as their sacrificial candidate against President Calvin Coolidge.

Three words ripped the convention apart: Ku Klux Klan.

Dormant for nearly a half century, the KKK sprung back to life in 1922 as a vehicle for small-town prejudice against blacks, Catholics, and, of course, Jews. Approaching four million members (who paid $10 annual membership fees plus extra charges for short-sheeting), the Klan emerged as a political force battling immigrants, urban sophisticates, and anything that smacked of change. A convention resolution denouncing the Klan by name failed by a single vote as the floor of Madison Square Garden was interrupted during the balloting by dozens of fistfights. Only the arrival of a thousand extra policemen averted a full-scale riot.

Everyone was obsessed with the Klan in early July when Freeman dropped by the offices of the venerable show-business weekly the *New York Clipper* to announce his return to New York. Just as singers who can replicate any note are said to have perfect pitch, so was Freeman blessed with Superior Swindle. Name a topic—and Freeman could invent a hustle on the spot to theoretically make some coin from it. The creativity of his gags and rackets almost gave him as much pleasure as the actual money.

Chatting with a *Clipper* editor, Freeman began marveling at the size of KKK rallies: "The idea of a crowd of 75,000 all alone in a big field and going home the way they came! It's enough to make a smart showman like me cry out loud. I've been in crowds much less than 75,000 and made them pay."

Joking around, Freeman played with the fanciful idea of charging admission to cross burnings: "Can you see what I could do with a bunch of K's like that—mostly all rubes or dressed-up small-town guys? If they are wearing hoods and cloaks, so much the better; but make this plain that I ain't a-going to take any hoods or cloaks in exchange [for admission]. Anyway, I don't wear light clothes."

Then Freeman kleverly konceded the one barrier to his becoming a konvincing klansman:

"I hear the Ku Kluxers ain't never known yet to pet a Bernstein. McCarthy? Worse, eh? Well, if I change my name, what am I going to do about my face? I can't change that. How about this? I'll call myself the Honorable Freeman Bernreid and not appear in person. Instead, I'll get some of the best workers in the East and have them there as my representatives. That's better. I thought so."

B y now, Freeman's guiding philosophy had become sink or swindle. His frauds—both real and imagined—regularly popped up in his monologues in *Variety*. He proposed knocking on mansion doors on the North Shore of Long Island to announce to the lady of the house that the British pound had risen to $4.98. And, for convenience, Freeman would be offering a $5 bill for a pound of gold. "Ain't that a pip?" he said to Sime Silverman. "Did you ever hear of any old house in the country that couldn't dig up a pound of gold in some shape or other—old watches, charms, emblems?"

Another racket that he pitched to *Variety* was called the Washington Dollar Gag. (There's no evidence that Freeman ever tried this, but he certainly was amused at the possibility.)

The scheme was to find a road on a tourist route that ran along a stream in a small town like Easton, Pennsylvania. After hiding a young confederate in the underbrush on the other side of the stream, Freeman would flag down the cars of travelers. "Gentlemen," he would say, "do you know that you are right now at the point where George Washington threw the dollar across the Susquehanna? What can they say? Then we do business. If they have one silver dollar they may throw it across just the same as Washington did. . . . I change their $5 bill and they throw the dollar over. If they gave it a kick it would have to land on the other side and the kid in the grass cops."

For the gullible, Freeman planned for just $1 more to show them Washington's original coin (a silver dollar on which he rubbed dirt to obscure the date). And if they were true rubes, Freeman's idea was to follow up by offering to sell them the authentic silver dollar—thrown by George Washington himself—for the bargain price of $97.40.

Then there was the hustle that he sketched out to Sime over a chop and a mug of New York's best Prohibition ale at Billy LaHiff's Tavern on West Forty-Eighth Street, a show-business hangout so new that it still offered Freeman credit. The idea, which Freeman intended to sell to a restaurateur like LaHiff, was to let eateries trim food costs by serving "small portions but on plates with magnifying-glass bottoms."

The Escoffier of the Magnifying Glass tried to steer *Variety* into running a weekly feature called "Great Men Freeman Bernstein Knows." The Prince of Wales—who had just dined, danced, and poloed his way through Long Island society on his second visit to America—would have been the initial topic of the column. "Of course, the Prince knows me," Freeman assured *Variety*. "He calls me Berny. If I hadn't got caught in a jam when he was over on Long Island, I would have steered that guy around for a good time."

Beneath the bluster, Freeman was doing hard time in both his marriage and his career. "I always was a mark for blondes," he confided to Sime, who had his own weaknesses for redheads. "Gee, what those blondes have done to me!"

Slow horses probably did more damage to Freeman's fortunes than fast dames. But he did admit that he wished he had put aside enough money to buy stocks on margin or, at least, have a big bill to put on the outside of his Michigan roll. His lack of financial prudence galled him. As Freeman put it, "I should have saved up my money when May was working."

May, in fact, decided in the fall of 1924 at age forty-three to come out of retirement with a new vaudeville act after calculating the odds that her husband would ever again become a good provider. Rejecting Freeman or her brother-in-law Sam Bernstein as her manager, May decided to go with a family that she could actually trust—her own.

In a symbol of her estrangement from all things Bernstein, May selected Herman Levine, married to her youngest sister, Elizabeth, as her manager. A veteran of the minor leagues of vaudeville, Levine initially announced that May would tour on the prestigious Keith-Albee circuit after a few warm-up performances. But bookings proved to be sparse for the former vaudeville headliner, whose Dresden Doll beauty had faded with the passing years.

Playing upstate New York towns like Frankfort and Kingston ("Extra Added Attraction"), plus doing a split week in Hoboken, failed to put a star on her dressing room door. Plucky to the end, May resorted to the crutch for flailing performers everywhere . . . an animal accompaniment. Her one-eyed Pomeranian joined her onstage for a few performances to sing a solo.

And that's how a vaudeville career ends—not with a bang but a bark.

Freeman also briefly gave way to his inner Ziegfeld. He booked dancers and showgirls on six-week contracts for a revue at Manhattan's largest restaurant, the Knickerbocker Grill at Forty-Second Street and Broadway. The restaurant's slogan was "Meet Me in the Lobby of the Knickerbocker Grill." But on opening night, Freeman was not around to meet anyone, and the booking was canceled.

The dance team was ready to sue Freeman for six weeks' back pay when they were introduced to the facts of life—Freeman was judgment proof. With $100,000 worth of unpaid claims against Freeman, the dancers had a better shot at out-stepping Fred and Adele Astaire. As *Variety* reported, "The dancing team, in particular, said that they should have known better than to do any business at all with Freeman, but that he had proved so convincing and offered so many promises of reforming . . . that they were inveigled into accepting the contracts."

Freeman was irate over the *Variety* story—shocked at its inaccuracy. "Listen you bum," he told Sime, "don't you ever print in *Variety* again that I only owe $100,000. What do you want to do besides, ruin my credit too? You know that counting the track, the crap joints and Mt. Vernon, I owe over $250,000. . . . So don't you ever try to make me look small in your dirty stories about me."

D espite his membership in the Grifter's Guild and the Swindlers Syndicate, Freeman was late to the wildest con man
convention of the 1920s. The Florida land rush created the biggest
bubble since William Procter and James Gamble began selling
soap. Freeman had been too busy trying to pick up easy coin in the
Caribbean to notice the large peninsula at the southern tip of the
United States.

Even in New York, Freeman ignored the signs for too long.
Dozens of times, he walked by the billowing palm trees painted on
the giant illuminated billboard at the corner of Fifth Avenue and
Forty-Second Street that beckoned, IT'S ALWAYS JUNE IN MIAMI. A
1922 article in the *Saturday Evening Post* captured the frenzy of
Florida real estate speculation: "The publisher of the leading Miami
paper declares that in some sections of the city, the soil is so fertile
that if a shingle is planted in it before sunup, it will grow into a
fully equipped bungalow by nightfall." Miami building lots, which
required only a 10 percent down payment, might be sold and resold
ten times in a single day. Florida real estate had become the Dutch
tulip mania with a suntan.

When Freeman finally headed to Florida in September 1924,
the lure was rebirth rather than real estate. A sun-drenched spot
like Palm Beach was one of the few places on the globe where his
reputation had not preceded him. "What I need this winter is a
flash joint where $25 spread around the first day in staking will
make any one in the place say what I tell them to about me," Freeman told Sime Silverman. In his conversation with *Variety*, Freeman
considered using burnt cork to help him impersonate an Egyptian

prince. But instead he decided to pretend to be "a banker from Burmah, the only American banker ever there. . . . And, bo, if I am going to be a banker from Burmah, you can figure up for yourself how far I expect to go with one."

But Palm Beach gave him a cold shoulder. That chill breeze sent him down the coast to Miami with an idea as appealing as a gin rickey in a frosted glass. In the warmest city in America, Freeman planned to repackage himself as the Ice Cube Man. He had survived Moscow so he knew something about refrigeration—and the rest he could improvise.

It wasn't hard to bamboozle the *Miami Herald*, which reported in early December, "Mr. Bernstein has just returned from Mexico city, where he completed the erection of one of the largest cold storage plants in the world. He has also recently erected large refrigeration plans at Santo Domingo city, and at Curaco [*sic*] in the Dutch East Indies."

Like most of Freeman's serious quests for cold cash, this one boasted a surface plausibility. As recently as 1920, Miami's reputation for winter hospitality melted in the face of a severe ice shortage. With local refrigeration plants unable to meet the demand, the city was forced to import frozen water by choo choo from as far away as Chattanooga. So the newspapers took Freeman seriously when he announced—in the words of the *Herald*'s headline—"$1,000,000 STORAGE PLANT FOR HIALEAH." Showing off his knowledge of refrigeration science, Freeman boasted to the *Miami News* that, because of the extreme temperatures, all the workers at the ice plant needed to be imported from Scandinavia.

Needless to say, it would be a cold day in hell before the South Florida Cold Storage & Ice Corp. ever got around to building the refrigeration plant. Even as Hialeah waited for the iceman to cometh, the newly incorporated city just inland from Miami had other reasons to celebrate. On January 16, 1925, as the *Miami Herald* swooned, "The greatest crowd that ever saw a race track open its gates to the sport of kings marked the opening of the Miami Jockey Club's new oval."

The first racing day at Hialeah (so close to the Everglades that it employed its own snake catcher) attracted seventeen thousand spectators, including Al Jolson, Will Rogers, Joseph Kennedy, and future heavyweight champ Gene Tunney. The *Herald*'s racing reporter gushed, "To print the names of all America's leading citizens who were present would require the reprinting of the elite directory."

Amid the crowd of racing gentlemen, one titan of the turf so towered over his fellow thoroughbred fanciers than he deserved his own elite directory. As the *Herald* put it, "Freeman Bernstein, who is constructing a refrigerating plant at Hialeah, was there, introducing new friends to many of his New York friends."

Between races, Freeman was probably peddling real estate to the out-of-towners. That was as much a local custom as worrying about snakes. At one point, Freeman claimed to own eight thousand acres near Miami and another twenty-two thousand around the state. *Variety* headlined, "F. BERNSTEIN HITS TOWN TALKING IN MILLIONS," but the subhead expressed the requisite skepticism about Freeman's underwater lots: "From Claims Made Has Nearly All of Florida Under Option."

Mostly, though, Freeman's fortunes were in as much of a deep freeze as his refrigeration plant. Sime spotted the showman whom he described as "the genius of Times square" tossing a quarter onto the sidewalk. "I ain't gone nuts," Freeman explained. "It's my last quarter and I want to hear the ring."

Nothing was working. Freeman, in fact, seemed to spend most

of his time thinking up rackets that he never carried out, like peddling the rights to operate a hot dog stand in front of Grant's Tomb or setting up the Booze Bureau for National Information. That scheme would advise tipplers for a dollar "what booze to get to keep out of the hospital." Of course, with Freeman there always had to be an angle. His notion was to tell restaurants and speakeasies, "You better give us a free pass to eat here for a year or we'll steer this business away."

Freeman, though, could serve as his own Better Business Bureau when he had to. Arriving in Nassau in the Bahamas at six in the morning, he took a taxi to the recently rebuilt New Colonial Hotel on Bay Street, a favored watering hole for American rumrunners during Prohibition. Everything was hunky-dory until the moment when he signed the hotel's guest register. Upon seeing the word "Bernstein," the desk clerk recoiled in horror saying, "Nothing today."

Instantly grasping that this was a restricted hotel, an irate Freeman asked, "Nothing what? Where do I wash without a room?" The supercilious keeper of the keys snarled, "In the wash room."

Never one to shrink from a fight (unless he was ducking a creditor or a process server), Freeman demanded at the top of his lungs to see the manager. He was incessant enough that the yawning majordomo eventually showed up at the front desk. "The only room we've got is $35 a day and without bath," the manager said. Even though he would be paying the modern equivalent of $500 for a chamber pit with a chamber pot, Freeman readily agreed. "That's my room," he said. "And I wouldn't care if it cost $1,000 a day. When I want a room I want a room. To hell with a bath."

That night Bathless Bernstein was dining in the hotel restaurant with two horseplayer friends: bookmaker Jimmy Beatty and

Honest John Kelly, who one year had dropped $55,000 at Belmont. Alerted to the presence of these two high rollers in his dining room, Frank Munson, the owner of the New Colonial, wandered by the table to pay his respects. That was the opening that Freeman needed. "Listen," he said. "Take a good look at me. Have I got to pay four times as much as the rest of this mob just because I'm a Jew?" Freeman's rate was immediately reduced.

The man who became the de facto head of the Anti-Defamation League of the Bahamas later explained to Sime Silverman (who played down his own Jewish heritage in the pages of *Variety*), "That's me, Freeman Bernstein, always using my own name on hotel registers, but judiciously."

There comes a point in the life of a confidence man when he loses confidence in his own rackets and resorts to cons so obvious that they become a sign of desperation. The equivalent would be a once slick-fingered pickpocket stealing from a blind news vendor. For Freeman, a low point came when he tried a variant of the "Waiter, there's a fly in my soup" restaurant gag favored by vagrants and starving artists around the world.

On June 17, 1925, a few months after he returned from Nassau, Freeman was enjoying the great outdoors at Aqueduct Racetrack. After four races, Freeman was riding high on his version of a winning streak: He was breaking even. In celebration, Freeman wandered over to the Jockey Club for a sandwich as he tried "to figure up whether the books would pay me or get nothing."

He took one bite of his lunch—and discovered a way to put a bite on the restaurant. "As I started to eat," Freeman later recalled, "I felt something sharp and the blood started to flow from my mouth. I was in a panic. So much happens to me I at first thought it was all coming out at once, but I put my hand inside against my cheek and pulled out of a hunk of glass that had been in the sandwich."

Maybe it was an accident. But Freeman always believed in the be-prepared gospel memorably expressed by Tammany Hall leader George Washington Plunkitt: "I seen my opportunities and I took 'em." He began screaming, so afterward he would have dozens of witnesses who had seen the blood. Then he headed off to see a doctor who, as Freeman put it, "congratulated me for having the toughest cheek he had ever heard of." That should not have come as a surprise because Freeman always had cheek.

All through the twenties, Freeman had been honing a new skill out of necessity—convincing blue-chip law firms to take his cases on contingency or in exchange for a gilt-edged Bernstein promissory note. "I called on some lawyers, quite a good firm . . . and you get what's coming to you from them," Freeman told *Variety*. "Haven't an idea in the world what I'll get out of it, but must get something."

Freeman's faith in the justice system was a touching testament, but legally naive. He sued the Queens County Jockey Club, which owned Aqueduct, and restaurant operator Thomas Healy, contending, "A medical examination and X-ray photographs . . . showed that glass had been swallowed causing serious internal injuries."

But for all its sharp edges, the case moved through the New York courts at a pace that even Charles Dickens would have considered languid. Healy died in 1927, prompting the dismissal of Freeman's complaint before it was ever heard. Short on cash and still dreaming of a racetrack payoff, Freeman got his law firm to appeal to a higher court on the grounds that he should be allowed to sue Healy's heirs for damages. In 1928, three years after Freeman's lethal sandwich, he hit the glass ceiling: The Supreme Court of

New York, Appellate Division Second Department, rejected appellant Bernstein's plea.

Like a Russian grand duke standing ramrod straight as he operated an elevator at Macy's, Freeman was obsessed with keeping up appearances.

Trying to impress a potential mark with his success in Florida real estate, Freeman slapped down a $100 bill—his entire net worth—to pay a $3 breakfast check at the Hotel Astor. As the waiter returned with $97 in change, a friend stopped by the table to welcome Freeman back to New York. Spying the pile of bills on the silver tray, the friend immediately put the touch on Freeman for $75. To his credit, Freeman lived by his version of the Shakespearean code: Always a borrower *and* a lender be. So cheerfully, yet tearfully, he forked over the $75 on the spot.

In Florida—with everyone out to con suckers—the trick was getting away with whom you pretended to be. "Down there in Miami you've got to put up a front," Freeman said. "Always a front. That's all they go by. Either you're in or you're broke." Freeman explained these verities of life in Florida in the shocked tone of a Wall Street shoe shine boy decrying uninformed speculation in the stock market. "Well, if you're broke what chance have you got? Not a chance," said Freeman. "They don't even see you."

By early 1926, thousands of invisible people were making the rounds on Flagler Street. The Miami land boom had lasted about as long as a touchdown run by the Galloping Ghost, Red Grange. Property sales had stalled due to a sharp drop in winter visitors and a capsized ship closed Miami harbor to deliveries of construction materials. As Freeman wrote *Variety* from Miami, "I don't know whether this Florida thing is a push over or bust."

Freeman was enough of a connoisseur of the cashless society

to bet on the bust. "Went flat at the track," Freeman recounted, "and when I commence to look for money in the city the people I knew started asking for it first when I was a block away." Things had gotten so bad, Freeman said, "Can't go very far with a marker here; they all use them."

In fact, the best way to be regarded as prosperous in Miami was not to be in Miami. "If you hang around too much it's a cinch you're broke or you wouldn't be hanging around," Freeman said. "Simple, ain't it? . . . But if you say, 'Guess I'll go up north for a few days and take care of things,' then go, that's the coin sign, for you can't travel without money."

Freeman was enough of a traveling man to make frequent trips back to New York, even if he sometimes had to stop off in Atlanta to borrow the train fare to go the rest of the way. In July 1926, Freeman tried the water route—sailing to Europe with May. How he financed this effort to join the Lost Generation has been lost, but presumably he got lucky at the track or found where May was stashing her dwindling savings. As the *Long Island Daily Press* reported, "Mr. and Mrs. Herman [*sic*] Bernstein of Cedarhurst, sailed a few days ago for a month's tour of Europe. On the vaudeville stage Mrs. Bernstein is professionally known as 'May Ward.' For the present she is living quietly in Oakland avenue . . . forgetting the footlights."

In reality, Freeman's European itinerary was not the stuff of the Society Page. He was planning to run several horses during the racing season in Vienna, and he had everything fixed . . . whoops, wrong word . . . arranged with three rival jockeys to guarantee a spirited competition that would end with victory for the Bernstein silks. But, as with so many other things with Jews in Vienna, it did not end well. After Viennese racing officials learned of the planned rigged race and betting coup, they suggested to Herr Bernstein that he take his horses and gallop out of Austria fast.

Whenever Freeman returned from Europe, he made the rounds of his family in New York, dropping off gifts with the indiscriminate enthusiasm of Kris Kringle on a bender. Freeman's niece, Sylvia Potofsky, recalled him showing up in Fort George with "fancy dresses that I couldn't wear to school . . . and I remember an English suit for my older brother that had short pants when American boys wore knickers." Other times there might be a huge stuffed elephant hanging from the apartment doorknob or a hand-carved wooden circus with removable heads on the animals so that a child could put a lion's mane on a zebra's body. If the cards had fallen Freeman's way on the return trip, Freeman might peel off a $10 bill from his roll for each of the three Potofsky children. The cash, of course, went into the family grocery fund the moment Freeman stepped out of the apartment.

But increasingly Freeman's visits to his sisters (Becky Potofsky, Jennie Feinberg, and my grandmother Rose Shapiro) ended with him sleeping on the sofa rather than taking the train back to Cedarhurst to argue with May over money. In fact, he used my grandmother as his banker of last resort. He had deposited with her a ring featuring three large diamonds, each in its own platinum setting, surrounded by diamond chips. Whenever Freeman needed money, he would stop by my grandmother's house in the Bronx to pick up the ring. He would immediately head for a favored pawnshop. Then, the next time he was flush, Freeman would redeem the ring and return it to my grandmother. Through some miracle of Freeman's fiscal flimflam, the ring remains in my family, passing from my father's youngest sister, Myrtle, to her Paris-based son, Neil Hollander, and his wife, Régine.

This ring cycle was part of a marriage in which increasingly Freeman and May had only one thing in common—a passion for hiding money from each other.

"Have you seen May?" Freeman asked Sime Silverman in mid-October. "I know that woman is under cover with coin but she won't open up for me. You can tell her I've got to go away for a stretch and you can fix [it] for a thousand. Don't stand to let her send you to Sam. Sam'd let me go."

A tone of regret crept into Freeman's monologues with *Variety* as he began to sense that there was something pitiable about a man in his fifties depending on the kindness of blood relatives and bookmakers. Although Freeman never used this precise terminology, he knew he was addicted to the adrenaline rush of the turn of the card or the posting of racing results. "Any habit is terrible," Freeman said, "but the betting habit worse of all. . . . See my condition. Something awful may happen to me if I can't get a bet down."

At least in New York, Freeman could wager on the ponies for nothing since the bookies would always extend him credit in the long-shot hope that a big win would allow him to pay off some of his markers. "Of course, I don't get any coin out of it," Freeman conceded, "but don't you see, it keeps my habit going and lets me have peace of mind."

With the New York tracks about to close for the winter, Freeman in his desperation began considering a proposition that made his sporting blood run cold. "Maybe I could beat that football thing," Freeman said as he expressed a thought soon to be echoed by gamblers everywhere. "They tell me there's a lot of saps in college towns. I'll slip a colored muffler around my neck and mix. . . . Ain't it terrible when a guy has been through as much as I have [and] he's got to go up against college boys to make a living?"

Then, for almost the first time in his life, he expressed a hint of envy for his brother Sam, who had chosen the steadier life of running the vaudeville booking agency that Freeman had given him a decade earlier. "I should have been the biggest man on Broadway," Freeman said, "and I guess I would have been if I had stuck on Broadway. Just a cluck, kid."

14

Think of the great pairings of the twenties: Burns and Allen, Ruth and Gehrig, Gallagher and Shean, and Lindbergh and the *Spirit of St. Louis*. Plus, of course, Herbert Hoover and Freeman Bernstein.

Not political by nature, Freeman grasped the biggest truth about presidential campaigns—millions of dollars flowed through party coffers with minimal accounting. That's why he had tried to sell the Democrats in 1916 on paying him to produce a movie glorifying Woodrow Wilson. Now with Hoover running in 1928 against New York Democratic Governor Al Smith, Freeman concocted a Jewish angle to pick up some Republican coin.

In normal times, Freeman might have been expected to gravitate to Smith, an anti-Prohibition "wet" whose campaign song was "The Sidewalks of New York." Back in the days when he was running the Trocadero in Fort George, Freeman always went out of his way to ingratiate himself with the Democratic sachems down at Tammany Hall. Then there was his friendship with Wilson's right-hand man, Joe Tumulty, whom he knew from his days in Bayonne.

This history should have made Freeman a Democrat for life—as it did with his wife, May. She was so enraptured with Smith that she came out of retirement to make political speeches on Long Island.

While history recalls the Smith campaign as rich in symbolism (he was the only Catholic to be nominated for president before John Kennedy), the 1928 race at the time seemed as satisfying as a Prohibition-era dinner topped off with toasts of sarsaparilla. Columnist Walter Lippmann captured the political tedium: "The two platforms contain no differences which could be called an issue."

The Jewish vote was in flux during the 1920s with affluent German Jews maintaining their traditional allegiance to the pro-business Republican Party while recent immigrants schlepped to the polls under the straight-ticket guidance of the big-city Democratic machines. As late as 1920, Republican Warren Harding won more than 40 percent of the vote in Jewish neighborhoods. Since Hoover basked in the glow of his humanitarian record directing postwar relief efforts to avert famine in Europe, Republicans nurtured hopes of at least equaling Harding's share of the Jewish vote.

Freeman always lived on the hopes and dreams of others. Even though he was born in Troy and spoke unaccented English, Freeman convinced the Hoover campaign to think Yiddish. As *Variety* reported, "Freeman Bernstein, a Democrat by training, indulged in a little concession dough from the Republican National Committee during the campaign. Freeman got the hunch Jewish patriarchs who couldn't read English might be interested in a little folder about Herbert Hoover in Yiddish."

The Yiddish pamphlet was actually written by Abraham Burstein, a Manhattan rabbi with literary pretensions who published poetry and contributed doggerel to the Conning Tower column in the *New York World* under the pseudonym "Cleric."

Burstein also had the prose style of a Soviet writer penning panegyrics to Stalin. He headlined the English portion of the bilingual four-page flyer "The Modern Moses of War-Stricken Europe . . . HERBERT HOOVER . . . He led ISRAEL out of the SLAVERY of STARVATION and DESPAIR." The accompanying drawing depicted the two biblical figures shoulder to shoulder—allowing astute voters to figure out that Hoover was the prophet without a beard. The back page of the handbill contained a final message for the wavering faithful: "THE JEW CANNOT AFFORD TO FORGET HIS FRIENDS."

Freeman collected his cut from his Republican friends by arranging the distribution of millions of these election-eve handouts in Jewish neighborhoods in New York, Philadelphia, and Chicago. But that was the only thing that paid off. The original Moses may have carried the Sinai Desert, but the Modern Moses only received about one-quarter of the Jewish vote.

W hile still paying for his listing in the New York *City Directory* as a theatrical agent, Freeman embraced a new calling that required neither embossed business cards nor gilt lettering on a frosted-glass door. Freeman's roster of vocations had grown long: carnival operator, theatrical manager, vaudeville agent, movie mogul, boxing promoter, oil stock hustler, and racehorse owner. But now he took on the most Runyonesque identity of them all— proprietor of a floating crap game.

"In my special racket, being the bank for roulette or dice, I ain't got no superior," Freeman boasted to Sime Silverman. "All I need are my own dice and a wheel. A bankroll could be used but may be taken a chance on by an expert fence leaper. If they break for you at the start, who knows whether I had a roll?"

Just to make sure that everything broke for Freeman so that he wouldn't have to show off his skills as a portly fence leaper, he came equipped with two sets of dice. He explained, "One set [was] for general use and the other set for myself in case things should go so bad to force me to extremes."

Freeman—who always boasted an instinct for self-preservation—sensed that his unorthodox business methods would not play with Manhattan sophisticates. (Anyway, the Biltmore Garage wants a grand and Freeman ain't got a grand on hand.) Instead, what he needed was a rural setting where the rubes would hail him as Honest Bernstein.

The proprietor of the newest established floating crap game in New York (State) had a few other site specifications before he settled in for the summer tourist season. As he told Sime, he needed "a location in the woods, where running is easy and trees are plenty." He found the ideal business location in the Adirondacks, where no one read *Variety*: "The spot looked as though laid out for me. Besides a railroad track running into it was a lake alongside and three automobile roads with a couple of Indian trails." All these exit routes meant that it would require a posse of pitchfork-waving gamblers to track him down in case of an honest misunderstanding over payment.

Fortunately for Freeman, the Adirondacks turned out to provide the setting for a perfect marriage between supply (his wheel and his dice) and demand (yokels yearning to take a chance on chance defined by Honest Bernstein). As he put it, "Pretty soon I was giving away coins in the street to what looked like poor people but they ain't—just former customers of mine."

Always a sporting man, Freeman briefly paused in his benevolent rounds among small-town paupers to drop in on Jack Dempsey's training camp in Saratoga Springs. According to the *Philadelphia Inquirer*, Freeman was one of the "old timers" from the fight game concerned about the former heavyweight champ's lackadaisical workouts as he prepped for a bout against Jack Sharkey. (Dempsey, in fact, knocked out Sharkey in the seventh round at Yankee Stadium in the last victory of his career.)

"Old timer" Bernstein, now in his midfifties, had achieved emeritus status as a ghost of Broadway past. When a play called *The Barker* about carnival life opened at the Biltmore Theatre, *Variety* headlined its insider commentary "'BARKER' TO FREEMAN IS OLD HOME WEEK." The opening sentence captured the reaction of this canny carny operator: "'Oh baby, but I got an inch to make a pitch when I seen that "Barker" show at the Biltmore,' cooed Freeman Bernstein, the pet of Times Square."

The Barker starred Walter Huston as Nifty Miller, the hard-bitten manager of a tent show ("Colonel Gowdy's Big City Show") who dreams of his son Chris becoming a lawyer. Instead, Chris becomes entwined with a snake charmer named Lou, played by Claudette Colbert in her first extended Broadway role. At the final curtain, respectability wins out as Chris marries the ever charming, but now snake-less, Lou and becomes a lawyer.

New York Times theater critic Brooks Atkinson noted that *The Barker* mourned the passing of an era: "Nowadays, they say, the carnival business is losing its vogue. Are radios and flivvers to blame, as one character in 'The Barker' complains? Or (save the mark!) is the country older?"

Variety theater critic Freeman Bernstein (who was also losing his vogue) brooded that Claudette Colbert was selling herself short by wasting her talents on snake charming. "A total loss, snake charming," he said. "If she's out for big money, I'll show her how. You can tell her about me, bo, and say it will only be business. Make that certain. That dame is a looker, ain't she?"

Freeman, however, was impressed with playwright Kenyon Nicholson's talent at chiseling a true-to-life portrait of chiselers. "Brings back the old times, a play like that," he said. "Who wrote it? A college professor? On the level? Where? Columbia? Lord help them students up there. He ain't never been with no carnival? Not a grifter? Honest? Well, he done pretty well, I say."

But it didn't take long for Freeman to realize that the feverish fascination of writers with the wrong side of the law was bad for business.

Did newspaper readers need to know all the details when Arnold Rothstein (the gambler who fixed the 1919 World Series) was gunned down in a Manhattan hotel room? Why did these amateurs have to find out that Rothstein was rubbed out because he refused to pay up after an all-night card game in which someone else had marked the cards?

"I certainly am for that censoring of plays and books. And newspapers," Freeman told *Variety* in late 1928. "They are showing up every racket. . . . When I started to read about that Rothstein thing and the way the papers talked about small time cheaters with marked cards against Rothstein, it gave me a pain-in-the-neck."

It wasn't that Freeman had direct ties to Rothstein, who ran with a much tougher crowd. What irritated Freeman were the newspapers "educating suckers" about the existence of marked cards.

"We boys must spend day and night to think out our stunts so that we can eat, only to find them on stage or in a book or like that Rothstein business, spread all over newspapers," he said. It got so bad that Freeman was forced to make the ultimate sacrifice: "I threw away all my markers and strippers."

Without cards, without dice, what's a fellow to do? As Freeman was the first to admit, "I've run out of rackets."

He had already survived a close call—an indictment for grand larceny. The details from his arrest on March 26, 1927, are sketchy, other than the graft involved $30,000 in betting slips and post-dated checks. Freeman always claimed that the whole thing was a paper tiger because "the man that held my paper sold it to another bookmaker." Freeman managed to come up with enough coin to settle with the shortchanged bookmaker—and the charges were dropped ten days later.

As his career opportunities were narrowing, Freeman had little choice but to return to his roots. Nearly forty years after he got his start apprenticing himself to gamblers at Saratoga, Freeman was back trying to take the uncertainty out of picking winners from the *Daily Racing Form*. The problem was making a buck off it. "That race fixing is expensive," he complained to Sime Silverman. "I don't mind putting down a bet for the jock, but when you must bet for the trainer, the jock's valet and the trainer's secretary, besides taking the worst of the odds, you ain't got money enough to bet for yourself."

Freeman's dreams of long shots galloping home at long odds kept fading in the stretch. The problem was less the greed of the jockeys and more his own ineptitude at mastering the nuances of the Sport of Kings. Every time Freeman tried to fiddle with the finish of a race, the notes came out sour. There had been that fuss in Vienna that forced Freeman to waltz out of town and even more nagging difficulties on the way to the Winner's Circle in Winnipeg.

Freeman's Canadian comeuppance came after Bernstein Stables acquired a four-year-old horse named Cas Welch with a history of limping home at the back of the field in claiming races. After establishing the nag's dismal track record at Aurora Downs in Chicago, Freeman moved him to Polo Park in Winnipeg in mid-1927. Working with Joe Reed, a bent trainer, Freeman tried to set up a betting coup for Cas Welch to win. But the jockey they wanted to compensate in advance for welching in the stretch had a quaint view of sportsmanship. Instead of pocketing Freeman's generous gift to his retirement fund, the judgmental jock went racing to the authorities.

The verdict of the stewards at Polo Park was swift. In fact, it arrived far more swiftly than any horse that Freeman ever owned. Presiding Judge G. W. Schilling ruled, "For attempted bribery and other corrupt practices owner Freeman Bernstein and trainer Joe Reed are ruled off the turf and the horse Cas Welch barred from further racing." That was enough for the prissy *Winnipeg Evening Tribune* to claim that a "dastardly plot was nipped in the bud and the guilty ones were justly punished."

Freeman could take a rebuff like this in stride, but for a horse like Cas Welch it raised the specter of the ultimate finish line. (Not to worry: Cas Welch kept running out of the money at Polo Park.)

Eighteen months later, in January 1929, Freeman tried to pull off a similar stunt in the anything-goes capital of North America: Tijuana, Mexico. Freeman miscalculated, though, by forgetting that Canadians make a fetish out of going south to escape the snow. His own nemesis—Racing Judge G. W. Schilling—was moonlighting by taking on a similar wintertime role at the Jockey Club in Tijuana.

When Freeman began racing his string of eleven horses in Tijuana, Judge Schilling wasted no time in banning the Bernstein Stables for the "inconsistency" of its ponies. As *Variety* explained, "'Inconsistency' in horse racing is equivalent to saying that Freeman's horses were over-educated; that they might have read the odds before going to the post."

Freeman had won his own version of the Triple Crown by being banned from tracks in three foreign countries (Austria, Canada, and Mexico). It took a lot of doing to be judged too crooked for Tijuana. That was like being shunned by the Marquis de Sade for being too much of a libertine.

Freeman had also been warned off by racing authorities in Chicago. But that only came out when *Variety* started writing that Freeman owed Sophie Tucker $650.*

In early 1929, Tucker was one of the biggest stars in show business in terms of talent, fame, and girth. During a recent tour of England, the Duchess of York (the mother of Queen Elizabeth) led the cheers at one of her performances. And now as Sophie headed west to make her first talkie (*Honky Tonk*) for the Warners, her every move was major news for *Variety*.

A gossip item in the weekly's Inside Stuff–Vaudeville column praised the performer for her continuing loyalty to her agent Bill Morris and songwriters Jack Yellen and Milton Ager as she hit Hollywood. "That's Soph," the unsigned column declared. "Her one error in life, from the record, was letting Freeman land her for $650 cash. And Soph wants to know where Freeman is so she can

---

* This story vindicated my father's memory—which I, of course, had doubted— that the Last of the Red Hot Mamas helped out Freeman financially in his later years.

ask him for it. Anytime Soph, when returning, sees a drove of men chasing another man, she should fall in line, they are Freeman's creditors."

A week later, Sime caught up with Freeman wearing two coats (a cloth garment over an expensive fur) on a mild day in late February. "Of course the sun is shining now and it makes me a little warm," Freeman admitted, "but I have got to wear that fur coat to keep it. Somebody found out where I was living and sicked the sheriffs onto me."

But what bugged Freeman, or so he claimed, was *Variety* "digging up old stuff like that Sophie Tucker's squawk for a lousy $650." He explained that he had borrowed the money from Soph in Chicago to keep his horses from being repossessed: "Another sheriff. My life has been mixed up with sheriffs."

Freeman portrayed himself as an innocent victim of Soph's generosity. "When I found I had to move the hosses, my bankroll had melted," he said. "I looked up Soph. It was in Chicago and Soph was there, working. So I knew she had money and nothing to do with it. I needed $325 and that was what I was going to ask her for first, but I said, says I, 'Freeman, be smart. Ask for $650. She will cut it in half and you will be safe.'"

Instead, Soph crossed him up by coming across with the full $650. "If she had done as I thought she was going to," Freeman calculated, "I would only owe her $325, so Soph really cost me $325, didn't she?"

That was Freeman's story until, about six weeks later, it wasn't.

In the revised version he gave *Variety*, Freeman had tipped off Tucker (a part-time gambler who sang songs like "Life Is Just a Game of Poker") about one of his horses running at Aurora Downs: "I says to Soph, 'Buddy, I'll stake you to the best thing that ever was pulled off on this course. . . . If it doesn't go over I'll give you your money back. That's how sure it is.'"

Of course, a Freeman sure thing was as reliable as a 1929 stock tip. The filly got left at the post and Soph was left muttering "some of these days" over the $650 she lost. Even worse for Freeman, the track judges decided that his horses had too high an IQ for Chicago. They told him that they don't want horses that "look backward at the far turn or know how to stand still at the post."

In his haste to get his brainy steeds out of Chicago, Freeman somehow neglected to square accounts with Tucker—or so he said. But he remained unrepentant, telling Sime Silverman, "If you write Soph, don't tell that dame anything. Let it die. She's in the big money now and should forget nickels and dimes."

Many con men, grifters, and hustlers flourished during the 1920s and 1930s. But what separated Freeman from commonplace cheaters and chiselers was his ability to convince leading citizens—the pillars of propriety—that his deals were on the level. His diction may have been crude, his Panama hat was stained, and his manners would have sent Emily Post into a swoon, but Freeman managed to convey the impression that he was an honored figure on Broadway. And, for the most part, that act worked as long as he stayed far away from Broadway.

Less than three weeks after taking office on March 4, 1929, Herbert Hoover announced that he would sell the presidential yacht, the *Mayflower*, as a way to save the Treasury $300,000 a year. Freeman, whose nautical knowledge stopped with all-night poker games aboard ocean liners, immediately tried to lease the *Mayflower*. His plan was to turn it into a floating restaurant with dancing, entertainment, and enough presidential memorabilia to give the enterprise a patina of patriotism. But Freeman's Hoover connections had become too waterlogged to pull this off, even though he graciously offered to split the profits fifty-fifty with the government.

Freeman's next gold-plated scam . . . err . . . generous scheme was to hold a benefit concert in Boston to raise money for the B'nai B'rith's $2 million national fund-raising campaign. Working with Aaron Fox, the brother of the founder of the Fox Film Corporation, Freeman arranged to rent the Boston Garden for two performances on Sunday, April 14. When Fox, a vice president of the movie company, came to Boston a few days in advance to promote the concert, Freeman accompanied him and was billed as his "personal secretary" by the *Boston Herald*. (A brief pause to imagine Freeman taking dictation.)

"I want to say that the concerts will be among the most successful ever given in the east," Fox assured local reporters. "I understand that the executive committee expects nearly 50,000 men and women from all over New England to attend." After the press conference, at which he also announced the support of the Gillette Safety Razor Company, Fox stepped into an adjoining room at the Ritz-Carlton Hotel for what he thought was a private meeting. Instead, he was surprised by a testimonial dinner presided over by his hardworking assistant, Freeman Bernstein.

The concert was headlined by Cantor Josef Rosenblatt, a world-renowned tenor who always performed in a yarmulke and black frock coat. Formerly the cantor at the First Hungarian Congregation Ohab Zedek in New York, the deeply Orthodox Rosenblatt shifted to show business in the mid-1920s when a failed investment in a Jewish newspaper left him owing $150,000. Resisting offers to join leading opera companies because he would have to shave his beard, Rosenblatt also turned down a chance to play Al Jolson's father in *The Jazz Singer*, since the role would have required him to sing *"Kol Nidre"* in a secular setting. At the Boston Garden, the diminutive Rosenblatt sang a mixed repertoire that ranged from Jewish blessings (*"Elohaynu"*) to Irish classics ("Last Rose of Summer") to tunes of his own composition ("Jewish Lullaby").

Sharing top billing were stars from *Roxy and His Gang* on the NBC Blue network. Impresario S. L. "Roxy" Rothafel presided over radio's leading variety show. It was broadcast from his Roxy Theatre—a New York movie palace so lush that a little girl asked in a *New Yorker* cartoon, "Does God live here?" Roxy decided at the last minute not to make the trek to Boston but sent a cellist and four singers to round out the program.

Even though the total attendance (with tickets ranging from fifty cents to $3) turned out to be eighteen thousand at the two performances rather than the fifty thousand Fox had exuberantly predicted, the B'nai B'rith anticipated a hefty check. Except with Freeman doing the bookkeeping, the concerts mysteriously lost $5,000.

Boston ticket broker Abraham Shapiro, who had been reassured by Freeman's connections with Roxy and Fox Film, was taken for about $300 in unpaid commissions. "For 37 years I have been selling tickets to the public. . . . But this is the first time in my career that I have been gyped," he told the *Boston Herald*. But the proprietor of the Shapiro Book Store in the theatrical district stressed that he was not the only victim of that "double crosser" named Bernstein: "I don't think that he paid even Cantor Rosenblatt, who is a world famous concert artist. I hear they owe a lot of money to others who were in on the concert."

With this reputation—among his fellow Jews, no less—Freeman

sensed that he was a has-been in the Hub. But his Boston massacre also taught him another business lesson: Beantown was thick with suckers. Freeman was never big on aliases (about the only time he adopted one was when he was peddling bogus oil stocks from Mexico City as "Harmon Beggs"), but he realized that the best way to play Boston again was under an assumed name. What he needed was a new identity—and a guarantee that no one from the B'nai B'rith or a fan of Cantor Rosenblatt would recognize him.

Without even resorting to a baptismal font, Freeman was reborn a month later as Roger O'Ryan. (His only prior connection to Ireland was that May's mother, who died long before they married, had been born in County Cork.)

Displaying a mastery of blarney that would make a leprechaun blush, Freeman arranged for an eight-day rental of the Boston Garden for an Irish Fair with . . . a Bernstein specialty . . . no money down. The first promotional ads appeared in the Boston papers in mid-May promising "SOD FROM EVERY COUNTY IN IRELAND—IRISH FIDDLERS AND WHISTLERS—HUNDREDS OF IRISH COLLEENS." Plus an "Irish Corned Beef and Cabbage Dinner SERVED FREE Every Afternoon Direct from Dinty Moore's Kitchen." All this Hibernian hoopla for an admission charge of $1 tops during the evening and as little as two bits during the day.

As opening night (Saturday, May 25) grew closer, the promised attractions blossomed like a field of four-leaf clovers. Boston's leading Irish pol, former Mayor James Curley (the inspiration for *The Last Hurrah*), was supposed to give the welcoming address. The *Boston Globe* breathlessly announced, "Babe Ruth and the entire Red Sox and Yankee teams are to be special guests of the Fair." An Irish village of cottages would be erected inside the Boston Garden with donkeys, hens, and razorback hogs imported from across the sea. And every paying customer would be encouraged (for a small fee) to chip a piece off a full-size replica of the Blarney Stone, though Freeman often gave the impression that the rock was the real thing.

As was so often the case with Freeman . . . sorry, Mr. O'Ryan . . . the Irish Fair was more sham than shamrock. Every piece of sod bearing the name of an Irish county (Cork, Kildare, Clare, Tipperary) had been carefully dug up from a pasture behind a barn in Franklin, Massachusetts. The razorback hogs hailed from New Jersey. The place mats for the Irish stew had indeed been lifted from Dinty Moore, but the food itself was being cooked by an off-duty Boston cop. And the Irish Colleens were all local showgirls.

But the real problem with the Irish Fair was that O'Ryan had the luck of a Bernstein.

Local Irish societies spread the rumor that the organizer of the fair was of the Hebraic rather than the Hibernian persuasion. With attendance on opening day just three thousand (and with only seven reporters showing up for the free lobster dinner for the gentlemen of the press), Freeman tried to save everything through the force of his personality. Dressed in evening clothes and wearing a derby hat, he would stand in front of the Boston Garden every night greeting patrons. "Short, fat and bald," as the *Boston Herald* put it, "he presented an unusual spectacle at an Irish fair, but there he kept his post, occasionally passing out a cigar or giving a friendly handclasp."

When pressed about his heritage, Freeman employed the Leopold Bloom defense without making specific reference to *Ulysses*. He insisted that he had grown up in Dublin and had spent eleven years—clearly an Emerald Isle record—earning his degree from Trinity College. (His presumed double major: cards and horses.)

As for the moniker Roger O'Ryan, Freeman later insisted to *Variety* that it was all an innocent misperception. "I didn't take that name," he said. "Someone wished it on me, I guess. I know they wouldn't want a Freeman Bernstein to get behind an Irish Fair anyway, so I said nothing."

The Irish Fair limped to a close on schedule Sunday night, June 2, without either Babe Ruth or former Mayor Curley ever stopping by to tour the Irish village, sample Dinty Moore's stew, or ogle the Colleens. Making matters worse, Freeman was belatedly discovering that Bostonians were not the hicks that he had assumed.

With the gate receipts already attached by creditors and the performers not yet paid, Freeman and his alter ego Roger O'Ryan quickly realized that Irish eyes would soon be frowning—and raced for South Station. En route, in a show-business ritual older than vaudeville, O'Ryan and Bernstein decided to break up their act. Dropping his Irish alias, Freeman headed south to parts unknown alone, unable even to retrieve his luggage from his Back Bay hotel.

This is where Freeman on-the-run stories normally end. In the past, about the worst that happened was that showgirls would have to rustle up train fare to get out of Scranton or some junior diplomat would cable New York with an ineffectual warning about Freeman's "gift for making black look white."

But Freeman misunderstood Boston—especially when the locals got their Irish up. Jurisdictions like New York considered it a minor infraction to hightail it out of town with unpaid show bills. In contrast, Massachusetts, true to its joyless Puritan heritage, regarded such evasive showmanship as a felony.

The day after the fair closed, twenty-five of the chorines who had been Colleens marched to the State House on Beacon Hill demanding their back pay. The attention-getting protest worked. The resulting front-page headline in the *Boston Herald* shouted, "OWNER OF IRISH FAIR MISSING; 'COLLEENS' CLAMOR FOR WAGES" while the subhead blared, "300 EMPLOYEES SEEK BERNSTEIN, ALIAS O'RYAN."

The jig was up: Judge Elijah Adlow issued a warrant for Freeman's arrest.

Tragically, this legal complication emerged just as Freeman was poised to find salvation. He had become envious of the heavenly success of British evangelist Gipsy Smith's revival meetings at the Boston Garden that, in the estimate of the *Boston Globe*, attracted "a quarter of a million weeping, salvation-smitten, human souls." Having failed with both the B'nai B'rith and Irish Catholics, Freeman figured that he needed another way to get right with God.

Aside from the Salvation Army bands in Times Square, Freeman's acquaintance with fire-and-brimstone preachers had been limited. But then he remembered Steamboat Bill, a local black fighter blessed with limited talent but an unlimited willingness to take a fall in a fixed fight—or, as he called it, "do a horizontal." Steamboat Bill, whose real name was S. J. Worrell, claimed to be a minister, and when times were tough in the canvas-back trade, he offered to marry couples for fifty cents a "hitch."

That was enough for Freeman to imagine that his bankroll could be born again. During the final days of the Irish Fair, Freeman had been already arranging (on credit, of course) for the printing of the advertising for his next Boston attraction. The posters featured a drawing of a turbaned black evangelist with one arm raised toward heaven in exhortation and the other arm reaching through fleecy clouds to send a red devil fleeing. Huge lettering identified the pastor: "Steamboat Bill, the Live Wire of Gospel."

But Freeman Bernstein had become the Dead Battery of Gospel Promoters. Not only were the Boston police after him, but Freeman (or "Mr. O'Ryanstein," as the *Boston Herald* now called him) had also become a figure of ridicule throughout New England.

The *Herald* instructed its readers in the difference between a "confidence man" (someone whose blatant dishonesty sometimes lands him in jail) and a "grifter" like Freeman, who is "less bold but more agile of mind [and] usually grafts his shabby schemes on the sentiment as well as the credulity of men and women." The advantage of being a grifter, the *Herald* explained, is that he almost always gets away with it because his "dupes" are unwilling or unable to prosecute. But this time, things had turned grim for a grifter.

When interviewed by the *Boston Herald*, not even Mr. O'Ryanstein's known associates would vouch for his honesty. "That guy—there's nobody like him," said Sam Bernstein, who was still running the vaudeville booking agency. "He comes to me with this 'Irish fair.' He says I should send him up three acts. I did. Then he says I should come up Monday to see the fine business—Ha!—that guy's my brother—I'm telling you. Then he wires me to come Tuesday—not Monday. Then he says wait until Wednesday. And then—can you beat it—he wires me not to come at all. A fine guy—and I gotta pay them acts I sent him."

Sam also captured Freeman's flamboyance, the sense that everything had to be the best, even if he had no idea how he would ever pay for it. The Irish Fair could have been done on the cheap, but not by Freeman. As Sam put it, "He's gotta go and have a lot of what painted around the place? Irish cottages—ah—them cottages—$4,500 for the painting."

Pressed about the whereabouts of Boston's leading fugitive,

Sam made clear that he was not his brother's keeper: "Where is he now—how do I know? Say, lissen—he's on his way to Africa—Germany—Porto Rico—he's down watchin' the ponies—"

At the offices of *Variety*, the speculation was that Freeman remained somewhere near New York. "He won't go abroad because if he did they'd never let him back in the country again," said Sime Silverman. "Anyhow, he's left stranded troupes all over the world and there's no place for him to go. That guy never eats in the same restaurant twice. He wore a cloth overcoat over a fur coat all last winter: If he left the fur one home, some one would attach it, and if he wore it on the street, they'd take it away from him."

The intrepid *Herald* correspondent also canvassed the gang at Lindy's, which he helpfully described as "the Broadway delicatessen from which Arnold Rothstein walked to his death." The general attitude of the noshers about Freeman was summarized as "Him as a Ryan? What's the gag?"

The gag was that Freeman couldn't dodge an indictment for grand larceny the way he could duck a process server. Freeman quickly resorted to his favorite "In Case of Emergency, Break Glass" ploy by attempting to douse the fire with a proposal to settle. The *Herald* reported that O'Ryanstein floated the offer "through Boston friends," though it strained credulity to believe that Freeman had any pals left in the land of the bean and cod. Reckoning the worth of a Bernstein promise, 270 performers from the Irish Fair tried instead to recover their back pay with a benefit concert at the Boston Garden, donated free by the embarrassed managers who had trusted Roger O'Ryan.

Having gotten away with so much for so long, Freeman became jaunty in his overconfidence. He soon popped up in *Variety*'s offices and started going home again to his wife, May, in Cedarhurst.

When the Boston authorities in late June tried to extradite Freeman on the cheap by wiring a warrant to Long Island, the Cedarhurst police chief nixed the request by pointing out that defrauding performers was merely a misdemeanor in New York. Freeman probably regarded it as a victimless crime.

But the Boston police soon dispatched Sergeant Cornelius Ring to Cedarhurst to collect in person the man who dared shortchange the Irish Colleens and their fellow performers. And this time Freeman learned how inconvenient the two words "grand larceny" could be for a lifelong grifter.

Roger O'Ryan's involuntary return to Boston in August 1929 proved to be temporary. Freeman had honed a skill that would serve him well during the coming decade—the ability to convince lawyers with political clout to take his cases without the usual retainer. His Boston attorney, Joseph Walsh, represented city councillors and was a prominent supporter of James Curley in his efforts to win back the mayoralty. By highlighting Freeman's purportedly clean record (no jail time in America), Walsh got his client released to return to New York to attend to his business dealings pending trial.

Freeman was aware of his upcoming January 20, 1930, court date—so aware that he made two separate trips to Cuba in January. Getting back was never difficult, just a six-hour crossing on an excursion boat like the *General Cobb*. But Freeman delayed long enough so that when he arrived back in Key West on January 16, about the only way that he could have made it back to Boston in time would have been with the airborne help of Colonel Lindbergh.

So it fell to Walsh to explain to an unamused Judge Williams of the Suffolk County Criminal Court that his client had been unavoidably detained in Havana. In truth, as *Variety* soon reported,

Freeman was playing Commodore Bernstein aboard a borrowed yacht, the *Calumet*, docked in Miami Beach.

In his business dealings—idiosyncratic as they were—Freeman had always tried to walk his version of a crooked line. He lied to bill collectors, scoffed at lawsuits, and skedaddled out of the way of sheriffs wanting to repossess his assets. But aside from a few strategic errors (like his time in the Tunnel in Brussels and the judicial confusion over betting slips in 1927), Freeman had avoided any activity that would lead to any more serious legal jeopardy than being escorted out of town.

But all that changed when Judge Williams banged his gavel and pronounced that the absent Freeman Bernstein had defaulted on his indictment for grand larceny. Freeman was not only banned in Boston but would face jail time if he ever returned to Massachusetts.

In tandem with the October 1929 stock market crash (*Variety* headline: "WALL ST. LAYS AN EGG"), Freeman had begun his long downslide.

15

Towering forty-three stories over Eighth Avenue and Thirty-Fourth Street, the New Yorker Hotel claimed to be the world's tallest hotel when it opened on January 2, 1930. The twenty-five hundred guest rooms invited superlatives: They required four hundred carloads of furniture and the hotel's bedsheets—if laid end to end—would cover thirty-two acres. Prominent Hungarian-born artist Louis Jambor painted the two oversize murals dominating the lobby: One harked back to the Dutch settlement of New York while the other was a visual ode to the skyscrapers of modern Manhattan.

When the developers began excavating the site during the boom times of 1928, the business plan was to give the garment trade its own luxury hotel. Out-of-town buyers could get off their trains at Pennsylvania Station, walk through a tunnel to the New Yorker Hotel, and drop their bags before visiting the fashion showrooms and the wholesale outlets in the West Thirties. An advertisement in *Vogue* in early January 1930 proclaimed, "The New Yorker offers something *decidedly new* in hotels . . . an individualized service which makes you a *privileged* guest . . . provides you a friendly, informal hospitality that's refreshingly old-fashioned in spirit, strikingly modern in manner!"

For all the comforts offered by the New Yorker Hotel, business travelers sometimes found it hard to adjust to the bustling city. A sleep study conducted for the hotel by the Psychological Laboratory at Colgate University found that one-fifth of the guests lay awake for at least part of the night. The most common reasons for insomnia were the clatter of the taxicabs and the rumble of the trolley cars. Of course, the dismal business climate contributed to the sleeplessness.

The hotel itself proved initially immune to the ravages of the Depression. Maybe it was the location or the friendly, informal hospitality, but celebrities soon whirled through the hotel's revolving doors. Evangelist Aimee Semple McPherson rested there after her run-in with U.S. Customs, which had accused her of snipping off the labels from Paris frocks to avoid import duties.

The convention business also thrived. During an April dinner speech to a gathering of fire insurance executives at the New Yorker Hotel, Police Commissioner Grover Whalen bragged that New York had become one of the safest cities in the country, with much lower levels of assault and theft than Chicago, Detroit, or Cleveland.

Theft of services was an unforgivable offense at the New Yorker Hotel. A week after Whalen's address, the hotel struck a blow for justice by getting a twenty-eight-year-old Philadelphia man sentenced to thirty days in a workhouse. His crime: walking out on a $30.10 hotel bill for a week's stay.

Freeman loved hotels with a passion that he normally reserved for fast horses and slow bill collectors. He was still luxuriating in the memory of those blessed few weeks in 1920 when he lived "on the cuff" at the Plaza Hotel. To be precise, he lived on the cuff at the Plaza until the house detectives collared him for sneaking out the back exit. So it was only natural that Freeman gravitated to the New Yorker Hotel—especially since any new business establishment, even a shoe shine stand, attracted his patronage in the hopes that the owner would be inexperienced enough to offer him credit.

The New Yorker Hotel boasted sixteen hundred employees. All Freeman needed was to find one cashier or desk clerk trusting enough to cash his checks. Despite his recent setbacks, Freeman's marksmanship in quest of a mark was dead-on. Over three days, between June 24 and June 26, Freeman passed enough rubber at the New Yorker Hotel to fund a tire factory. Three checks for $4,000 added up to serious coin.

Despite the subsequent interest of the New York City Police Department, some of the details of the racket have blurred with time.

The bogus checks were all written to Freeman by a "Sol Mayer" and drawn on the J. S. Fried and Company. Even though J. S. Fried and Company had a Financial District address at 80 Wall Street, it was, in reality, a gambling joint masquerading as a brokerage house. The bucket shop was owned by the three Silinsky brothers (the name J. S. Fried had been borrowed from a clerk in a clothing store) and it made money by taking commissions on the wagers it handled. The firm added to its profits by sometimes paying off winning gamblers with checks that had a little bounce in their step.

The identity of Sol Mayer proved harder to puzzle out. Several Sol Mayers lived in New York in 1930, and the closest one owned a wholesale underwear and hosiery company on West Thirty-Second

Street, a few blocks from the New Yorker Hotel. But that connection is elusive since Freeman never fancied boxer shorts who couldn't take a punch.

Searching bygone newspaper clips for Sol Mayer and then Solomon Meyer, I came across a Meyer Solomon. And, coincidentally, he was running a downtown betting shop that was affiliated with J. S. Fried. Meyer Solomon, in fact, often served as a "betting commissioner," a neutral figure who watches from the fringes of a high-stakes card game to certify that everything is kosher.

Solomon (who also used the moniker "Meyer Boston") had actually been playing at the table the night of Arnold Rothstein's final card game. "Rothstein lost about $300,000," Solomon testified during the 1929 murder trial arising out of the case. "He gave I.O.U.'s for it. He made out a lot of them." As for Solomon himself—whom the newspapers described as "a small nervous man"—he walked away with $8,000.

So what happened with Freeman at the New Yorker Hotel?

Asked about it years later, Freeman said vaguely, "That was the matter of that baseball pool or something like that. I was at the New Yorker. There was a lot of paper. I was okaying the drafts."

It seems probable that Freeman and Meyer Solomon were running the baseball pool out of a hotel room—and the two of them didn't have the cash to pay off the winners. Maybe they lost big when the last-place Red Sox split a doubleheader with the Tigers on June 24. Or took a pasting on the twenty-fifth when the Yankees (two home runs by Babe Ruth and another from Lou Gehrig) demolished the hapless St. Louis Browns, 16–4, in the Bronx.

For men of the world like Freeman and Solomon, the obvious next step would have been to appeal to the kindness of the New Yorker Hotel. Solomon had brought along a sheaf of beautifully embossed blank checks from the J. S. Fried and Company that looked like they were drawn on a firm that rivaled J. P. Morgan. Calculating that it didn't matter who signed the bogus checks, since everything rested on persuasiveness of the J. S. Fried logo, Solomon transposed his name to scrawl "Sol Mayer."

Waiting until the banks closed, Freeman in all likelihood wandered down to the lobby of the New Yorker Hotel in search of an understanding cashier. I can see him confiding that he was a wealthy sportsman temporarily short of funds in a gentleman's game. Freeman pulled off impersonations like this all the time— and it wouldn't have taken much to convince an obliging hotel employee to tide him over until his brokerage house (J. S. Fried) opened in the morning.

Maybe a few Cuban cigars or even a $20 bill accidentally left on the cashier's window helped establish the bonds of trust. But within a few minutes, a smiling Freeman was headed upstairs with $750 in cash. The graft worked so well on June 24 that Freeman and Solomon pulled variations of the same stunt the next two nights to keep the baseball pool solvent.

Leaving the hotel on June 26, Freeman probably felt like he had hit a grand-slam homer, especially since he assumed that he faced no jeopardy over the kited checks. The responsibility obviously rested with "Sol Mayer," who had signed the checks that he had cashed. And good luck to the house dicks at the New Yorker Hotel in finding Mayer.

Freeman, who had talked himself out of scrapes on three continents, never imagined he could get into serious legal trouble in his hometown. But Freeman did not yet understand that the easy money days of the twenties were gone—and in the Depression, no hotel would write off $4,000 in rubber checks.

By the summer of 1930 more than four million Americans were out of work, and everyone was reeling from the plunging elevator collapse of the economy. Well, almost everyone. Responding to criticism that at $80,000 he was earning more than the president, Babe Ruth replied, "What the hell has Hoover got to do with this? Anyway, I had a better year than he did."

Times were so tough that Freeman couldn't even rustle up the money to travel. Sounding like a swell missing his annual Grand Tour, Freeman told *Variety* in August, "Accustomed as I am to spending the summer in Europe, I ain't used to this stay-at-home thing. . . . [But] there ain't no dough around for nobody. I found that true because I got none, and when Freeman can't dig dough, you know, kid, the works are in."

With little to do at home in Long Island, Freeman was reduced to, as he put it, "rehearsing starvation for two and three days at a time, as I'm too stout anyway." The missing meals led to Freeman brooding about his mortality, even imagining his funeral at Frank E. Campbell, the leading Upper East Side mortuary. As Freeman put it, "I got so desperate that I thought of going up to Campbell's and getting a rate, just so I would chisel a little at least for May on the way out."

The black-crepe mood may have been brought on by the worsening health of Sime Silverman, who was doing a slow fade-out as he battled tuberculosis. When the next Freeman monologue appeared in *Variety* three months later, it carried for the first time a byline other than Sime's. Freeman treated Joe Bigelow, his new amanuensis, as a peach-fuzzed youngster: "What's your name? Do you live with your folks? Have they any money?" The article contained a few vintage lines such as Freeman's bravado over losing a wad at Saratoga: "But that's okay. I have made and lost too many millions to be squawking over $1,200 or one rough summer."

An era was ending for both *Variety* and Freeman. A few pranks still carried Sime's imprint: *Variety*'s twenty-fifth-anniversary number in late 1930 listed Freeman as the manager of the Palace, which was about as likely as Sir Bernstein of Troy being welcomed at Buckingham Palace. The issue also contained a letter from Freeman to Sime dripping with mock outrage: "I suppose my reputation has been ruined by this lousy 'Variety' more often than any rep anyone ever had. I didn't know I had so many reputations to ruin until you started it."

The letter ended with Freeman's promise, "So long, lousy. Will write again in 1955."

Nothing ruins a reputation faster than a felony warrant. Displaying little respect for the man whom *Variety* called the "Pet of Times Square," the New Yorker Hotel had grown petulant about getting its $4,000 back. Instead of resorting to bill collectors (who were rather busy during the Depression), the hotel resorted to District Attorney Thomas C. T. Crain, a Tammany Hall favorite.

On October 25, Freeman and the elusive Sol Mayer were indicted on three counts of grand larceny. Freeman was arrested the same day, with bail set at $3,000 (about $43,000 today). After three nights enjoying the comforts-of-home service provided by the municipal jail chillingly known as the Tombs, Freeman finally found a trusting bail bondsman (the Grand Central Security Corporation). And on November 6, Honest Freeman Bernstein pleaded "not guilty."

Awaiting trial (which was postponed until November 1931), Freeman tarried in Hot Springs, Arkansas, a wide-open mob town that had become Al Capone's favorite watering hole. But in 1931,

Capone was stuck at home in Cicero, Illinois, preparing for his federal trial on income tax evasion. Still, Freeman probably checked into the Arlington Hotel (Capone's favorite) and gambled at the Ohio Club, where the bar and casino were hidden behind a cigar store to fool Prohibition agents. And Freeman undoubtedly recognized familiar faces from Broadway like Owney Madden, the tough-guy founder of the Cotton Club, who had relocated to Arkansas to escape a corruption investigation back in New York.

Freeman, in fact, was spending more time on the road than Odysseus. At home on Long Island, May Ward tried to adapt to a solitary life. Almost fifty, she had made her final appearance on the New York stage in early 1929 in a benefit for the Actor's Fund headlined by Ethel Barrymore, Will Rogers, Eddie Cantor, and Chico Marx.

Instead of vaudeville, May was playing to a smaller audience. She found solace in her animals—a menagerie that included seventeen dogs. The nightly din from this canine chorus grew so incessant that her neighbors in Cedarhurst took her to court as a public nuisance. Given a choice between her dogs and her home, May stayed loyal to a girl's best friends. She and her dogs moved in 1930 to a bungalow in a quiet neighborhood near the water in East Rockaway.

Even though she was licensed to keep no more than six animals, her unsanctioned kennel quickly grew to well over a dozen small dogs, including a blind one. The Pomeranians, Pekingese, and poodles had become her life—and when a dog became sick, she took blankets downstairs to stay with her canine companion through the night.

After a neighbor complained in 1933, the local health officer, Dr. Arthur Jaques, set out for 29 Third Avenue in East Rockaway to enforce the law. But Dr. Jaques's bark turned out to be worse than his bite. Moved by the former vaudeville star's love for her dogs, he helped her craft a successful appeal to the village board (everyone on Third Avenue signed her petition) that allowed the animals to stay.

Getting Freeman to stay was another story. By that time, he was on the lam on the other side of the world.

E very life has turning points—and mostly they go unrecognized at the time. But Freeman knew the consequences when he failed to appear for trial on the bum-check charges on November 4, 1931. He was now wanted in New York for a new felony—jumping bail. And he couldn't go home again.

Why did he do it?

Freeman later insisted that he had been given incorrect instructions by the court officer: "I went down to Hot Springs when he told me I could go away for six or seven weeks." That seems as plausible as Freeman being delayed because he was flagpole sitting or in the middle of a dance marathon.

Approaching his sixtieth birthday, Freeman probably figured that he didn't have time to do time. Nobody was writing show tunes about the lush life at Sing Sing. In mid-1931, two prisoners had been stabbed to death and a third badly wounded at the prison. As for the food . . . well . . . it had been twenty years since Sing Sing had even served turkey for Thanksgiving.

Always an optimist, Freeman may have assumed that his legal problems would blow over if he took a powder for a few months to raise the cash to pay off the New Yorker Hotel. Then there was his family to think about. Already, his youngest sister Becky's husband, Samuel Potofsky, was urging her to avoid her scapegrace brother. If Freeman went to prison upstate, there was no guarantee that his sisters and his brother Sam would be there on visiting day.

So he fled. He popped up in Hawaii in February 1932 as *Variety* reported, "Somehow Freeman Bernstein got to Honolulu."

But Freeman, who was having problems with his entrances and exits, arrived just as the Massie Affair was convulsing Honolulu. Thalia Massie, the well-born and emotionally flighty wife of a navy officer, had made the dubious claim that she had been attacked coming home from a party. The subsequent assault trial of five local men (two native-born Hawaiians and the others of Chinese and Japanese ancestry) ended with a hung jury. In early January, her husband, her mother, and two navy officers kidnapped one of the accused assailants in hopes of beating a confession out of him. Instead, they accidentally killed him. As a result, the vigilantes (three navy officers and a society grande dame) were indicted for kidnapping and murder.

Freeman was just getting acclimated to the islands when newspapers began bannering headlines like "HONOLULU BOYCOTTED BY FLEET." It is hard to imagine three words more dispiriting to a grifter than "Shore Leave Canceled." Freeman jokingly told *Variety*, "My scheme was to grab a concession for the high tide rights. Then I intended to charge a fare to bathe at high tide. I was just about to close the deal when those assault things started to happen."

With his plans out to sea, Freeman decided to head back to the mainland, since he felt safe as long as he avoided the New York area. "Under the conditions as I unfortunately found them over there," Freeman said, "I had no time to operate and all of my finesse went bust, leaving me with a short bank roll and a hell of a hard luck story. It was the story and 50% of the roll that got me on the boat."

He washed up in San Francisco worse for wear. As *Variety*'s San Francisco correspondent described him in March, "Mr. Bernstein looked quite nifty. . . . His panama hat seemed second hand and his trousers were once white, but he had been shaved and his cherubic face wore that Bernstein grin that can't be dodged."

A month later, Freeman was in Tokyo. Or, as *Variety* wrote, "Freeman Bernstein is post-carding his Broadway friends to let them know that everything's hotsy-totsy in Japan." In fact, Freeman was staying at the hoity-toity Imperial Hotel, the Frank Lloyd Wright art deco treasure that had survived the devastating 1923 Tokyo earthquake.

Freeman frequently bragged about having been "all over the world, leaving each country by request." Now, by the process of elimination, Freeman had found in Japan a new country ripe for the plucking.

When Bernstein-san showed up in 1932, Japan was far down the road toward militarism but had yet to turn its angry glare toward America. Instead, China was the target. The Japanese army had established a puppet regime in Manchuria, but the victory soon left Tokyo hungry again. So the Japanese initiated a four-month war against Shanghai that included an unprecedented bombing campaign of civilian targets launched from an aircraft carrier.

Back home in Tokyo, though, the Japanese remained infatuated with American movies. When Charlie Chaplin visited in May, the son of the prime minister was scheduled to take the Little Tramp to sumo wrestling. Except nationalist fanatics assassinated the prime minister (Inukai Tsuyoshi) on the day of the match.

Freeman missed that drama because he had left Yokohama a few weeks earlier aboard the Canadian Pacific's *Empress of Russia*, en route to Vancouver. By tradition, passengers aboard luxury liners leaving Japan would throw paper streamers to their friends on the shore as the ship sailed. I can see, if I squint hard enough, Freeman tossing his streamer to the police officer who escorted him to the dock or maybe the house manager from the Imperial Hotel who was waving an unpaid bill. Reflecting his reduced circumstances, Freeman traveled in second class ("cabin class")—and declared to customs officials that he was carrying $50 when he arrived in Vancouver.

Freeman probably never read *A Man Without a Country*, but he may have seen the 1917 or 1925 movie version. Now he was living the life of a stateless nomad. He tried a few weeks in the Panama Canal Zone, loosely administered by the United States, before sailing to Los Angeles (again in cabin class), arriving on July 29.

The City of Angels was celebrating its coming-of-age party—the 1932 Olympics were opening the next day with a speech by Vice President Charles Curtis at the newly erected Coliseum. It is likely that Freeman had some graft going as he checked into the Ambassador Hotel. In fact, just snagging a downtown hotel room was an accomplishment, especially when—in Freeman's case—he presumably had no intention of paying for it.

A bloodhound when he scented coin, Freeman had to be thrilled to discover that the town was thick with rich foreigners with a shaky grasp of English (the Japanese held a reception in his hotel) and fun-loving out-of-towners like the sixteen delegations of fez-wearing Shriners. Let other sportsmen waste time cheering the track-and-field exploits of Babe Didrikson (two gold medals and a silver). Let other hustlers be deterred when the Los Angeles Police announced that sixty detectives would be working the hotels. For Freeman Bernstein—the homeless world traveler—all that mattered was that the game was afoot.

W hatever hustles he tried at the Olympics, Freeman afterward put on his own track-and-field exhibition by fleeing faster than the naked eye. Vanishing for nearly a year, he disappeared completely from the pages of *Variety*, police blotters, and immigration records.

The best clue to his whereabouts can be found in the title of a memoir that, late in life, Freeman announced he was writing: *The Trials and Tribulations of a Transgressor: An Inside Story of Kings, Queens, Sultans, Maharajahs and Movie Moguls I Have Hobnobbed With*. (The book was never published—and quite possibly the few trusting souls who sent $2 in advance to Freeman Bernstein are still waiting for their copies.)

The years from 1932 until 1935 were Freeman's Sultans and Maharajahs period.

This was when the photograph of the Man in the White Suit . . . Freeman complete with pith helmet . . . appeared in the *Times of Ceylon*, the leading newspaper in the British colony. But Freeman didn't limit himself to safe billets where the only threat to an American on the run was malaria. If money were to be made, he would go to the ends of the earth.

Literally.

As *Variety* later recounted, "One of the stories of his far away wanderings had him touring a show through Mongolia, traveling by camel, oxen or other means and accepting furs in lieu of admission." Outer Mongolia in the 1930s was a land where the entertainment options ranged from Communist Party meetings to the occasional circuses. Alas, few mementos of the Ulan Bator theatrical scene from that era have survived. And, in any case, they probably would not have been English-language playbills emblazoned with "Free-man Bernstein Presents . . ." But the Mongolia expert whom I con-sulted (really) said that the story of Freeman demanding furs as the price of admission was quite plausible.

Finally, in mid-August 1933, *Variety* tracked the Mongolian Showman down in a fur fur better place . . . Shanghai. Slightly mangling the reasons for his road trip, *Variety* announced, "It appears Freeman recently jumped bail following a pinch over a stock transaction and headed for China. It's figured that by now Freeman has offered to take over the Chinese army versus Japan on a percentage basis."

Freeman had arrived too late to save the Chinese army. Under the terms of the 1932 Shanghai Ceasefire Agreement, the Chinese army had retreated from the area and the city of three million was now under the "protection" of the Japanese. But daily life, with all its vices, went on pretty much as before for the fifty thousand for-eigners in the International Settlement.

A 1934 tourist guide, *All About Shanghai*, conjured up "a blatant cacophony of carnality from a score of dance halls; scarlet women laughing without mirth; virgins in search of life; suicides; mar-riages . . . Communists plotting; Nationalism in the saddle; war in Manchuria!" And we haven't even mentioned opium and overwrit-ing in guidebooks.

In years to come, Freeman would brag to relatives back in New York, "Did I ever tell you the time that I met the Grand Rabbi of China?" When Freeman was in Shanghai, about eight thousand residents of the International Settlement were Jewish. Nearly all of them had fled Stalin's Russia for political or health (not being shot) reasons.

Everyone in the International Settlement had a past—and

many of their stories made Freeman seem like a refugee from a choir loft. White Russians were responsible for as much as 85 percent of the crime in the International Settlement. The two quasi-legal gambling houses were controlled by crime syndicates: an American-owned group with Mexican front men and a Portuguese operation secretly funded by the Chinese.

Freeman was enough of a realist to grasp that in Shanghai you don't run a racket without permission. At the noisy red-brick American Club at 209 Foochow Road, where gambling mostly revolved around shaking dice for drinks, Freeman probably swapped tales of show business with salesmen dreaming of making China safe for Colgate toothpaste. And just in case Freeman got any ideas about grifting, the American Club offered a direct view of the Central Police Station.

Every monarchy has its creation myth. King Arthur won his crown by extracting a sword from a stone. Freeman became the Jade King of China by scoring some stones.

Freeman later explained, exaggerating the duration of his reign, "For the past ten years I have been a frequent visitor in all parts of China making a specialty of buying and selling jade. This has caused me to be known throughout Europe and America as 'The Jade King of China.'"

Why jade?

Freeman certainly knew his jewels after a lifetime of pawning them. America was becoming enraptured with the green-eyed gem. About the time when Freeman was first fleeing to Asia, a giant green pagoda, carved out of an eighteen-thousand-pound block of Burmese jade, went on display at Radio City in Rockefeller Center. The promotional exhibit for jade also featured a choker made of translucent stones appraised at more than $100,000.

In his ramblings through Asia, Freeman made it to Burma. "Precious jade does not come from China," Freeman knowledgeably told the *Los Angeles Times* in 1936. "It comes from Burma, the home of the baby elephant."

The self-crowned Jade King went on to explain, "In the interior of Burma, there are approximately 200 miles of mountains containing jade and about six different mines. It is blasted out of the mountains and driven sixty-five miles into the city where it is placed aboard schooners and shipped to three parts of the world, where it can be cut into stones. These are Canton, Shanghai and Peiping, China."

In Shanghai, small-stakes gambling may have financed Freeman's start in the jade business, but he obtained his working capital by borrowing sales techniques from the glad-handers at the long bar at the American Club. His targets were the only innocents in Shanghai—Americans fresh off the boat. Freeman met every ocean liner with his jade japes as his loud sales pitches competed with opium touts shouting in pidgin English, "Wantchew chow opium."

But Freeman couldn't make a living off the tourist trade looking for cheap gewgaws. To land customers for his better jade pieces, he had to land back in America. That carried risks from the pending arrest warrants and—more ominously—the curiosity of customs agents.

Freeman preferred slightly circuitous routes across the Pacific to lessen suspicion. In late summer 1933, Freeman spent two weeks in first class aboard the Canadian-owned *Empress of Asia*, disembarking in Victoria, British Columbia, before the Jade King entered the United States by train. At the end of that year, Freeman tried the *General Pershing*, a small converted United Fruit Company freighter, slowly plying the route from Manila to Portland, Oregon.

Always accompanying Freeman on these transpacific crossings was Benny, a Sealyham terrier weighing about twenty pounds. Benny was a jewel smuggler's best friend. Freeman pampered the dog, telling Mae West, "I treat him the best—the best. I feed him lamb chops and everything." But when the *Empress of Asia* and the *General Pershing* neared port, Benny's diet switched over to mineral supplements: jade, sapphires, and diamonds.

Freeman would waltz through customs—a loud, cigar-smoking businessman accompanied by a lovable ball of white fluff. Later, in the privacy of a hotel room or train compartment, the jewels would be retrieved, using traditional natural processes. Small wonder Freeman would say when asked about his four-legged sidekick, "Why we're pals, ain't we, Benny."

Jaded from his travels, Freeman had a hard time settling down on his visits to America. He popped up in Los Angeles and Reno before *Variety* spied him in May 1934 "on a ranch near Las Vegas writing his show biz experiences."

I would have loved to see Freeman channeling his inner Ernest Hemingway. The way I picture it: Freeman would be on horseback before dawn, riding out into the desert to glory in the sunrise before returning to the ranch for a hard day roping words at the typewriter. Evenings would be spent at the local saloon, swapping tales of the literary life with other writers, grumbling about meager advances and the inability of the American bourgeoisie to recognize true artistic merit.

Yet somehow Freeman never found his muse under western skies—and the memoir remained unfinished.

Reliving the thrilling days of yesteryear may have reminded Freeman of his first adventure, selling cheap jewelry to miners during the Klondike gold rush. Maybe, he figured, the same gag would work in 1934. Freeman had the cheap jade—his leftover pieces—if only he could find the miners.

All roads led to his friend Jack Munroe, an old-time Canadian boxer known as the Cape Breton Miner. The high point of Munroe's ring career came in 1904 when he lost to Jim Jeffries (whom Freeman later put on the vaudeville stage) for the heavyweight championship. A hero during the Great War, Munroe was described by the *Toronto Star* as "an amiable, smiling fellow, who took life by the scruff of the neck and shook a strenuous living out of it; a modest winner, a good loser."

Rather than hanging around ringside as an aging pug, Munroe spent the 1920s successfully prospecting for gold and silver in northern Ontario. Now he was a successful mining official and the mayor of the tiny township of Elk Lake, about four hundred miles north of Toronto.

In late July, Freeman tried to relocate to Canada, listing Jack Munroe as his sponsor at the border crossing in Sault Ste. Marie. (Asked for next of kin, Freeman gave the name of his brother Sam.) Accompanying Freeman at the border was thirty-one-year-old Jerome Wiseman, who was fresh off the boat from Yokohama and presumably bringing in more jewelry. Both men told Canadian officials that they intended to embark on new careers in mining in Elk Lake, although it must have strained credulity to imagine Freeman—both stouthearted and stout—wielding a pickax or bending over to pan for gold.

Thomas Wyatt, the immigration clerk at this remote outpost, had other ideas. He barred Freeman and Wiseman from Canada. His verdict probably had little to do with Freeman's criminal record or even that the would-be miners listed "Jewish" as their race and "Hebrew" as their religion.

Rather, Wyatt relished the power of "no." He rejected more than three-quarters of border-crossing applicants that month (including Methodists, Lutherans, and Presbyterians). His motivation, perhaps dictated by the government in Ottawa, may have been the fear that footloose Americans might take Canadian jobs amid the dire economic realities of the Depression.

International borders rarely daunted Freeman. He had acquired a useful companion in his travels—the cloak of invisibility. He had learned how to cross international borders even when his papers were not in order. Proud as he was to be no longer shackled by visas and passports, the skill was born of necessity. In 1932, the State Department had opened a file labeled "Bernstein, Freeman—Fugitive from justice (Grand Larceny)."

O n March 14, 1935, Freeman Bernstein—fugitive from justice—turned himself in after more than three years on the run.

Returning to the East Coast for the first time since he jumped bail, Freeman was staying in Washington at the Parkside Hotel ("Reasonably Priced Apartments in a Real Downtown Location"). In his furnished room at the Parkside, Freeman received an urgent telegram about his brother Sam. "My brother was dying," Freeman later explained, "and I called up [the police] because I knew they wanted me."

Freeman and Sam had fought and feuded, complained to *Variety* about each other at the top of their lungs, and had once even run rival nightclubs across the street from each other in Fort George. But they had also grown up sharing a room in tenements on River Street in Troy; they had gone from running seedy carnival games to sharing a vaudeville booking office on Broadway; and fifteen years earlier, they had shared the sons' burden of burying their parents, Hyman and Yetta.

Now, Freeman's older brother had only weeks to live because of worsening diabetes. For Freeman, who was devoted to his family, there was no agonizing over his decision. He dropped a dime and a roll of quarters on himself to phone the New York City Police Department with an offer to surrender.

The police department sent Detective Grover Brown—their expert on financial crimes who had been investigating loan sharks—to haul in Freeman, whose misdeeds were more at the minnow level. But bail jumping was a serious enough offense to get Freeman sent to the Tombs awaiting trial.

Even in the can, Freeman kept hitting the wrong numbers. District Attorney William Dodge was in the midst of a crusade against prostitution (Polly Adler was arrested), crooked bail bondsmen, and the numbers racket. As a result, two hundred numbers runners and low-level gamblers were stuck in the Tombs, unable to raise bail. The overcrowding at the jail led to a breakdown in the informal policy of segregating nonviolent prisoners from hard-core criminals.

Freeman spent twenty-nine days in the Tombs mastering the art of doing time. Affable and generous, never putting on airs, Freeman's jailhouse persona was an extension of his Broadway one. On May 3, his lawyers (White & Stillman, a theatrical and sporting firm on Forty-Second Street) arranged for a suspended sentence and five years' probation because of Freeman's age. In exchange, Freeman agreed to repay the New Yorker Hotel an initial $1,000 in May and the rest gradually . . . very gradually . . . over time.

He also posed for two mug shots as Prisoner No. 86221. The

side view gives him the debauched look of an emperor on a counterfeit Roman coin. The head shot emphasizes Freeman's multiple chins and his rumpled suit as he looks shiftily to the side, radiating ire at the camera.

Freeman's anger could have been directed at the fates because his brother was facing his last days. Sam died on May 9 at the age of sixty-four. The paid notice in the *New York Times* described Sam as a "beloved husband" and "brother of Freeman Bernstein." Sam's three sisters were never mentioned.

Freeman was also featured in the opening sentence of the obit in *Variety*. Although it was not spelled out in the three-paragraph item, Sam's on-again-off-again partnership with Freeman colored almost everything about his career: "[Sam] Bernstein was a pioneer of Sunday night vaudeville concerts, starting them in 1906 in the H.C. Miner outlying theatres. On other occasions he operated the Trocadero Music Hall in New York and Lagoon Island Park, near Albany. He built the Bergen Point theatre at Bayonne, N.J., and for a long period imported circuses and outdoor shows to South America."

Sam's death was a moment of reckoning for Freeman, especially since he still faced an outstanding felony warrant in Boston dating from the ill-fated Irish Festival. After the New York district attorney's office wrapped up the details of the suspended sentence, they handed over Freeman to the Boston police.

Detective Cornelius Ring—the same gumshoe who had nabbed Roger O'Ryan in Cedarhurst in 1929—hopped the New Haven Railroad in late June to collect Freeman the Felon. Boston had no interest in paying to lodge an over-age, out-of-state criminal in prison. All the local DA wanted was the money that the Irish Colleens were owed. In the depths of the Depression, Freeman somehow came up with enough coin for his second round of restitution, probably borrowing from relatives or collecting an early bequest from Sam's will.

Finally, after six years of nervously looking over his shoulder for a copper, Freeman was a free man. Free, that is, as long as he kept on the good side of his probation officer.

He was also broke, jobless, and short on schemes. As Freeman put it on July 27, 1935, in a back-from-Shanghai letter to *Variety*, "I read by the Broadway columnists that Broadway isn't Broadway any more, and the only place I can find the guys I used to know is under N.Y. to L.A. in your sheet. Everything is changed—everything but the muggs I saw in a peek through your window."

Amid the sweltering heat of summer, Freeman offered *Variety* his latest Rube Goldberg notion—a vaudeville show that moves through the theater district, presenting each act in a different air-cooled lobby. "[We] open in the Paramount lobby," he explained. "After an even 30 minutes, we cross the street to the State, with a stop-over intermission in the air-cooled Astor Lobby. From the State it's just a short hop to the Palace, but we don't stay long there because it breaks my heart to see the Palace in its present shape."

With Sime Silverman gone (he died in Los Angeles in 1933 just after launching *Daily Variety*), the muggs at the paper's office in New York may have been heartbroken to see Freeman in his present shape. Twenty-four years earlier his first monologue (proposing a Broadway dating service) had appeared in Sime's new weekly: "No one in New York needs to be lonesome for little Freeman Bernstein is here."

Now, two years after Sime's death, the string had come to an end. That July 27 letter was the last time that the distinctive voice of Freeman Bernstein appeared in the pages of *Variety*.

——————

Camping in Sam's old office at 1560 Broadway at the corner of Forty-Seventh Street, Freeman kept thinking that there must be money in the writing game. Every day he read in the columns about some famous writer going to Hollywood. Just from hanging around the cigar store—hoping somebody would stake him to one—Freeman got the sense that the movies were paying through the nose for good stories.

Not only did Freeman have the stories, but some of them were even true.

So with his brother dead and the memories of the slamming cell doors in the Tombs echoing in his ears, Freeman embarked on the oddest project of his career. He set out to tell his story his way: the fictional tale of what might have been if only the breaks had gone his way and if only the fates had allowed him to cut the cards.

With the help of a shaky typist (likely Sam's secretary), Freeman composed a thirty-page story that he imagined being sold to the movies. It was typed (with a wildly wandering capital "M") on the back of borrowed letterhead from ARROW LIQUOR and WINE WHOLESALE DISTRIBUTORS, Inc. at 1619 Broadway. The manuscript—titled *Blue Money*—was eventually placed in an oversize envelope lifted from WILBAR PHOTO ENGRAVING COMPANY on West Fifty-Second Street.

The survival of *Blue Money* is nothing short of a hand-of-God miracle, a sign from on high to a nonbeliever (me) that Freeman Bernstein wanted his life story told. The unopened 1935 envelope from Wilbar Photo Engraving was found by an archivist in 2008 in a forgotten file cabinet that *Variety* was about to discard as the paper moved to smaller offices. Instead of being buried in a landfill beneath fifty tons of garbage, the manuscript of *Blue Money* eventually materialized in the show-business archives of Emerson College.

When Freeman began writing, he only had a hazy idea of what a movie script looked like. So *Blue Money* was filled with awkward references to scenes and a lack of quotation marks. But from the opening sentence of the first scene, it provided a snapshot of Freeman's blues over money. Never had autobiographical fiction been so transparent:

> At the office of Fred Howard, the theatrical broker on 47th Street and Broadway, are his chief clerk, Pat Currans and his secretary Kitty Lee. The time is the first week in July, hotter than hell . . .
>
> Howard is at his desk smoking a big Manila cigar. He sees at first glance on his desk a bill from the telephone company, on reading same there is a notice that if the same isn't paid by two o'clock this afternoon, the phone will be disconnected. He then rings for his secretary immediately and orders Miss Lee to fix a draft drawn on Seattle for the amount. . . . This will give us at least three weeks, they will have a hell of a time finding this draft paid, as the man on whom I am drawing this was dead four years. . . .
>
> His office rent is due for the last two months and he immediately send[s] for his chief clerk and says Pat find a spot in Canada where I can draw a draft, where there is no railroad. Pat a Canadian says that Elks Lake, a lonely spot in the mining country of Ontario. It will take a month to find this place. Allright says Howard

draw up a draft on the Royal Bank of Canada, Elks
Lake, Ontario for three months rent on this office.

Freeman . . . sorry, Fred Howard . . . is also five weeks behind
on his room bill at a fashionable hotel. But Howard fends off
Mr. Jeffries, the hotel manager, by tipping him off that Warner
Brothers stock is about to move and offering him a sure thing on a
horse. Since this story is Freeman's invention, Warner Brothers
immediately jumps two points and the horse gallops home victorious at four-to-one odds.

In real life, Freeman was obsessed with betting coups. His old
friend Isidore Bieber—a Broadway ticket scalper who had hustled
his way into owning the B.B. Stable—almost pulled one off in
1934 at the Empire City track in Yonkers.

Bieber raised the odds on his best horse (Anna V.L.) by pairing
the filly with an unknown apprentice jockey (R. Moon). Only a
few insiders knew that Bieber had been training Moon in secret for
just this race. But word leaked out just before post time—maybe
because Bieber bet too conspicuously—and winning tickets for
Anna V.L. paid off just seven-to-five.

Freeman borrowed the outlines of his plot from the B.B. Stable.

In Freeman's version, the horse was named Blue Money. And
his alter ego, Fred Howard, had been training him in secret at the
beach. As Howard explains, "I have a horse that no one knows
anything about, he never started. He won two races in Canada
with the cheap horses. I will have him in the Fifth Race Handicap
to-morrow, ought to be 50 to 1. . . . This horse will be eating his
supper while the other horses in the race are at the eight pole."
And, for good measure, the jockey will be an unknown apprentice
who mastered his craft at tiny tracks in Canada.

To raise $10,000 for his betting coup, Fred Howard asks Mr. Jeffries to assemble a group of wealthy hotel guests who have sporting blood in their veins. There is Mr. Rubin ("a gentleman from Shanghai"), Mr. Lion ("a retired business man"), and Mrs. Ball ("the widow of a former director of a Pittsburgh Steel Company"). Especially Mrs. Ball: "a very charming lady."

The merry widow is smitten with Fred Howard from the moment she spies him in the hotel elevator. Like many fledgling authors, Freeman struggled to write a credible love scene: "Mrs. Ball asked Mr. Howard if he was single, he says he never was loved in his life, he never had his arms around the lady's waist. Well, you can start right now, you will be the pupil and I the teacher. Fred blushed."

They were off to the races in more ways than one.

The next day, Blue Money wins by ten lengths. The betting ring collects $660,000 (with half going to Fred), as "the bookies have not been so hard hit in a good while." In celebration, "Mrs. Ball kissed Fred and squeezes him. More wine is served. . . . Mrs. Ball is now calling Howard, Fred."

The sparks from the romance between Fred and Mrs. Ball ("Blanche") leap off the typed page. Clark Gable and Claudette Colbert in *It Happened One Night* had nothing on them. Before long Blanche is telling Fred, "I have been a widow now for three years and I am too nice to be alone. I need your companionship, you are my ideal, my sweetheart. . . . Fred gave Blanche a kiss that was full of dynamite, a kiss that Blanche will remember always."

To cool things down (the Hays Commission had begun aggressively censoring movies), Freeman arranged for the happy couple to get married immediately. But, in truth, maybe a cooling hotel fire hose was also needed: "After a couple quarts and celebrating, Blanche feeling a little tipsy asked Fred if he could send down to his room for his pajamas. Why, Fred says that is old-fashioned, honey. Honeymooners don't wear pajamas anymore. Kiss me, says Blanche. Then Blanche asked if they will wear nighties, hell no, nothing, nature is the grandest thing."

Just when it was looking like the role of Blanche had to be played by Mae West, Freeman introduced a subplot drawn from life. His life.

As word of Fred Howard's double windfall (Blue Money and a rich wife) spreads along Broadway, the hotel lobby quickly fills with Fred's pals: "He is met by all the boys, that is one at a time . . . and not one was turned away. Fred was touched plenty, but he just smiled."

Yes, it sounds biblical—the silent, smiling saint giving alms to down-and-out horse players and plungers. But that was Freeman's credo: If you're touched by good luck, you help out those who put a touch on you.

Fred Howard harbored a dark secret, one that Freeman could appreciate. Fred's fame had attracted Jerry Sands, a ghost of misadventures past:

> Jerry is an old acquaintance of Fred's, that is a cellmate, they had both done time in Joliet. It seems that Fred had got into difficulties on leaving college and was sentenced for one year for passing a worthless check. Jerry was doing four years for grand larceny.
>
> Jerry says to Howard, you know that this newspaper notoriety on your big winnings and marrying Mrs. Ball, the multi-millionairess might open the eyes of the bondsman out in Chicago, as you know you slipped the bond on that second rap. Oh, hell that is outlawed, says

Fred is that what you came up to see me about. No, I came up to get a thousand dollars from you, I need it very badly. . . . Well, you aren't going to threaten me, Fred says to Jerry. Absolutely, no there is nothing copper about me. Well, I am going to give you a thousand dollars and I want you to keep away from me."

But paying hush money rarely pays. Especially since most of the members of the Joliet Alumni Association are now hanging around the lobby of Fred's hotel. In a sentence that captures the anguish long hidden beneath Freeman's confident exterior, he writes about his alter ego, "He can't sleep as his mind is on the old rap, he has to see someone of the old mob, he must not high-hat anyone of them."

Since *Blue Money* wasn't designed to be a gangster movie like *Manhattan Melodrama*, Freeman quickly erases the storm clouds hanging over Fred Howard's happiness. Fred sends an emissary to Chicago to pay off the old warrant. And he is rewarded with the kind of telegram that Freeman must have fantasized about: "Bringing dismissed indictment papers with me and also a letter from the district attorney to you, congratulating you on your good fortune and hard work."

This letter allows Fred Howard to successfully appeal his case to the only judge who matters—his new wife. "Come sit down in that chair, and let me confess, now that I am vindicated, I have nothing to hide, Howard said. . . . I endorsed a check for a pal of mine who went to college with me. It was only for $50.00. Well that endorsement jammed me up. I was put in jail, was bailed and skipped my bail. I was then indicted and all these years was a fugitive for helping a friend. But now I am a gentleman again and you see I am complimented by the district attorney."

This passage mirrors Freeman's self-image. He only went to the can after "helping a friend" by endorsing a rubber check. But now all the jailhouse stigma has been washed clean so that Fred can become a gentleman again. And reflecting Freeman's embarrassment over his scanty education, Fred Howard is, of course, a college man.

At this point, two-thirds through the scenario for *Blue Money*, Freeman abandons dramatic tension to revel in the fantasy of being rich.

Who could blame him?

Picture Freeman in reality: his face drenched in sweat, his suit worn, his tie stained, bravely scribbling at a desk in a shabby office filled with ghosts of his brother. He is subsisting on handouts from relatives and his relations with his wife, May, are presumably troubled since he never seems to go home to Far Rockaway. Okay, it isn't Dostoyevsky in Siberia. But it ain't Faulkner in Hollywood, either.

In *Blue Money*, Fred Howard gives full attention to ritzing his wardrobe so that he can be worthy of his new bride. In a ritual Freeman knows well, Fred retrieves his gold cuff links, watch, and stickpin from hock. A tailor is summoned to measure Fred for two suits with a dozen more promised if these were satisfactory. Sulka ("Shirtmakers and Haberdashers," 512 Fifth Avenue) rushes a salesman over with shirt samples and dozens of ties. To round out the Sulka order, Fred buys multiple sets of silk underwear. For, next to himself, Freeman loved Sulka best.

The result of this head-to-toe refurbishment: "Fred called his valet. In his dinner suit he looked the millionaire that he was."

A millionaire in the 1930s had responsibilities—especially when pals were in trouble. As a favor to a dying friend, Fred buys for $400,000 a circus (The Bostock Shows) complete with sixteen elephants, sixteen camels, about one hundred lions and tigers, twelve specially made Pullman cars, and enough canvas to cover an entire city. Fred also picks up for $40,000 a gym near Broadway, the Piping Exhibition Company Fighting Club.

Freeman could have given his alter ego a nightclub, a yacht, or even a movie studio. Instead, he opted for a circus and a fight club. It is telling that, even when Freeman created air castles, they were the fantasies of a sporting man who longed for the smell of liniment at ringside and sawdust under a big top.

When Fred Howard hears that the hotel in which he and Blanche have been living is teetering on the edge of bankruptcy, he buys it as well. As Freeman tells it, "Mr. Jeffries was so dumbstricken at the proposition, he said . . . how can I repay you. Mr. Howard speaks to Jeffries, you have made me the happiest man and I intend to make you the same if it's in my power. I shall never forget you Mr. Jeffries, you have a third interest in this hotel now."

The final scene of *Blue Money* (labeled "TENTATIVE FINISH") shows Fred Howard in the library of his hotel suite "smoking a large Corona-Corona cigar." Fred takes a satisfying puff and reflects, "Haven't done so bad for myself and for my pals, now that all my bills are paid that I know of." He inventories his life as a "millionaire, hotel owner, owner of a circus and not forgetting a fight club and plenty of Liberty Bonds left in my wife's vault."

In fact, Fred muses at fade out, "Next to my pal Blue Money, Blanche is the sweetest girl in the world."

During the heyday of vaudeville, *Variety* and a few other weeklies maintained a registration service for performers. Say you had a new comedy act that ended with the patient hitting the doctor over the head with the medical man's mallet. You would mail the script and maybe a photograph to *Variety*'s Registration Department. A clerk would time-stamp the envelope and file it. If somebody in Buffalo started doing a doctor skit that ended with the misplaced whack of a doctor's mallet, the original performer had ironclad evidence that he originated the act.

By 1935, this informal system had been replaced by the Writer's Guild registry for movies and other copyright mechanisms. Barely wheezing, vaudeville had much graver respiratory problems than the stealing of acts. *Variety* maintained its registry out of habit (as a hat tip to its origins) with barely a half-dozen scripts trickling in each year.

When he completed his draft of *Blue Money*, Freeman didn't know where to send it. So he mailed it to *Variety*—the place where, when he had to go there, they would take him in. Freeman scrawled on the manila clasp envelope from Wilbar Photo Engraving, "Registry Department, Variety."

On August 19, 1935, the unopened envelope was logged into *Variety*'s system. Then it was placed in a file cabinet that eventually was shipped from New York to *Variety*'s main office in Los Angeles. Freeman's literary masterpiece—a window into the soul of a con man with the heart of gold—sat unread in that file cabinet . . . for nearly seventy-five years.

16

Freeman always shaded the truth in the quest of a good story. If he were a novelist, this tendency to embellish would have made him an unreliable narrator. But as I discovered in reanimating Freeman's life, there was always a kernel of reality behind his most outlandish claims.

Which is why I believe Freeman's insistence that he visited Nazi Germany in 1935. But I'm getting ahead of the story. For in his varied and vivid retellings, Freeman always insisted that the Bogus Nickel Caper began in Shanghai.

In late 1933 or early 1934, a Jewish vaudevillian on the lam in the Orient sat down over drinks with an acquaintance from the German embassy to try to sell him jade. In those early days of the Third Reich, most members of the German diplomatic corps were not heel-clicking fanatics demanding racial purity in their business dealings.

During the conversation, Freeman remarked that he "was getting hold of a little nickel . . . out of the [jade] ore that came out of Burma, Rangoon." As soon as Freeman uttered the word "nickel," the Nazi diplomat reacted as if he had been offered a canteen of water in the middle of the Gobi Desert. The German announced that his government wanted a large quantity of nickel and would pay top reichsmarks to get it.

Freeman replied, "The only place where there is any nickel . . . is in Canada and they supply the world." He could have dropped matters there. Instead, Freeman hinted that he might know the right people in Canada and promised to investigate on his return to America.

Even then, Freeman had a glimmer of a plan.

Any country intending to invade Poland and France needed Canadian nickel. An essential ingredient in high-grade stainless steel, nickel had been used during the Great War for guns, ammunition, and armor plating. In 1916, Germany thrilled to the exploits of the U-boat *Deutschland* as it evaded the British blockade to bring home 360 tons of Canadian nickel, which the kaiser's men had acquired in New York.

Under Hitler, the Germans in 1934 switched to nickel coinage (which could be easily melted down) as a ruse to acquire this strategic metal for ostensibly peaceful reasons. The Nazi government also banned the private use of the metal for most purposes—which meant that all imported nickel was, in effect, war material.

Canadians grasped the connection between the vast nickel mines around Sudbury, Ontario, and German rearmament.

In 1934, legislation was introduced in Parliament (although not passed) requiring the government "to forbid the export of nickel to be used for war purposes." The Toronto *Globe and Mail* declared in a biting May 1935 editorial, "Canada remembers with a bitterness

still unhealed that Canadian soldiers were killed in France by German shells and bullets hardened with Canadian nickel—nickel
mined while Canada was at war with Germany." With Canada
providing 90 percent of the nickel available on the world market,
the *Globe and Mail* sniffed, "It takes no very advanced mathemati-
cian to work out how far Herr Hitler's rearmament program could
have gone in these last two years without nickel from Canada."

After Mussolini invaded Abyssinia in October 1935, the
League of Nations slapped a boycott on Italy as punishment for its
aggression against Haile Selassie's African kingdom. But Canada's
resulting ban on the export of nickel hit Il Duce with all the force
of a plateful of Chef Boyardee's canned ravioli. Since the United
States was not a member of the League of Nations, exporters only
needed to ship railroad cars filled with Canadian nickel across the
American border so the cargo could be rerouted to Italian ports.

In a world on the brink of war—with Japan in Manchuria, Italy
in Ethiopia, and Germany poised to reoccupy the Rhineland—
everyone wanted to nick some Canadian nickel. But only Freeman
Bernstein . . . broke and recently out of the can . . . had a line into
the best Canadian nickel. Or, at least, Freeman had concocted a
con to make it look like he did.

Writing *Blue Money* may have sustained Freeman with the
dream of swaddling himself in Sulka and entertaining
himself with his own circus, but it didn't pay the rent. Then again,
Freeman—even when he was flush—never paid the rent.

Faced with severe cash flow problems (no cash, no flow), Freeman mulled his options. Gone were the days when he could riffle
through May's purse in the middle of the night in quest of coin.

About the only thing he had left to pawn were pawn tickets. And somehow Freeman at age sixty-two couldn't picture himself pushing a wheelbarrow on a government construction site as part of President Roosevelt's WPA.

Then the nickel dropped for Freeman: He remembered that conversation with the Nazi diplomat in Shanghai. He had even been given a letter of introduction to a shadowy figure at the German embassy in Washington. Scraping up train fare, Freeman headed south for a rendezvous on Embassy Row. "On arrival in Washington I telephoned my man," Freeman later wrote. "His secretary took my message and then informed me that his boss would see me in an hour. I arrived at the appointed time and after my introduction, my friend was very eager in obtaining nickel scrap for Germany."

That was enough to send Freeman off in quest of what he called a "million dollar deal." It was also enough to send Freeman off to the Third Reich in September 1935 with his samples of high-grade Canadian nickel—samples that, unbeknownst to the Nazis, he had bought from a shop in Lower Manhattan.

Having braved the Soviet Union during Lenin's purges and having taken a C(r)ook's tour through the backwaters of Asia, Freeman was fearless enough to enter the Führer's realm. He also was motivated since he had been promised a $1,000 initial payment from the Germans if he could guarantee a supply of Canadian nickel.

For all his world traveler credentials, Freeman faced two problems so serious that getting there wouldn't be half the fun: no passport and no money.

Under the terms of his release from jail in New York, Freeman had surrendered his passport and had to report to his probation officer monthly. For anyone else, this would be an impediment to foreign travel. "I had no business to leave here," Freeman later admitted. "I had only 30 days to go over and come back. . . . I had no passports, you see. I came through without a passport." Explaining his ability to elude immigration authorities, Freeman boasted, "I know how to do business. I have been across for 25 years."

Freeman had never been so hard up since he first discovered the joys of card games on ocean liners. With only $110 to his name, Freeman was placed in the humiliating position of only being able to afford a $106 ticket to Bremen . . . in steerage. As Freeman wrote, "This is the first time in my many ocean voyages that I was compelled to take steerage, so this inconvenience preyed on my mind." Especially since he was forced to share his third-class room with a heavy-drinking Swede who was returning home on vacation after fifteen years in America.

"This gentleman was very fond of the ambruic [*sic*] fluid," Freeman recounted. "So instead of going to bed he would imbibe all night. Of course the circumstances were such that any sleep for me was impossible as I was persuaded too often to assist with his libation. This first night after quite a few drinks under his belt he became charitably inclined. He insisted on loaning me fifty pounds of his English money to tide me over, which I freely accepted under the circumstances, and I gave him an I.O.U."

What Freeman did next was so in character that . . . even if there had been no corroborating details . . . I would have been convinced that he did sail to Hitler's Germany.

The Swede, for understandable reasons, slept late the following morning. So Freeman left his hungover friend behind in steerage to go directly to the purser with his borrowed £50 to change "my quarters to first class so I could enjoy a good breakfast and have a little rest at the same time." For the rest of the voyage, Freeman enjoyed Swedish pancakes at breakfast while his benefactor was pancaked in third class.

(Freeman, by the way, insisted that he repaid the IOU two months later.)

Germany in 1935 was surprisingly open to foreigners, even Jews. William L. Shirer (who had been a Berlin correspondent during this period) wrote in *The Rise and Fall of the Third Reich*, "A foreigner, no matter how anti-Nazi, could come to Germany and see and study what he liked—with the exception of concentration camps." Louis Katin, a journalist with the *Palestine Post*, took a three-day bike trip through northern Germany in October. Katin did not pretend to be an Aryan: "I defy anyone to look more Semitic than myself." Aside from the inescapable photographs of Hitler in every hotel room, Katin was never harassed and witnessed nothing more ominous than a sign in a village: WARNING . . . JEWS IN THIS PLACE.

But in the fall of 1935, German Jews should have shed their last illusions that they could ride out the storm. In mid-September, shortly before Freeman arrived, the Reichstag unanimously rubber-stamped the Nuremberg Laws, stripping citizenship from German Jews and forbidding marriage with Aryans. The *New York Herald Tribune* reported in late October that desperate Jewish business owners were selling their assets at one-fifth of their value or less. During this period, Shirer sadly noted in his *Berlin Diary*, "Many Jews come to us these days for advice or help in getting to England or America, but unfortunately there is little that we can do for them."

Freeman, who claimed to have stayed at the Hotel Adlon in Berlin before moving to Düsseldorf, almost certainly attended synagogue in Nazi Germany for a mournful Rosh Hashanah (September

28–29) and may have still been there for Yom Kippur on October 7. Although there were no major outbreaks of Brownshirt violence, Jewish leaders in Cologne warned worshippers not to be conspicuous by wearing top hats in the streets on the way to synagogue. The Nazis also arrested Leo Baeck, the leading rabbi in Berlin, on the eve of Yom Kippur because they had learned that he had written a sermon refuting the Nuremberg Laws.

Freeman apparently departed Nazi Germany with the $1,000 earnest money that he had been promised since he booked his return to New York on the *Île de France*. In first class.

E ven before Freeman left for Germany, he knew that he needed a confederate in Canada—a businessman with connections in the metals trade whose flexible business ethics rivaled his own. It was a job description that fit Meyer Brenner like . . . well . . . a prison cell.

When Freeman met Brenner in Toronto in 1920, the Canadian was a callow twenty-nine-year-old playboy interested only in fast horses, faster cars, and looting his father Nathan's scrap metal business. Maturity arrived for Meyer Brenner a year later when Toronto detectives jumped onto the running board of his Rolls-Royce to arrest him for fraud. Brenner had used company funds to bet heavily on the British pound, only to be caught short when the sterling collapsed. On the hook for $700,000, Brenner did what Freeman would have done in similar circumstances—he cooked the books. And was sentenced to seven years in prison.

Inheriting his father's firm after being released from Saskatchewan Penitentiary in Prince Albert, Brenner applied for a stockbroker's license by boldly claiming that he had never been convicted of a criminal offense. The resulting indictment for securities violations did not prevent him from continuing to offer hot investment tips in publications like the *Canadian Jewish Review*: "SUDBURY BASIN MINES . . . should sell much higher in view of the possibilities of the properties they are holding."

Despite his continual legal scrapes (everything from fraud to intimidating witnesses), Brenner emerged as a pillar of the Toronto Jewish community—organizing the Hudson Tennis Club, the leading Jewish sporting club in the city. Meyer Brenner & Company ("Iron, Steel and Metal Merchants") radiated an aura of prosperity with offices in the Toronto Harbour Commission Building, a Beaux-Arts classic sitting on reclaimed land near the waterfront.

During the summer of 1935, Freeman paused in his artistic labors sculpting the manuscript of *Blue Money* to telephone Brenner about a sure thing with a bigger payoff than a racing coup. Freeman told him, "I have got a chance for you to make some money. I have got an order and if you get down here I will give you a chance to make a dollar."

The Canadian metals magnate made four trips to New York in July and August. For his meetings with Freeman, Brenner always stayed in a $5 room at the Biltmore Hotel, adjacent to Grand Central Station. Whether sitting with their heads close together in the hotel restaurant or sharing a restorative drink in Room 1148 at the Biltmore, the two conspirators looked like an unlikely pair: Freeman's multiple chins and slow-moving girth contrasting with Brenner's long, angular face and lean tennis-champ body.

The outlines of the nickel sting were in place by the time (9:34 p.m.) Brenner checked out of the Biltmore on the evening of August 15 to catch the overnight train back to Toronto. Brenner would eventually put up the operating cash and they would split the profits fifty-fifty as Freeman's reward for coming up with the nickel swindle.

When Meyer Brenner returned to New York on November 12 for a planning meeting with Freeman at the Biltmore Hotel, the two men chortled over the idea of hustling Hitler. Freeman stressed to Brenner that any nickel going to the Nazis would be used for ammunition: "They are going to kill all the Jews there in Germany and you better send them plenty of pig iron and mess it up with tin cans and have them packed and pressed."

Both men were keenly conscious of being Jewish. Brenner would soon embark on a futile battle to win admission for his Hudson Tennis Club to the WASP-only Toronto Tennis League. When the religious-based rejection became public, a Presbyterian minister told the *Toronto Star*, "It's just the sort of Jewish persecution that is going on in Germany." Freeman, of course, had been sensitive to the plight of Jews in Europe since his visit to Polish relatives in 1921—after which he described to *Der Tog* the desperation of Jewish immigrants trying to get to America.

Freeman and Brenner were also men of the world. While they would love to see the Nazis ensnared in their nickel racket, they were con men out to get the best price, not secret agents.

So they floated word in New York that they were selling more than two hundred tons of high-grade Canadian nickel—a mother lode at a time when worldwide exports equaled forty thousand tons, and almost all of that was allocated under existing contracts. The metal would be in the form of nickel cathodes: one-inch-square pieces that were ideal for coating the insides of bombs and protecting the barrels of guns from rust.

All they needed was a buyer so desperate to acquire Canadian nickel that the purchaser would agree to a few idiosyncratic conditions. For example, the bill of lading from Canada would have to be marked "scrap metal" instead of "nickel." This sleight of hand with the paperwork was necessary, Freeman would explain, to get around the de facto Canadian embargo on the unauthorized export of nickel.

Successful swindles depend on the complicity of the mark. Freeman knew that the key to pulling off the con was getting the purchaser to agree to a false bill of lading while still paying full freight for the nickel. That way, a series of irregularities could be explained away as an effort to evade Canadian customs. Both buyer and seller would be on the hook since illegally exporting strategic materials like nickel from Canada was a grave offense. The entire transaction required honor among thieves—which was a credo that Freeman never had signed up for.

Freeman would later begin telling his version of the nickel swindle like this: "I first met Otto Kafka, president of Otto Kafka, Inc. . . . [when] Kafka was then acting as an agent for the German Reichstag and engaged in exporting for the Nazi Party materials to be used for the purpose of warfare." Freeman went on to claim that he had been given Kafka's name in Düsseldorf as the Nazis' preferred metals agent in New York.

Otto Kafka (cable address: "OTTOKAF") was Franz Kafka's first cousin. Yes, that Franz Kafka.

Rather than being regarded by his literary cousin as a trial or an annoyance like a cockroach, Otto Kafka was seen as an inspiration. As the family's most successful émigré in the New World, Otto Kafka served as the model for a major character in his cousin's 1912 novel *Amerika*. "Particulars of Otto Kafka's life and aspects of his personality may be discernible in the character of Senator Edward Jakob," Anthony Northey writes in his academic study *Kafka's Relatives*. "In the novel he moves with great resolution towards any goal he has set himself. Nothing seems to deter him. . . . Otto Kafka possessed similar traits."

Born in Prague in 1879, Otto Kafka hopped a freighter to Buenos Aires when he was eighteen. After killing a man in Argentina in 1906, Kafka fled to New York where he got his start at Warner Brothers. That was, of course, Warner Brothers, the corset makers. Finding the corset trade too confining, Kafka soon ended up in the export department of the Cambria Steel Company. Before long, in only-in-Amerika fashion, Kafka was running his own company (Vulcan Steel Products), exporting to neutral countries in Europe while the Great War raged.

Even though still a subject of Austria-Hungary, Germany's ally, Kafka excelled as an America-based war profiteer. When the United States entered the war in 1917, Kafka had a net worth of $500,000 (about $9 million today). But the War Department quickly deciphered the secret of his success: "Kafka's cables were intercepted and it was definitely proven that he was trading through neutral countries for the benefit of Germany." Kafka's estranged wife, Alice, also told authorities that her husband "was violently pro-German; that he glorified and justified the sinking of the *Lusitania* and in the loss of American lives aboard the steamer."

In August 1918, Kafka was imprisoned as a dangerous enemy alien. The *New York Times* noted that he was "one of the wealthiest enemy subjects resident in this city." He was not paroled until January 21, 1919, more than two months after the Armistice with Germany was signed.

Kafka never fully recovered from his foolhardy bet on the

kaiser. In a bitter 1923 divorce trial, he claimed his fortune had vanished, partially because of his wife's extravagance. But by 1934, Kafka had scrambled back to his familiar niche as a war profiteer. His sale of shipbuilding steel and plating to an unnamed European power (presumably Germany) was considered such a major transaction that it was featured in the stock-market column of the *New York Herald Tribune.*

On January 8, 1936, Meyer Brenner telephoned Otto Kafka from Toronto to offer him more than two hundred tons of bootleg nickel. Laying it on thick, Brenner told Kafka that he would soon be hearing from a "thoroughly reliable" business associate.

Thirty minutes later, the Thoroughly Reliable Freeman Bernstein showed up at Kafka's office at 2 Rector Street lugging a twenty-pound bag of nickel samples just purchased from his favorite small-time dealer in Lower Manhattan. Like an Arrow-collared businessman, Freeman crisply ticked off the deal terms: thirty-two cents a pound for the nickel cathodes to be delivered to either a Canadian port or an American port no farther south than New York. Kafka or his associates could inspect the nickel in Canada and be assured of the validity of the title.

Freeman was persuasive: Kafka's secretary typed up a deal memo for the sale of 225 tons of nickel cathodes. A key provision called for Freeman to "agree to facilitate in every conceivable way . . . inspection by giving our agents full access to the material wherever located."

At times, though, Freeman's manner did not fit the business recommendations of *How to Make Friends and Influence People.* Freeman was cagey about his office address and suggested that he might be living with relatives in Poughkeepsie. Scheduling a follow-up meeting in Toronto with Kafka and Brenner proved tricky since Freeman kept saying that he first had to go to Pennsylvania to collect

$2,000. And, as the Reliable Mr. Bernstein prepared to leave Kafka's office with the deal memo, he suddenly asked to borrow $100. After telephoning Brenner in Toronto, Kafka reluctantly handed Freeman the one hundred smackers, though it took him five hours to raise the cash.

The trio of nickel fanciers (Messrs. Kafka, Brenner, and Bernstein) was supposed to meet in Toronto on January 19, but Freeman did not show up as planned at the Royal York Hotel. A few hours later, Freeman called Kafka (collect) from New York with an explanation: He had missed him in the crowd at Grand Central Station and, as a result, had no way to pay his fare. Once again, after checking with Brenner, Kafka wired $25 to Freeman (care of: Western Union, Grand Central Station) so that he could take the overnight train to Toronto.

When Freeman finally straggled into Toronto, Kafka insisted on changing the deal memo. "I told Mr. Brenner," Kafka later recounted, "that since apparently Mr. Bernstein was ambulant, since he had no definite place of business, I could not possibly contract with him for the purchase and sale of the material offered; however, that I would contract with Mr. Brenner."

Freeman might have argued that he did have a fixed place of business—anywhere that he could make collect calls and receive money from Western Union. But he agreed to the changed terms of Kafka's contract: Brenner was now listed as Freeman's "agent" and the merchandise was "consigned to [a] German port."

Even though Kafka returned to New York with a signed agreement in his pocket, negotiations were, in fact, just beginning, for Freeman and Brenner were already scheming to do better than Kafka's offer.

Their nickel lode was attracting the kind of fortune seekers who quested after the Maltese Falcon. Otto Kafka could have doubled for the sniveling Joel Cairo while Freeman himself was, of course, the rotund and devious Kaspar Gutman. In fact, Gutman's line from the 1929 Dashiell Hammett novel summed up the life philosophy of everyone caught up in the Great Nickel Chase: "I do like a man that tells you right out he's looking out for himself. Don't we all? I don't trust a man that says he's not."

Metals dealer Stephen Meade had also caught the nickel bug. The Hungarian-born Meade (who looks very Mittel-European in a surviving photograph of him on a white horse in riding gear) was the author of the indispensable classic *Meade's Manual on Steel and Metals*. But the finances of Meade Steel and Metals Company were shaky—and the thirty-nine-year-old Meade was struggling to satisfy the social ambitions of his wife, who imagined him as an American diplomat. Meade did maintain strong international relations with one foreign nation: Mussolini's Italy. As he later bragged, "The banks have recommended me as the only man with whom the government should deal directly."

While there were other bidders, none of them matched the eagerness of the Italians in trolling for nickel in New York. Romolo Angelone, the commercial attaché at the consulate, was willing to go as high as forty-four cents a pound for two hundred tons of nickel cathodes—and was dangling a $100,000 line of credit to back up his offer. In fact, Angelone boasted, "We have millions of dollars."

The Italians also had millions of delivery problems. To avoid the League of Nations boycott, the nickel would have to be shipped to the Austrian free port of Trieste. Germany was out of the question as an intermediate destination for the Canadian nickel heading to Italy. An agent for the Italians explained in a letter to Meyer Brenner, "It will not be possible for us to accept this material for shipment to Hamburg, Germany, for the reason that we cannot obtain any binding assurances that the merchandise upon arrival will not be seized by the German Government. . . . A recent shipment of 110 tons of this material was actually seized by the German Government upon arrival in Germany."

(In early 1936, Mussolini and Hitler were not yet buying their jackboots at the same shoe store. Both dictators dreamed of dominating Europe and were wrestling for influence over Austria. It took the Spanish Civil War, launched in July 1936, to create the Axis of fascist powers.)

Freeman and Meyer Brenner must have been overjoyed by their good fortune. With a few rumors, they had created a bidding war for their Canadian nickel. Already, the price per pound had jumped from thirty-two cents to forty-four cents. Every new potential buyer meant that Freeman and his Canadian co-conspirator could credibly threaten to scuttle the deal if anyone objected to their terms.

The problem, as with so many of Freeman's rackets, was getting paid. Otto Kafka, in theory, controlled the nickel, since he had the deal memorandum with Brenner, acting as Freeman's agent. In reality, Kafka was as broke as Germany after the Treaty of Versailles. Kafka had sneered at no-fixed-address Freeman, but his claims to business legitimacy were equally dubious. As Kafka confided at the time, moaning about the calls to Toronto, "My telephone bill is large and my telephone was disconnected."

Kafka's chances of obtaining a personal line of credit were less than the odds of obtaining privacy on a party-line telephone. At the same time, Stephen Meade kept having to fend off desperate clients: "The Italians want to buy and the Austrians want to buy, and nobody seems to have nickel."

Nobody, except Otto Kafka.

But Meade recoiled at Kafka on sight, especially after the shady Nazi agent began their conversation by demanding to be reimbursed for prior expenses: "I spent $1,500 in Canada. I tracked this down and I got this material. Now, if you can give me $1,500 I will make a deal with you." Meade snapped back, "You can't get it. If you want to sell nickel that is one thing, if you want to borrow money that's another thing."

Yoked together like two prisoners on a chain gang, Meade and Kafka headed to Montreal on February 3 to try to negotiate a joint deal with Freeman's Toronto-based partner Meyer Brenner. (Mr. Bernstein was in Toronto on other nickel business at the time.)

When they were finally seated across from each other in the club car, Otto Kafka ordered drinks and a full dinner with everything going on Meade's tab. Short of cash himself, Stephen Meade began shouting at Kafka, "You are a crook. I don't say that you are a crook at heart, but you do things which are crooked in the commercial sense of the word."

But it wasn't until they arrived in Canada that Meade recognized a real crook. After meeting Meyer Brenner for the first time, Meade said to Kafka, "This guy impresses me as a racketeer." Kafka responded with the warning, "You have to handle this man like a silk glove."

In truth, Meade would soon need an army of silkworms to handle Brenner. Meade may have thought that he was a hard bargainer by the standards of the American Society for Metals, but now he was dealing with three gentlemen who had spent time behind bars: Freeman, Brenner, and Kafka.

However, for the moment, it was Kafka who faced a metamorphosis. By the time the meeting in Montreal was over, Stephen Meade had a newly signed contract for all the nickel at thirty-five cents a pound. And Kafka was left on the scrap heap. Freeman and Brenner had figured out that—despite Kafka's Nazi ties—they didn't need him to sell to Germany or anywhere else. In fact, when Kafka tried to write a new contract on the spot, Brenner dramatically ripped it into tiny pieces.

What about our old friend Freeman Bernstein, the Pet of Times Square, the Jade King of China, and the Dark Knight of Nickel? How had he been spending his time in Toronto?

Exuding prosperity, Freeman had printed new stationery for F. Bernstein Metals with the same office address as Meyer Brenner. But beneath the fancy letterhead, Freeman was reduced to staying in third-class hotels and once was forced to return to New York on a bumpy bus.

But mostly, Freeman spent his time in Toronto arranging the little things needed to make the nickel deal work. Little things like inspection, packing, shipping, and . . . oh yes . . . coming up with the metal specified in the contract with Meade.

In his labors, Freeman was assisted by business associates of Brenner, mostly Jewish, though not the sort you would be apt to find on the dais at a B'nai B'rith dinner. Particularly useful was John King, who was later described in legal documents "as being in his early 30's, about 5'6" tall and weighing around 145 pounds. He appeared to be of Jewish nationality." The well-dressed King (his natty wardrobe was often contrasted with the shabbiness of Freeman's suits) not only served as an efficient lieutenant, but he also boasted such useful skills as being able to command day laborers loading metal in a warehouse.

In early February, King dropped by the offices of Toronto junk-metals dealer Pincus Mehr, who specialized in the resale of the materials like the carcasses of Model T Fords and crumpled bumpers from discarded Maxwells. Mehr quoted King a price of $8 per ton for what was known in the trade as a Number Two Bundle—automotive scrap and old railroad tracks pressed into seventy-five-pound blocks. Anticipating a large shipment from Pincus Mehr, King then contracted for storage space in Toronto with the Terminal Warehouse Company and Verral Storage.

Meanwhile, the owner of F. Bernstein Metals arranged with Kaplan Custom Brokers to handle a shipment of unspecified material that he would soon be exporting. With a flurry of activity, Freeman also purchased 561 wooden packing cases from the Brochard Box Company suitable for shipping nickel and retained a weight inspector for the cargo (James Madden).

Everything now depended on the one firm that could queer the deal—the impartial metal analysts who would certify the purity of the nickel.

On February 3, Freeman telephoned the Charles Warnock Company, a Montreal-based concern with a tiny outpost in Toronto, just a single room divided by a partition. The secretary, Miss Willis, referred Freeman to James Keane, the only inspector currently in the office. Freeman discussed with Keane the rates for analysis of an unidentified metal cargo. The phone call ended with Freeman's implicit promise to soon send business Keane's way.

It sounded like a standard business conversation similar to thousands that occurred that day in Toronto. Except, in reality, both Freeman and Keane were playing parts in a play produced for the benefit of Miss Willis and anyone else who might have overheard them in the cramped Warnock office.

Keane, who was known as a "tough mug," had just joined the

Charles Warnock Company. Meyer Brenner had either known or sensed that Keane's loyalties were subject to the whims of the free market. So, at an earlier secret meeting, Brenner and Freeman made him an offer that did not require much metallic analysis to accept. Keane would get $5,000 in two installments if he took a permissive approach to certifying that the nickel cargo was genuine.

On February 10, Pincus Mehr sent seven freight cars loaded with Number Two Bundles rumbling across Toronto. Accompanying them was an eighth car filled with broken automobile brake drums. Their destination: the warehouse space that had been reserved by James King. Payment terms: King gave Mehr $2,101.17 in cash, with the money coming from the Meyer Brenner nickel supply fund.

Keeping the charade going, Freeman wrote on February 13 to the Charles Warnock Company ("Attention: Mr. Keane") requesting that a representative be sent "in order to sample a quantity of Cathodes." The letter, typed on the fine stationery of F. Bernstein Metals, set out rigorous conditions: "You are to open every tenth container at random and take two samples out of each."

But, oddly enough, Keane kept running into obstacles when he tried to comply with these instructions. When Keane visited the Verral warehouse on February 14, King informed him that the nickel wasn't yet ready for inspection. Three days later, Keane was told to go to the Terminal Warehouse where he found King supervising a team of laborers hoisting three-foot-square boxes filled with some form of heavy metal. As Keane later recalled, "King told me it would be very difficult to obtain samples at the time due to the position of the cases, but volunteered to take them for me in order to save time."

Moved by this altruistic gesture, Keane returned at the end of the day to pick up the scientifically selected samples. The trusting metals inspector accepted without hesitation King's assurance that the nickel samples had been randomly taken from ten different cases. Keane, the picture of innocence, later claimed, "I had no knowledge at the time as to what the cases contained."

When Freeman received the testing results from Keane's firm, they confirmed his hopes: The cathodes contained more than 99 percent nickel with a smidge of iron. Of course, Freeman shouldn't have been surprised—that figure was identical to the makeup of the bag of nickel cathodes that he bought from his favorite metals dealer in New York.

Desperate for immediate shipment of the nickel, Stephen Meade made two trips to Toronto to confer with Meyer Brenner at the Primrose Club, the city's leading meeting place for Jewish businessmen. Even though the Toronto playboy could never entice Meade into a friendly game of billiards, he proved adept at snookering the New York metals dealer.

Take the way Freeman's partner, Brenner, swatted down Meade's concerns that an obscure firm (Warnock) was doing the metals analysis. Meade couldn't understand why Brenner wasn't using the industry leader, Canadian Testing Laboratories. In a tone that suggested that Meade must have arrived in Toronto on a turnip truck, Brenner explained that Canadian Testing was under the thumb of the nickel cartel. "They might pass word along to the nickel company," he said, "and we would not want to be in a position to be questioned."

Meade had a secret of his own: His company was on the rocks—and we're not talking about a nickel mine. At the beginning of February, the balance in the Meade Steel and Metals Company account at Irving Trust was just $992.94. Even with the help of a credit line from Irving Trust, Meade could only buy one freight car load at a time. What this meant was that instead of Meade being able to sell the nickel in a single two-hundred-ton batch from his home base in New York (with the Nazis as likely purchasers), he had to scramble to find paying customers before the metal left Canada.

The first Canadian National freight car (CN 580963) filled with Pincus Mehr's finest lumbered out of the Terminal Warehouse on February 19, heading for the U.S. border. Its bill of lading said that it contained seventy-three cases of nickel cathodes. Two days later Meyer Brenner and his assistant, Leo Bochner, met with Stephen Meade in New York to show him the results of the Warnock metal analysis proving that the cathodes were as pure as Ivory Soap (99.44 percent nickel). Satisfied with the Warnock findings, the bill of lading, and the weigh master's report, Meade, using borrowed money, scrawled a check for $21,965.85 to Meyer Brenner as the agent for Freeman Bernstein.

But nickel smuggling carried risks. Immediately after returning to Toronto, Brenner called Meade to warn him that a railroad official was in his office asking suspicious questions about the cargo. The only solution, Brenner said, was to divert the freight car onto a siding and wait for a few days.

Sensing that his buyer, Meade, was becoming skittish, Brenner immediately raced down to New York with his secret weapon: Freeman Bernstein of F. Bernstein Metals.

Meeting at the Biltmore Hotel, they told Meade how lucky he was that the freight car hadn't continued toward the American border. As Freeman put it, "Because the government is investigating, we want to lay low for a little while, but the car will eventually be shipped to a seaport. This will eliminate suspicion on the part of the government."

In truth, the Canadian Mounted Police were keeping a close watch on CN 580963 now en route to Halifax. On February 29, the Mounties impounded the freight car in Brockville, halfway between Toronto and Montreal. But after holding the freight car for three days—and giving it a closer inspection than it received in Toronto—the Mounties couldn't figure out a reason to block the export of Canada's best scrap metal.

Just to be on the safe side, Brenner had also employed political clout: Samuel Factor, the first Jewish MP from Ontario, intervened regularly with the Canadian Ministry of Justice. As Factor wired Brenner at one point, HALIFAX CUSTOMS AUTHORITIES HAVE RECEIVED BY TELEGRAPH INSTRUCTION FROM OTTAWA TO RELEASE CAR 580963.

With one freight car inching its way toward Halifax and seven more waiting to be loaded in Toronto, Meade had everything— except a buyer for his two-hundred-ton stash of what he naively believed to be impossible-to-get Canadian nickel. In early March, Meade made several sales calls at 25 Broadway to African Metals, a subsidiary of the Belgian corporate octopus that controlled the copper mines of Katanga. African Metals had no compunction about reselling to the Nazis or anyone else.

Meade—ever the patsy—brought with him a bag of nickel cathodes, the same well-traveled pieces that Freeman had originally purchased just a few blocks away. In his eagerness to make the sale to African Metals, Meade claimed that the weigh master, James Madden, had seen the cargo and recognized it as nickel. In reality, Madden later said that he had never checked the contents of the freight cars: "It would have been a lot of work to sample any [cases] in the car after they were loaded nailed [shut]. . . . The temperature was 6 or 7 degrees below zero, so things hustled along."

Just as General Winter defeated Napoleon at the gates of Moscow, so too did the harsh Canadian climate help bring victory to Freeman and Brenner.

Meade's strongest selling point was the metallic analysis describing the cathodes as more than 99 percent pure nickel. But following standard business practice, African Metals required additional sampling. No problem for Freeman, since he had the inspection racket down pat in Toronto. John King salted preselected bags of scrap metal by putting the nickel cathodes on top. When James Keane, the bent metals inspector, came by the warehouse for a new round of testing, King steered him to the right bags.

On March 7, African Metals formally accepted Meade's offer to buy the bulk of his nickel at a price of 43.33 cents per pound with delivery to Hamburg guaranteed. By the end of the month, Meade had made other sales to Anglo American Metals and Ferro Alloy Corporation (shipping to Hamburg through Gothenburg, Sweden) and the International Selling Corporation (destination: Rotterdam, Holland).

Stephen Meade must have been overjoyed. He was picking up a middleman's profit of about eight cents on each pound of metal he sold—so his theoretical reward for doing business with Freeman and Brenner totaled more than $32,000.

But it was Freeman who had the right to sing "Happy Days Are Here Again." Two years after he got the first inspiration for a racket in Shanghai . . . four months after he and Meyer Brenner figured out how to hustle Hitler . . . two months after he was staying in fleabag hotels in Toronto . . . Freeman had pulled off the biggest heist of his career.

Stephen Meade deposited six checks adding up to $149,682.04 in Meyer Brenner's account at the Bank of Nova Scotia. Brenner then wrote four checks to F. Bernstein Metals with the last one dated April 6. Freeman's take was $116,588.35 (the equivalent of about $2 million today). Freeman was miraculously, uncharacteristically, and all too briefly rich.

Freeman had learned an enduring lesson during his two decades booking vaudeville shows and circuses—when to get offstage. Sensing that certain metal dealers might soon find ways to express their displeasure with him, Freeman decided that this was a perfect moment to take a slow boat to China.

To do so legally, Freeman was back in court in New York City on March 3, 1936, successfully petitioning to lift the rigorous terms of his probation over those bum checks at the New Yorker Hotel. He would now be permitted to leave New York State at will (instead of by sneaking across borders) and only had to report to his probation officer by mail every three months. Freeman was a free man until 1938, when he had to appear in court in person to show his repayment record.

The first shipment of nickel left Halifax on March 13 on the freighter *Liberty* en route to Hamburg. A second load followed on March 23 aboard the *Drottningholm,* stopping at Gothenburg before it docked in Hamburg.

From his days as a silent movie producer of historical epics, Freeman would have known how to film the scene in Hamburg:

The camera would pan the waterfront as stevedores lowered the packing cases from Toronto's Brochard Box Company onto the dock. Hulking in the background would be a squadron of Nazi SS men in black uniforms with polished boots and sidearms guarding against sabotage. A German government official with a pince-nez and a clipboard would be standing ready to inspect the precious hoard of Canadian nickel. As a dockworker cracked open the first packing case, there would be a moment of baffled silence as out tumbled burlap bags filled with rusted railroad tracks, mashed Canadian auto bodies, and dented tin cans. That moment of puzzlement would quickly give way to jackbooted rage as the Nazis slowly realized that they had been hustled by two Jews from North America.

In reality, the owner of the cargo, African Metals, hired a local photographer, the aptly named Otto Reich, to document the hoax on the Third Reich. The photographer took a dozen pictures of the imported goods displayed against a brick wall on the Hamburg docks. While Reich's images are fuzzy—especially eight decades later—you can tell that the cargo is scrap metal.

Pincus Mehr's Number Two Bundles had safely arrived in Hitler's Germany. The Nazis would not be making any nickel-plated armor or ammunition from this shipment.

17

The 1936 crossing from Hong Kong to Seattle by way of Manila was one of the last ocean voyages of Freeman's life. And the saddest. For he had just learned that May Ward had died.

The July 5 cable—sent care of the Dollar Steamship Lines ("Orient and Round the World")—had chased Freeman from Shanghai to Hong Kong. Once Freeman received the news from New York, he raced to make the evening departure of the *President Jefferson*, which had been delayed in port for three days for repairs. It would take Freeman three weeks to get to New York, but in his grief it was the only thing he could do.

Freeman had left New York in April because he had decided that returning to Asia as the Jade King was safer than waiting around Broadway to be nabbed for the nickel deal. He knew that May had been battling a long illness (presumably cancer). But he never imagined that they wouldn't be celebrating their thirtieth wedding anniversary together in December. He never imagined that May would be dead at fifty-five before he returned from the Orient.

During their three decades of marriage, Freeman and May had gloried in nights out on the town at Hammerstein's Roof. They had reveled in fur coats and (soon-to-be-hocked) jewels. They had, between them, filed for bankruptcy four times. They had hit the heights of vaudeville (star billing for May and her Dresden Dolls) and the depths (busted in Hartford). They had turned May into a silent movie star and then watched as their celluloid dreams were cut to ribbons by a censor's scissors. And they had raised their champagne flutes in celebration on the high seas before fleecing the gullible with their Anniversary Hustle.

Sure, they had bickered for decades over money, going through each other's pants and purses at night looking for coin. Their marital theme song might well have been "Oh Promise Me" attached to a stack of IOUs. As Freeman once said, "Well, I don't blame May. She always stood for my touches, and often I nearly took her roll."

The marriage wasn't always Fred Astaire and Ginger Rogers dancing their way across Rio. They hit the rocks for a while when the charlatan Sig Wallace mesmerized May while Freeman screamed, "White slavery." And, in May's defense, perhaps Freeman tarried a little too often in the Caribbean with traveling troupes filled with blondes.

But through it all, they stayed together (mostly) because they understood each other (completely).

As May told her husband early in their marriage, "Freeman, I always get you before you start." Both May and Freeman were clever, crude, fun, and fearless. Hungering for the limelight, they shared the same resilience in the face of bill collectors, bankruptcies, and bad breaks. And through it all—even the sad times when May was left with only her dogs for company and Freeman was down to one shabby suit—they had displayed a zest for life and an optimism that the next phone call, the next dice roll, the next racket would make everything right.

The funeral was small. The paid death notice for May Bernstein in the *New York Times* noted that the services would be held at her home in East Rockaway. The only obituary for the vaudeville star appeared in *Variety*—and it ran a mere fifteen lines. It summarized her career in just two sentences: "Miss Ward was a singer and derived her billing from the Dresden doll costuming and production background in which she appeared. Her act usually included a line of girls."

She was buried in a Jewish cemetery (Mount Judah) in Queens as May Bernstein. Her tiny estate, just $500, was left to her husband. Freeman later dedicated his memoir to "my beloved wife May Ward Bernstein." He also described the soubrette whom he first booked into the Trocadero for three nights in 1905 as "my inspiration, she was from the day I set eyes upon her."

Freeman finally made his way home to New York in early August. His mourning was private—very private—because, as he feared, he had been indicted for grand larceny over the bogus nickel deal. And the police were rumored to be staking out the Bernstein house in East Rockaway.

On July 21, a Manhattan grand jury had charged Freeman along with his four Canadian confederates: Meyer Brenner, Leo Bochner (the courier for Brenner), James Keane (the crooked metals inspector), and John King (who had bought and loaded the scrap metal). The indictment asserted that the five men had conspired to "defraud a certain corporation called Meade Steel and Metals Company" by selling them "not nickel cathodes, but, on the contrary . . . scrap steel."

By defining New York–based middleman Stephen Meade as

the victim, the DA's office had taken the subsequent buyers and Nazi Germany out of the equation. It wouldn't have mattered legally, since the United States still had normal commercial relations with the German Reich in 1936 and wasn't abiding by the League of Nations boycott of Italy.

Worried far more about the police league than the League of Nations, Freeman cut short his funereal visit to New York and took off for California one step ahead of the sheriff. He had vamoosed by the time probation officer Abraham Simon got around to actively searching for him on August 21. When Simon arrived at the small house in East Rockaway, Sam Bernstein's widow met him. May Ward's sister-in-law proved to be as uncooperative as a nervous witness to a mob slaying: "She was unaware of Freeman Bernstein's present whereabouts at the time and had not heard from him for approximately one month and did not know when he would return."

Freeman had headed west with a dwindling supply of cash— despite having landed the biggest fish in a lifetime trolling for suckers.

Meyer Brenner had nicked most of his roll. Yes, $116,000 had been deposited in the Toronto account of F. Bernstein Metals at the Bank of Nova Scotia. But Brenner could make withdrawals and had bled Freeman dry. Freeman grumbled that every time he asked Brenner for his share of the Nazi loot, "He sent me some chili con carne: that's what I got."

The switcheroo symbolized Freeman's career. In Shanghai, he came up with the idea of swindling the Nazis over nickel. In Germany, he got the name of the original fall guy (Otto Kafka). But because he didn't have the cash or the connections in Canada to pull off the racket on his own, Freeman had to bring in Meyer Brenner. And, as Freeman sadly discovered, Brenner was not a business partner to be trusted.

Freeman had left Canada with $10,000 in his pockets. But traveling to China first-class cut into his coffers, as did acquiring the precious stones (and the sparkling paste) needed for his comeback as the Jade King. In Los Angeles, with the help of the Pacific Finance Corporation, the sporty Freeman splurged on a second-hand Ford convertible with a rumble seat. And Freeman could never say no to a touch, which contributed to his cash woes. As he put it, "You understand that I am no piker when I have money."

But for the first time in his life, Freeman was running scared. His time in the Tombs had left him with a fear of doors that only locked from the outside. Freeman stayed at the plush and private Garden of Allah Hotel in Los Angeles for a while under an assumed name. He was so nervous about being arrested that he asked a friend to write a dunning letter to Canada on his behalf because Freeman worried that his handwriting might be recognized. The note on the Garden of Allah stationery told Freeman's Toronto solicitor and longtime friend, Richard Greer, "I am in hock here and to wire me two hundred. I am using the name of L. Adley."

Using an alias was not up Freeman's Adley. He had spent more than six decades facing up to what life offered as Freeman Bernstein, the grifter with the heart of gold. He had too much pride to slink around for long, pretending to be someone else. Also, anonymity was bad for business. The Jade King couldn't drum up customers by pretending to be a commoner operating under an assumed name.

Freeman jettisoned his nom de guerre in the most public way possible—by giving an interview to the *Los Angeles Times* in December 1936 about the jade business. Billed as "Freeman Bernstein, world traveler and 'jade king' of Shanghai, China," he was holding court at the El Mirador Hotel in Palm Springs. But in a catch-me-if-you-can challenge to the police, Freeman announced that he would soon be departing on a jade-hunting jaunt by taking a clipper ship to Manila and then flying on Royal Dutch Airlines to Bangkok.

Ever since he ran his first carnival on an island in the Hudson River, Freeman had been playing dodgeball—ducking landlords and dunning phone calls, legal writs, and grand larceny indictments. But he had always assumed that if he could disappear for a while, it would all blow over.

That was part of his rationale for making this second trip to the Orient in late 1936. Returning from Bangkok to Los Angeles, he discovered to his horror that the New York district attorney's office was still serious about tracking him down. In addition, Stephen Meade—who had been forced into bankruptcy by the nickel deal— was spending every nickel that he could round up on private detectives to locate Freeman.

Now a peddler like his father—albeit with a bag of jade— Freeman washed up in Boise, Idaho, with a bad case of the flu and an even sicker exchequer. In desperation, he wired Dick Greer in Toronto, hoping that the solicitor could squeeze some money out of Meyer Brenner. But the Western Union lines from Canada remained silent. Eventually Freeman had to bail out of Boise because, as he later explained, he was "dodging coppers."

Throughout his career, Freeman understood how easily appearances are confused with reality. Which is why he gravitated to Hollywood, the town of glittering surfaces. After coming up with a bit of cash from either a touch or a jade sale, Freeman returned to L.A. like a potentate. The room at the Garden of Allah (this time under his own name) and the chauffeured limousine all suggested that he was a successful businessman without a care in the world.

The masquerade worked when he went calling on Mae West on

the night of February 18. She immediately sensed that it was jade in his pocket and he was glad to see her. But Mae West, who picked up on Freeman's flimflam, never sensed that he was one bad break from a breadline. There was a big difference between describing Freeman as "shady"—as she did in her autobiography—and dismissing him as seedy.

Even Freeman's arresting officers were gulled by his facade of prosperity. From the moment Detectives Johnnie Erickson and Jack Koehn pulled Freeman over in his chauffeured limousine in front of the Brown Derby, they knew that they were dealing with a celebrity felon rather than a run-of-the-mill fugitive. That was why Freeman was put on display the next morning (Friday) for a press conference instead of being left moldering in a cell block trying to make a nickel phone call to a lawyer.

The script that Freeman wrote overnight in his bunk at the Hall of Justice was a far more professional literary vehicle than his film treatment, *Blue Money*. Freeman understood how to appeal to the guys with press cards in their fedoras better than most Broadway publicists. For decades, he had created headlines as easily as Tin Pan Alley created hits. "You mustn't pay attention to newspaper reports after I give an interview," Freeman cautioned Dick Greer in a letter. "Yes, Dick, I put on a show for them and I thought it was pretty good."

Freeman's stroke of genius was to heil Hitler himself rather than just talking vaguely about the Nazis. In all of the 1936 correspondence surrounding the nickel deal, there were no references to the Führer nor was Herr Hitler ever mentioned during Freeman's conversations with Meyer Brenner and Otto Kafka. But meeting with reporters at the L.A. jail on Friday morning, Freeman suddenly played the Schicklgruber card.

In every interview, Freeman invoked Hitler more often than a speaker at a German American Bund rally. As he told the *Los Angeles Times*, "I went visiting in Germany about a year ago. They introduced me to Hitler at Dusseldorf. Der Fuhrer was pretty down in the mouth, because the iron embargo passed by the United States had hurt 'em badly. He begged me to find some metal. Then I moved to Canada and established offices to handle his order."

The idea that Hitler—preoccupied with rearming the Rhineland and the 1936 Berlin Olympics—would make a personal appeal to a Jewish swindler from New York is as ludicrous as the Führer taking time to memorize his Torah portion for his bar mitzvah. But Freeman flogged the Hitler connection as a way of elevating his own importance. Mostly he portrayed himself as a martyr of the Nazis and his prosecution the result of trumped-up German justice. But now and again, Freeman forgot himself and made it sound like his idea of fun was fly-fishing with the Führer. His malady might be called Con Man Confusion—a grifter's desperation to impress so intense that sometimes he dropped the wrong name and it clanged like an anvil.

Ever since he wiggled out of his first arrest in Troy a half century earlier, Freeman knew firsthand that the law balances on the head of a technicality. His thin veneer of legality was that the Canadian export documents from the Nazi nickel had been marked "scrap metal." Freeman soon convinced himself (mostly) that Hitler had gotten precisely what he paid for. He wrote to Dick Greer in Toronto from his cell in the Hall of Justice that never had there been a "more legitimate transaction in the world than the one [I] made with the Nazis. The scrap market today is three times what I charged them."

Of course, Freeman and Meyer Brenner had paid Pincus Mehr in Toronto $2,100 for his bundles of rusted auto bodies, railroad tracks, and brake drums. And they then sold the junk metal for nearly $150,000—a markup of more than seventy times.

F reeman was performing different kinds of math as he adjusted to his first weekend in jail. He counted his daily meals and came up with only two: hot dogs for breakfast and lima beans cooked with pork for dinner.

Mostly Freeman was calculating the odds on making his hefty $25,000 bail. Having already skipped bail twice, he reckoned that any bondsman would demand at least fifty cents on the dollar. Freeman knew that his L.A. friends wouldn't come up with $12,500, despite the confident courtroom assertions of his lawyer, John E. Ford. And, for the first time in his life, Freeman faced the reality that—even if things got desperate—he couldn't call May or his brother Sam for help.

He also worried about having enough shekels to avoid being sent back to New York in shackles. Battling extradition would require unusual legal maneuvers and a hearing before Republican Governor Frank Merriam. Pretty soon his attorney was going to realize that the limousine and the Hollywood name-dropping were Freeman's props—and, in reality, his high-profile client didn't have the personal resources to fight a $2 parking ticket.

His oldest friend in the world, John Considine (who had hired Freeman in 1906 to book vaudeville acts for his Sullivan-Considine circuit), was in and out of the hospital at age seventy-five with heart problems.

So everything depended on the Jade King's connection to authentic Hollywood royalty—Joseph Schenck, the cofounder of 20th Century-Fox, whom Freeman had known since the new century was in its swaddling clothes. The two men had gone their separate ways since Schenck (in partnership with Marcus Loew) had operated an amusement park in Fort George next to Freeman's Trocadero Music Hall. But even though Schenck never came up with Freeman's bail money, he proved to be a potent ally.

As a New Yorker who only followed politics when there was a buck to be made, Freeman didn't know that Joe Schenck had played a major role in getting Frank Merriam elected governor in 1934.

In his chronicle of the 1934 gubernatorial race, *The Campaign of the Century*, Greg Mitchell described Merriam as "an old war-horse as out of step with trend-happy California as a silent movie.... He was sixty-eight years old and looked every day of it. Behind his back many of Merriam's associates called him Old Baldy." Merriam had been finishing out a lackluster political career in the largely ceremonial post of lieutenant governor. But Old Baldy was elevated into the top job upon the death of the incumbent governor in June 1934.

What turned this California election into an epic contest was the August 1934 Democratic primary victory of utopian radical Upton Sinclair with his plan to End Poverty in California (EPIC). Suddenly, the Bolsheviks were at the gates—and the only thing standing between California and a purported Red takeover was Frank Merriam.

With Louis Mayer detained in Europe, someone had to take the lead in protecting Hollywood against Upton Sinclair's left-wing insurrection. "It was none other than that inveterate womanizer, master of the malaprop ('Don't cut off the hand that lays the golden egg') and exemplar of Hollywood decadence—United Artists president Joseph M. Schenck," Mitchell wrote. In apocalyptic statements to the press, Schenck warned that Sinclair's election "would be the end of California." And to punctuate the threat, Schenck announced that he would immediately move his studio to Florida if Sinclair became governor.

Schenck never had to leave Hollywood, since three days after the election Upton Sinclair began dictating his latest book, *I, Candidate for Governor: And How I Got Licked*. But now more than two years later, Governor Merriam again needed Hollywood support as he planned to run for another term in the increasingly Democratic state. So Merriam was ready to follow the guiding principle of politics: Never cross your supporters unless you really have to.

Schenck's big gift to Freeman was providing him with an unlikely attorney—Greg Bautzer, a twenty-five-year-old nightclubbing clotheshorse who soon would be dating Lana Turner. Up to now, Bautzer's only significant case had been the divorce trial of a C-list starlet. His office at 6253 Hollywood Boulevard was so small that Bautzer and his law partner put a name plaque on a closet door to suggest that there was a second room.

Bautzer, who was on the same party circuit as Schenck, understood how Hollywood worked. When he graduated from USC Law School, he immediately borrowed $5,000 to set himself up in private practice. Rather than spending the wad on a law library, Bautzer acquired the wardrobe of a matinee idol. Lunching at the Brown Derby every day in a different suit, tipping the maître d' lavishly to guarantee a prime table, the handsome young lawyer soon became a well-known man about town. As James Gladstone wrote in his biography of Bautzer, *The Man Who Seduced Hollywood*, "He devised a plan based on dressing to impress potential clients. He thought that if he looked successful, it would bring in business."

Bautzer immediately realized that he needed a two-pronged strategy to fight Freeman's extradition. A plausible legal argument was required to give Merriam a fig-leaf justification to turn down the routine request to return the prisoner to New York to stand trial on felony charges. But Bautzer also needed to remind the governor that Freeman's influential supporters were California voters and campaign contributors while the Manhattan DA's office was three thousand miles away.

Even though he was young, inexperienced, and distracted by Hollywood nightlife, Bautzer was a smart enough lawyer to find the biggest flaw in Freeman's indictment: Every important step in the carefully orchestrated plot to defraud Meade Steel and Metals Company had taken place in Toronto. As Bautzer argued in one of the first legal filings of his career, "Assuming, for the sake of argument, that a crime was actually committed, the state of New York is absolutely without jurisdiction, since all the transactions were conducted in Canada, and more important, payment to Bernstein made on the Bank of Nova Scotia, a bank located in Toronto." Bautzer added that "the Canadian authorities . . . refused, when the matter was presented to them, to institute any criminal proceeding, contending that the matter was civil in nature."

In mid-February, the Manhattan DA's office sent two detectives to Los Angeles to escort Freeman home in anticipation of Governor Merriam granting the extradition request. Grover Brown, the police department's expert on financial crimes, was familiar with the fugitive: The detective had retrieved him from Washington in 1935 after Freeman had turned himself in for jumping bail on the bum check charges. His partner, Detective Charles Dinegar, had worked on the Lindbergh kidnapping case and had recently recovered for Mrs. Irving Berlin a $300 gold cigarette case inscribed TO ELLEN WITH MY LOVE ALWAYS, IRVING.

Staying in plush hotels (the Biltmore in Los Angeles and the

Senator in Sacramento), Brown and Dinegar were secretly thrilled that New York had decided to reward them with an extended California vacation. But in their frequent telegrams and letters back to the DA's office, the two detectives kept stressing the existence of hidden forces at work delaying Freeman's extradition. As they complained in a joint letter, "It appears that the governor was looking for a way out and had seized upon the [legal] subterfuge."

Beyond such legal niceties, Freeman had already made the strongest possible case for his own freedom with his jailhouse press conference. He was, after all, a victim of vengeful Nazi justice. Sending Freeman back to New York would be like exiling Donald Duck to Siberia.

The anti-Hitler publicity barrage worked.

A March 7 telegram was sent to the governor by Robert Butts, who identified himself as the president of the Young People's League for Anti-Nazi America: OUR ORGANIZATION COLLECTIVE BELIEVE THIS PROSECUTION TO BE FURTHER INDICATION OF HITLER PERSECUTION OF JEWS. Octogenarian Los Angeles civic leader John Randolph Haynes wrote Merriam to say, "Anyone who can gyp one dollar or one hundred thousand dollars from the emissaries of a nation which has destroyed freedom of speech, press, assembly and religion should receive a gold medal and praise."

The governor's top aide, Frank Cochran, wrote a confidential memo in early March advising against extraditing Freeman: "The newspapers have carried stories of this case intimating that this is an attempt by the German government, or their representatives in New York, to persecute a Jew, and I understand that several influential Jews in Hollywood are friendly to this individual and feel that this is merely an attempt to persecute him."

Brown's and Dinegar's notes to the Manhattan DA's office were filled with warnings about Hollywood's growing support for Freeman. They wrote on March 9, "The Motion Picture interests as personified by Mae West and Nick Schenck have interested themselves in Bernstein." (Nick Schenck, Joe Schenck's younger brother, was the president of the Loews Corporation, founded by Marcus Loew.) Another note featured disturbing news: "From confidential sources we learned that Al Jolson contributed $200 to the fund being raised on behalf of Bernstein." Meanwhile, the two New York gumshoes discovered that Bautzer was trying to obtain an affidavit from the Department of Justice proving "that Kafka was a German spy and in the employ of Adolf Hitler." (The document from Washington never surfaced.)

Freeman had hoped to get out of the can following Bautzer's March 9 hearing in front of the governor. Instead, Freeman's can opener vanished when Merriam gave both sides thirty days to file additional legal papers. The delay proved a disappointment, since Freeman had been afflicted with painful neuritis in his arms and legs from the chilly nights in the steel and concrete fortress. Even though his bail had been reduced to $15,000, Freeman still couldn't come up with it.

So, in characteristic fashion, Freeman set out cheerfully to make the best of a bad situation. If he had to do extended time on a weight-loss regimen of two meals a day, he would do it with a smile on his food-deprived face. Just as Freeman in happier times had no problem chatting up the Duke of Windsor, so too was he willing to give the most downtrodden of drunks and pickpockets a dose of the Bernstein charm.

All this led to one of the oddest, but most genuine, tributes that Freeman ever received. A neighbor at the Los Angeles Hall of

Justice—a scribbler known as the "Prison Poet"—dashed off a few lines in Freeman's honor:

> There isn't a person in this whole jail
> When to barber you go, greets you a "hail"
> For all have heard and read your story
> And know that man that made Hitler "gory."
> Suffice to say whatever your trouble
> You haven't been a cheap air bubble,
> For you've spread your money and big cigars
> From the lowest prisoner to those that were stars.

Although his fellow prisoners didn't know the details, Freeman fiercely adhered to the code of those who spend their lives on the wrong side of the law. Initially sounded out about a possible deal that involved ratting out everyone else in the Nazi nickel racket, Freeman refused to play stool pigeon to win his freedom. As he scrawled in a jailhouse note to Greer in Toronto, "The first quick [offer] they made to me is if I gave the lineup they will have me exonerated. Not me, Dick. Am not built that way."

Sensing that their prized fugitive was slipping away from them, the two New York detectives visited Freeman twice in his cell at the Hall of Justice. As Brown and Dinegar reported in a March 26 letter to District Attorney William Dodge, "We advanced several arguments designed to impress upon Bernstein the necessity of coming back to New York voluntarily, but we found that he was more concerned about the parole warrant. He again reiterated his belief that he would beat the metal case, but was afraid that he would be severely punished for the parole violation."

Freeman understood that he was facing double jeopardy in New York.

Under the terms of his probation agreement on the bum-check charges, he was obligated to appear before a Manhattan judge on March 3, 1938. But if he showed up in court, he would be immediately arrested on the nickel charges. Without a rigged wheel or crooked dice, Freeman couldn't figure out a way to win. By his reckoning, the best he could do would be to sit in the Tombs for months (once again unable to raise bail) while his lawyers tried to prove that the Nazis had really wanted to buy scrap metal instead of nickel—and that the entire deal took place in Canada.

Freeman did make a tentative offer to Brown and Dinegar to return to New York to stand trial on the plugged-nickel charges if the DA would drop the parole matter and, more important, guarantee that he would face minimal bail. But Freeman's heart wasn't in it. When the two detectives asked Freeman to put his proposal in writing, the prisoner suddenly developed writer's cramp. As Brown and Dinegar theorized in their letter, "We gathered that he wanted time to talk with Schenck and Considine."

Perhaps inspired by a new board game called Monopoly, Freeman in the end opted for a California "Get Out of Jail Free" card.

The final legal filings in the extradition case strengthened Bautzer's argument that this was a case for the Mounties rather than the Manhattan DA's office. Meyer Brenner, who had been resisting Freeman's pleas for bail money, did deliver a last-minute telegram from Toronto: ALL PURCHASE PACKING WEIGHING AND INSPECTION OF METAL MADE IN CANADA STOP ALSO CONTRACT EXECUTED AND ALL SHIPMENTS AND PAYMENTS MADE IN CANADA STOP.

Freeman's ailing friend John Considine (who contributed $1,700 toward his legal bills) proved a game-enough trouper to compose an implausible affidavit under oath. Considine—who had once got away with shooting an ex-sheriff in Seattle—claimed that Freeman had written him ten letters postmarked Toronto while the nickel deal was taking place. Of course, Considine couldn't produce any of them since "said correspondence . . . was of a personal nature and was therefore discarded and destroyed."

Considine, in fact, rose from his sickbed to serve as a star witness during a successful three-hour hearing on Freeman's fate in Governor Merriam's office on April 7. The freedom-for-Freeman outcome was summarized in this headline from the *New York Post*: "Bernstein the Junk Dealer Ties a Can to Hitler & Co."

While Merriam prepared a formal letter to New York Governor Herbert Lehman rejecting extradition, Detectives Brown and Dinegar telegraphed the DA's office with the news: BERNSTEIN EXTRADITION DENIED. REASON AFFIDAVITS UNABLE TO PLACE BERNSTEIN IN NEW YORK.

Paperwork delays kept Freeman in his blue denim prison uniform for an extra day. But when he faced the newspaper boys on April 8, Freeman mugged for the flashbulbs with the joy of the showman who once claimed that he had arranged a British match race for Man o' War. "Give me a cigar, boys, and I will tell you all about it," Freeman announced as he held court from a desk in the Hall of Justice. Before long—with a fresh cigar between his teeth—he was raising his right hand in a mock Nazi salute in a picture that appeared on the front page of the *Los Angeles Examiner*.

Retelling the Nazi saga, Freeman stressed a new name: the Commander in Chief of the Luftwaffe. After he once again described Hitler "on bended knee" pleading for nickel, Freeman name-dropped,

"General Goering also did some pretty hard begging." Then Freeman added a line that summed up his con man's belief that the Führer got what he paid for: "I knew Hitler didn't have anything on me."

As Freeman got ready to walk into the Los Angeles sunlight, he said, "Not only is California justice the real thing, but so are the people. I have decided to make Los Angeles my home." He even talked about opening up a high-end jade shop for discriminating customers in Beverly Hills.

After seven weeks in the big house, Freeman was a free man. Or, at least, as free as he could be with the knowledge that he still had a date in a Manhattan courtroom on March 3, 1938.

Once again Freeman was famous, as he was during the years when *Variety* lovingly chronicled his escapades on Broadway. Of course, not all the portrayals would have pleased him. The United Press wire story described him as a "mammoth individual with big jowls and three chins." And the headline in the *Wisconsin State Journal* in Madison veered toward the anti-Semitic: "Jew Denies Gyping Hitler in Junk Deal."

But Freeman was also a Jew who wanted to send a Bronx cheer special delivery to Berlin.

That's why he would have been pleased by a letter of protest forwarded to Governor Merriam by the American Chamber of Commerce in Berlin. These U.S. businessmen were prospering from their see-no-evil dealings with the Nazis. Their letter complained about "the fraudulent delivery of nickel cathodes to Germany approximately a year ago" and demanded to "know the reasons for Bernstein's release."

The underlying message in the letter sent from the chamber's offices at 56 Unter den Linden was: We don't handle justice like that here in Berlin. Especially when a Jew hustles Hitler.

18

In 2000, I escorted my father—then past ninety, slow moving but eager to get around—to the New York Public Library to search for himself and his family in a microfilmed copy of the 1910 census. The years leading up to World War I had been a prosperous time for my father's family, and he was on a quest to discover whether his parents owned or rented the house in which he was born, the vintage farmhouse at 500 Audubon Avenue in Upper Manhattan.

My father probably mentioned that his uncle Freeman had owned a theater nearby in the Fort George section of Manhattan. But it never occurred to me . . . why should it? . . . to walk the sixty feet to the card catalog to look up Freeman Bernstein. Twenty steps and then bending over to open the old-fashioned library file drawer. That was all it would have taken to vindicate my father's fascination with his wayward uncle. For if some strange hunch, some magnetic lure of family history had propelled me forward, I would have discovered Freeman's forgotten masterwork. Sitting unread in the stacks of the public library for more than six decades was a 1937 self-published and self-serving booklet titled *Was Hitler's Nickel Hi-Jacked?*

Not until 2011—seven years after my father died—did I discover the existence of what Freeman had billed as "The STORY of the CENTURY." My archaeological find was made possible because the *New York Times* in the 1930s dutifully recorded in agate type every new book that was sent to the paper, even self-published pamphlets. A listing in the November 28, 1937, *New York Times* drily summarized Freeman's autobiographical account as "an American businessman's experience in dealing with Hitler." (The *Times* probably would have described *Moby-Dick* as "an American maritime man's experience in dealing with a large white mammal.") That ancient newspaper clip belatedly led me and my wife, Meryl, to the New York Public Library's catalog.

At the time, my journalistic career was going through a temporary phase that theater folks might euphemistically describe as "between engagements." The Bureau of Labor Statistics would have preferred a blunter description: "Unemployed." But everything changed when a library attendant handed me Freeman's magnum opus. As I began reading with amazement, I said to Meryl, "They say that when times are tough, you can always depend on your family. But this is ridiculous."

That was the moment, if you're wondering, this book began.

In 1937, Freeman left L.A. lockup bristling with anger at Meyer Brenner. Not only had the Toronto scrap metals dealer looted Freeman's account at the Bank of Nova Scotia, but he also refused to contribute bail money. In fact, when Brenner's lawyer, Joseph Singer, briefly visited Freeman in jail, he gave him $5, the sort of tip that a high roller might drop on a shoe shine boy.

As a free man, Freeman was at liberty in more ways than one.

Financially, he was back in his natural state—flat broke. With his benefactor John Considine in the hospital, Freeman barely had enough for carfare, let alone a convertible. In that April 23 letter, Freeman explained, "I am going to give up that car today. I have paid for half of it, but John Considine being sick and being back on the payments, I am not going to be worried about a car right now."

For all his glib talk about opening up a refined jade shop in Beverly Hills, Freeman's finances were too jaded for such a burst of respectability. In the past, a desperate Freeman could always figure out a way to wangle his way back into show business—a carnival, a circus, a trip south of the border, a rigged game of ring toss . . . anything. But now, Freeman conceded, "I cannot get in the show business here as I haven't got the dough and as I tell you that you wear your friends out after you go to them once or twice."

In his new home at the Marsden Apartments near Hollywood Boulevard, Freeman reviewed the last year or so of his life in an effort to answer the existential question: Who can I sue?

Even though the William Morris company had always cashed his checks (a triumph of hope over experience), Freeman recalled that he had urged novelist and screenwriter Rex Beach to sign with the talent agency. Like Freeman, Beach had sought his fortune in the Klondike gold rush, returning with enough stories to earn the moniker "the Victor Hugo of the North." As Freeman filed a $5,000 nuisance lawsuit against the William Morris Agency, he must have known that he faced better odds panning for gold in the Los Angeles River.

Freeman always prided himself on his self-reliance, boasting to his Toronto friend Dick Greer, "No man has ever supported me!" That's why during the summer of 1937, Freeman realized that he would have to write his way out of the corner. After all the headlines about his tying a tin can to Hitler, Freeman figured that it was time to tie a feed bag to the free publicity.

His first step was hiring (a word that in Freeman's lexicon did not necessarily imply payment) old-time Broadway publicist Maurice B. Haas to provide the literary polish and spit shine. *Variety* had described Haas as an "ex-scribe, ex-horseman [and] ex-boulevardier." Fate may have washed Haas (like Freeman) up on the West Coast, but his heart belonged to Times Square. As Haas once put it, "I'd rather be broke on Broadway then have a ten-spot anywhere else, any time."

The fruit of their literary collaboration was a forty-seven-page booklet printed on slick paper with a heavy cardboard cover, a little smaller than the *Reader's Digest*. A photograph of Adolf Hitler wearing a brown shirt and a Nazi pin stared menacingly from the cover. Directly below the Führer was an oversize red question mark. It punctuated a query that was on everyone's lips: *Was Hitler's Nickel Hi-Jacked?* And the answer was available to anyone who would plunk down four bits wherever dubious brochures were sold.

The pamphlet began with Haas's four-page retrospective of Freeman's career, written with the ballyhoo of a magazine cover predicting flying cars: "His uncanny faculty of anticipating the public wants, likes and dislikes enabled him to foster many new ideas of entertainment as well as promotions which have netted him many millions of dollars." Haas then listed some of the performers Freeman had put on the stage: "Al Jolson at $20 per week, Will Rogers, who received $40 per week; Eddie Cantor received his first job from him at $20 a week, and Sophie Tucker received $10 for just working on Sunday."

The biographical sketch ended with an ode to Freeman's late-in-life status as the most peripatetic world traveler since Magellan. As

Haas wrote, "I can truthfully say that he is known intimately by cap-
tains and pursers of every steamship line in the world." Left unsaid
was that Freeman probably owed money to every purser on every
steamship line in the world.

When Freeman (with the help of his amanuensis) began to tell
the tragic tale of a nickel deal gone bad, he faced a daunting artistic
problem: He couldn't decide how to present his story in a way that
was both sensational and made him look good. So Freeman the
Unreliable Narrator veered in all directions like a wobbly marathon
dancer. On one page, Freeman came across as a bigger foe of the
Nazis than Winston Churchill and the Anti-Defamation League
rolled into one. But a few pages later, reflecting his Con Man Confusion, Freeman was name-dropping Joseph Goebbels and buddy-
buddying Adolf Hitler.

In the preface, Freeman depicted himself as an unyielding foe
of fascism: "In writing the full account of my dealing with Herr
Hitler and the German Government, I do not wish to pose as a
martyr in the eyes of the American public, for the fact that I am of
Jewish faith and having been an accessory to a hoax perpetrated on
Herr Hitler . . . I offer no apologies for my conduct to Herr Hitler
and the German Government."

If only Freeman had maintained this high-minded tone through-
out his booklet. But fidelity to the truth was never his style—especially
when he thought there was money to be made by embellishing it. So
Freeman shamelessly invented details to turn "The STORY of the
CENTURY" into the biggest heist since Jason stole the Golden
Fleece.

In Freeman's latest version of the story, the nickel deal was so
vital to the Nazis' war plans that not only was he summoned to
Germany in September 1935 (plausible), but that also the Führer

demanded to personally inspect the nickel samples (about as likely as Freeman rolling craps with Joe Stalin).

When Freeman docked in Bremen, he was taken off the ship by the German police (always plausible in Freeman's case). And then he was escorted to the Hotel Adlon in Berlin, where supposedly the only food available was starvation rations of sawdust-filled pumpernickel bread and American condensed milk. (There were periodic German food shortages in 1935, but going hungry at the Adlon was as likely as getting short-sheeted at the Connaught in London.) With Hitler on the move, the Nazis provided Freeman with a chauffeured limousine to catch up with the Führer in Düsseldorf. (A standard courtesy offered to all Jewish guests of the Reich.)

Arriving early in Düsseldorf, Freeman did what any Aryan might do if given a few extra hours: "I strolled around the town and found in the Jewish quarters a restaurateur who saw that I had a good breakfast."

So with blintzes on his breath, Freeman joined the crush at Town Hall in Düsseldorf at ten fifteen, expecting to wait hours to see the Ruler of the Third Reich. But all it took was twenty minutes. As Freeman recounted the story, "At last, the thing I had tried so many times to picture in my own mind was coming to pass; evidently the room to which I was taken was Hitler's office. I knew how many Americans had tried to see him but failed . . . so I realized I was quite a privileged character to be admitted to the august presence."

Wait, it gets worse: "As I entered Hitler's office he was seated behind a large flat top desk. I was introduced just as I entered, giving him the Nazi salute."

I would have loved to have seen how Groucho Marx might have played this Heil Hitler scene.

The entire passage makes me cringe, even though I doubt that Freeman actually met Hitler. Why did he write it? A theory: Freeman had become a confidence man who had lost confidence in the future. He had become a grifter losing his grip. And that desperation—that need to impress strangers—led him in alarming narrative directions.

As a fledgling author, Freeman struggled with literary pacing. The story bogged down for a few pages as the Führer sent out the nickel samples to be assayed. During the long wait in Hitler's outer office, Freeman recalled that Hermann Goering "seemed to take an exceptional interest in me personally, possibly due to the fact of his hatred for the Jewish faith."

But it became all smiles and *sieg heil*s when Freeman's nickel checked out as good as promised. But then a new obstacle blocked German-Jewish rapprochement—Freeman's demand for his promised $1,000 down payment in American dollars. Hard to believe, but the German Reich didn't have a grand on hand.

Or so Freeman claimed.

Picture the scene: Freeman and the Führer—two men of the world with large, yet unfilled, dreams—chatting amiably as they waited for the $1,000 to be flown to Düsseldorf from Cologne. Even though Freeman only spoke a smattering of German, the Führer was fluent in English, a biographical detail mysteriously overlooked by later historians of the Third Reich.

Not surprisingly, given their overlapping interests, the conversation soon turned to America and the Jewish problem. Freeman offered his own solution, which was an appeal to German self-interest with a few extracts from *The Protocols of the Elders of Zion* thrown in. The idea, like some of Freeman's old monologues in *Variety*, was alternately astonishing and appalling:

Herr Hitler, the majority of the wealth in America today is in the hands of former German Jews and I think you are too smart a man to drive money out of Germany. Of course, I do not want to tell you what to do, Herr Hitler, as you are a smart man and a brave man, but if I were you I would cater to the Barney Baruchs, the Guggenheims, who control the smelting business in the world; Mr. Morganthau, Treasurer of the United States, and men like Governor Lehman of New York State, who I know if you would ease up, you could get all the assistance necessary to challenge the world. As you are one of the biggest men today, why not cater to the big money?

When Freeman finished his ode to the power of Jewish Money, the Führer laughed and said, "Well, we'll get along and God will help us." Then, as Freeman told it, "Hitler said that he would decorate me some day as I had come to his rescue and he expected me to return in a couple of months for a social visit. I said goodbye and good luck to all around the room and gave them the Nazi salute and left the portals of Germany's superman."

Actually, Freeman didn't get far. At the terminal in Düsseldorf, a Nazi customs officer purportedly pocketed Freeman's $1,000 down payment from the nickel deal just before he was to board his train to Brussels. Furious, Freeman raced back to Town Hall demanding to see the Führer. He had to settle for Goering, who sent Freeman back to the station with two soldiers to successfully recover his money.

The story was almost certainly fanciful, but it is nice to imagine Freeman as the only Jew ever to leave Nazi Germany with his exit tax personally refunded by Hermann Goering.

Around this point in the narrative—completely out of the blue—Freeman offered a testimonial to his true loyalties. Stapled with no explanation into the text of the pamphlet was an October 1937 note to Freeman from the Santa Monica Lodge of the B'nai B'rith. The letter thanked Freeman for "the wonderful and inspirational talk you gave us. . . . Your talk was one of the best that this lodge has even listened to and will long remember."

Meanwhile back at the nickel racket: Freeman then devoted four pages to the loading of the "scrap metal" in Canada, without ever mentioning his co-conspirator Meyer Brenner. Everything was hush-hush: "Owing to the embargo on merchandise going into Germany we were compelled to be very secretive and ship to Rotterdam, Holland."

But somehow—and, yes, this strains credulity—there were soon rumors that something was rotten in Rotterdam. Having built his career around fast exits, Freeman knew when to skedaddle: "Fearing that someone may have double-crossed me, I immediately paid all bills, closed my office in Toronto and . . . chartering a plane, I left for Portland, Oregon, and in a few days took ship General Pershing to Manila."

By now (page 32), readers may have been getting restless waiting for the solution to the mystery that originally prompted them to plunk down fifty cents: "Was Hitler's Nickel Hi-Jacked?" So Freeman, who could always intuit when an audience's attention was flagging, provided his answer in a single run-on sentence:

> During the prohibition era I had heard numerous times of the word "hi-jack," the meaning of which I was informed meant that a shipment of alcohol or whisky on its arrival was found to be water, but surely did not

think this could happen with supervised shipments of merchandise.

Freeman appeared to have been the victim of one of the oddest coincidences in maritime history: A ship carrying nickel to the Nazis was hijacked by another freighter that, by chance, was carrying precisely the same weight in scrap metal. No wonder Freeman concluded, after a lifetime of failed rackets, "All is not gold that glitters."

Then Freeman, in a head-spinning ideological shift, spent eight pages denouncing Nazi Germany.

Forgotten was Freeman's Nazi salute, the promised medal from the Führer, and the planned social visit to Berchtesgaden. Instead, Freeman began vying with Walter Winchell as America's staunchest opponent of the Third Reich:

> Those concentration camps are "Chambers of Horrors." "The Hole of Calcutta" are palaces compared to them. Not only the Jews are put there, but those poor Catholic Priests, the Sisters of Mercy and Sister Superiors are living a life of hell.
>
> They are given the rottenest of foods after the maggots get their first chance, then these human beings get what is left.
>
> It is really impossible to describe the pitiful conditions existing in these concentration camps.
>
> Whole families have been known to disappear over night from their neighborhood. No one knows whether to a concentration camp or to a morgue. . . .
>
> The Jew in Germany is now in the period of annihilation.

There are no Jewish children attending school with Nazi children.

There is not one professor of yesterday of the Jewish race holding forth in the schools today. . . .

Everything is being done to discourage the Jew so that he will leave Germany forever.

At the rate of the number of Jews who have left Germany in the past two years, it is with absolute truth that I say the Jewish race will soon be no more in Germany for generations to come.

Freeman's dire prophecy may have been inspired by his (probable) visit to Hitler's Germany. Or he may have derived it solely from the 1937 news clips ("BERLIN CURTAILS JEWS' USE OF PARK BENCHES") that dotted the final pages of his pamphlet. But, as Freeman learned from his days in silent movies, the last reel matters far more than the opening scene. And so Freeman hoped to win credit for his mid-pamphlet conversion to anti-Nazi fervor.

Sales of *Was Hitler's Nickel Hi-Jacked?* were modest—and only seven copies are known to remain in existence. But Freeman's literary efforts did inspire a small, but loyal, fan club: The Manhattan district attorney's office bought four copies.

On the back page of the pamphlet, Freeman included an ad promoting the coming sequel: "Watch for Story of My Life . . . 'FORTY YEARS OF ESCAPADES' . . . Entitled 'THE TRIALS AND TRIBULATIONS of a TRANSGRESSOR' . . . An Inside Story of KINGS, QUEENS, SULTANS, MAHARAJAS AND

MOVIE MOGULS I HAVE HOBNOBBED WITH . . . Out Soon by FREEMAN BERNSTEIN . . . Price $2.00."

But even when Freeman was trying to make an honest living as a literary man, the trials and tribulations of a transgressor continued.

On December 13, a few weeks after Freeman became a published author, Dr. Berthold Frey rushed to the Marsden Apartments on an early-morning emergency call. The Vienna-trained physician found Freeman gasping for breath and "unable to pass gas to any extent." Dr. Frey noted "indications of a severe heart condition" but refrained from telling Freeman about "the gravity of his case for fear of psychologically inducing another attack." (This may have been the only time Freeman was ever regarded as psychologically vulnerable.) The doctor's prescription: three weeks of bed rest and round-the-clock nursing care.

With the ever-loyal John Considine paying the bills, Dr. Frey visited Freeman twice a day for almost two weeks. Responding to a second emergency call on the day after Christmas, the doctor found that Freeman's "cardiac symptoms seemed more pronounced." Dr. Frey quickly discovered the reason behind Freeman's deteriorating condition: The patient was rambling around the apartment and even—horrors—sometimes leaving home. Dr. Frey, a harsh taskmaster, took away Freeman's bathroom privileges and ordered him to spend the next six to eight weeks in bed.

How sick was Freeman?

Dr. Frey in a legal deposition stated that Freeman's "heart could not, with any degree of certainty, stand the strain of many more such attacks." The physician declared that Freeman's late-December 1937 electrocardiogram showed "severe myocardial damage . . . as well as evidence of coronary thrombosis."

In layman's terms, Dr. Frey was saying that it would be

inadvisable for his patient to bet on tomorrow's races since he might not be around to collect. And—just to be on the safe side—Freeman should keep his loaded dice on his bedside table in case he needed to roll them to get through the Pearly Gates.

As a cynical investigator (think Sam Spade), I sought a second and even a third medical opinion. Miraculously, a copy of Freeman's EKG from 1937 still survives—and I showed it to two cardiologists. Dr. George Philippides, a friend, concluded, "This was a minor heart attack that caused minimal damage." Dr. Mark Sotsky, a relative, concurred: He noted that the electrocardiogram was ambiguous, showing either mild deterioration or a relatively healthy heart.

Despite this modern medical consensus, I am convinced that Freeman believed that he had a serious heart attack. Overweight and afflicted with ailments ranging from bowel problems to the neuritis he developed in jail, Freeman was approaching his sixty-fifth birthday, the official retirement age set by Franklin Roosevelt's new Social Security Act. Reluctant to ever display weakness, Freeman nonetheless passed word to *Variety* in January that he was "set for long rest on doctor's orders."

Not until mid-February did Dr. Frey permit Freeman to rise from his sickbed for a few minutes at a time. He suggested Freeman might consider moving to a sanitarium in Palm Springs or the nearby desert. Instead, Freeman worried about getting his just desserts on the other side of the continent. On March 3, Freeman was obligated, under the terms of his probation, to report to Judge Otto Rosalsky in Manhattan. In person. Or else.

As the deadline approached, Freeman consulted with his lawyer, Greg Bautzer, who was a trifle preoccupied at the moment. The *Los Angeles Times* reported on February 13 that Bautzer was seen at a horse show in Pacific Palisades "with a new titian-haired beauty decorating his arm." The decoration was Lana Turner on the cusp of her seventeenth birthday. The young, handsome, impeccably dressed Bautzer was her first lover. As the MGM actress wrote in her autobiography, "Greg was loving and patient with me, even though I had no idea how to move or what to do."

With Freeman, Bautzer knew he had to move fast. On March 2, the legal Lothario telegraphed the chief probation officer for Manhattan courts: DOCTORS CERTIFICATE RE BERNSTEIN EN ROUTE AIRMAIL HOLD ANY ACTION LETTER FOLLOWS.

The follow-up letter featured Dr. Frey's dire diagnosis of Freeman: "His condition is such that any procedure involving him in great stress, either mental or physical, might well bring on a further anginal attack and possibly cost him his life." Dr. Frey was suggesting that the rigors of heading east in manacles could sentence Freeman to the death penalty for the crime of writing bum checks.

The medical argument might have convinced a judge in New York that Bail-Jumper Bernstein was a frail old man, except that Freeman made a baffling decision in late March that jeopardized his freedom. Instead of continuing his convalescence under the warming desert sun in Palm Springs, Freeman opted for the ice-cube cure.

Accompanied by a nurse, Dorothy McKichney, Freeman was driven fifteen hundred miles north to continue his recovery at the most obscure health spa in North America—the Gull Lake Sanitarium in Gull Lake, Saskatchewan. Rounding out the party was a Filipino chauffeur, Macario Gaming, and a Scotch terrier named "First and Last." The Los Angeles–based chauffeur and his auto were almost certainly lent by John Considine, while the dog was Freeman's most loyal retainer.

Why Gull Lake, a tiny dot on the map ninety miles north of the Montana border?

With Freeman, the simplest explanation was always that he was running a racket—and had figured out a way to defraud Canadian rustics in the middle of the Depression. When Freeman was released from the L.A. jail in 1937, he thought about trying his luck in Toronto or Winnipeg. As the luckless Jade King put it then, "I can make more money around Canada than I can here right now."

Another possibility: Dorothy McKichney, who had relatives in the area, was providing Freeman with more than just nursing services.

It is certain that the weather in Gull Lake was not an attraction—unless Freeman had developed a late-in-life passion for curling. The curl-your-hair Saskatchewan temperatures only edged above freezing for two days during all of March.

Soon after being exposed to Gull Lake's restorative frigid air, Freeman was stricken with his third heart attack in three months. He was immediately transferred to the eighteen-bed Gull Lake Union Hospital where he remained for five days. On March 30, Dr. John Mathewson scrawled a brief "To Whom It May Concern" note stating that Freeman was afflicted with "heart disease and fecal impaction." I will resist the temptation to draw larger psychological conclusions from the revelation that the most openhearted of confidence men, my great-uncle Freeman, was suffering from acute constipation.

Freeman left Gull Lake by car a week later, declaring a modest bankroll of $11 (about $180 today) when he crossed the border at Turner, Montana. But by the time Freeman reached Butte on April 13, he was a fabulous invalid. He booked a suite at the Finlen Hotel, which had been modeled after Freeman's favorite Broadway watering hole, the Hotel Astor.

In the late 1930s, Butte was a fading mining boomtown as

the Depression chilled worldwide demand for minerals. Copper mines pitted downtown and the air was so acrid that Dashiell Hammett fictionalized Butte as "Poisonville" in his 1929 novel, *Red Harvest*.

Freeman's arrival in Butte prompted a two-column story in the *Montana Standard*: "MAN WHO SHIPPED HITLER NICKEL WHICH ARRIVED AS SCRAP IRON VISITOR HERE." The article portrayed Freeman as a vaudevillian and circus man "who topped off a colorful career in an affair with Hitler—costing him his freedom for several weeks." These days, according to the un-bylined story, "Bernstein has been knocking about from one part of the universe to another, with dogs as his pet fancy."

The unsuspecting reporter fell for Freeman's flimflam. "First and Last," who Freeman claimed to have purchased for one hundred pounds in Edinburgh, was supposedly the sire of a Scottish terrier in the Black & White Scotch ads. The article stated as fact that Freeman's arrest in Los Angeles on the nickel charges was "at the request of the German ambassador in Washington." As for the nickel itself, it had been "pirated somewhere between Canada and Germany."

Even though Freeman continued to insist that he had been granted an audience with Hitler himself, he also sounded as passionately anti-Nazi as any soapbox orator in Union Square. "No one knows how many Hitler has already put to death," Freeman thundered. "People disappear and nothing is ever learned regarding their fate. Hitler is a cannibal—nothing less."

Wherever he went—from Japan to jail to Germany—Freeman went out of his way to ingratiate himself with the locals. This back-slapper style reflected both his natural gregariousness and a grifter's belief that new friends might someday become newer marks.

Even though he was lingering only a day or two in Butte, Freeman was careful to tip his hat to the local tourist board. "There is only one Butte," he told the *Montana Standard*. "I have circled the globe many times and mixed with kings, princes and paupers. But there is no place like Butte."

When Freeman finally returned to Los Angeles on April 20—with the beauty of Butte only a fading memory—a surprise awaited him: a fugitive warrant for his arrest from New York. Newly elected Manhattan District Attorney Tom Dewey was in no mood to forgive and forget. Already eyeing the White House in 1940, the young racket-busting DA would pursue any case that would guarantee headlines. And after pulling a fast one on the Führer and then beating Dewey's predecessor at the extradition game, Freeman was still front-page fodder.

The *Los Angeles Times* treated it as a Page One story ("Charges Laid to Nazi Plot") when Freeman voluntarily surrendered to the police on April 24. But Freeman soon discovered that it was hard to blame Hitler's henchmen for his 1930 decision to write rubber checks to the New Yorker Hotel. Nor were German agents responsible for Freeman still owing $2,000 in restitution.

Freeman soon had a new enemy: Judge Louis Kaufman. Despite pleas from Freeman's ladies-man lawyer, Greg Bautzer, Judge Kaufman set a high bail of $5,000. With Freeman quickly running out of funds and friends (and bail bondsmen wary of a bail jumper), the most coin that he could scrape together was $1,500.

So on April 29, Freeman entered a familiar sanitarium, a reducing spa that offered just two meals a day and ample time for meditation. Freeman was back among his friends at the Los Angeles County Jail as he waited for Governor Merriam to rule for a second time on his extradition to New York.

19

From black-and-white movies and cinematic imagination, we can envision how prisoners were transported cross-country in the late 1930s. The steamy coaches, the burly guards with sidearms, the handcuffs and leg chains, along with the contemptuous stares of the law-abiding passengers.

But Freeman didn't travel steerage even when two detectives were escorting him back to New York in late July 1938 on a fugitive warrant.

After taking the Union Pacific's Sunset Limited from Los Angeles, the detectives allowed Freeman to stop over for two days to recuperate when the train pulled into New Orleans. Instead of regaining his strength at a grimy railroad hotel with stained rugs and paper-thin walls, Freeman was housed at the Roosevelt with its block-long lobby and its fabled Sazerac Bar, which had been Huey Long's favorite watering hole. The only deprivation the prisoner faced was that the hotel's Blue Room, the leading supper club in New Orleans, was closed for renovations.

The detectives (Grover Brown, who had been gumshoeing

Freeman since 1935, and David Lynch) were relaxed guardians. They permitted Freeman to give an interview to the New Orleans *Times-Picayune*. The front-page story—a tribute to Freeman's enduring gift for self-promotion—portrayed him as the happiest prisoner this side of a monkey house:

> "The Jade King of China," between chuckles and puffs on a cigar, told here Friday how he sold eight carloads of tin cans and pig iron to a Nazi representative for $250,000. Freeman Bernstein, also known as "the man who tied a can to Hitler and Company," stopped at The Roosevelt for a two-day "rest" before continuing in custody of two police officers from New York.

Freeman faced no objections from his police escorts when he claimed that he was being brought back to New York to face the music for putting a plugged nickel in Hitler's nickelodeon. It was so much more dignified to depict himself as a victim of German injustice than to admit the truth—that he was being bounced backed to New York for writing bum checks.

Boasting that he was "glad" to have defrauded the Nazis, Freeman went back to his old story about how he had fulfilled the contract for "scrap metal" by providing the Germans with precisely what they had ordered. "Anyway," Freeman chortled as he went for the punch line, "there's a little nickel in tin cans."

Freeman had every reason to revel in the attention from the *Times-Picayune* and to luxuriate sitting in the Roosevelt's bar under the Paul Ninas murals of the New Orleans demimonde, probably with a Sazerac in his hand.

It had been a dispiriting three months for Freeman.

Governor Frank Merriam had been primed to again reject extradition after his top aide, Frank Cochran, reminded him in a memorandum, "You no doubt will recall the previous extradition proceedings involving the question of the purchase of nickel by an agent of the German Government which you denied." And Greg Bautzer had submitted a sheaf of medical testimonials to the governor describing Freeman as if not at death's door, at least close to the window.

What undermined Freeman's case was his own folly in taking off for the Gull Lake Sanitarium. Stanley Fuld, the assistant New York DA handling the case, pointed out in a legal filing that Freeman's doctor had recommended that he restore his health in a sunny, dry climate. "We now discover," Fuld stated with horror dripping from the printed page, "that this fugitive did not enter a sanitarium 'either on the desert or possibly in Palm Springs,' but went on a jaunt to Saskatchewan, a distance of about twelve hundred miles. It became very apparent that this fugitive was—and is—fully able to travel whenever he chooses."

Governor Merriam had been swayed in 1937 by the public opposition to extraditing Freeman by such major Hollywood powers as studio head Joe Schenck and stars like Al Jolson and Mae West. But this time around, only Bautzer chanted "Freedom for Freeman."

The few letter writers who weighed in while the governor was contemplating extradition all had scores to settle with Freeman. The California Northern Hotel Association passed along an angry complaint from the New Yorker Hotel expressing frustration over the delay in winning justice on the bad-check charge. And the Pacific Finance Corporation wanted assistance from the authorities in recovering the $142.92 still owed to them on the 1929 Ford convertible that Freeman had once owned.

In the end, after a series of procedural delays, Bautzer won what was probably the best deal possible. Governor Merriam agreed to send the fugitive back to New York with one major condition: Freeman would be permanently off the hook on the nickel deal. On July 19, District Attorney Tom Dewey agreed to the compromise by telegram: HE WILL NOT BE TRIED FOR INDICTMENTS BASED ON METALS THEFT . . . NO ACTION TO BE TAKEN AGAINST BERNSTEIN EXCEPT IN CONNECTION WITH VIOLATION OF PROBATION FOR WHICH EXTRADITION NOW SOUGHT.

Frank Merriam signed the extradition papers on Saturday, July 23. Three days later, Freeman and his two guardian detectives began their slow trip east. Any illusion that Freeman nurtured that he would be treated gently on his return to New York vanished by the time he was escorted to police headquarters. Placed in a lineup, he was harshly quizzed by Police Captain Richard Kennelly. And the topic—despite the terms of Freeman's extradition—was Canadian nickel.

"Are you a friend of Chancellor Hitler?"

For Freeman that question was as loaded as a pair of dice in a rigged crap game. By mid-1938, Adolf Hitler's local fan club was confined to the Boys in the Bund in Yorkville and a few other German neighborhoods. Yet Freeman's sense of self-importance depended on name-dropping. For without a connection to the famous and powerful, Freeman was just another two-bit con artist in a shabby suit standing in a police lineup.

"Yes," Freeman replied in a confident voice. "I have met Chancellor Hitler five times in Germany in the last three years." As embarrassing as that boast was—both then and now—Freeman, at least, didn't claim that he advised the Führer to swallow Austria and to cast a covetous eye at Czechoslovakia. Prodded by Captain

Kennelly, Freeman went on to assert his own connection to royalty: "I am known as the jade metal king."

The explicit understanding during the negotiations over extradition was that Freeman would face minimal bail on his return. But Judge James Wallace, presiding over the Court of General Sessions, apparently hadn't gotten the message. After a prosecutor detailed the DA office's eighteen-month struggle to bring Freeman back to New York, Judge Wallace said the chilling words, "I'll not fix any bail. Lock him up."

For the fourth time since he jumped bail in 1931, Freeman heard the jailhouse doors lock from the outside.

Sitting in his airless cell in the Tombs, the normally suspicious Freeman didn't grasp that he had been set up. The no-bail-for-Bernstein verdict had been prearranged by the DA's office. An internal memo described Freeman as "an old-time con-man and swindler." And Stanley Fuld—the assistant district attorney who had become Freeman's nemesis—wanted "it made clear to Bernstein that his only hope lies in 100% cooperation with us. He has a great deal of dope which will be of considerable assistance to us against the co-defendant. . . . This should be impressed upon him."

Freeman soon learned that he had a choice: rot in the Tombs for a month until he could see another judge or serve up Meyer Brenner. For Freeman, the answer didn't demand the lengthy deliberation that Jack Benny brought to the question: "Your money or your life?"

Sure, Freeman had built a code around not ratting on a fellow grifter.

But Meyer Brenner was different. He had looted Freeman's bank account in Toronto, despite the promised fifty-fifty split on the nickel deal. Brenner had refused to send money to Los Angeles in 1937 even though Freeman was begging for help with bail. And when Freeman was recovering at the Gull Lake Sanitarium in Saskatchewan in March 1938, Brenner had advised him by wire: "return to California perfectly safe."

(Los Angeles was indeed "perfectly safe" for Brenner, who remained in Toronto, but not for Freeman, who returned to face a fugitive warrant from New York.)

After two sleepless nights in the Tombs, Freeman agreed to assist the authorities in their efforts to lure Meyer Brenner across the Canadian border. Freeman's reward for his cooperation: He was released from jail on $2,500 bail. The money came from Freeman's nephews—theatrical agents Abe and Joe Feinberg, who were the sons of Freeman's oldest sister, Jennie. Unable to even afford the scrap paper to flesh out a Michigan roll, Freeman temporarily moved in with his sister and her husband, Louie Feinberg, in Peekskill, an hour north of Manhattan.

When the final legal details for his probation were hammered out in mid-September, the freed Freeman expressed his thanks in an effusive telegram to Frank Cochran in Sacramento: TERRIBLY GRATEFUL TO YOU AND THE GOVERNOR WILL YOU BE GOOD ENOUGH TO EXPRESS MY GRATITUDE TO HIS EXCELLENCY WILL BE BACK SOON TO VOTE FOR HIM.

But Freeman soon discovered that he had a demanding new job . . . as a stool pigeon. By mid-October, he was installed in Room 335 at the Park Central Hotel (Seventh Avenue and Fifty-Fifth Street) on the same floor where gambler Arnold Rothstein had been gunned down in 1928. Freeman loved bustling hotels with many escape routes in case of a financial emergency. But these days, he was too dispirited to swim laps in the hotel pool or to drop by events like the metropolitan bridge championships. Freeman even skipped an inspirational Sunday morning lecture by octogenarian Villa Faulkner Page titled "This Is Another Day."

For Freeman, another day meant another attempt to get Meyer Brenner. On Friday, October 21, he gave a detailed deposition to Stanley Fuld against Brenner and his associates. Far from a reluctant witness, Freeman even urged the prosecutors, "Listen, rush up . . . and get the fellows that was hooked in with me." Fuld had a simpler idea: Freeman could entice Brenner across the border to New York so he could be arrested.

That evening, with the police listening in on the extension, Freeman made a five-minute person-to-person call to his elusive co-conspirator in Toronto. The dialogue (recorded by Sergeant George McNulty) went like this:

Bernstein: Hello, is that you Meyer?

Brenner: Yes. Hello, Freeman.

Bernstein: Are you coming down here?

Brenner: No, not right now.

Bernstein: For Christ's sake, what's the matter with you?

Brenner: Why?

Bernstein: I thought you were coming down.

Brenner: No, but I will as soon as I get out on Tuesday. . . .

Bernstein: I will be at Peekskill, Louie Feinberg's. You will be down here Tuesday?

Brenner: Yes. There is a letter up here today.

Bernstein: From who?

Brenner: I think from the D.A. to the [police] detectives' office. I want to find out about it today. What did they want there today?

Bernstein: It don't mean a God damn thing to me, and you have nothing to fear down here. Now, do you think you will be down here Tuesday?
Brenner: Yes . . .
Bernstein: Now listen to me, I've got to have a sit-down-and-talk with you, and you come down here.
Brenner: All right, make it Tuesday. . . .
Bernstein: Good-bye.

Meyer Brenner probably sensed something odd in Freeman's vehemence about holding an immediate sit-down in New York. But what had to have set off clanging alarm bells was that Freeman had telephoned person to person—and didn't seem worried about paying the charges. When Brenner also considered that the New York DA's office was in cahoots with the Toronto Police, he judged it too risky to cross the American border.

Even as Freeman was fast becoming a ward of the district attorney's office, he thrashed about trying to find someone else to finance his three-meal-a-day habit. Proving yet again that the most gullible marks are those who have already been gulled, Freeman turned to the name at the top of his personal Sucker List—Stephen Meade, who had gone bankrupt as the fall guy in the nickel deal.

True, Meade had once sent private detectives searching for Freeman, which probably led to his arrest in Hollywood in 1937. But Meade had come to realize what everyone on Broadway had known for decades—there was no point in suing Freeman, since you could never collect. Which was why Meade turned to Freeman for help in trying to collect from Meyer Brenner.

Freeman also saw Brenner as a target for . . . let's not mince words . . . blackmail.

On November 2, Freeman composed a "Dear Meyer" letter that veered wildly from self-pity to overt threats. "You promised to send me some money, but you didn't keep your word," Freeman began. ". . . I am sick and broke and in desperate mood. Since I have been in New York, I saw Mead[e] and got some money from him. I have been down to the DA's office . . . and they want to pay me to make a statement. Don't stall me further or you will be in a lot of trouble. A little money now will be well spent."

Freeman took the train to Toronto a few days later in hopes of reaching a mature understanding with Brenner. Freeman pictured two seasoned businessmen recognizing their mutual self-interest. Instead, Brenner stiffed him.

Back in New York—and frantic for money—Freeman wrote Brenner on the stationery of the Park Central, "When I was in Toronto on Sunday you were to wire me money the next day. No money from you so I took more money from Meade[e] yesterday and signed an affidavit at the D.A.'s made out by them. . . . You know I am sick and desperate, but you let me starve. Too bad if you are hurt, even if my statement is not true."

A week later (November 17), Freeman composed a third version of his dunning letter. This time Freeman adopted a more-in-desperation-than-anger tone: "You didn't come through. Signed more papers. Can't help it. I don't want to hurt you, but don't care what I do to get money. I'm starving. They gave me more money and made me sign putting you into it. Why didn't you keep your promise and send me more money."

Three years earlier, Freeman Bernstein and Meyer Brenner—the Jade King and the Metals Maven—had laughed uproariously at the Biltmore Hotel over their scheme to fleece the Führer. The two Jews pictured the look on the face of the Nazis in Hamburg when they discovered that they had paid inflated nickel prices for rusted Canadian brake drums and discarded auto bodies.

It wasn't just a fantasy. They had not only pulled it off, but also gotten paid richly in advance. For Freeman, this was the grandest racket of his career. Better than his early days on Broadway, better than creating a movie studio with borrowed money, better than those trips to the Caribbean with blond show girls, and certainly better than smuggling in jade pieces from the Orient.

Now Freeman—sitting alone in his hotel room, not far from a Broadway that he no longer knew—heard on the radio that Europe was moving closer to war, just two months after Neville Chamberlain had promised "peace in our time." And Freeman himself, worried about his heart and his stomach, felt old and tired and broke.

But Meyer Brenner was now in no condition to help. On November 23, just a few days after Freeman's most recent letter had arrived, the bent metals dealer was arrested in Toronto at the request of Tom Dewey's office. Brenner was to spend the next six months in and out of jail in Canada fighting extradition to New York.

As 1938 flowed into 1939 along the Great White Way, New Year's Eve was built around anticipation for the coming World's Fair. All over Manhattan, the World Fair's theme song, "Dawn of a New Day," was played as often as "Auld Lang Syne." But for Freeman, who had moved to cheaper quarters at the Hotel Abbey on West Fifty-First Street, there was no dawn to brighten the new day—there was no sunlight to break through the gloom tornado that followed him everywhere.

Freeman's prospects were so bleak that the DA's office soon put him on work relief. As Stanley Fuld explained in a March 20 memo, "[Bernstein] has indicated that he has been borrowing from friends and acquaintances for the last eight months and sees little likelihood of continuing such borrowing. Payments of $25 to be given to Freeman Bernstein are, in a sense, compensation for the fact that he cannot return to California. His age and state of health prevent his being detained in a house of detention for witnesses."

Freeman might have enjoyed the irony of his final con—getting the City of New York to pay him to sit in a hotel room waiting to testify against Meyer Brenner. Except the $25-a-week payoff (about $425 today) was barely enough to keep him in cigars.

Canada extradited Meyer Brenner to New York on April 24. But even as Brenner enjoyed Yankee hospitality as a guest in the Tombs, the case against Freeman's accomplice began unraveling like the stitching on a jailhouse uniform. Stephen Meade was the first thread that snapped. The bankrupt Meade admitted in an amnesiac deposition on June 5 that because of his nickel nightmare, "I went through so much misery . . . that my mind is absolutely blank and I couldn't recall anything."

During the spring of 1939, Freeman began fading into oblivion. It wasn't that he ran off to the World Fair on opening day, April 30, and never returned. But the boy who grew up in the tenements of Troy and craved the limelight since he put Gentleman Jim Corbett on the vaudeville stage in 1902 was confronted with the worst fate imaginable for a showman—the audiences stopped caring.

Variety stopped mentioning the onetime Pet of Broadway. No credulous newspaperman quoted Freeman on his supposedly first-hand impressions of Hitler and the Nazi menace. Even the district attorney's office, Freeman's erstwhile employer, temporarily lost interest in their prize witness as they struggled to assemble a case against Meyer Brenner that they could take to a jury.

In a city of more than seven million, Freeman Bernstein had

become just another face in the crowd. The 1940 census showed Freeman living at the Hotel Abbey in a $60-a-month room, which represented more than half of his stipend from the DA. He listed his profession as theater manager but acknowledged that he had been unemployed for the prior 312 weeks (five years).

Freeman's value to Assistant District Attorney Fuld in preparing a case against Meyer Brenner was dwindling as fast as Republican hopes of ever defeating Franklin Roosevelt. Freeman's contradictory statements became a topic of ridicule in the legal filings of Meyer Brenner's attorney, Irwin Weinstein. Particularly damaging to the prosecution's case was that Freeman never mentioned Brenner as his accomplice in what Weinstein mockingly referred to as "his famous book" and his "masterpiece."

But Freeman was not granted his freedom until June 4, 1941, when the district attorney's office formally dropped all charges against him. Approaching his sixty-eighth birthday with few enduring ties to New York beyond his family, Freeman headed west in hopes of reviving his nonexistent career. Or, more realistically, in hopes of living out his final days in the Hollywood sun.

Freeman rented an inexpensive room at 1745 North Gramercy Place in Hollywood, probably sharing a hallway with the usual assortment of hopeful screenwriters, failed actresses, and fading figures from the silent movie days. But in my mind's eye, I can see Freeman flowering again now that he had a new audience to beguile with his stories of maharajas, potentates, and the Broadway of yesteryear.

My imagination fixates on a particular day: August 9, 1941. Dressed in his best suit and dreaming of schemes, Freeman made his way to the nearest Western Union office. Every inch a slightly soiled boulevardier, Freeman would have flirted with the young woman behind the desk as he scrawled the messages for two cele-bratory telegrams to New York.

The first wire (CONGRATULATIONS AND BEST WISHES FOR A LONG LIFE PROSPERITY HEALTH AND HAPPINESS) went to my father on the eve of his wedding. The other telegram—which I read now with both a smile and a tear—was delivered to my mother: BEST WISHES TO THE NEWLYWEDS SMILES CHEER AND SUNSHINE GALORE.

The Sunshine Kid signed himself, COLONEL FREEMAN BERN-STEIN. I have often wondered whom the eternal con man was try-ing to gull with the dubious title of "Colonel." My father knew that Freeman's major military credential was that he had been investi-gated by the War Department after World War I. My mother (Edith Herwitz) would have asked my father for the details about the supposedly illustrious war hero in the family. Which is why I finally concluded that Freeman added the "Colonel" to his name as a flourish to impress the Western Union clerk.

Colonel Freeman Bernstein's military career was not quite over. In the patriotic flush after Pearl Harbor, Freeman reported to the local Hollywood draft board to register on April 27, 1942. The army dutifully noted that the gray-haired recruit was five foot six and weighed 168 pounds. Even though Freeman added two years to his age (claiming seventy), the army was skeptical as a clerk scrawled on Freeman's registration card: "Birthday year unknown. Waiting for passport."

Shortly after Freeman's actual sixty-ninth birthday on August 15, *Variety* gave him the kind of present that he would have treasured—a mention amid the prime real estate of its Hollywood Chatter column. The item ran directly under brief updates on Errol Flynn heading for Mexico City and Sophie Tucker houseguesting with Fanny Brice. Regarding Sime Silverman's favorite Broadway character, *Variety* reported, "Freeman Bernstein around after five-week illness."

Freeman had moved closer to the center of the action, taking a room in a small stucco building at 1748 Orchid Avenue, a block from Hollywood Boulevard and Grauman's Chinese Theatre.

Despite the innate optimism that had carried him through life—the dream of once again flashing a big roll—Freeman also recognized the intimations of his own mortality. Whenever he went out, he carried with him a letter filled with instructions on what to do in case of sudden death.

On December 1, Freeman wangled a meeting with movie director William K. Howard. The Ohio-born Howard had worked with the best actors: directing Spencer Tracy in *The Power and the Glory* (1933); Helen Hayes in *Vanessa: Her Love Story* (1935); and Carole Lombard in *The Princess Comes Across* (1936). But now, as an example of the capricious justice that had always governed the film business, Howard was reduced to grinding out B-pictures for Monogram Pictures, an independent studio scorned by the Hollywood establishment.

I wish I knew what business brought my great-uncle to William K. Howard's suite at the Hollywood Plaza, a residential hotel just a few hundred feet from where Freeman had been arrested in 1937 after leaving Mae West's apartment. Maybe Freeman was putting the touch on an old friend or reminiscing with the Hollywood veteran. But I like to think that Freeman was there to pitch a screenplay—maybe a version of *Blue Money* or, better yet, the prewar saga of how a Jewish vaudevillian had hustled Hitler.

Trying to close the last deal of his life, Freeman was felled by a fatal heart attack. The in-case-of-my-death letter that Freeman had been carrying proved sadly prescient. Following his instructions, his modest funeral was held at the Malinow and Simons Mortuary on Venice Boulevard.

Newspapers around the country ran wire-service obits with headlines like "Man Who Gyps Hitler Is Dead in Hollywood." But only *Variety* gave Freeman a proper send-off. Headlined in the distinctive argot of show business ("Freeman Bernstein, Fantastic Vaude Figure of Yesteryear, Dies in H'wood"), the obituary called him "one of the most fantastic yet colorful characters known in and out of the vaudeville field that was."

What would have pleased Freeman more than anything was *Variety*'s portrayal of him as a con man with a heart of gold: "Bernstein had the native ability to borrow cash and his credit was considerable because when he was again in the chips he paid off. For that reason, perhaps, he could always borrow up to $500 in any branch of the William Morris agency. Several years ago he returned to N.Y. from a trip loaded with money he disgorged from all pockets and even his shoes. That was one time that he took care of his creditors."

Freeman was buried in Mount Carmel Cemetery just outside Los Angeles. There "this fantastic vaude figure of yesteryear" rested forgotten—aside from my father and a few other family members—for more than seventy years.

Epilogue

On a sunny March day, the kind of California day that had brightened Freeman's final years, I set out to visit the grave of my great-uncle. I soon discovered that the Mount Carmel Cemetery shares only one characteristic with Forest Lawn . . . the residents of both places are dead.

Located in a Latino neighborhood in Commerce, south of the Santa Ana Freeway, Mount Carmel has the look of shabby abandonment without ever inspiring a poetic elegy. After telephoning an off-site office, I had been furnished with the combination to the locked gate and directions to find Freeman's final resting place at the rear of the small cemetery.

Accompanied by my wife, Meryl, I parked my rental car in the shadow of a rotting metal warehouse—the kind of warehouse where I could imagine Freeman storing Pincus Mehr's scrap metal. Clutching a blue hydrangea plant that I had bought at a nearby flower shop where no one spoke English, I began a methodical search for Row 25 East, Grave No. 33.

Row 25 East was easily located near a memorial arch inscribed

UNITED HEBREW BENEVOLENT SOCIETY. But the graves ended abruptly long before No. 33. Instead of gravestones, there was nothing but a mangy clump of dirt, dead leaves, small pieces of plywood, and stray paper.

In exasperation, I called the cemetery office, demanding new coordinates to find Freeman. "The grave is exactly where I told you it was," said the cranky male voice on the other end. "You just have to kick some dirt and leaves around to find it."

He was right. Buried under several seasons of debris was a muddy footstone, about the size of a paperback book, marking Freeman's grave. It was so modest that there was not even enough room for a full name—just "F. Bernstein 1942." Only ten letters and four numbers to commemorate sixty-nine years of a self-made American life—filled with schemes and scams, hustles and hijinks—lived loudly and lustily on four continents.

With a bottle of water from the car and pocket tissues, Meryl and I did our best to clean Freeman's footstone.

Standing over his grave, I searched for the proper words to say. I am not religious enough to recite a prayer or a blessing. But I wanted to pay tribute to this man whose story fascinated my father and now me. I wanted to find words that would comfort the old showman, the cigar-smoking fight buff, and *Variety*'s voice of Broadway. Words that could somehow bridge eternity.

Looking down at the nondescript footstone of F. Bernstein 1942, I said softly, "You are remembered."

Acknowledgments

This book was born in 2010 over lunch at a religious shrine—the legendary temple of smoked fish, Barney Greengrass: The Sturgeon King.

Allan Potofsky, a second cousin living in Paris from a branch of the family that I didn't know existed, had looked me up on a visit to Manhattan. He was doing genealogical research on behalf of his sister, Donna Ritter. Over sturgeon, eggs, and onions, Allan happened to mention, "The only interesting thing I ever heard about our family is that my great-uncle once cheated Hitler on a nickel deal."

I had heard the same implausible story from my father—and that was how the quest began.

The idea for a book about a Broadway con man who fleeced the Führer was championed by my agent, Flip Brophy, at Sterling Lord Literistic. For the more than ten years that she has represented me, Flip has been everything that a writer could hope for—responsive, encouraging, understanding, and creative.

David Rosenthal appreciated from the beginning the funny, quirky story that I was trying to tell. Even when I exasperated him with missed deadlines in my dogged efforts to do Freeman Bernstein justice, David proved adept at mixing the right amount of pressure, guilt—and, yes, tolerance—to inspire me to do my best work. In addition to his sensitive editing of the manuscript, David sent me a series of funny e-mails that I may try to have published in a companion volume.

The enthusiasm of everyone at Blue Rider Press for the saga of Freeman Bernstein sustained me in the dark hours (every writer has them), when it seemed that this book would never be finished. I recall with pleasure Aileen Boyle, the head of marketing and publicity, telling me that she had a picture of Freeman on her office wall. While I have not yet met everyone who worked on *Hustling Hitler* at Blue Rider, I do want to single out my publicist, Marian Brown, for planning a great (knock wood) book launch. I want to thank Katie Zaborsky for overseeing the book's final editing and production. And I am deeply indebted to Muriel Jorgensen for her meticulous, yet sensitive, copyediting of the entire manuscript. Thanks go to Janice Kurzius as well for additional smart copyediting.

Now is the moment when I erect a well-deserved pedestal for my researcher—the talented, resourceful, and dedicated Alyson Krueger. Even though Alyson was writing regularly for the *New York Times* Style section and many magazines, she still found the time to pull off research coups like unearthing the original Yiddish transcript of an article about Freeman in *Der Tog* and then finding translator Harry Fuhrer to decipher the blurred microfilm copy. Alyson also fact-checked the manuscript while pausing to highlight her favorite jokes. But I am, of course, responsible for any lingering, inadvertent errors.

Writing this book put me in touch with relatives whom I had never met. Donna Ritter, whose interest in the extended Bernstein family was the initial catalyst for my research, was invaluable in giving me a brief family memoir by her late aunt Sylvia Potofsky and providing me with a family tree that I consulted constantly. Herb Rubenstein, another cousin, shared the fruits of his own genealogical research, as did Glenn Galer. Rounding out the Cousin's Club are Barbara Lowell and her daughter, Jane Evans, who displayed keen interest in hearing the latest wrinkles in the Freeman Bernstein story. The same was true of my first cousin Nancy Hollander.

Acknowledgments

My sister, Amy Shapiro, buttressed my recollections of the tales of Freeman that we heard growing up. We spent a memorable day going through World War II letters, and finding Freeman's wedding telegrams.

My far-flung relatives—the heirs of Hyman and Yetta Bernstein—have not been close in decades. During a delightful dinner in Denver, my first cousin Elisabeth Leistikow smartly observed, "We were the first generation who didn't have to be close to the family." Doing this book, though, has introduced me to Neil Hollander, another Paris-based cousin, and his wife, Régine. Not only did Neil help me decipher the family connection to Stutchin, which our great-uncle visited in 1921, but Freeman would have also enjoyed hearing himself discussed at Neil and Régine's Parisian apartment with a view of the Eiffel Tower out the window.

Jeannie Zandi, a relative of May Ward, deserves her own paragraph for leading me to the memorable photograph of the vaudeville star and her Dresden Dolls in mid-performance. I also want to thank Tom Kelly, another May Ward relative, for his help.

I have benefited greatly from the generosity of other writers. Jim Gladstone—who wrote a riveting biography of Freeman's lawyer, Greg Bautzer—consistently went out of his way to help me unravel Hollywood connections from 1937. Peter FitzSimons, the Australian biographer of Les Darcy, visited my apartment in New York for a memorable brunch (catered by Barney Greengrass) to discuss the doomed boxer. Attorney and novelist Jack Casey was an enthusiastic tour guide in Freeman's hometown, sharing with me his fascination with nineteenth-century Troy.

While I was investigating my family's roots in Troy, I also met with the late Jim Richard Wilson, who had curated the 2001 exhibit "Troy: An American Shtetl" at the Rathbone Gallery in Albany. Kevin Franklin, the historian of the Town of Colonie, spent a morning driving me around to show me the probable site of Freeman's first amusement park, which is now a highway on-ramp. As every researcher quickly learns, librarians and archivists are the grandest people on earth. I am grateful to so many people who assisted me along the way, from the National Archives to the State of California Archives.

Acknowledgments

John Fox was particularly helpful in obtaining Freeman's FBI files. The most amazing find came courtesy of the Emerson College Archives and Special Collections, which had preserved Freeman's 1935 film treatment, *Blue Money*. Dace Taube was particularly helpful in locating photos of Freeman from the collection of the *Los Angeles Examiner* at the Doheny Memorial Library at USC. And a hat tip to the Rensselaer County Historical Society, where I began learning about Troy, the city that forged Freeman.

This book would not have been possible without the amazing New York City Municipal Archives. I vividly recall my shocked glee on the day when a trolley was wheeled out for me containing two banker boxes filled with all of Freeman's 1930s legal files. The NYC Archives was my second home for four months as I went through the full documentation of the Nazi nickel deal. I especially want to single out the kindness of the late Leonora Gidlund, Barbara Hibbert, and Ken Cobb.

A few expressions of gratitude are a trifle more idiosyncratic. I would like to thank my eminent team of cardiologists, Drs. Mark Sotsky and George Philippides, for consulting on Freeman's seventy-eight-year-old medical records. I also want to mention my Mongolia experts, Rick Messick and Ann Altman, who confirmed that Freeman might have toured this off-Broadway locale with a show in the 1930s. And an ego-driven highlight of the production of *Hustling Hitler* was having my author's photograph taken by Nina Subin.

During the course of my research, my colleagues at the Brennan Center for Justice, where I am a fellow, have both expressed continued interest in Freeman Bernstein and have been indulgent about my newly developed fixation on vaudeville. So a shout-out to president Michael Waldman as well as John Kowal, Jeanine Plant-Chirlin, and my editor, Jim Lyons.

Melinda Henneberger, the editor of *Roll Call* and a dear friend, has been a fan of the book since the beginning. Jill Lawrence has been wonderfully supportive—asking nervously about the status of each chapter and eagerly spreading the word about my favorite con-man great-uncle.

A few other friends deserve to be honored for their special service to the creation of *Hustling Hitler*. Urban Lehner and Nancy Leonard (who squeezed in time to proofread the galleys) have been there from the beginning. Enduring thanks go to Josh Gotbaum and Joyce Thornhill (who was my designated Canadian sponsoring a freedom-of-information search in Ottawa). Ralph Schlosstein and Jane Hartley have been devoted friends. And Jane, now the American ambassador to France, provided her version of Yaddo-on-Seine by hosting me for a few days in Paris during an eating tour and the writing of an entire paragraph of the book.

Other friends who may have gotten tired of hearing about Freeman Bernstein but never showed it include Suzanna Andrews, David Weisbrod and Peggy Simon, Rita Jacobs and Jim Wetzler, Elaine Kamarck, Michelle and Steve Stoneburn, Mandy Grunwald, Ben Cooper, Jeff Rosen, Joe Klein and Victoria Kaunitz, Carla Rapoport, Susan Chira and Michael Shapiro, Jeff Greenfield and Dena Sklar, Amanda Howe and Ellen Qualls, Julia Baird, Rick Stengel, Christine Rosen, Terry Smolar, Liz Loewy, Joanne Hubschman, Kanti Rai, Alison Bender, Susan Hyde and Sean Smith, Rick Ridder, Judy Miller and Jason Epstein, Peggy Noonan, Mark Starr, Garrett Epps, Christine Doudna and Rick Grand-Jean, Pat Bauer and Ed Muller, James Hohmann, and John Martin.

I also want to salute three absent friends: Dotty Lynch, Gordon Stewart, and Henry Hubschman.

In writing this book about *my* family, I also have a tremendous debt to my wife's family. Meryl's parents, David and Adelle Gordon, still going strong in their nineties, have been supportive in every conversation about the book. Jesse Gordon and Meg Wolf—both knowing the joys and uncertainties of show business—are my target audience for tales of Freeman in vaudeville. Thanks, as well, to Jenny Rakochy. And Nate Gordon, the photo editor in the family, did a masterful job in restoring a damaged picture of pith-helmeted Freeman in Ceylon, as well as finding photographs of Mae West and Les Darcy.

As for young Ozzy Gordon and Sadie Gordon, I can't wait to start enlivening their storybooks with the saga of Freeman Bernstein.

This book—like my life—revolves around Meryl. Words cannot express how much she is reflected in the words in this book. She understood before

Acknowledgments

I did the magic in the story of Freeman and read over my shoulder the old grifter's 1937 tale of the Nazi nickel hijinks at the New York Public Library. She was, as always, my first and best editor. Every time I write a joke or feel pleased at a passage, I picture Meryl's smile. She is the wind beneath my wings, the song. . . no, no, no . . . I can't go full Khalil Gibran here. Instead, I will end with Meryl's fantasy of a production of *Freeman: The Rap Musical.*

As I write these final words, I mourn the passing of my parents, Salem and Edith Shapiro. This book, as I have said elsewhere, is a son's gift to his father. But I also imagine my parents' pleasure that a joyful photograph of them appears in this book, dancing at my wedding to Meryl.

Research and Chapter Notes

For four years, I lived with Freeman Bernstein on a daily basis. And, yes, it is hard to say goodbye to the cheerful grifter who was my great-uncle. But I do want to explain the research behind my effort to turn a forgotten vaude figure of yesteryear into a flesh-and-blood person on the printed page.

In writing this book, I consulted more than 2,500 newspaper clips about Freeman Bernstein, May Ward, and the events that shaped their lives. I also unearthed approximately 1,500 pages of documents from the amazing New York City Municipal Archives, the state of California, the War Department, the State Department, the FBI, and the Bureau of Investigation at the Justice Department.

Even though this book began with hearing my father's stories about Freeman, the only family papers that still exist are one page of recollections by his niece Sylvia Potofsky and two telegrams sent to my parents for their wedding in 1941.

Luckily, Freeman was a literary man. I, of course, drew wisdom from his 1937 autobiographical classic, *Was Hitler's Nickel Hi-Jacked?* Even more revealing on a psychological level was his 1935 film treatment, *Blue Money*, which was more a wish-fulfillment fantasy than a coherent story.

Advances in character recognition software (the computerized ability to recognize printed words) helped make this book possible. A decade ago, it would not have been possible to search documents like the *Troy Times* from the 1880s because they had never been indexed. As a result of twenty-first-century technology, I discovered thousands of newspaper clips that I never could have located before my father died in 2004.

All quotations in this book are verbatim. And all dates have been confirmed by newspaper articles or other documents.

Freeman, however, could be an unreliable narrator who trafficked in exaggeration and comic invention. He also told conflicting stories. As a result, I have taken great pains to work out what was the most plausible sequence of events. At times, I have also offered my best interpretation of the motivations behind Freeman's actions.

Like anyone trying to reanimate a character from a bygone era, I would have given almost anything for just an hour to ask Freeman questions through a haze of cigar smoke. In fact, I wish there was someone still living who knew my great-uncle well.

Fortunately, Sime Silverman, the founder of *Variety*, captured Freeman's argot in about fifty monologues over two decades. If my great-uncle has a voice in this book, it is partly because Sime recognized a century ago that Freeman Bernstein was an extraordinary Broadway character.

What follows is a chapter-by-chapter guide to the research that undergirds this book. To prevent these notes from becoming as tedious and lengthy as the references in a doctoral thesis, I have not listed most newspaper articles. Any researcher looking for a specific reference may e-mail me at waltershapiro@gmail.com.

CHAPTER ONE

I have primarily relied on the accounts of Freeman's arrest in the *Los Angeles Times*, the *Los Angeles Examiner*, the *Los Angeles Daily News*, and the *Los Angeles Evening Herald and Express*. Wire-service stories from the United Press and Associated Press were also helpful.

By chance, the *Los Angeles Times* ran a two-part series in late March 1937 on jail conditions, which allowed me to reconstruct Freeman's arrival at the Hall of Justice. The backgrounds of the arresting officers—Johnnie Erickson and Jack Koehn—were taken from news clips, mostly in the *Los Angeles Times*.

Mae West's autobiography, *Goodness Had Nothing To Do With It*, was the source of the details of Freeman's visit to the Ravenswood Apartments. Where there was a conflict between Mae West's twenty-year-old recollections and newspaper clips, I went with the contemporaneous versions.

CHAPTER TWO

The research was hearing my father's stories—and wishing that I had taken notes or remembered them better.

CHAPTER THREE

Beginning with the 1868 manifest of passengers arriving in New York and continuing through the 1870 census, I have been grateful for government documents that are easily retrieved from Ancestry.com. These documents allowed me to trace Hyman Bernstein's early years in America.

The details of the arduous crossings of the *James Foster Jr.* are primarily derived from newspaper accounts in the *New York Times* and the *Brooklyn Eagle.* I also used the online library at the Mystic Seaport museum.

Reconstructing Hyman and Yetta Bernstein's early days in Troy was made possible by listings in the annual Troy *City Directory*, articles from the *Troy Times*, and the 1875 New York State census. This mid-decade document listed "Framen Bernstein" as one year and ten months old in June 1875. From that exceedingly precise detail, I have concluded that Freeman was born in August 1873. But, it is an informed guess, since New York State did not use birth certificates until the 1880s.

In researching Jewish life in Troy in the late nineteenth century, I am indebted to the records from a 2001 exhibit at the Rathbone Gallery (now the Opalka Gallery) in Albany. Titled "An American Shtetl: Jewish History and Community in Troy, NY," it provided a context to understand the lives of my great-grandfather and the rest of the Bernstein family.

The initial account of Freeman's discovery of Saratoga comes from the introduction to *Was Hitler's Nickel Hi-Jacked?* I also drew upon *Such Was Saratoga* by Hugh Bradley (New York: Doubleday, Doran, 1940) and *The Sport of Kings and the Kings of Crime: Horse Racing, Politics, and Organized Crime in New York, 1865–1913* by Steven A. Riess (Syracuse, NY: Syracuse University Press, 2011). Details about anti-Semitism in Saratoga were plucked from *A History of the Jews in America* by Howard M. Sachar (New York: Alfred A. Knopf, 1992).

The Nellie Bly screed against "Our Wickedest Summer Resort" appeared in the August 19, 1894, edition of the *New York World.*

The news clip from the *Fairbanks Daily-New Miner* recalling that Freeman sold jewelry to the Klondike miners comes from his obituary, which appeared on December 2, 1942.

I have assumed that Freeman stayed in Skagway, which became the largest city in Alaska for the duration of the gold rush, because it was an arduous three-month journey to get to the actual gold fields around Dawson in the Klondike.

The story of Freeman's first amusement park comes from the Albany *Times Union* and the *Troy Times.* Kevin Franklin, the town historian of Colonie, New York, helped me pinpoint where on the Hudson River islands Camp Manhattan was located.

CHAPTER FOUR

Both Armand Fields's James J. Corbett biography and *Vaudeville Wars* by Arthur Frank Wertheim were indispensable in understanding how Freeman could book the former heavyweight champ into his theater at Bergen Point.

(As I wrote this section of the book, I imagined that a stirring Broadway musical could be built around the 1901 vaudeville strike and the benefit performance organized by the White Rats at the Academy of Music.)

Before *Variety*, the most dishy Broadway gossip appeared in the *Morning Telegraph*, which in those days covered show business as well as sports.

I reconstructed the backgrounds of the performers who appeared at Bergen Point through searches of various newspaper archives. Particularly helpful were show business publications like the *New York Clipper* and the *New York Dramatic Mirror*. In some cases, I found capsule biographies in Joe Laurie Jr.'s *Vaudeville: From the Honky Tonks to the Palace*.

I was stymied in my efforts to work out precisely how Charles Kanter was related to Freeman.

CHAPTER FIVE

May Ward's birth date comes from the 1900 census. The background about her parents was drawn from the 1880 census. The archives of Green-Wood Cemetery in Brooklyn provided the details about the 1891 death of Mary Southward.

Later in life, May Ward repeatedly said that she was initially on the stage at age thirteen, which would have been 1894. But I did not find any references to her as either May Ward or May Southward before 1897.

I was aided in understanding the early history of burlesque by a 1990 monograph by Robert C. Allen titled "'The Leg Business': Transgression and Containment in American Burlesque." Also very helpful was Rachel Shteir's *Striptease* and Robert C. Allen's *Horrible Prettiness*.

The Lost Amusement Parks of New York City by Barbara and Wesley Gottlock was invaluable in tracing the history of the amusement area in Fort George. The arrest of Eva Puck was taken from the 1904 annual report of the Society for the Prevention of Cruelty to Children.

Descriptions of theaters, including their seating capacity, were taken from various editions of *Julius Cahn's Official Theatrical Guide*, which are available online.

A website called Travalanche was helpful in researching the story of Mlle. Adgie and her lions. It is run by a writer who identifies him or herself as Trav S.D.

CHAPTER SIX

Just as I am indebted to Sime Silverman for keeping Freeman's voice alive, so I am grateful to his biographer, Dayton Stoddart. A website maintained by alums of *Variety* called *Sime's Site* was also very helpful.

The best capsule biography of John Considine is in *Vaudeville Old & New: An Encyclopedia of Variety Performers in America*, volume one, by Frank Cullen (New York: Routledge, 2006). The reference book is useful for other short portraits of performers like Maggie Cline.

The details of Freeman's wedding are taken from his December 6, 1906, marriage license.

The Papers of Will Rogers not only provide a rich layer of detail about his performances but they also provide short bios of everyone who appeared on a vaudeville bill with America's leading lariat tosser and joke teller.

CHAPTER SEVEN

Much of the story of John the Barber, the clipped hair clipper, is drawn from *Lord Broadway*, the Sime Silverman biography.

Harry Houdini's *A Magician Among the Spirits* offers a spirited diatribe against Madame Diss Debar. Also useful was a 1975 article in the *American Quarterly* by R. Laurence Moore titled "The Spiritualist Medium: A Study of Female Professionalism in Victorian America."

For Walter Wellman, the best source is his biography in *American National Biography* (New York: Oxford University Press, 1999).

CHAPTER EIGHT

Some of Freeman's lengthy monologues in *Variety* were unsigned. If they had the same tone and tenor of the Freeman stories bylined "Sime," I attributed them to the founder of *Variety*. Not until the 1930s, when Sime was dying, did anyone else put his byline on a Freeman monologue.

The size of May Ward's mortgage on the house in Mount Vernon is taken from her (what else?) bankruptcy petition.

The website BoxRec was indispensable for researching all details about the fight game and the fighters whom Freeman managed.

CHAPTER NINE

D. W. Griffith's The Birth of a Nation by Melvyn Stokes was my primary source for all material about the greatest triumph of the silent movie era. (Despite its repugnant pro-KKK theme, I was awed at the intensity of the movie when I watched it for the first time in researching this chapter.) Also helpful was *Silent Films, 1877–1996: A Critical Guide to 646 Movies* by Robert K. Klepper (Jefferson, NC: McFarland, 1999). For details on certain performers, I also consulted IMDb online.

In writing this chapter, I drew heavily on magazines chronicling the infant film business. Some catered to movie fans while others emphasized the commercial side. They include *Motion Picture World*, *Moving Picture World*, *Motion Picture News*, and *Photo-Play Review*.

The Joe Tumulty connection is largely based on a 1925 quote from Freeman in *Variety*: "You were in the White House when I used to call on Joe Tumulty." According to the Political Communication Center at the University of Oklahoma, the first political commercials (shown in tandem with movies) did not appear until 1940.

CHAPTER TEN

One of my favorite articles that I uncovered researching this book was a 1937 account of the life and loves and more loves of the man whom May Ward knew as Siegfried Wallace. This syndicated feature ("Glamorous Scoundrels of Today") by Asa Bordages first appeared in the May 18, 1937, *Milwaukee Journal*. But the story of the con artist who conned Freeman's wife is also based on dozens of contemporaneous newspaper clips. And—much to my amazement—the New York City Municipal Archives has saved a copy of May Ward's 1917 deposition about how she had been hoodwinked.

My telling of the Les Darcy story has been enhanced by Peter FitzSimons's biography and *The Magnificent Rube* by Charles Samuels on the life of promoter Tex Rickard. Also helpful was a 1996 article from the *Journal of Sport History* by Katharine Moore and Murray G. Phillips: "From Adulation to Persecution and Back: Australian Boxer Les Darcy in America, 1916–1917."

The first article I read on Les Darcy was the most poignant: "In Search of Les Darcy in America" by Ruth Park (1978), building on the research of her late husband D'Arcy Niland. It is available online at a website devoted to the work of D'Arcy Niland.

All prior accounts of Les Darcy's sad American journey depended on news articles that were saved in a scrapbook brought back to Australia by Darcy's manager after his death. Thanks to many new newspaper databases—and the ability to search documents that never had an index—I have been able to assemble a far more comprehensive record of Darcy's American tour. It is worth noting that my version of the story also puts Freeman in a far better light as a promoter who never wavered in his support of Darcy.

Details about Freeman warning of a German espionage ring are based on files from the War Department and the Bureau of Investigation at the Justice Department.

CHAPTER ELEVEN

In writing about the U-boat menace along the East Coast during the spring of 1918, I called upon *The United States in the World War: 1918–1920* by John Bach McMaster (New York: D. Appleton, 1920) and volume three of the *Annual Report of the Secretary of War, 1918*. Especially useful was another government publication by the Navy Department in 1920: *German Submarine Activities on the Atlantic Coast of the United States and Canada*.

World War I and its aftermath prompted the creation of the first major set of government files on the activities of the suspicious Freeman Bernstein. I remain grateful for the dutiful record keeping by the War Department and the Bureau of Investigation in the Justice Department.

The best explanation for how slowly the Doughboys were mustered out of the service was found in a study written by Benedict Crowell and Robert Forrest Wilson, *Demobilization: Our Industrial and Military Demobilization After the Armistice, 1918–1920* (New Haven, CT: Yale University Press, 1921). Invaluable for understanding the steady demand for vaudeville performers was Weldon B. Durham's *Liberty Theatres of the United States Army, 1917–1919*.

In War Department documents, J. R. Banta is referred to as "Major Banta." Since I could find no record of Banta's service in uniform, I assume that this was an honorary rank given to favored civilians working for the War Department.

CHAPTER TWELVE

The Anniversary Gag that Freeman and May Ward pulled on transatlantic liners is described in a colorful profile of my great-uncle that appeared in the New York *Sunday Mirror* on September 11, 1938.

Freeman's visit to Stutchin (Szczuczyn) is mentioned in his March 18, 1921, interview with *Der Tog*. I consulted a heartbreaking website that mourned the Nazi's destruction of Jewish life in Stutchin: www.szczuczyn.com. I found additional information in Celia S. Heller's *On the Edge of Destruction: Jews of Poland Between the Two World Wars* (Champaign: University of Illinois Press, 1977).

Rounding out my research on my ancestral home was an academic article by Piotr Wróbel in the March 2003 edition of the *Journal of Modern European History*. Wróbel's article is titled "The Seeds of Violence. The Brutalization of an Eastern European Region, 1917–1921."

CHAPTER THIRTEEN

For my crash course in the law of extradition, I drew upon a 1992 article by Ethan A. Nadelmann in the *N.Y.U. Journal of International Law and Politics*. Its title: "The Evolution of United States Involvement in the International Rendition of Fugitive Criminals."

The details about the raucous battle over the Ku Klux Klan at the 1924 Democratic Convention come from Robert K. Murray's glorious history called *The 103rd Ballot*.

The 1920s Florida land boom is discussed in detail in John Kenneth Galbraith's *The Great Crash 1929*. Even more fun was the reconstruction of the real estate mania in an article called "The Beauty of Bubbles" in the December 18, 2008, issue of the *Economist*.

Freeman's legal appeal in the glass sandwich case was rejected by the New York Supreme Court in February 1928. The case was called *Freeman Bernstein, Appellant v. Queens County Jockey Club and Another, Defendants*. And nothing would make me happier than if a contemporary lawyer cited the case as a precedent.

CHAPTER FOURTEEN

In researching Freeman's walk-on role in electing Herbert Hoover president in 1928, I was aided by an academic article by Sonja P. Wehtling in the September 2000 issue of *American Jewish History*. The article was called "Herbert Hoover and American Jewish non-Zionists 1917–28." Also helpful was Henry L. Feingold's book *A Time for Searching: Entering the Mainstream, 1920–1945* (Baltimore: Johns Hopkins University Press, 1995). In addition, I consulted David Bruner's biography *Herbert Hoover: A Public Life* (New York: Alfred A. Knopf, 1979).

The limited details surrounding Freeman's 1927 arrest for grand larceny come from his rap sheet in the district attorney's files obtained from the New York City Municipal Archives. Freeman also referred to his first American arrest in an interview with the DA's office on March 27, 1939.

The Sophie Tucker story, which vindicated my father's memory, came from three articles in *Variety* in 1929. I also consulted the entry for Sophie Tucker in the *American National Biography* shelf of reference books.

The Herbert Hoover Presidential Library and Museum helped me track down the history of the presidential yacht called the *Mayflower*.

CHAPTER FIFTEEN

The NYC Archives retained the DA's files from all of Freeman's bouts with the law—and they were invaluable in writing this and subsequent chapters.

Other aspects of how Freeman defrauded the New Yorker Hotel can be found in the state of California legal files from Freeman's 1938 extradition case.

The details about the baseball games that might have threatened the solvency of Freeman's sports book come from the amazing compendium of online box scores called Retrosheet.

In reconstructing Freeman's career as the Jade King of China, I consulted such books as *Empire Made Me: An Englishman Adrift in Shanghai* by Robert A. Bickers; *Voices from Shanghai: Jewish Exiles in Wartime China*, edited by Irene Eber; and *Carl Crow—A Tough Old China Hand* by Paul French.

Freeman's formula for smuggling jewels comes courtesy of Mae West's autobiography, *Goodness Had Nothing To Do With It*.

The best history of the Tombs in the 1930s that I discovered was Meyer Berger's two-part series in the August 30 and September 6, 1941, issues of the *New Yorker*.

The Emerson College Archives and Special Collections preserved Freeman's film treatment, *Blue Money*. The catalog describing the *Variety* Protected Materials Department Collection provides an invaluable history of the script registration system for vaudeville.

CHAPTER SIXTEEN

In understanding the military uses of nickel, I was aided by a 1992 journal article in *The Historian* by John Perkins called "Coins for Conflict: Nickel and the Axis, 1933–1945." A surprisingly good capsule history of nickel in wartime can be found on the website of Dartmouth Toxic Metals Superfund Research Program maintained by Dartmouth College and Dartmouth Medical School. Also helpful was John Fairfield Thompson's 1960 history of the International Nickel Company called *For the Years to Come*.

That said, the best sources for understanding the passions surrounding nickel in the mid-1930s were news clips on the debate over whether to embargo the strategic metal in the Toronto *Globe and Mail* and the *Toronto Star*.

I should note that the NYC Archives has retained three small nickel cathodes that Freeman used as his samples during the negotiations that led up to the hustling of Hitler.

When I began researching the nickel deal, I never dreamed that I would depend heavily on a literary study titled *Kafka's Relatives* by Anthony Northey. But it was indispensable in helping me write a capsule profile of the shifty Otto Kafka.

Notes

CHAPTER SEVENTEEN

Both the state of California and the Manhattan DA's office have retained all the legal correspondence and court filings surrounding the battle over Freeman's 1937 extradition.

B. James Gladstone's biography of Freeman's attorney, Greg Bautzer, *The Man Who Seduced Hollywood*, provided a rich portrait of a lawyer who was as colorful as his client. I also drew heavily on a memorable chronicle of the 1934 California gubernatorial race, *The Campaign of the Century*, by Greg Mitchell.

CHAPTER EIGHTEEN

Almost everything in this chapter comes from either the New York DA's files or the state of California files on Freeman's second extradition battle in 1938. Other details have been filled in through contemporaneous newspaper clips.

CHAPTER NINETEEN

A useful history of Huey Long and the Roosevelt Hotel in New Orleans can be found in an article by Paul F. Stahls Jr. ("Roosevelt Returns") in the July–August 2009 issue of *Louisiana Life*. Also helpful was Anthony Stanonis's *Creating the Big Easy: New Orleans and the Emergence of Modern Tourism, 1918–1945* (Athens: University of Georgia Press, 2006).

The two wedding telegrams that Freeman sent in 1941 were miraculously saved in a large box along with the letters that my parents wrote each other during World War II.

Bibliography

Allen, Robert C. *Horrible Prettiness: Burlesque and American Culture*. Chapel Hill: University of North Carolina Press, 1991.

Bartels, Jon. *Saratoga Stories: Gangsters, Gamblers & Racing Legends*. Lexington, KY: Eclipse Press, 2007.

Bernstein, Freeman. *Was Hitler's Nickel Hi-Jacked?* Los Angeles, 1937.

Berton, Pierre. *The Klondike Fever: The Life and Death of the Last Great Gold Rush*. New York: Alfred A. Knopf, 1958.

Bickers, Robert. *Empire Made Me: An Englishman Adrift in Shanghai*. New York: Columbia University Press, 2003.

Burns, George. *I Love Her, That's Why!* New York: Simon & Schuster, 1955.

Cahn, Julius. *Julius Cahn's Official Theatrical Guide*. New York, 1907.

Casey, Jack. *The Trial of Bat Shea*. Troy, NY: Diamond Rock, 2011.

Doherty, Thomas. *Hollywood and Hitler, 1933–1939*. New York: Columbia University Press, 2013.

Durham, Weldon B. *Liberty Theatres of the United States Army, 1917–1919*. Jefferson, NC: McFarland & Company, 2006.

Eber, Irene, ed. *Voices from Shanghai: Jewish Exiles in Wartime China*. Chicago: University of Chicago Press, 2008.

Erdman, Andrew L. *Queen of Vaudeville: The Story of Eva Tanguay*. Ithaca, NY: Cornell University Press, 2012.

Fields, Armond. *James J. Corbett*. Jefferson, NC: McFarland & Company, 2001.

Bibliography

FitzSimons, Peter. *The Ballad of Les Darcy*. Sydney: HarperCollins Australia, 2007.

French, Paul. *Carl Crow—A Tough Old China Hand: The Life, Times, and Adventures of an American in Shanghai*. Hong Kong: Hong Kong University Press, 2006.

Galbraith, John Kenneth. *The Great Crash, 1929*. New York: Houghton Mifflin, 1961.

Gilbert, Douglas. *American Vaudeville: Its Life and Times*. New York: Whittlesey House, 1940.

Gladstone, B. James. *The Man Who Seduced Hollywood: The Life and Loves of Greg Bautzer, Tinseltown's Most Powerful Lawyer*. Chicago: Chicago Review Press, 2013.

Gottlock, Barbara and Wesley. *Lost Amusement Parks of New York City: Beyond Coney Island*. Charleston, SC: History Press, 2013.

Grau, Robert. *The Business Man in the Amusement World: A Volume of Progress in the Field of the Theatre*. New York: Broadway Publishing, 1910.

Hammett, Dashiell. *The Maltese Falcon*. New York: Alfred A. Knopf, 1930.

Hay, Peter. *Broadway Anecdotes*. New York: Oxford University Press, 1989.

Houdini, Harry. *A Magician Among the Spirits*. New York: Harper & Brothers, 1924.

Jolson, Harry. *Mistah Jolson*. Hollywood: House-Warven, 1951.

Jones, Charlotte Foltz. *Yukon Gold: The Story of the Klondike Gold Rush*. New York: Holiday House, 1999.

Tiny. *Circus Queen and Tinker Bell: The Memoir of Tiny Kline*. Champaign: University of Illinois Press, 2008.

Koszarski, Richard. *An Evening's Entertainment: The Age of the Silent Feature Picture, 1915–1928*. Berkeley: University of California Press, 1994.

Laurie, Joe, Jr. *Vaudeville: From the Honky Tonks to the Palace*. New York: Henry Holt, 1953.

Marx, Harpo, and Rowland Barber. *Harpo Speaks!* New York: Bernard Geis Associates, 1961.

Meade, Marion. *Dorothy Parker: What Fresh Hell Is This?* New York: Penguin Books, 1987.

Mitchell, Greg. *The Campaign of the Century: Upton Sinclair's Race for Governor of California and the Birth of Media Politics*. New York: Random House, 1992.

Murray, Robert K. *The 103rd Ballot: Democrats and the Disaster in Madison Square Garden*. New York: Harper & Row, 1976.

Northey, Anthony. *Kafka's Relatives: Their Lives and His Writings*. New Haven, CT: Yale University Press, 1991.

O'Connor, Richard. *Bat Masterson*. New York: Doubleday, 1957.

Raines, Robert K. *Hot Springs: From Capone to Costello*. Charleston, SC: Arcadia Publishing, 2013.

Rittner, Don. *Troy: A Collar City History*. Charleston, SC: Arcadia Publishing, 1998.

Rose, Frank. *The Agency: William Morris and the Hidden History of Show Business*. New York: Harper Business, 1995.

Samuels, Charles. *The Magnificent Rube: The Life and Gaudy Times of Tex Rickard*. New York: McGraw-Hill, 1957.

Seidensticker, Edward. *Tokyo Rising: The City Since the Great Earthquake*. Tokyo: Charles E. Tuttle, 1990.

Shirer, William L. *Berlin Diary: The Journal of a Foreign Correspondent, 1934–1941*. New York: Alfred A. Knopf, 1941.

————. *The Rise and Fall of the Third Reich*. New York: Simon & Schuster, 1960.

Shteir, Rachel. *Striptease: The Untold History of the Girlie Show*. Oxford: Oxford University Press, 2004.

Smith, Richard Norton. *Thomas E. Dewey and His Times*. New York: Simon & Schuster, 1982.

Snyder, Robert W. *The Voice of the City: Vaudeville and Popular Culture in New York*. New York: Oxford University Press, 1989.

Stein, Charles W. *American Vaudeville as Seen by Its Contemporaries*. New York: Alfred A. Knopf, 1984.

Stoddart, Dayton. *Lord Broadway, Variety's Sime*. W. Funk, 1941.

Stokes, Melvyn. *D. W. Griffith's The Birth of a Nation*. Oxford: Oxford University Press, 2007.

Storry, Richard. *A History of Modern Japan*. London: Pelican Books, 1960.

Thomas, Hugh. *Cuba or The Pursuit of Freedom*. New York: Harper & Row, 1971.

Thompson, John Fairfield, and Norman Beasley. *For the Years to Come: A Story of International Nickel of Canada*. New York: G. P. Putnam's Sons, 1960.

Trav S.D. *No Applause—Just Throw Money*. New York: Faber and Faber, 2005.

Vazzana, Eugene Michael. *Silent Film Necrology* (Jefferson, NC: McFarland & Company, 2001).

Wertheim, Arthur Frank. *Vaudeville Wars: How the Keith-Albee and Orpheum Circuits Controlled the Big-Time and Its Performers*. New York: Palgrave Macmillan, 2006.

Wertheim, Arthur Frank, and Barbara Blair. *The Papers of Will Rogers,* vol. 2. Norman: University of Oklahoma Press, 2000.

West, Mae. *Goodness Had Nothing To Do With It.* Upper Saddle River, NJ: Prentice Hall, 1959.

Wharton, David B. *The Alaska Gold Rush.* Bloomington: Indiana University Press, 1972.

Credits for Photo Insert

About the Author

In addition to chronicling the hokum and hustles of his con-man great-uncle, Walter Shapiro has covered every presidential campaign since 1980. A columnist at *Roll Call*, Shapiro is also a fellow at the Brennan Center for Justice at NYU and a lecturer in political science at Yale. He won the 2010 Sigma Delta Chi Award for best online columnist for his work as a senior correspondent at *Politics Daily*. During his four decades covering politics, Shapiro has been a columnist for *USA Today*, and *Esquire*, and was the Washington bureau chief for *Salon*. He has been on the staff of *Time*, *Newsweek*, and *The Washington Post*. His book on the prelude to the 2004 Democratic presidential race, *One-Car Caravan*, was published in 2003. Shapiro served in the Carter White House as a presidential speechwriter. For a decade, he performed stand-up comedy at clubs in New York and claims that his onstage career is merely on hiatus. He lives in Manhattan with his wife, writer Meryl Gordon.